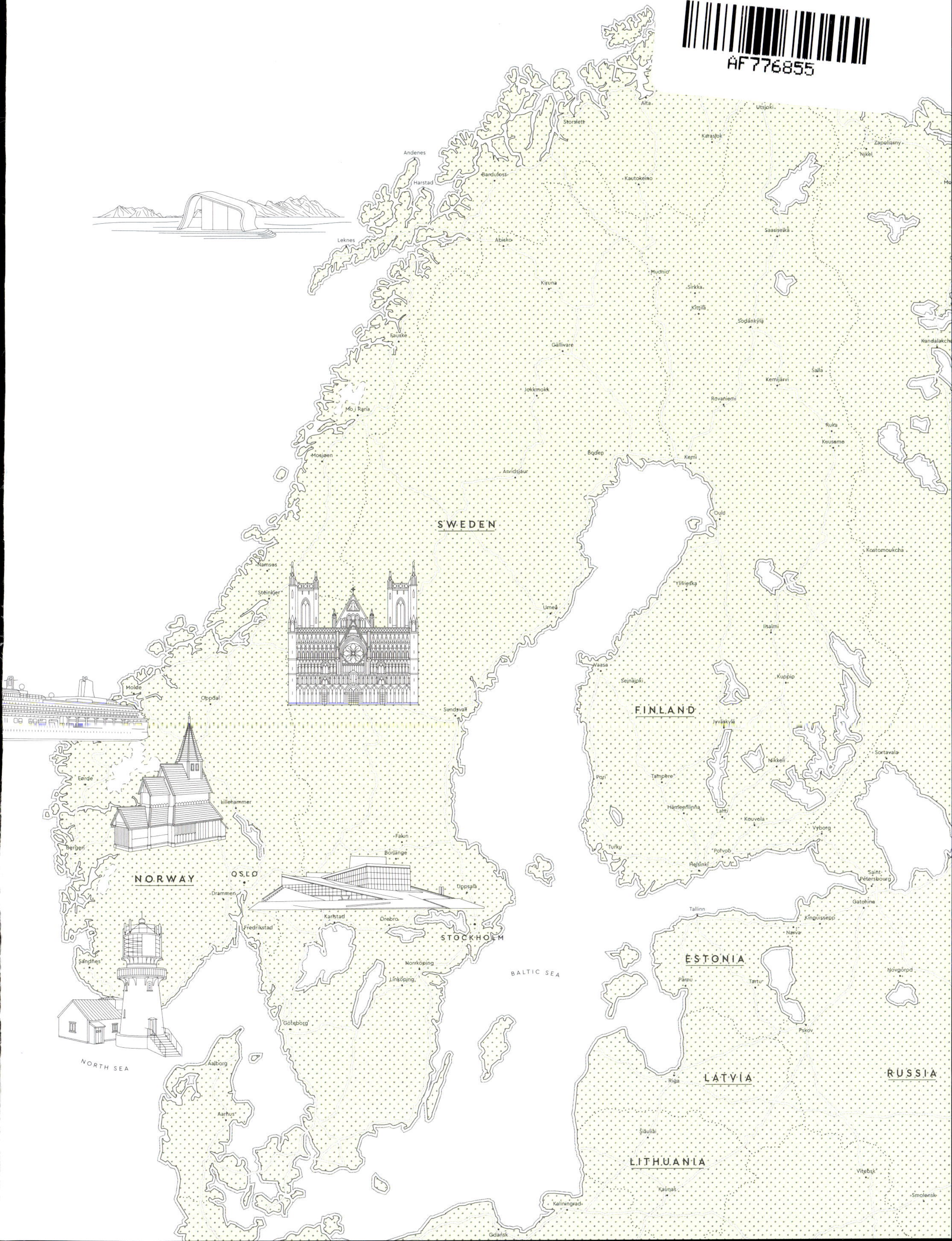
Alta
Utsjoki
Storslett
Karasjok
Zapolyarny
Nikel
Andenes
Harstad
Bardufoss
Kautokeino
Saariselkä
Leknes
Abisko
Muonio
Kiruna
Sirkka
Kittilä
Sodankylä
Fauske
Gällivare
Kandalaksha
Salla
Kemijärvi
Jokkmokk
Rovaniemi
Mo i Rana
Ruka
Kuusamo
Mosjøen
Boden
Kemi
Arvidsjaur
Oulu
SWEDEN
Kostomuksha
Namsos
Steinkjer
Ylivieska
Umeå
Iisalmi
Vaasa
Seinäjoki
Kuopio
Molde
Oppdal
Sundsvall
FINLAND
Jyväskylä
Sortavala
Nikkeli
Førde
Pori
Tampere
Lillehammer
Hämeenlinna
Lahti
Kouvola
Vyborg
Falun
Turku
Porvoo
Bergen
Borlänge
Helsinki
Saint Petersbourg
NORWAY
OSLO
Uppsala
Drammen
Gatchina
Tallinn
Karlstad
Örebro
Kingisepp
Fredrikstad
Narva
STOCKHOLM
Sandnes
ESTONIA
Norrköping
Novgorod
BALTIC SEA
Linköping
Pärnu
Tartu
Göteborg
Pskov
NORTH SEA
Aalborg
LATVIA
RUSSIA
Riga
Aarhus
Šiauliai
LITHUANIA
Vitebsk
Kaunas
Smolensk
Kaliningrad
Gdańsk

NORWAY

THE EXTRAORDINARY GUIDES

NORWAY

BRICE PORTOLANO

RIZZOLI UNIVERSE

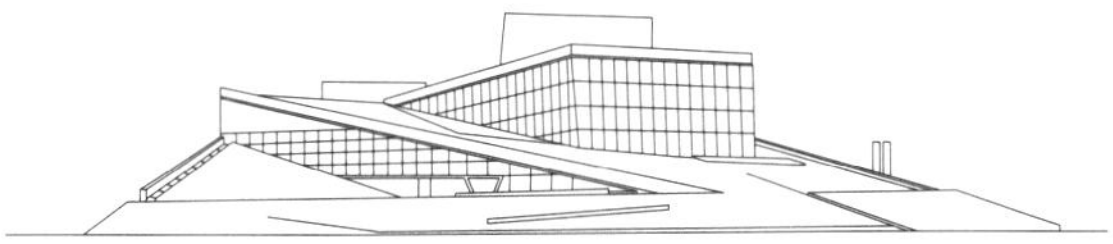

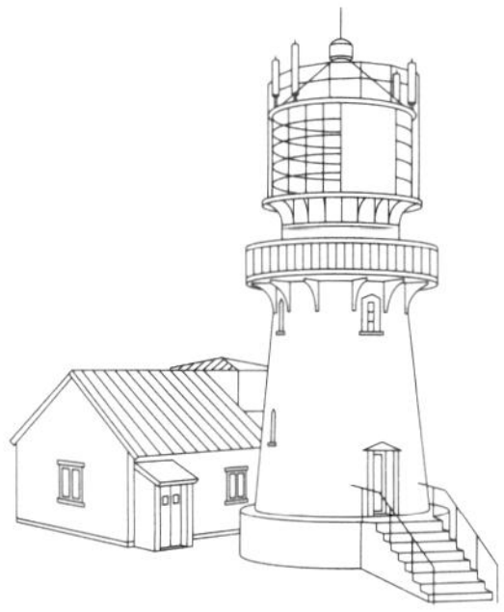

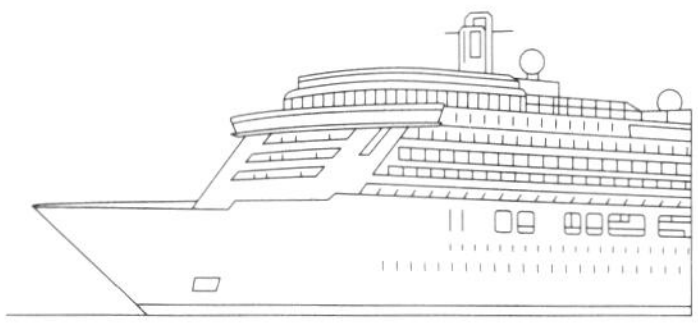

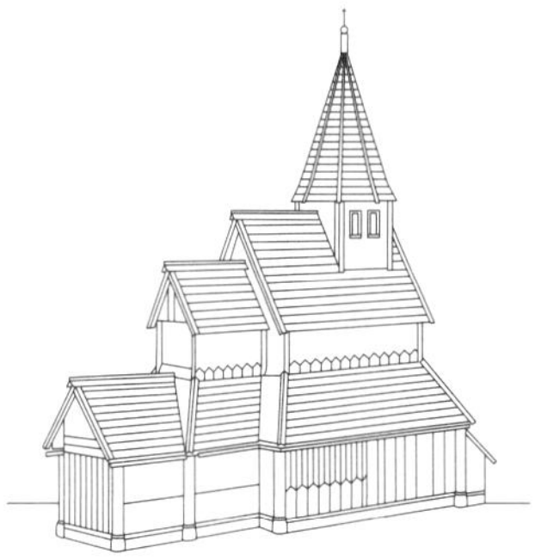

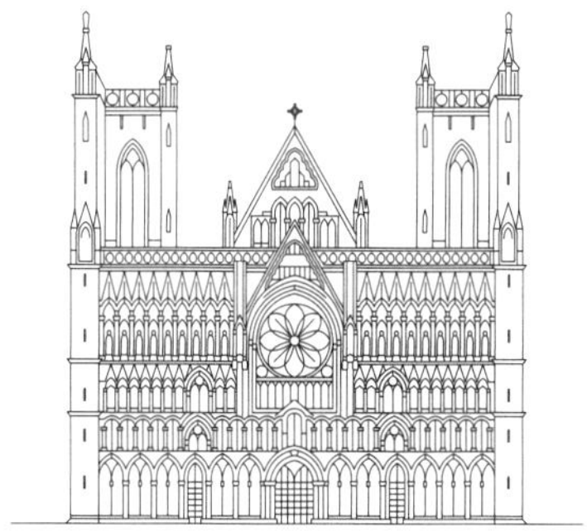

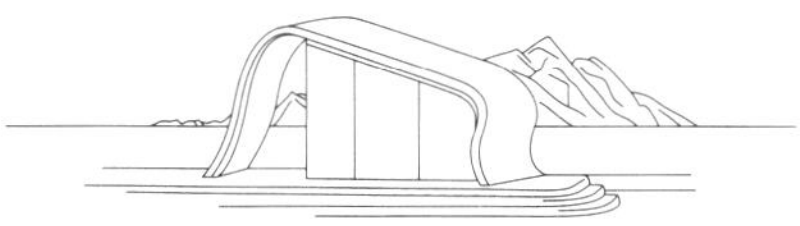

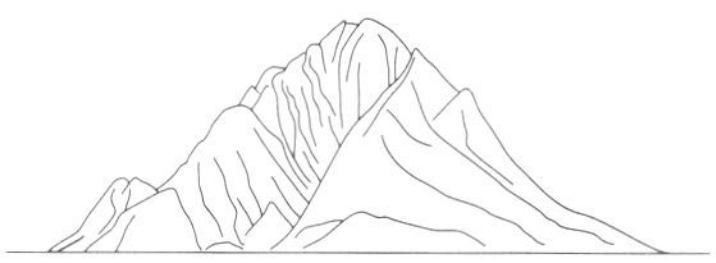

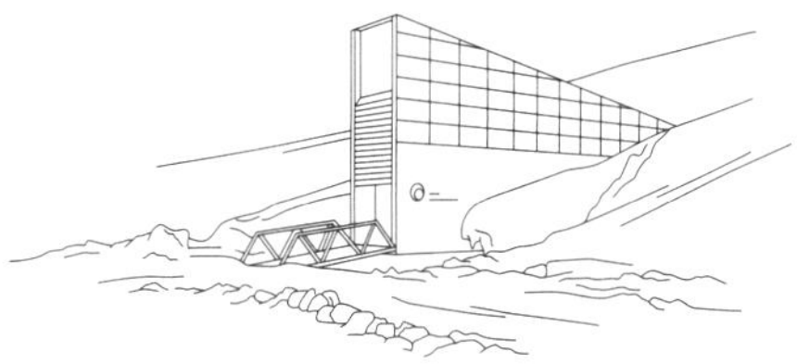

INTRODUCTION

The mere mention of Norway is enough to quicken the pulse of travelers and nature lovers alike—who doesn't dream of exploring the Lofoten Islands or being transfixed by the sight of the Northern Lights on their way to the legendary North Cape?

The land of fjords, Vikings, and polar bears owes much to its magnificent natural beauty and spectacular scenery. Visitors can expect a wow moment around every corner, although the Norwegians enjoy their country too—as keen ramblers and lovers of the great outdoors, they are so devoted to getting out into nature that a hike in the mountains is a far from uncommon suggestion for a first date.

Two expressions may help to explain the importance of outdoor life to Norwegians. Firstly, *Allemannsretten,* a guarantee of everyone's right to enjoy the natural world. Any rambler or hiker may cross private land and even camp there, as long as they leave no trace of their passing and pitch their tent a minimum of 165 yards (150 m) from any dwellings.

Friluftsliv means spending time in nature without disturbing or destroying it, a philosophy practiced by the great majority of Norwegians throughout the year, whatever the weather. The number of days that Norwegians spend out in the open air may even explain the country's leading position in the global ranking of the happiest nations.

The character of Norway's 5.3 million inhabitants has been deeply influenced by the nation's dramatic geography. More than two thousand five hundred glaciers are scattered across the country, with Jostedalsbreen, the most famous, being the largest glacial mass in Continental Europe. There is also no shortage of mountains: Galdhøpiggen, Norway's highest peak, rises 8,100 ft (2,469 m) above Jotunheimen National Park. Despite measuring some 1,088 miles (1,750 km) from north to south, no more than 3 percent of the country's land mass is suitable for agriculture, with the rest being taken up by forests, lakes, and mountains.

The twists and turns of the rugged coastline stretch out for some 51,580 miles (83,000 km), making it the longest in Europe. Coastal areas enjoy a fairly mild climate thanks to the warm currents of the Gulf Stream that protect them from winter ice formation. Before the twentieth century and the completion of the road and rail infrastructure, in the winter people preferred to travel by sea. As for the country's fjords, they are undoubtedly one of its most iconic features, with vertical cliffs that can rise to heights of 3,280 ft (1,000 m).

The first fishing and hunter-gatherer communities began to colonize Norway when the land became habitable at the end of the last Ice Age, around twelve thousand years ago. The population grew as the climate warmed but did not stray far from the coasts as the interior remained inhospitable. The Stone Age lasted until 1800 BCE in Scandinavia, as can be seen from tools that have been found with carved animal heads and numerous petroglyphs, especially in the area around Alta. Trade with Southern Europe developed during the Bronze Age (between 1800 and 450 BCE) but was of only very limited nature, leaving little trace in European records. The Iron Age that followed lasted until around 800 CE and trading relations increased during this period, with the Roman Empire supplying metals, pottery, and fabrics to Norway.

Norway's written history did not begin until later, with accounts of the Vikings and their many conquests. Harald I's defeat of the other Viking chiefs at the Battle of Hafrsfjord near Stavanger in 872 unified the country, and Trondheim, formerly known as Nidaros, became Norway's capital. The era of the Norse warriors and their many pillaging raids across Europe was to continue until 1066 and the death of Harald III. The influence of the Kingdom of Norway was further extended in 1261 with the annexation of Greenland and Iceland.

Norway's power began to wane after unification with Sweden in 1319, shrinking to the status of a mere province within Scandinavia. This heralded the beginning of a four-century decline that was precipitated by the arrival in Bergen in 1349 of a ship from England carrying the plague. It would prove too be a catastrophe for the whole country, with fields left untended and the economy in freefall. The departure of a large proportion of the workforce obliged the nobility to work the land themselves to ensure their survival. Norway had been devastated, and about a third of its population is estimated to have died from the Black Death (with mortality rates rising to 80 percent among the aristocracy), leaving the country seriously weakened politically, administratively, and religiously.

Norway was not to regain its status as an independent kingdom until 1905, nearly four centuries later. The egalitarianism that is deeply ingrained in Norwegian attitudes has its roots in this period that profoundly shaped the country's history. The leveling of the social classes caused by the Black Death also goes some way toward explaining the prevailing absence of hierarchy today in Norwegian society.

Norway has now become a liberal state with full employment. It is also a bastion of social capitalism, providing a blend of free market economy and state intervention. The low unemployment rate is underwritten by a tripartite federation of employers, unions, and the state, who maintain strong levels of cooperation in wage negotiations to sustain the high rate of employment. State benefits guarantee access to healthcare and education for all the residents of this Scandinavian nation that also ranks first in the world in terms of press freedom, according to the Reporters Without Borders World Press Freedom Index.

One major challenge that Norway is yet to confront is the post-oil era, however. Having been skyrocketed into the ranks of the world's most affluent countries by the discovery of oil fields off its coasts, this tiny fishing nation still relies heavily on hydrocarbon exports, which account for more than half of its total revenues overseas. Will Norway manage to choose wisely and ensure a smooth transition to a world with a drastically diminished appetite for fossil fuels? This is a complex challenge of great concern to the Norwegians, who remain extremely environmentally conscious and under no illusions about their quality of life, even if their lifestyle may be energy-intensive. The political decisions made between the present and 2030 will undoubtedly have lasting ramifications for twenty-first century Norwegian society.

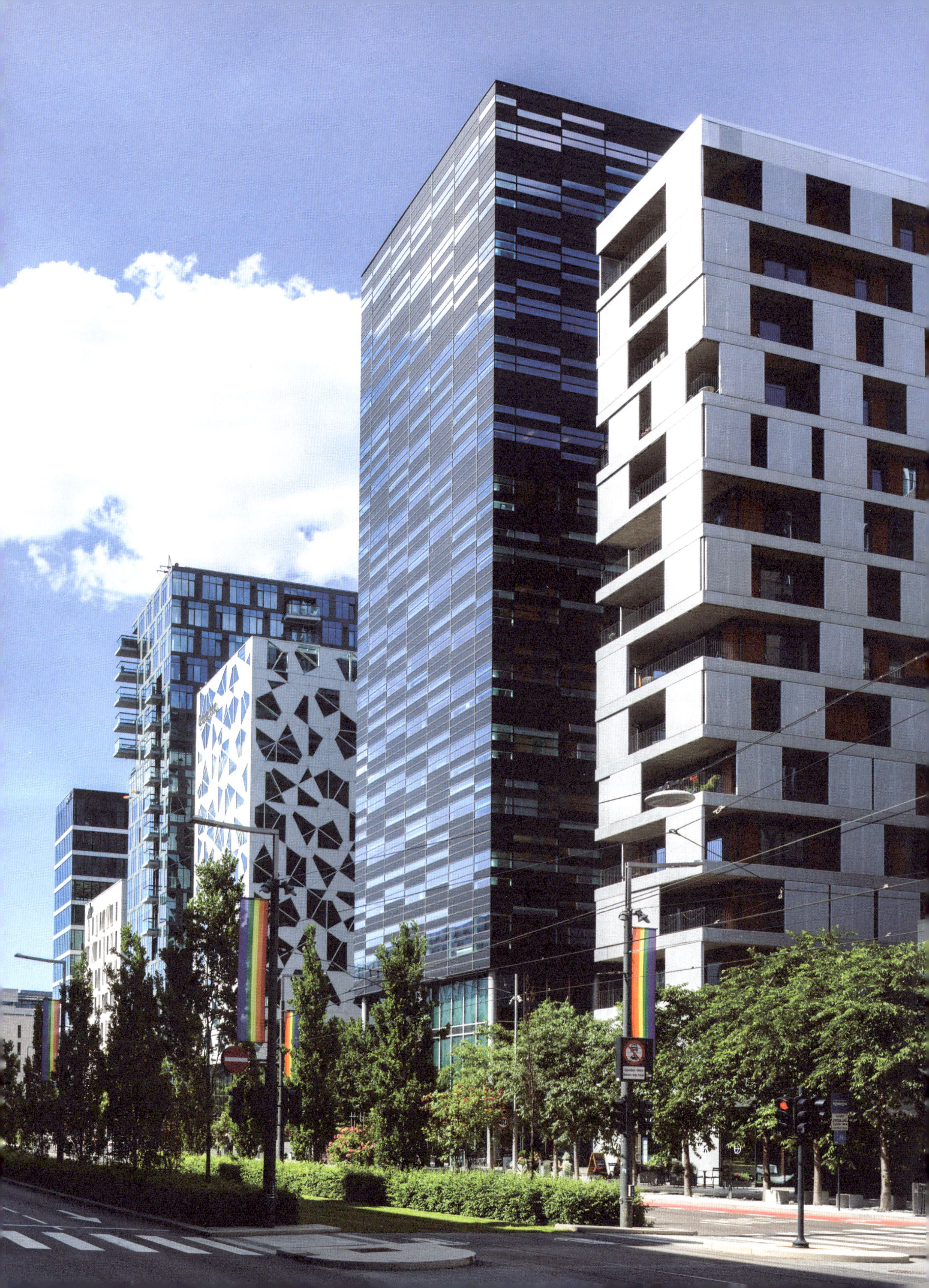

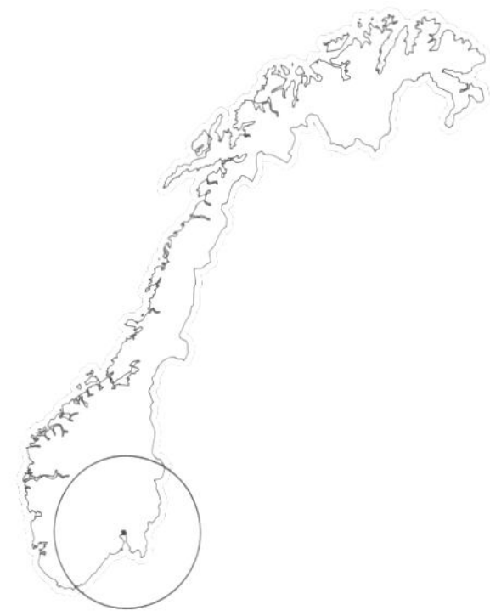

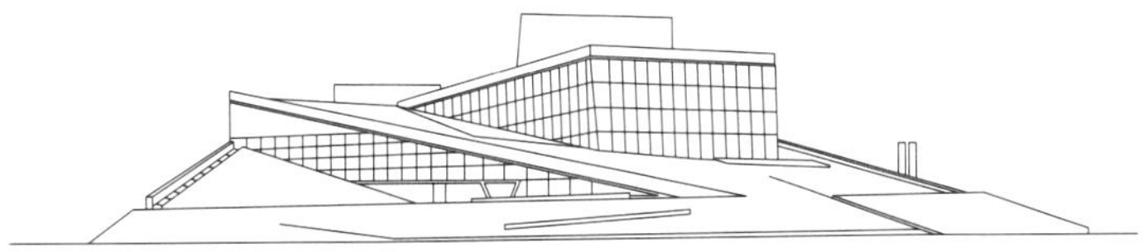

A DYNAMIC CAPITAL

OSLO

Vibrant yet understated, the Norwegian capital is well worth exploring for its many museums and lively harbor promenade.

P.10

Nine vessels dating back to the sixteenth century were excavated during construction of the Barcode Project on the old docks in the Bjørvika neighborhood.

OPPOSITE

Flowers bloom outside an old wooden house on Telthusbakken, a street famed for its eighteenth-century buildings.

Oslo has enjoyed higher population growth than any other European capital, with the changes that have taken place in recent years contributing to this. A once sedate, industrial town has now been transformed into a pleasant and highly dynamic metropolis with a rich cultural life.

The waterfront of the Bjørvika neighborhood has undergone a real transformation since Oslo Opera House opened its doors there in 2008, with highlights including the opening of the Deichman Bjørvika public library in 2020 and the Munch Museum in 2021. The old container port has had a complete makeover and now welcomes crowds of pedestrians during the long summer evenings. The promenades built beside the fjord attract locals who come to swim, take a sauna, or enjoy a meal before an evening of partying. The neighboring area of Aker Brygge was once a shipyard but has now been radically reimagined. Since 2022 it has been home to the new National Museum, whose treasures include one of the five versions of Edvard Munch's famous artwork *The Scream*.

Visitors may be surprised by the city's low volume of traffic: policies adopted in recent years have strongly disincentivized car use and encouraged residents to take public transport or to get about on foot and by bike—the ultimate aim being to banish cars from the city center completely. Many areas have therefore been pedestrianized, providing the opportunity for some pleasant strolling while exploring the heart of Oslo.

In the capital, which is surrounded by forests and hills, nature is never far away. Head away from the center for the hill of Holmenkollen with its ski jump and 360-degree panorama of the city and Oslo Fjord dotted with many islands. Oslo Vinterpark with eighteen ski runs (and ski-lift access even at night) lies on the northern slopes of the hill and can be reached via the metro. Of all the city's green spaces, however, Frognerparken may be the most pleasant, popular with locals who come here to play sports, take a stroll, or meet friends for a picnic.

A whole host of activities is also available on Oslo Fjord, adjoining the city center, including sea kayaking, swimming, and hiking. The city enjoys one of the most inviting natural settings of all the European capitals and is well worth a visit, whether to immerse oneself in Norwegian culture, to delve into the country's past through its many artists, or just to get a feel for the city before heading out to explore the great outdoors.

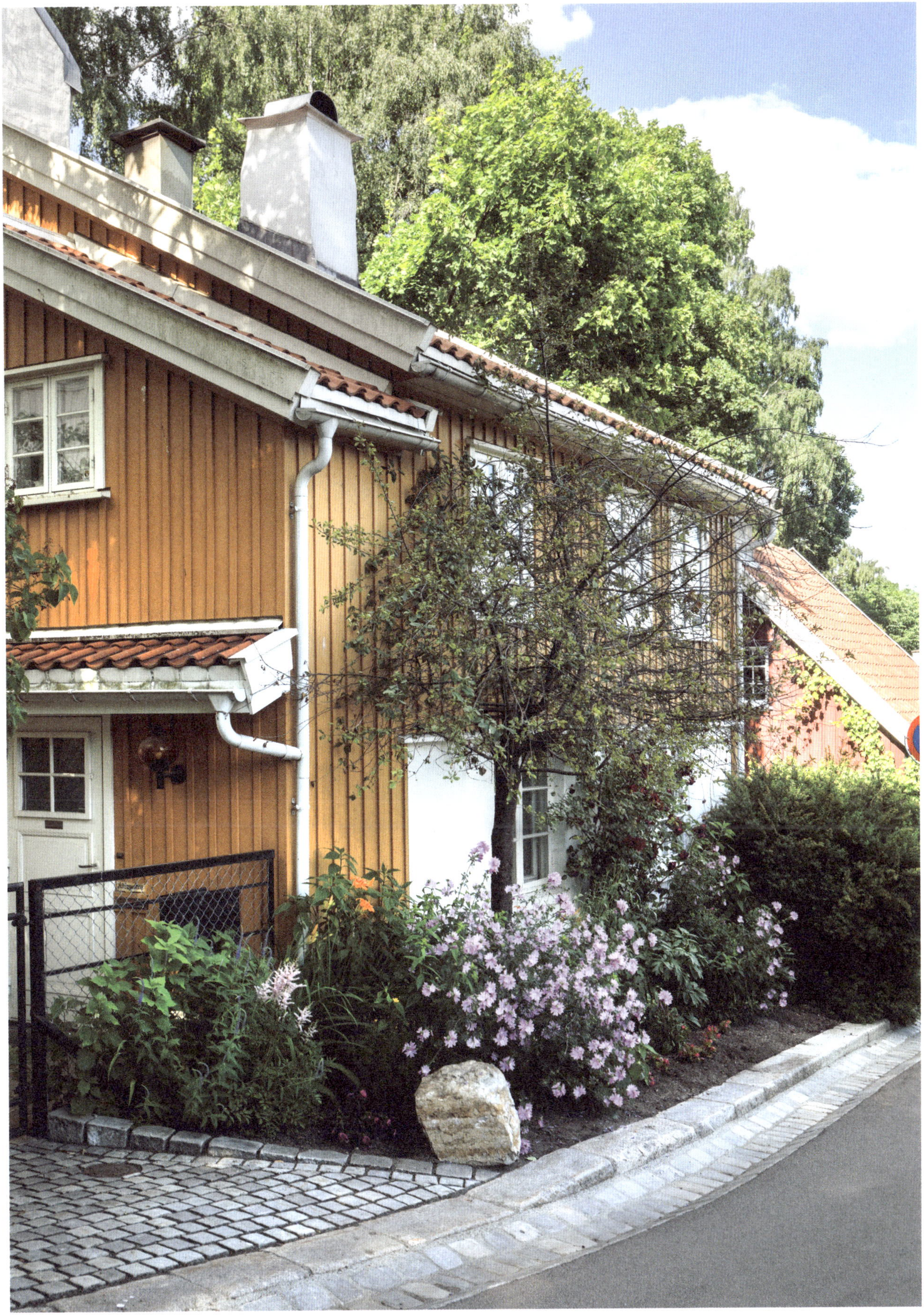

THE ESSENTIALS

01

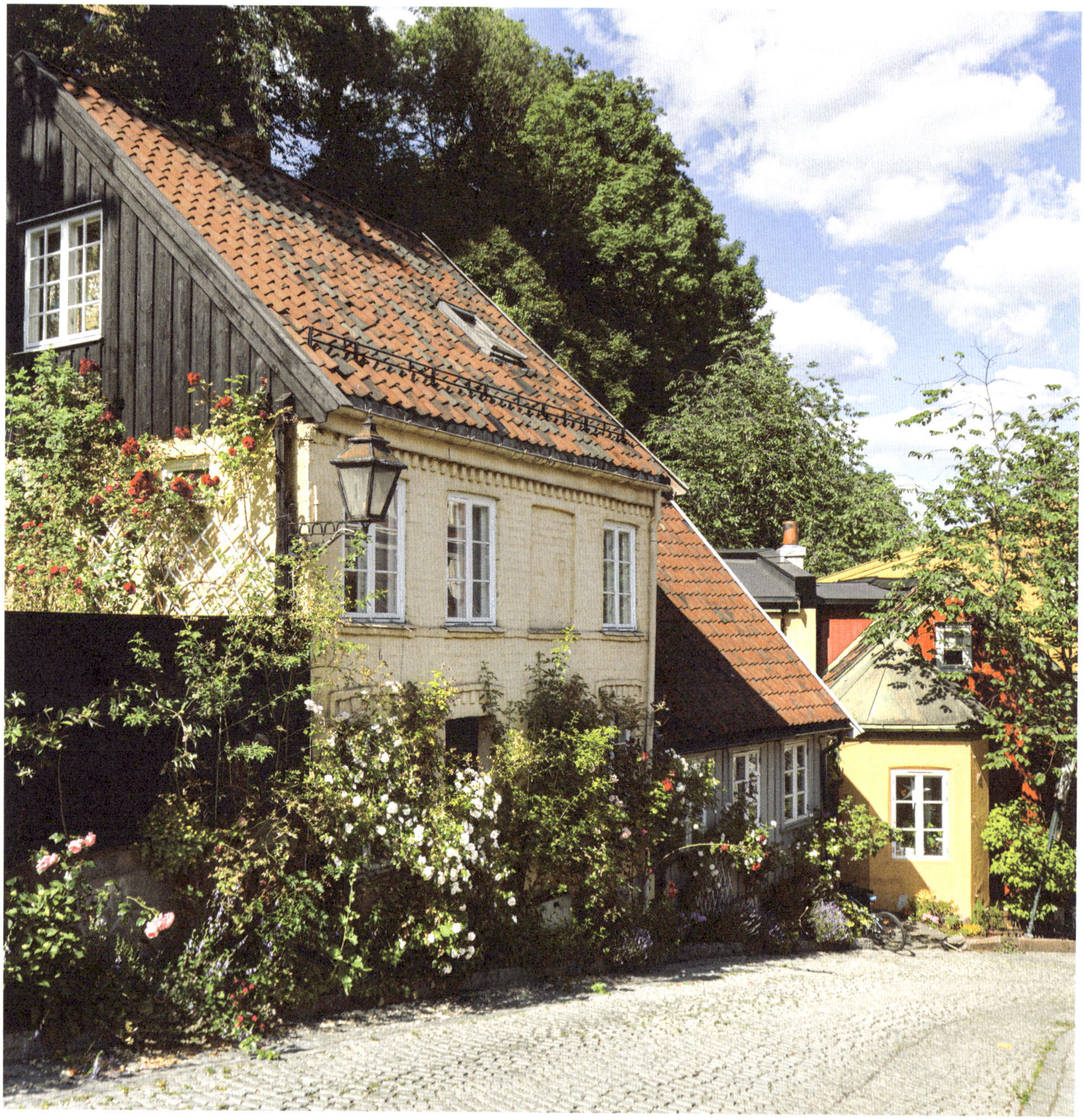

DAMSTREDET AND TELTHUSBAKKEN

Dating back to the late eighteenth and nineteenth centuries, the charming and picturesque streets of Damstredet and Telthusbakken are located on high ground in the center of Oslo.

02

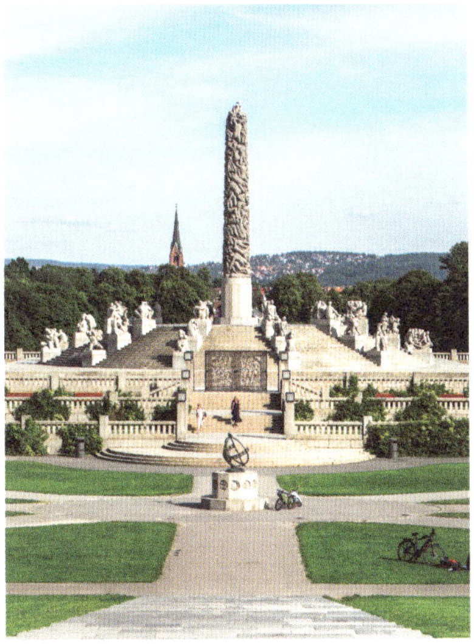

FROGNERPARKEN

This pleasant park lies close to the city center. Locals come here to play sports or eat a picnic lunch on the lawns.

03

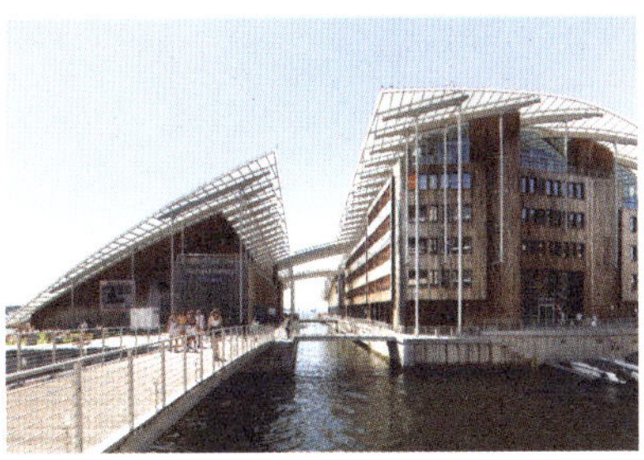

ASTRUP FEARNLEY MUSEUM OF MODERN ART

A private museum housing an extensive collection of modern and contemporary art from Northern Europe.

04

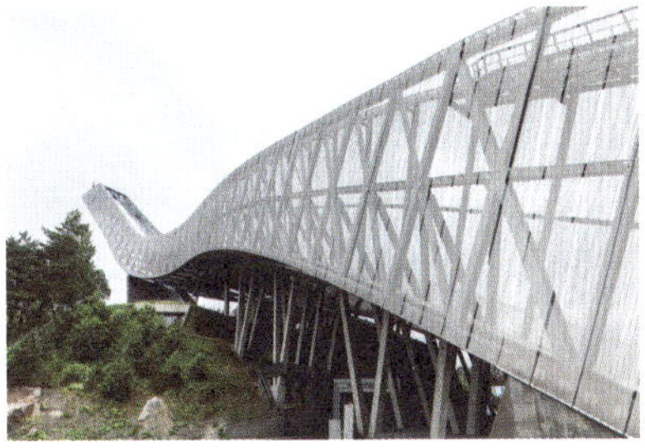

HOLMENKOLLBAKKEN

A ski jump in the hills overlooking the city with a unique vantage point to look out over Oslo Fjord.

05

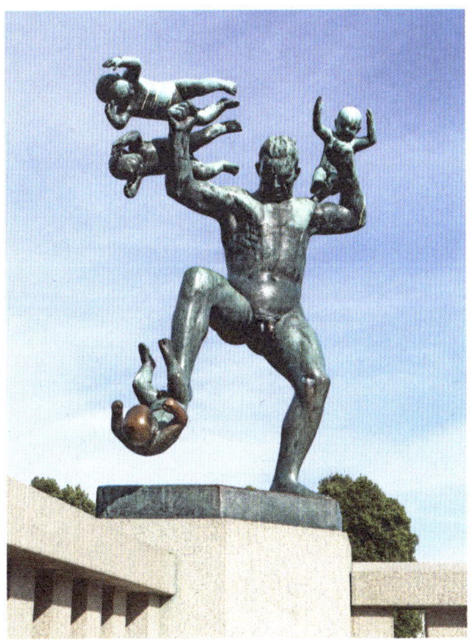

VIGELAND SCULPTURE PARK

This park dedicated to the work of Gustav Vigeland, Norway's most famous sculptor, is one of the most popular tourist destinations in the country.

06

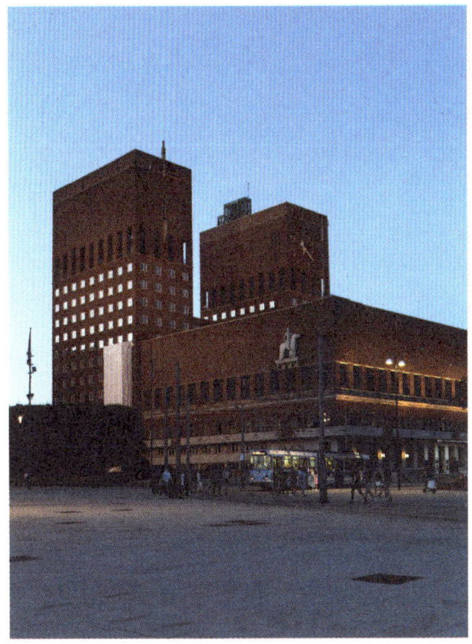

OSLO CITY HALL

The Nobel Peace Prize is awarded annually at a ceremony held in Oslo City Hall. There is no charge for visitors to access the site and view its historical artifacts and many murals.

07

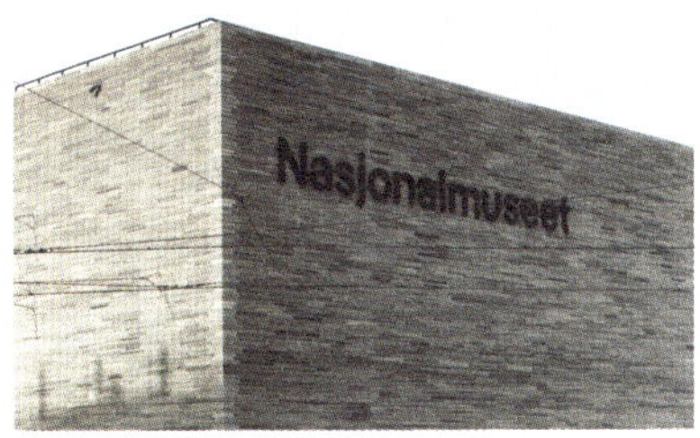

OSLO NATIONAL MUSEUM

Opening in 2022, this museum was built to replace the old National Gallery. It features the country's largest collection of works by Norwegian and foreign artists from the nineteenth century to the present.

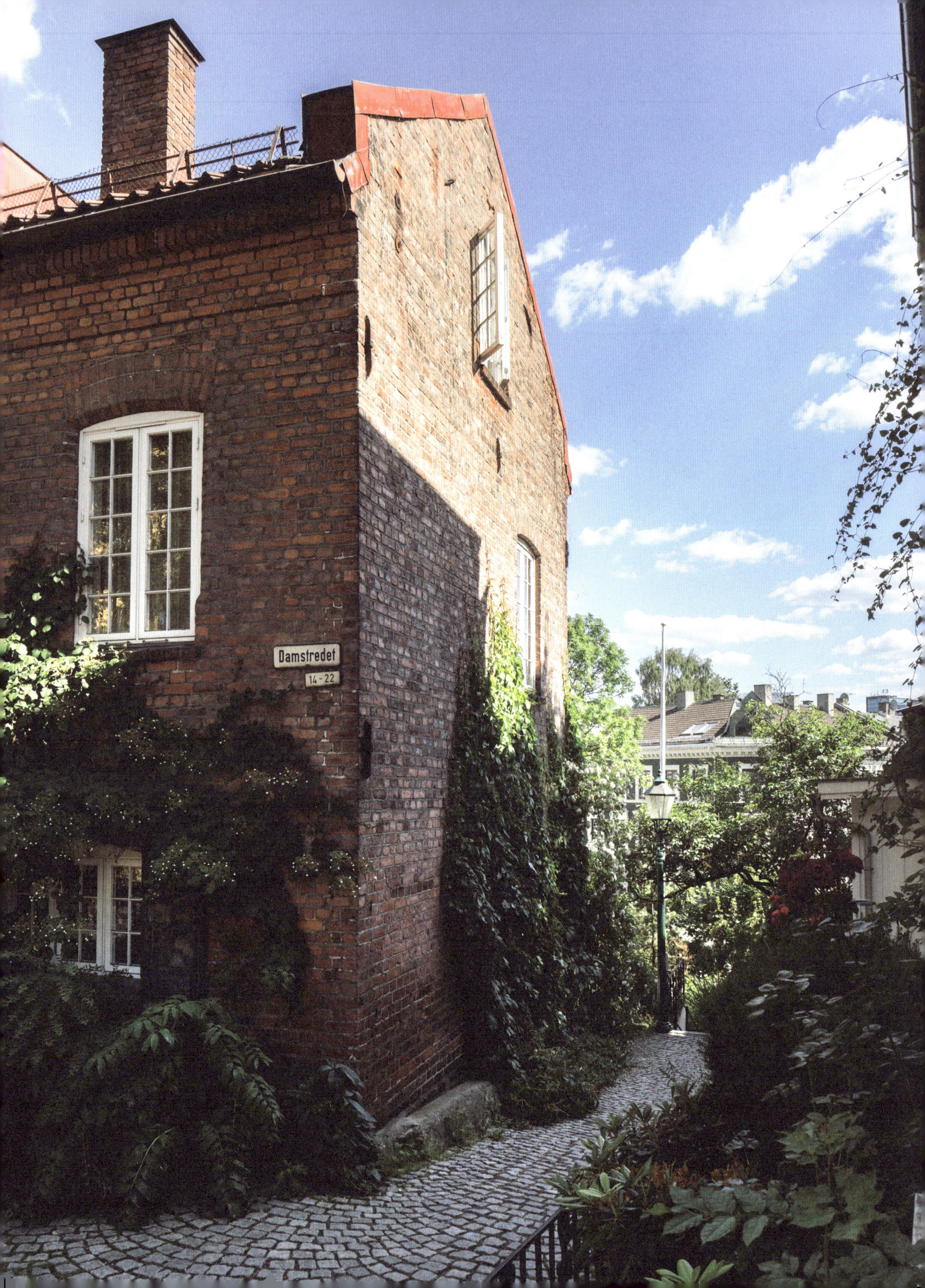
Damstredet
14–22

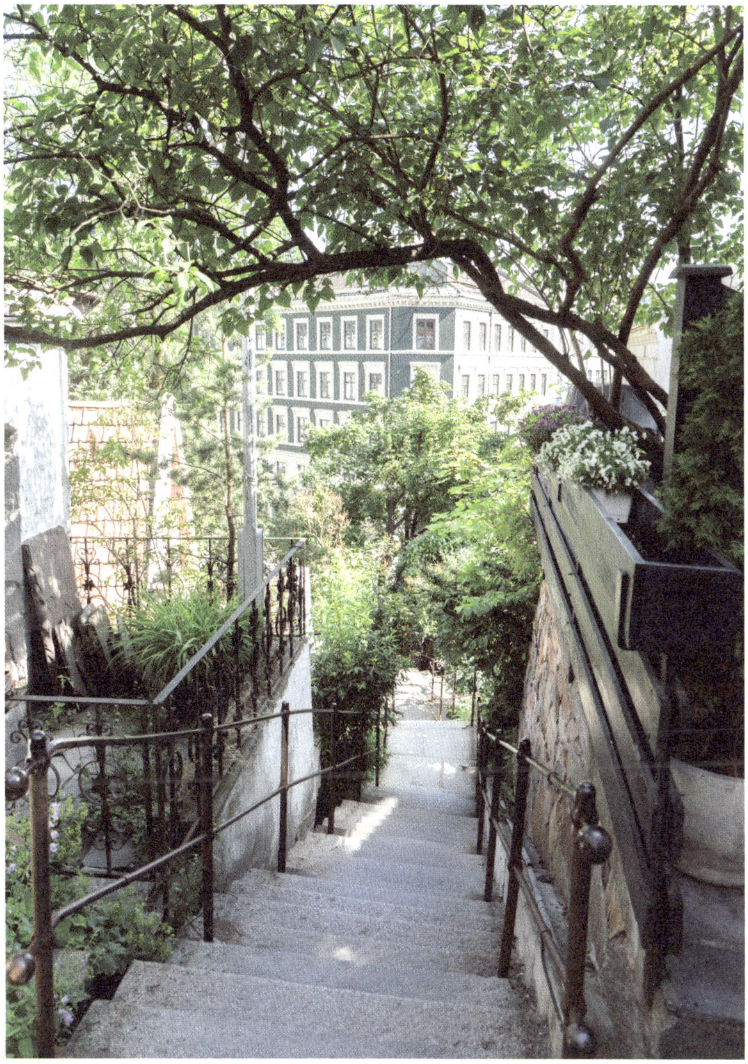

ABOVE

With its cobblestones and flights of steps, Damstredet feels like a mini version of Montmartre in Paris.

OPPOSITE

The local houses built of wood and brick offer a sharp contrast to the modern architecture of the city center.

HISTORY

EXCAVATING THE VIKINGS

PRECIOUS TREASURES FROM THE PAST

Archeological digs carried out in Oslo Fjord at the beginning of the twentieth century have unearthed an extremely well preserved Viking longship.

The Vikings' reputation as warriors has long preceded them. They had a formidable weapon at their disposal in the form of the longship, which enabled them to carry out the raids that terrorized parts of Europe. These were exceptional vessels for the time, allowing the Vikings to travel at speed to plunder the monasteries and abbeys of Great Britain and Ireland.

The Vikings also had no scruples about plundering burial sites, viewing Christians as "disciples of the white cross" and Christianity as a threat to the Viking belief system. Their many conquests across Europe may also be explained by their rapid population growth accelerated by the practice of polygamy, spurring the next generation to seek their fortunes overseas rather than carving up inherited land into ever smaller plots. While much about this race of merchants, explorers, and pirates is still shrouded in mystery, discoveries made during recent archeological digs have shed new light on their rites and culture.

In 1903 a farmer discovered an almost intact longship in a burial mound near Oseberg, south of Oslo. The mud encasing it had protected the wood from decaying over the centuries, and the vessel is now on display in the Viking Ship Museum in Oslo. Although it has been restored, 95 percent of the original wood has been preserved. Expert studies suggest that the oak vessel, which was 72 ft (22 m) long and 16 ft (5 m) wide, may have been constructed in 820 CE and would have achieved a top speed of ten knots. The remains of two women were discovered within the boat, their ages estimated at approximately fifty and eighty years. They were likely of high status as this kind of ship burial was reserved for warriors, clan chiefs, and their families.

Provisions and jewelry were often placed in grave sites, along with animals that had been specially sacrificed, and servants would sometimes even volunteer to accompany their deceased masters on the journey into the afterlife. Six dogs, two cows, fifteen horses, a chariot, tools, bedlinen, and five beds were recovered from the longship. Other valuable items had been stolen from the site, which would explain why parts of the skeletons were also missing.

The discovery is an impressive relic of the past, allowing us to imagine Viking life in much greater detail than previously.

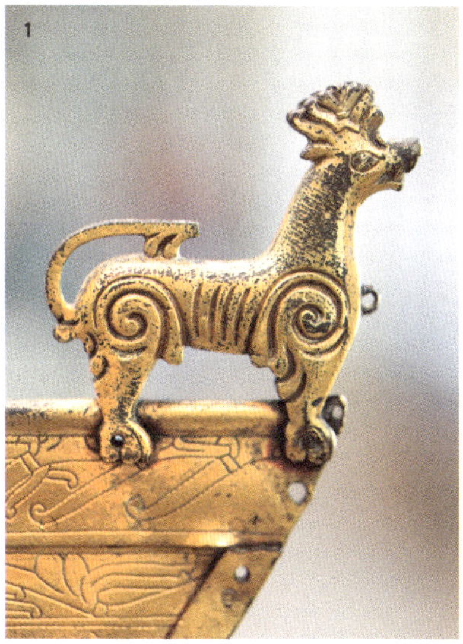

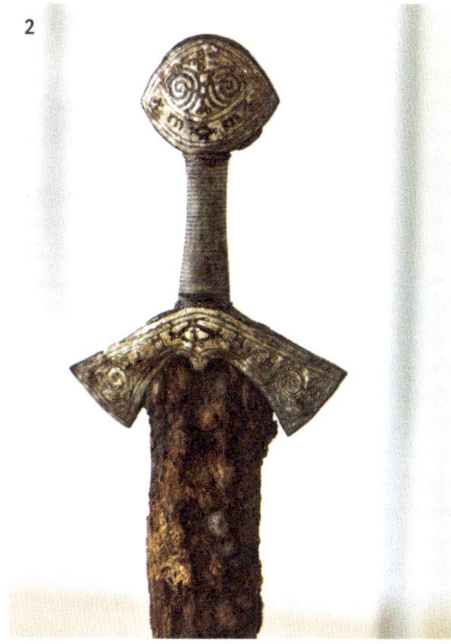

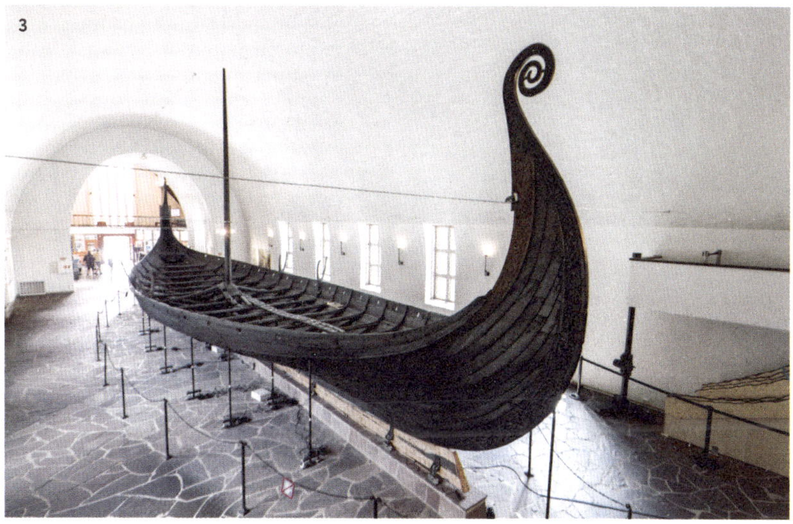

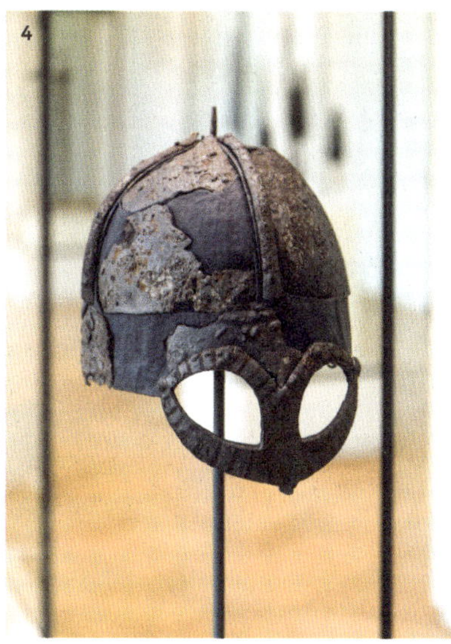

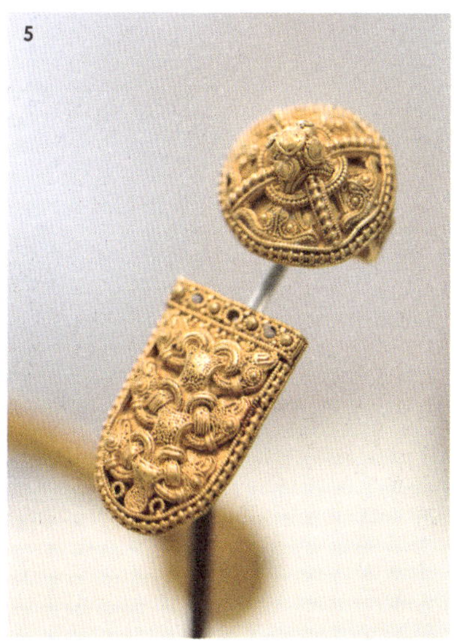

1/ MARITIME REMAINS

Detail from a gilded copper alloy weathervane from a ship's prow, dating from 1000–1050 CE. Museum of Cultural History, Oslo.

2/ WEAPON OF WAR

A decorated sword hilt with a forged blade. Manufactured overseas between 800–1000 CE.

3/ OSEBERG SHIP

The Oseberg longship was discovered in a burial mound in a remarkable state of preservation.

4/ NASAL HELMET

This combat helmet is typical of medieval armor from Northern Europe. It features a metal bar to protect the nose and eyes.

5/ GOLD SPUR

The upper part of a golden spur, found in a farmer's field in 1887. The decoration features gold filigree and beads soldered in highly detailed patterns.

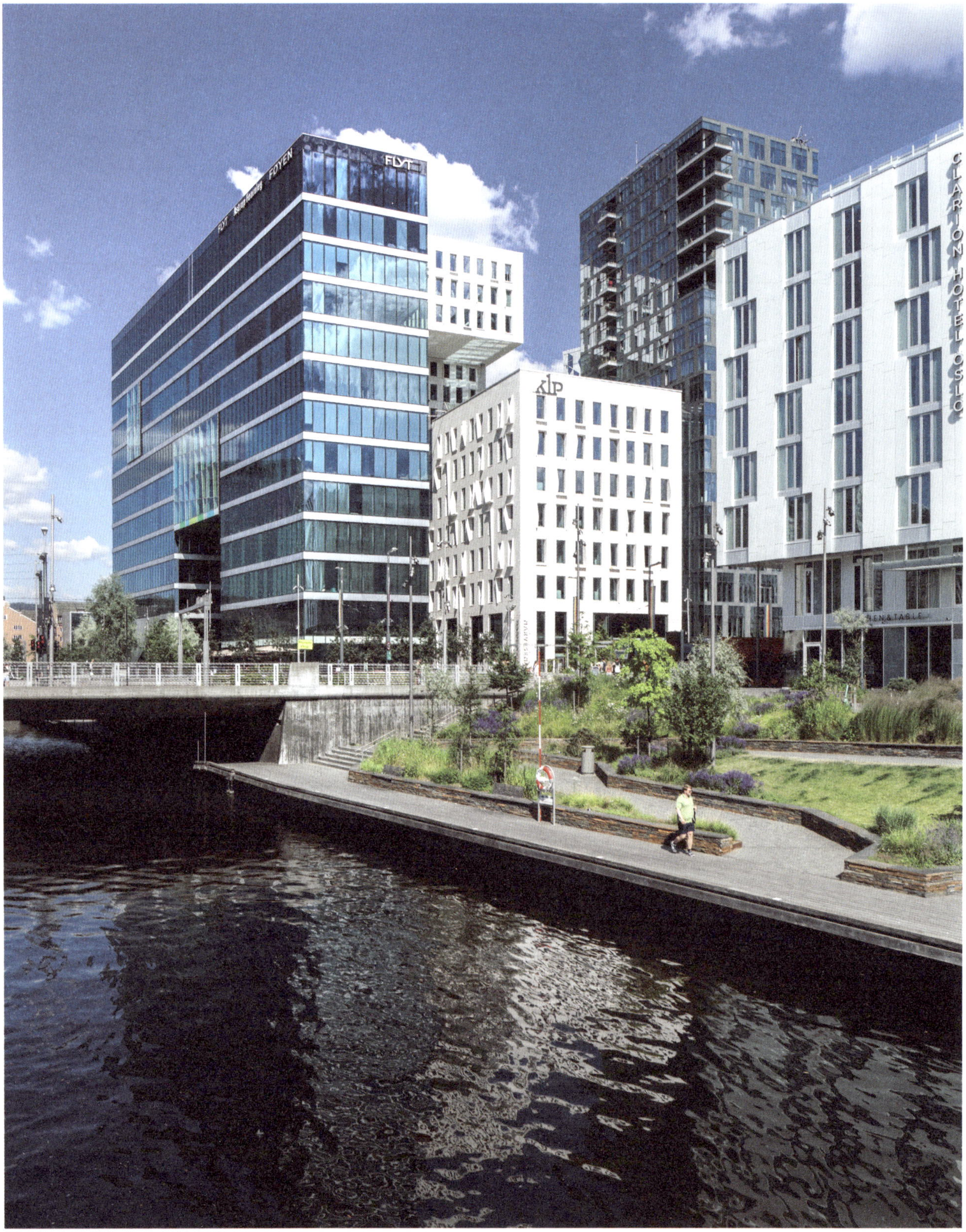

The buildings of the Barcode Project tower over the green spaces beside Oslo Fjord in Bjørvika.

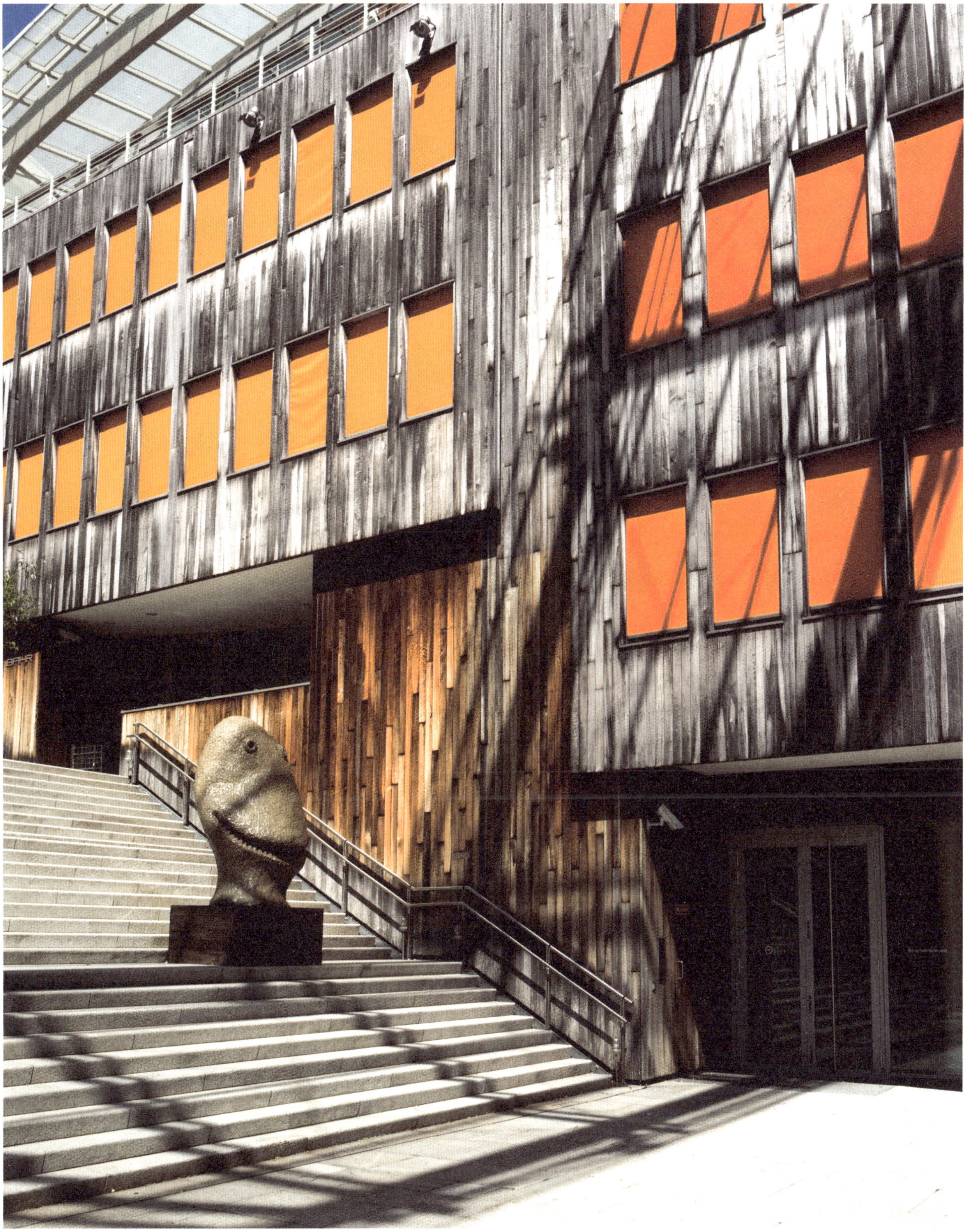

Visitors to the Astrup Fearnley Museum of Modern Art are greeted at the entrance by a sculpture.

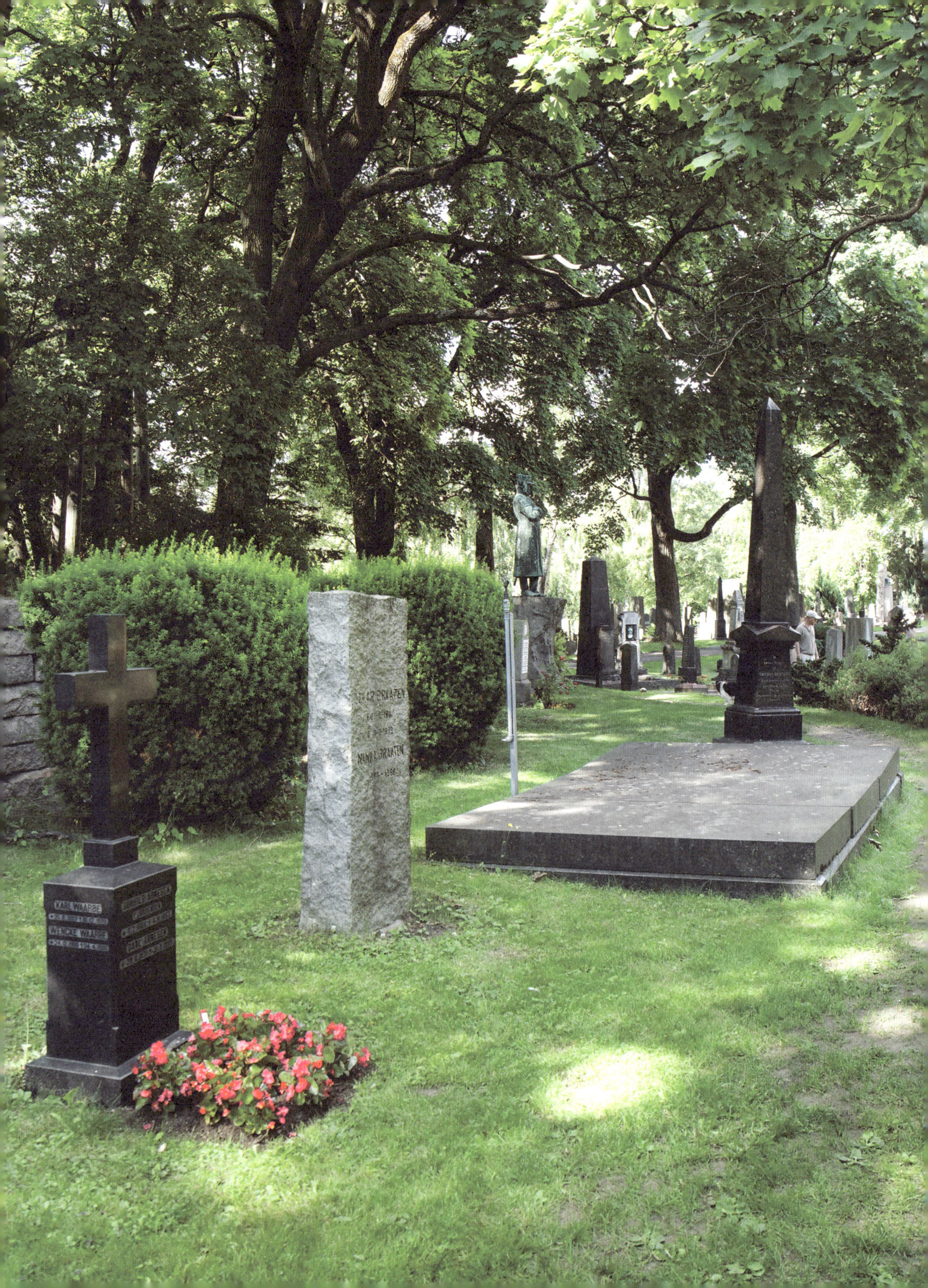
KARL WAARBE
WENCKE WAARBE
OSKAR BRAATEN
NANNA BRAATEN

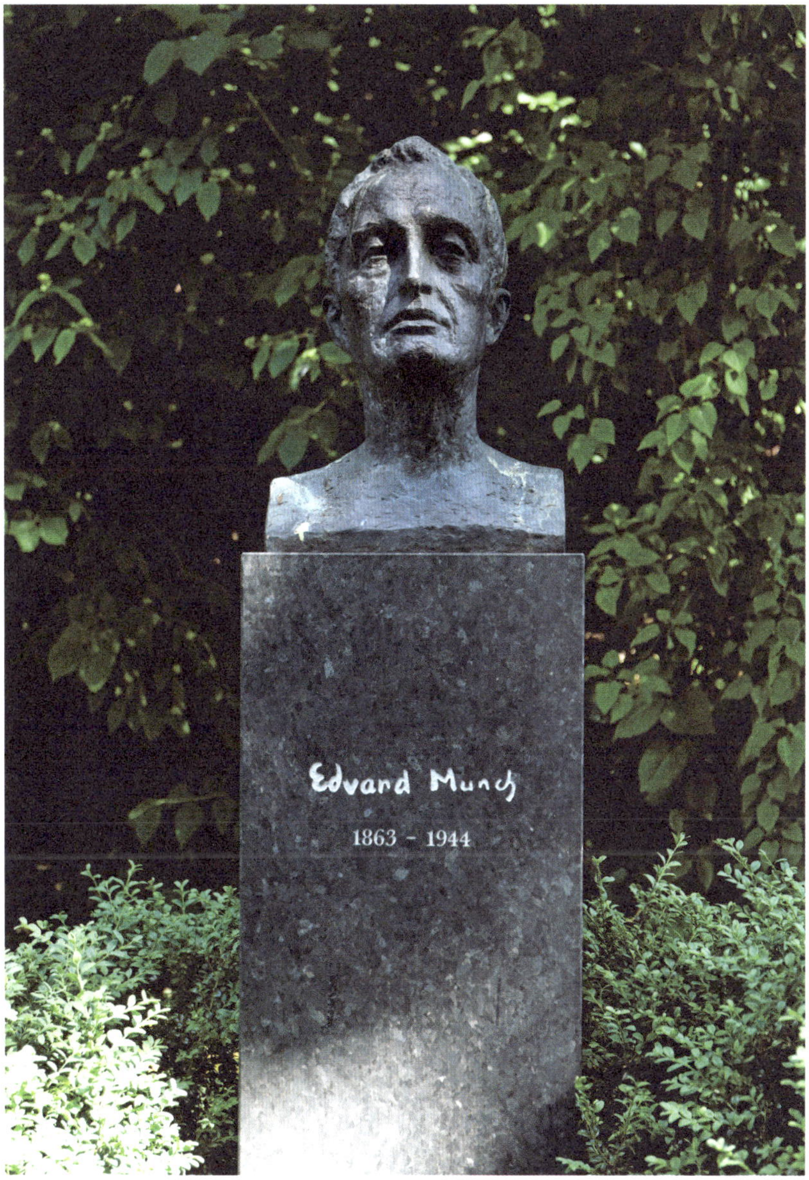

ABOVE

The famous Norwegian painter Edvard Munch is buried in Our Savior's Cemetery in the historic heart of Oslo.

OPPOSITE

The graves of many prominent figures from the Kingdom of Norway are to be found in this cemetery, which is located a stone's throw from Damstredet and Telthusbakken.

ARCHITECTURE

OSLO AND ITS ARCHITECTURE

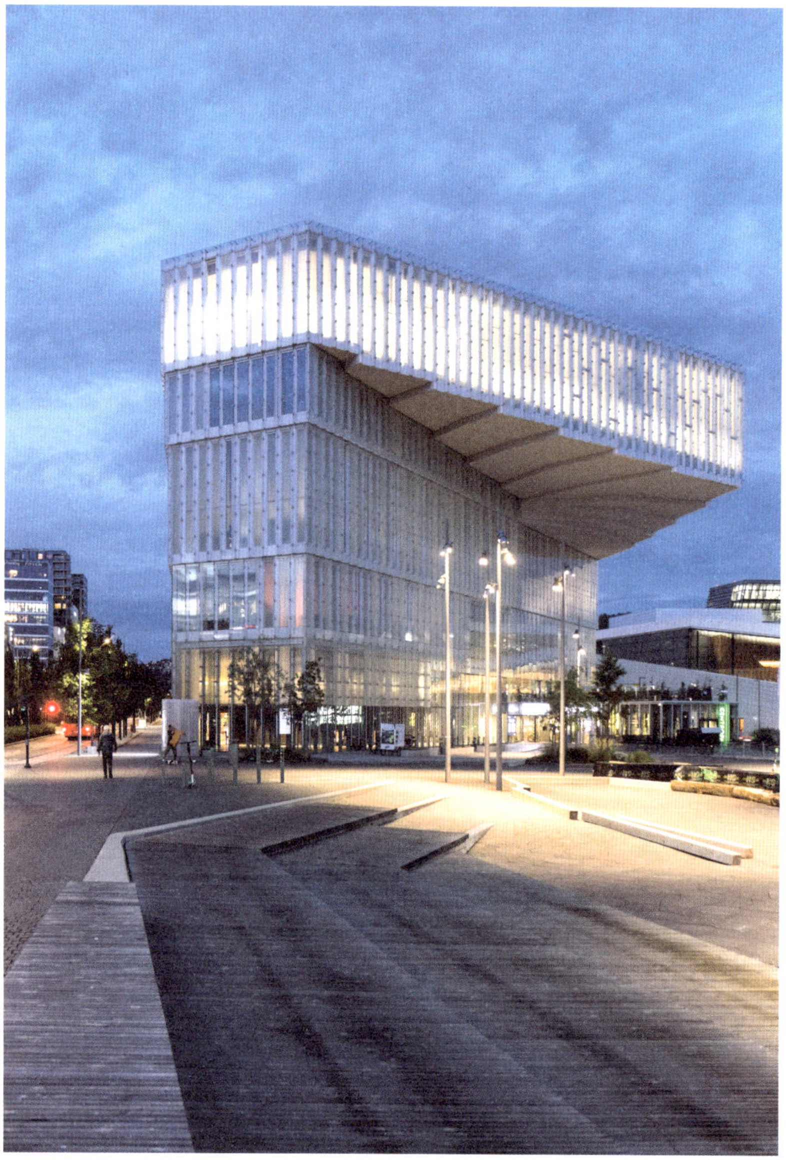

BJØRVIKA PUBLIC LIBRARY

Housing one of the most modern libraries in Europe, the building was designed by Bollinger+Grohmann and has won several awards for its architecture.

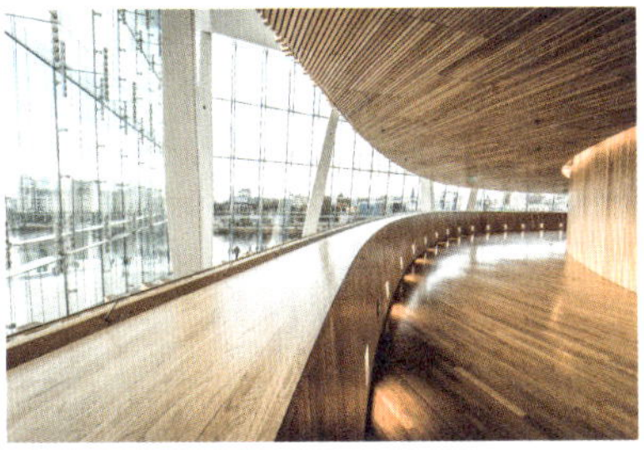

OSLO OPERA HOUSE

Interior of Oslo Opera House, inspired by Norway's natural surroundings.

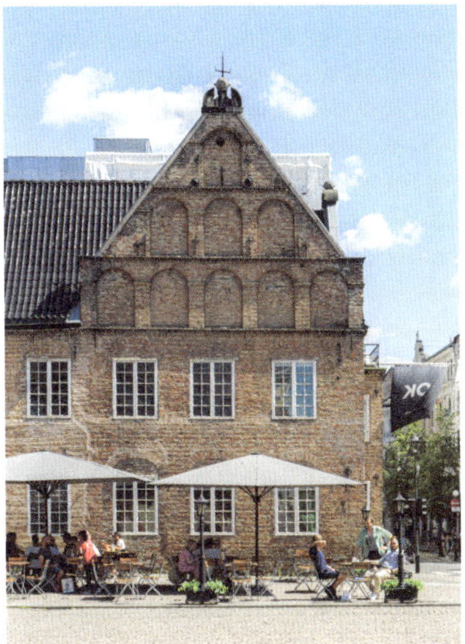

GAMLE RÅDHUS

Traditional Norwegian cooking is served here all day.

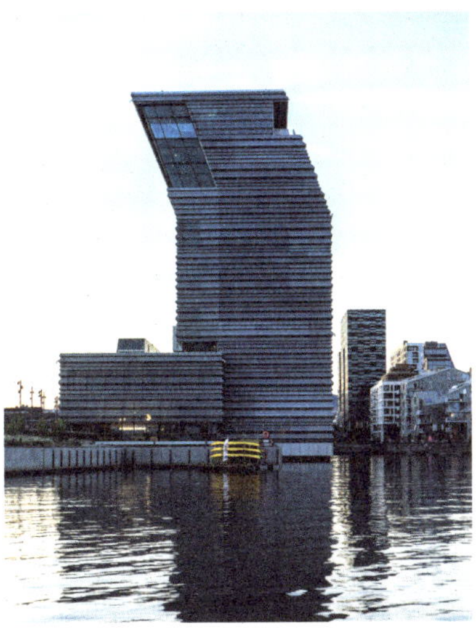

MUNCH MUSEUM

This museum situated beside the fjord is home to Munch's famous work *The Scream*.

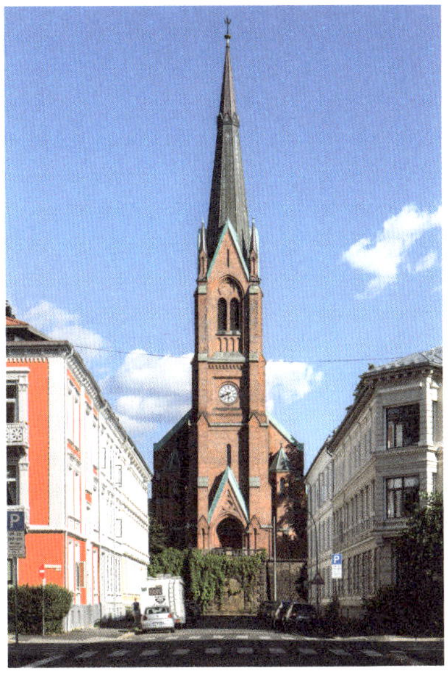

PAULUS KIRKE

This church in the Gothic Revival style opened its doors in 1892.

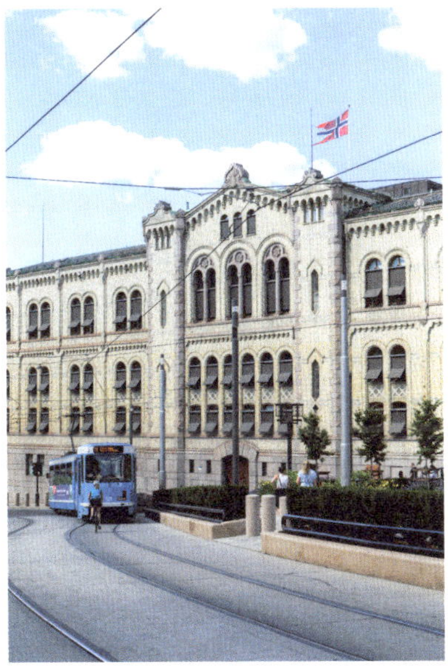

STORTINGET

The Norwegian Parliament building, designed by Emil Victor Langlet, was completed in 1866. It features a combination of styles inspired by French and Italian architecture.

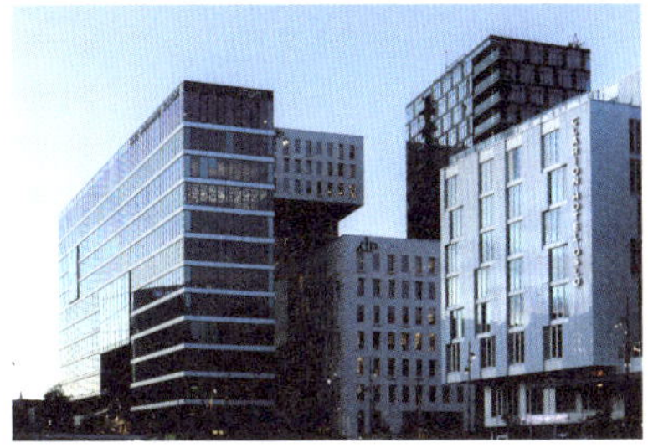

BARCODE PROJECT

The Barcode Project is a building complex in Bjørvika.

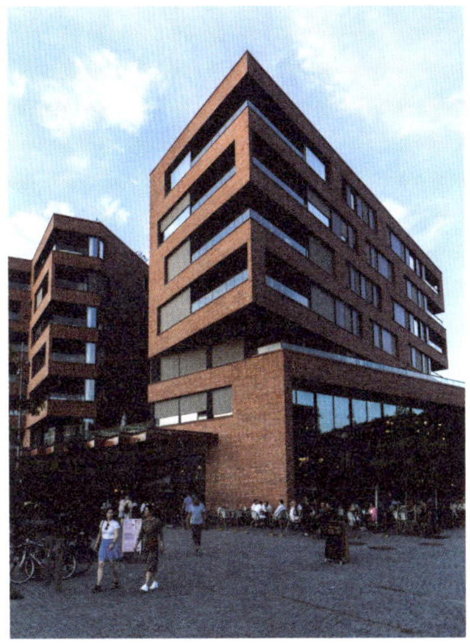

BISPEVIKA

Bispevika is a new residential district built on the site of the city's old port.

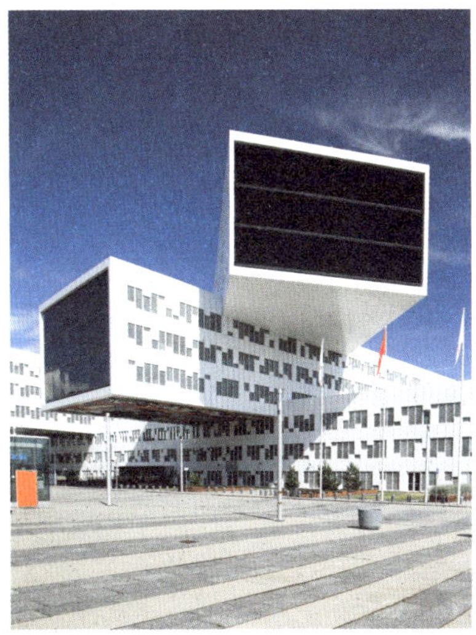

STATOIL

The offices of Norway's Statoil petroleum company (now Equinor) are noted for their modern architecture.

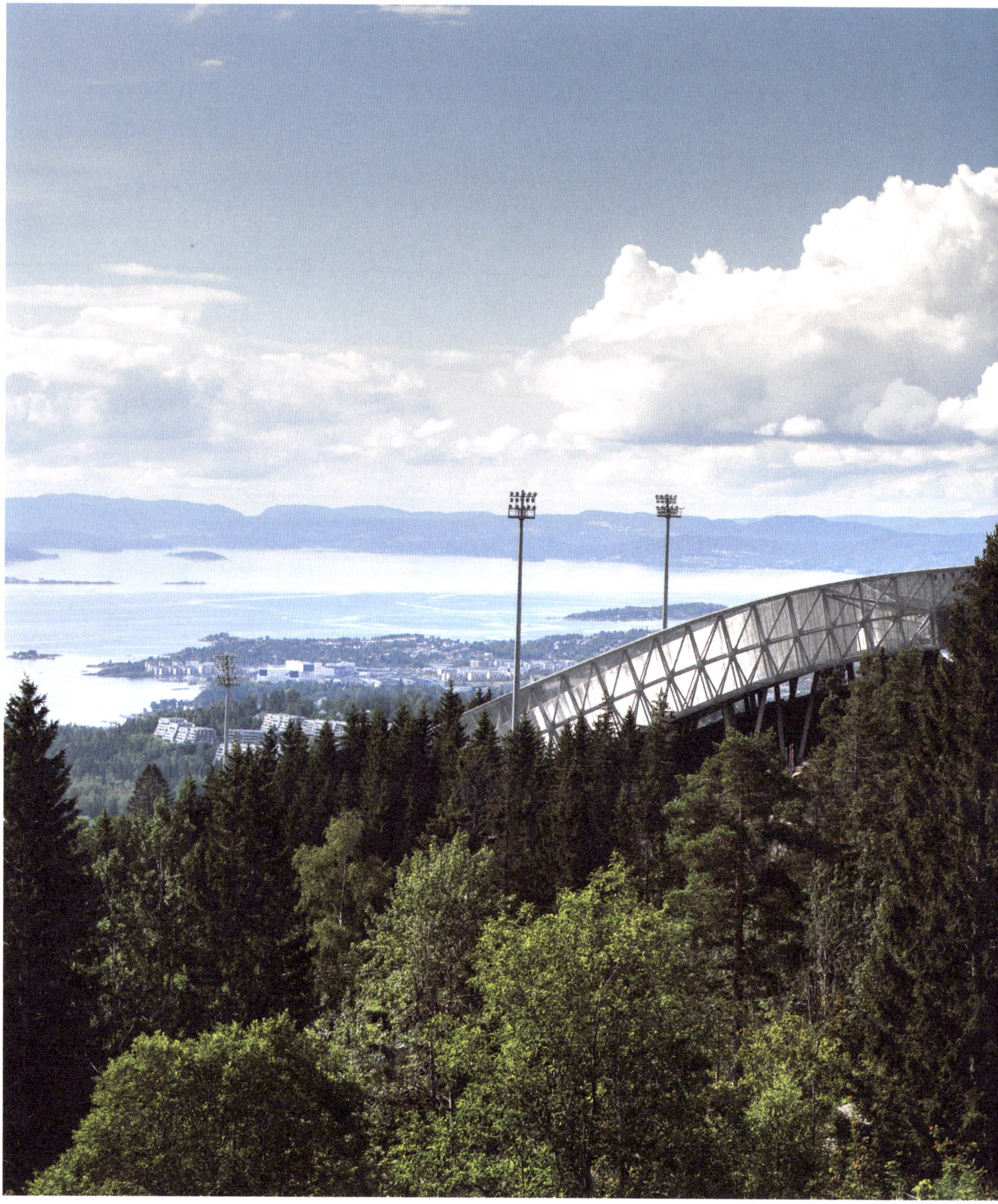

Holmenkollen ski jump, built on high ground beside the city, has played host to numerous competitions since its construction in 1892.

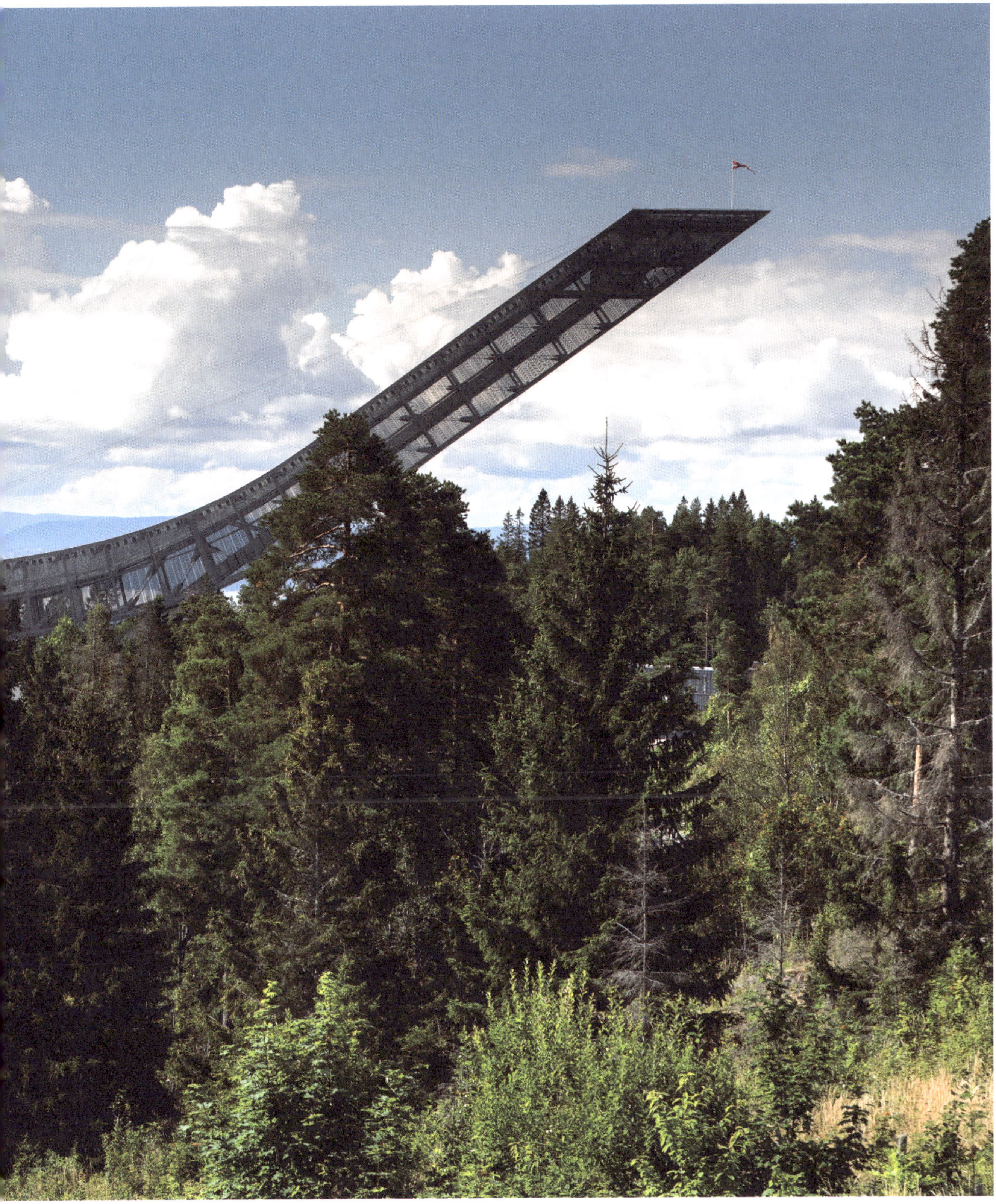

ARCHITECTURE

THE KISTEFOS MUSEUM

THE TWIST

The Kistefos Museum was built on the site of a former paper mill and now exhibits contemporary artists from all over the world.

The Kistefos Museum opened its doors in 1999 and features sculptures by numerous international artists, including Ólafur Elíasson, Anish Kapoor, Yayoi Kusama, Claes Oldenburg, Tony Cragg and Fernando Botero. These works were created especially for the museum and are displayed in one of the largest sculpture parks in Europe. They draw their inspiration from the old factory, its history, and its natural surroundings. Each year a new artist is invited to create a work to augment the museum's permanent collection. Some of these, such as Jeppe Hein's installation *Path of Silence*, a large sculpture that makes use of water and mirrors, are conceived on a grand scale, influencing how visitors move through the park.

The Kistefos Museum is the only wood pulp mill in Scandinavia to have preserved almost all of its buildings and manufacturing equipment. It also houses a historical museum with a host of treasures from the region's industrial past.

In 2019 the Kistefos opened a space that has since become iconic. The Twist, a 280-ft (85-m) high building designed by the Danish architect Bjarke Ingels, is at once a sculpture, an art gallery, and a bridge connecting opposite banks of the Randselva river. The center of the building features a ninety-degree structural rotation that creates an unexpected architectural sculpture. The exterior facade is clad in rectangular aluminum panels arranged in a fan pattern, creating a geometry of complex curves that reflect the river and the sun's rays. The interior space is paneled in the same way, with white-painted fir planks covering every surface from floor to ceiling.

Inside is a temporary exhibition space that guest artists adapt as the display is updated. The Twist has become a draw for many visitors from abroad and has won several prizes for its unique design, including, in 2020, the LCD Award that recognizes exceptional cultural spaces around the world.

It is this blend of historical museum, contemporary art gallery, and natural setting that gives the Kistefos its truly unique character. The museum also features a gift shop, café, and children's adventure park. It is quite easy to spend half a day here, or take a stroll in its peaceful surroundings and explore the many works of art scatted across the small, wooded valley. The museum represents a real breath of fresh air in gorgeous natural surroundings just an hour from the city of Oslo.

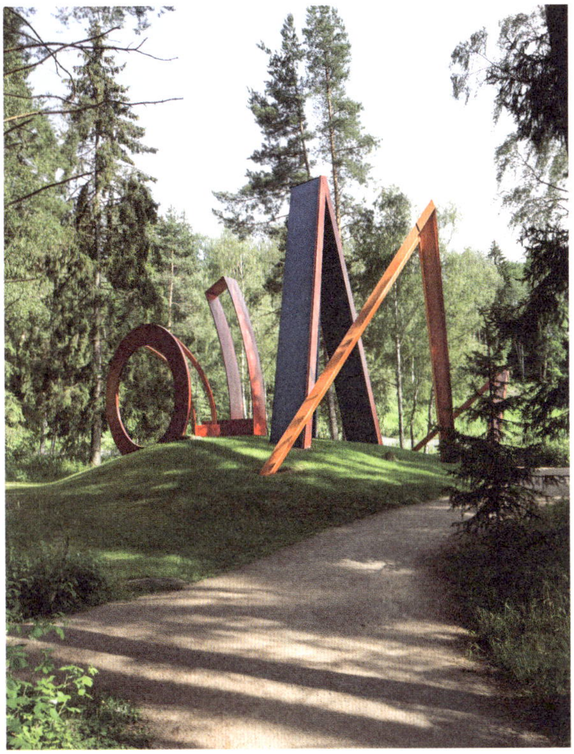

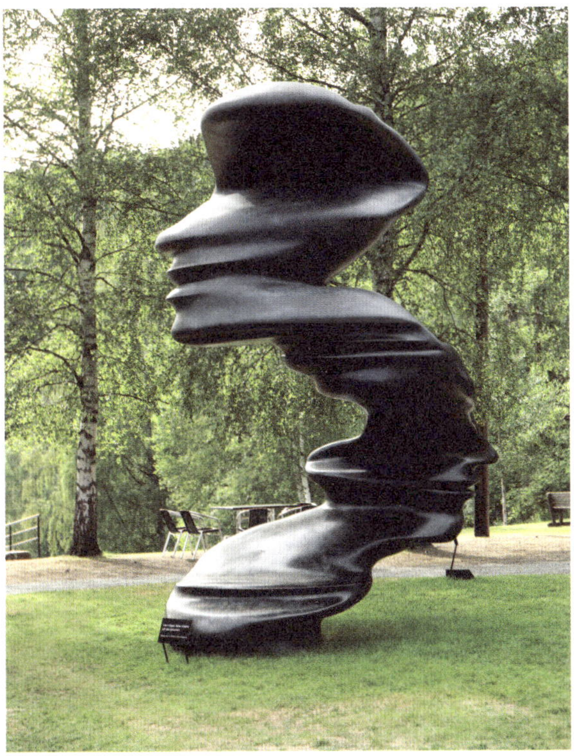

SCULPTURES

Tony Cragg's *Bent of Mind* (above) is just one of the park's fifty sculptures. The profiles of the two human faces change as the viewer moves around the work.

WATERSIDE LOCATION

Visitors can enjoy views of the river and the museum's natural setting from inside the gallery.

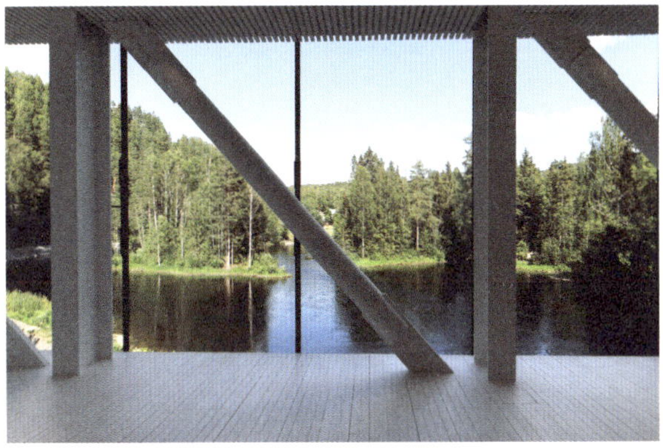

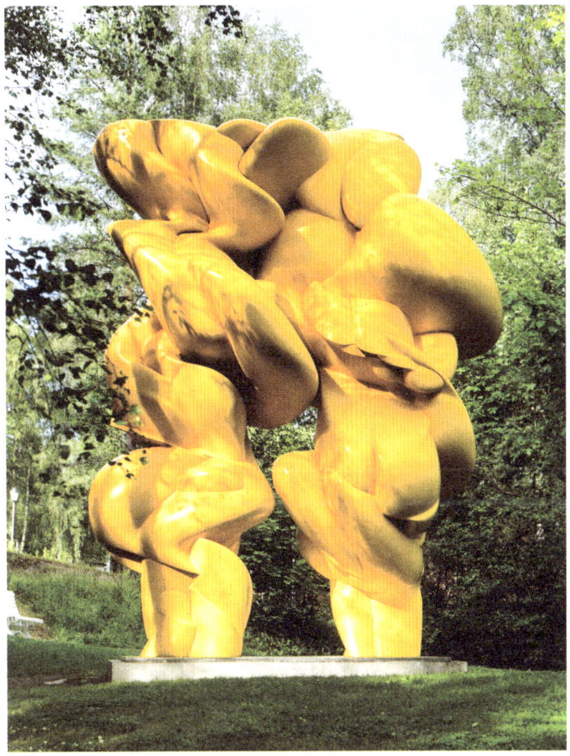

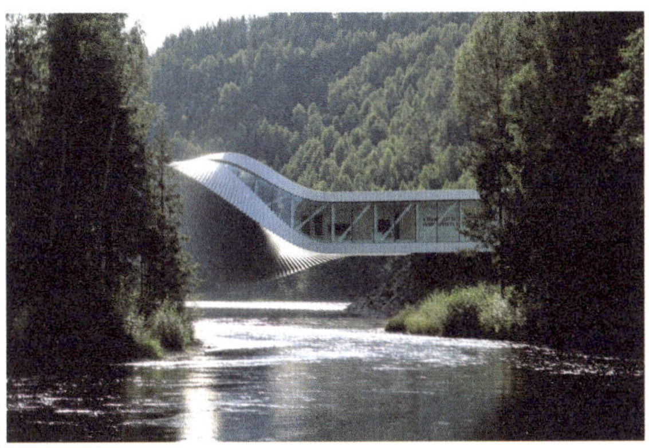

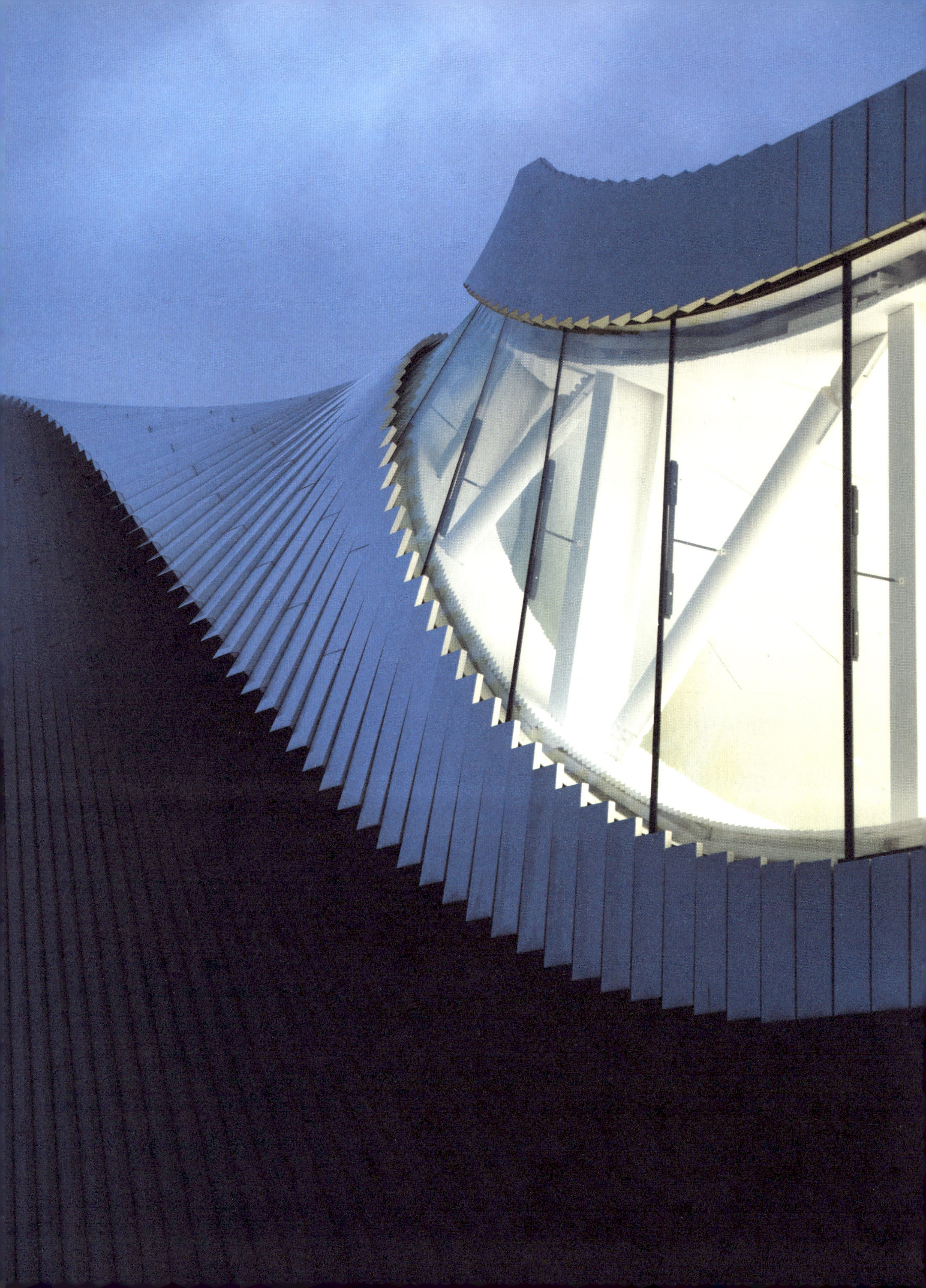

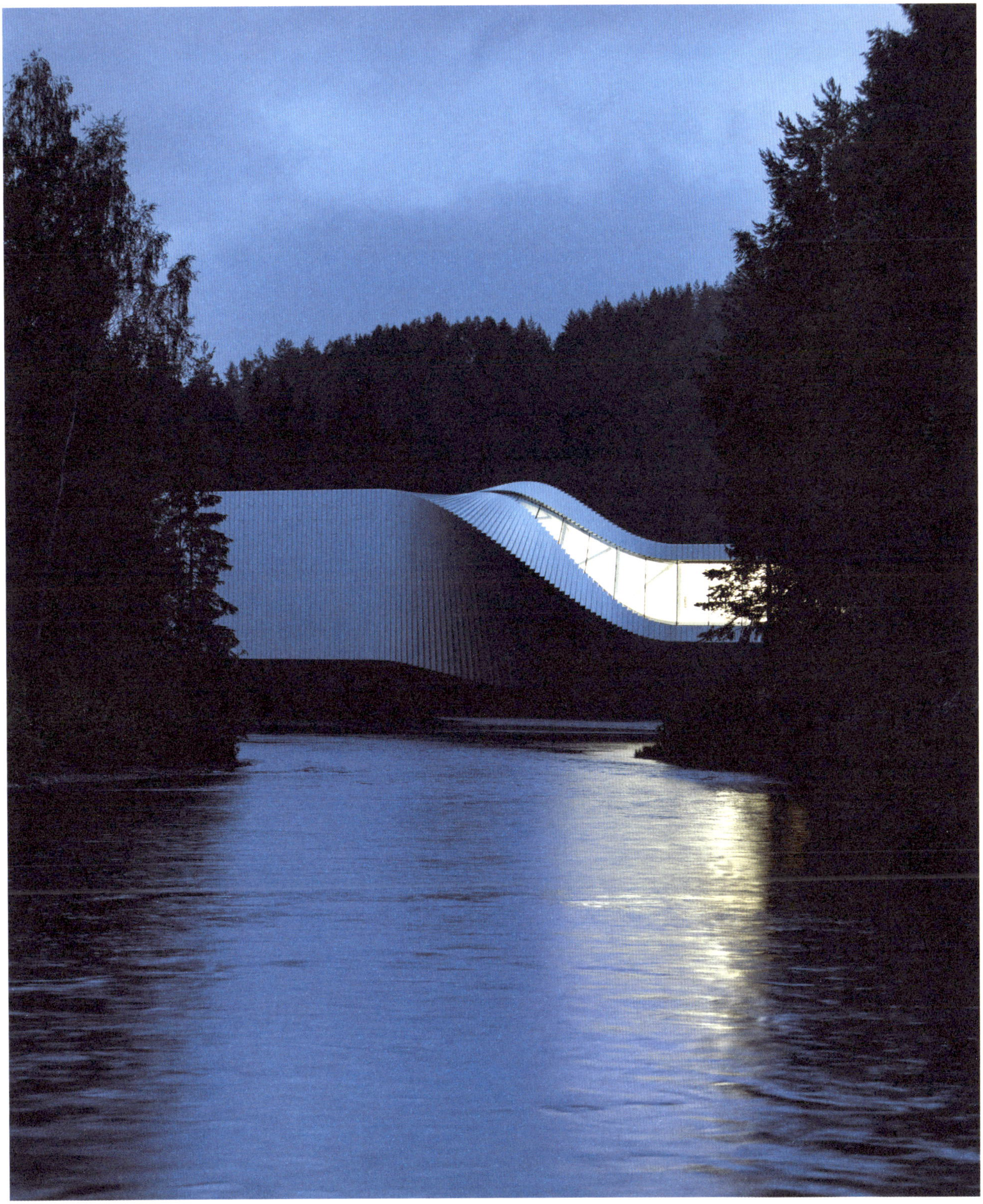

ABOVE

With its unspoiled natural setting, the Twist gallery resembles a structure from a sci-fi film.

OPPOSITE

The building's unique character is defined by its structural rotation.

DEEP DIVE

OSLO OPERA HOUSE

SYMBOL OF A BOOMING CAPITAL

Drawing inspiration from icebergs adrift on the sea, Oslo Opera House is one of the most iconic buildings in Scandinavia.

After a protracted national debate and four years of construction work, Oslo Opera House opened its doors in 2008. It now occupies a central position both in the city itself and in the minds of its residents. The building is used as an opera house, thoroughfare, and public square where local people can gather. Visitors are free to make use of the space as they wish as they roam around the entire structure, including even its roof, which is accessed via gentle inclines and from where there is a stunning view of Oslo Fjord.

With architecture inspired by icebergs, the opera house sometimes looks as though it is floating in the fjord. The exterior, clad in white granite and Carrara marble (an Italian marble renowned for its purity and whiteness), looks like shimmering ice, and the effect is only heightened in winter when condensation freezes on the walls and sparkles in the sun. Water, sky, and the surrounding buildings are reflected in its glass walls during the day, while the lights inside the Opera House are revealed as night falls.

The interior, which is paneled entirely in wood, is no less stylish. Its warm ambience has been exploited as a backdrop by a number of artists—Ólafur Elíasson, for example, created reticulated wall cladding that covered the roof pillars and reproduced the effect of melting ice. Other artists have also contributed to the project, including Pae White (who designed a curtain for the main stage that was inspired by crumpled aluminum foil), Linus Elmes and Ludvig Löfgren (the duo who created the foundation stone), and Kristian Blystad, a famous Norwegian sculptor. The main auditorium, which can seat an audience of one thousand three hundred and fifty, contains an immense central chandelier of LED lights mimicking a full moon, beneath which ballets and operas are performed to international acclaim.

Oslo Opera House was awarded the 2009 European Union Prize for Contemporary Architecture by the Fundació Mies van der Rohe as one of the first architectural projects in a rapidly expanding waterside development that has seen the construction of a host of modern buildings, including the Deichman Bjørvika public library, the Munch Museum, and the new National Museum.

Oslo's iconic Opera House is just one of the reasons why Norway has become a Mecca for travelers with a passion for architecture.

OSLO OPERA HOUSE

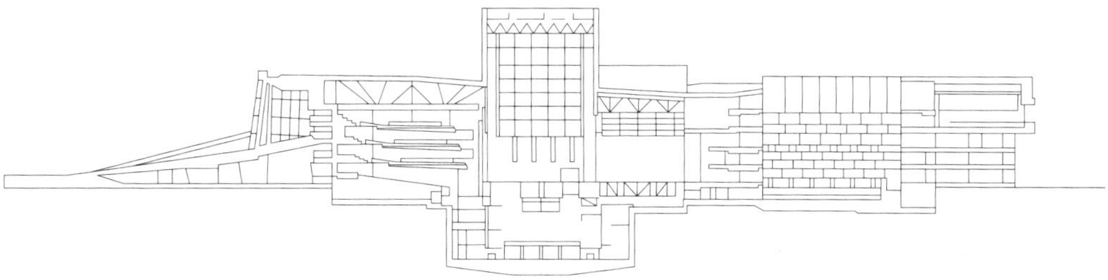

MODERN ARCHITECTURE

The Opera House has two auditoriums, seating 1,350 and 400 patrons respectively, as well as a 200-seat rehearsal studio. With a floor area of 829,900 ft² (77,100 m²), it is the largest cultural structure to be built in Norway since Nidaros Cathedral in 1070.

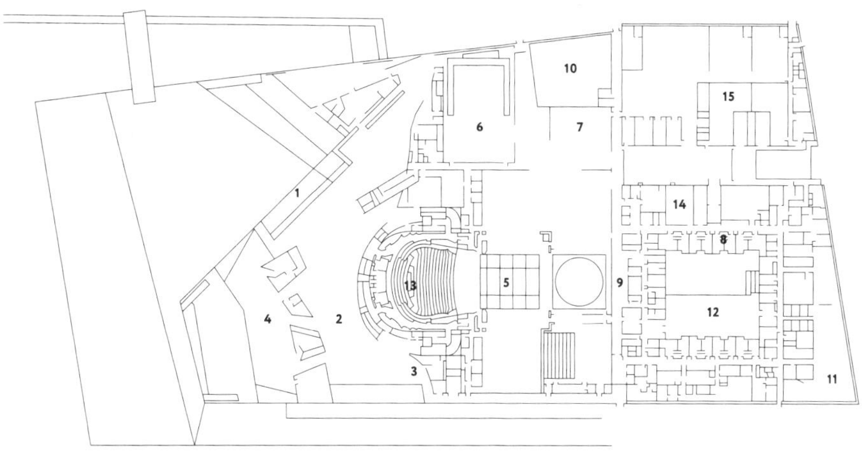

FLOOR PLAN OF THE OPERA HOUSE

1 Main entrance 2 Lobby 3 Café 4 Cloakroom 5 Main stage 6 Second stage 7 Assembly hall 8 Dressing rooms 9 Backstage area 10 Orchestral rehearsal 11 Technical room 12 Courtyard 13 First balcony 14 Opera rehearsal 15 Offices

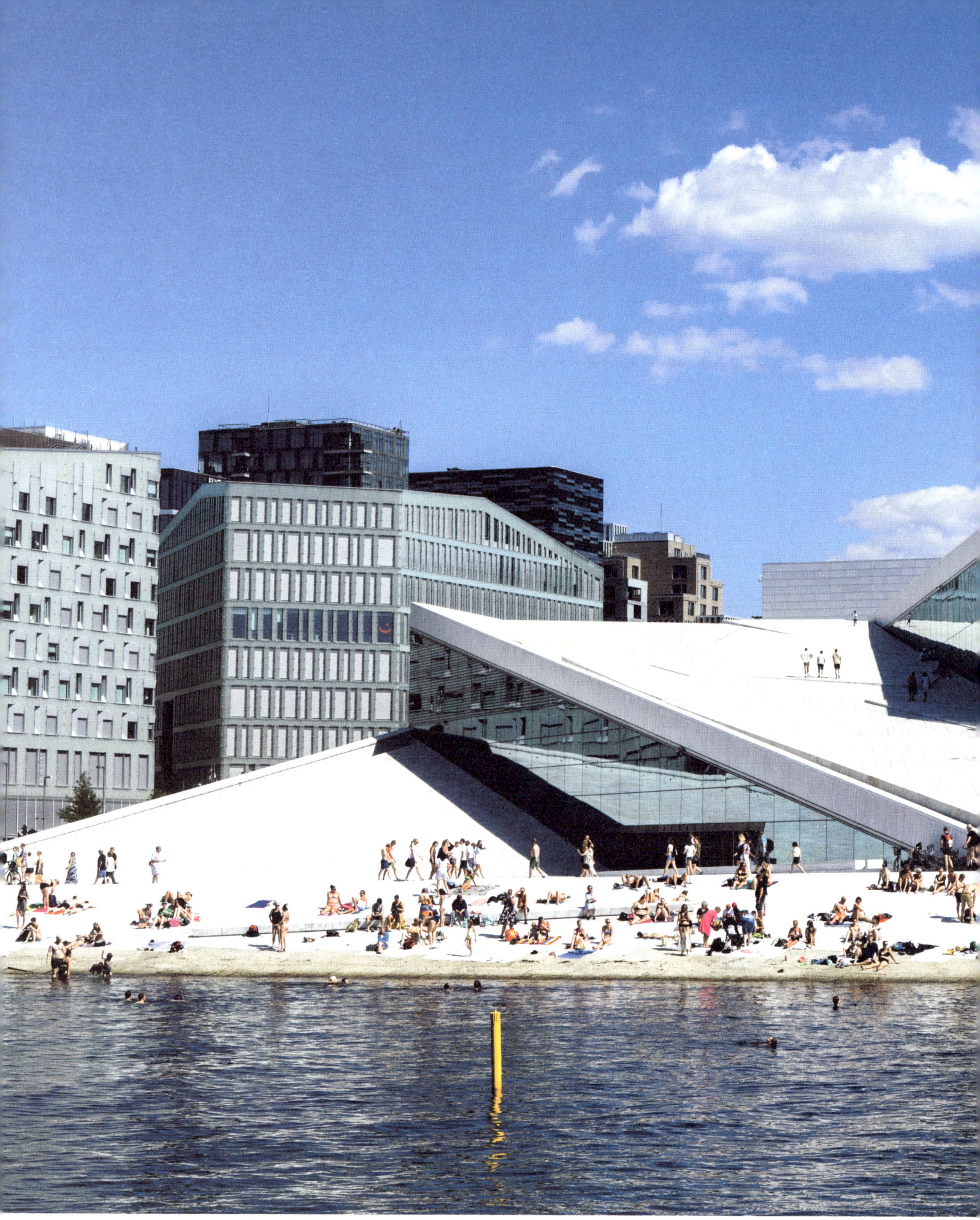

Oslo Opera House is transformed into a beach during the heat of summer as crowds of city dwellers come to swim in the cool waters of the fiord.

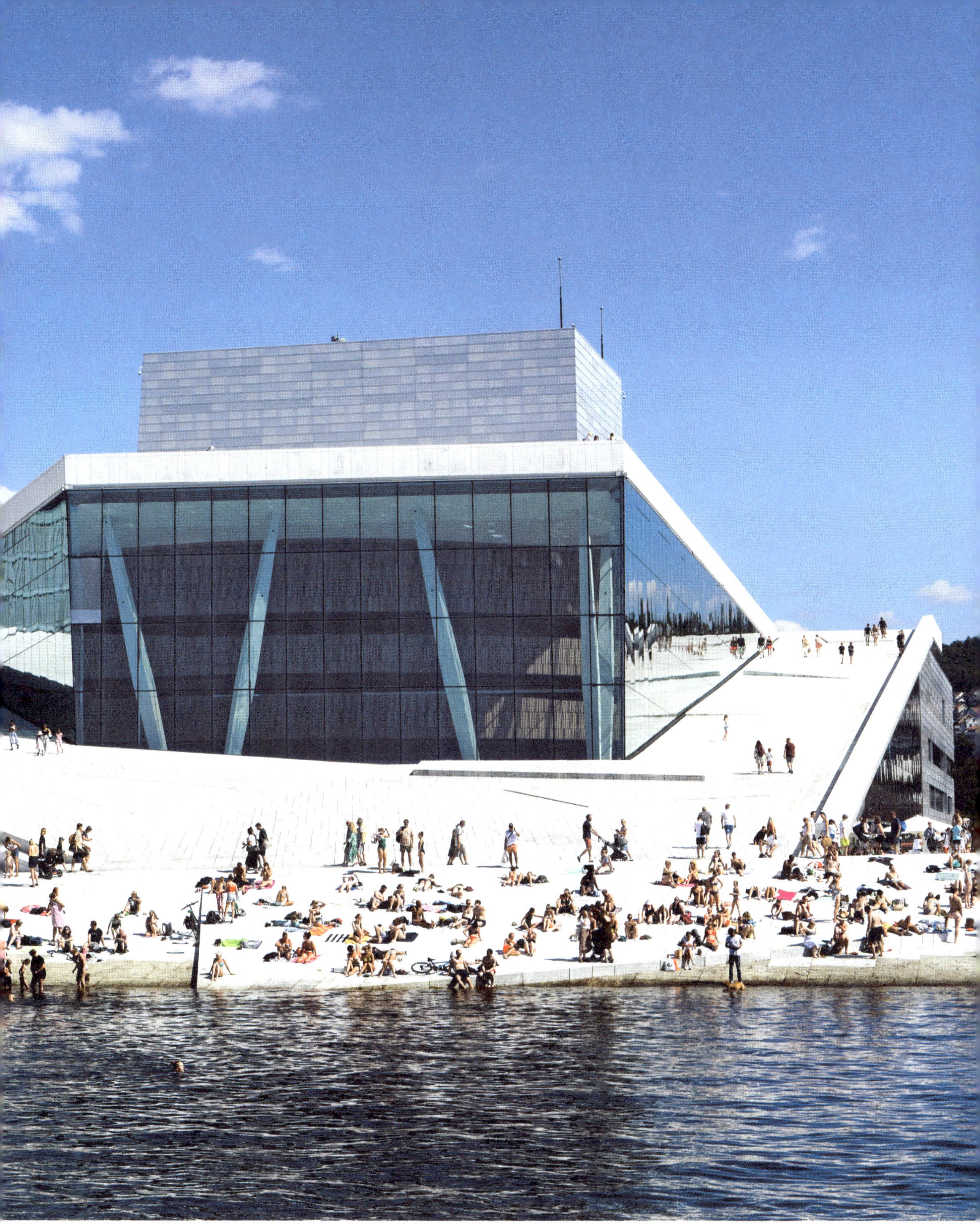

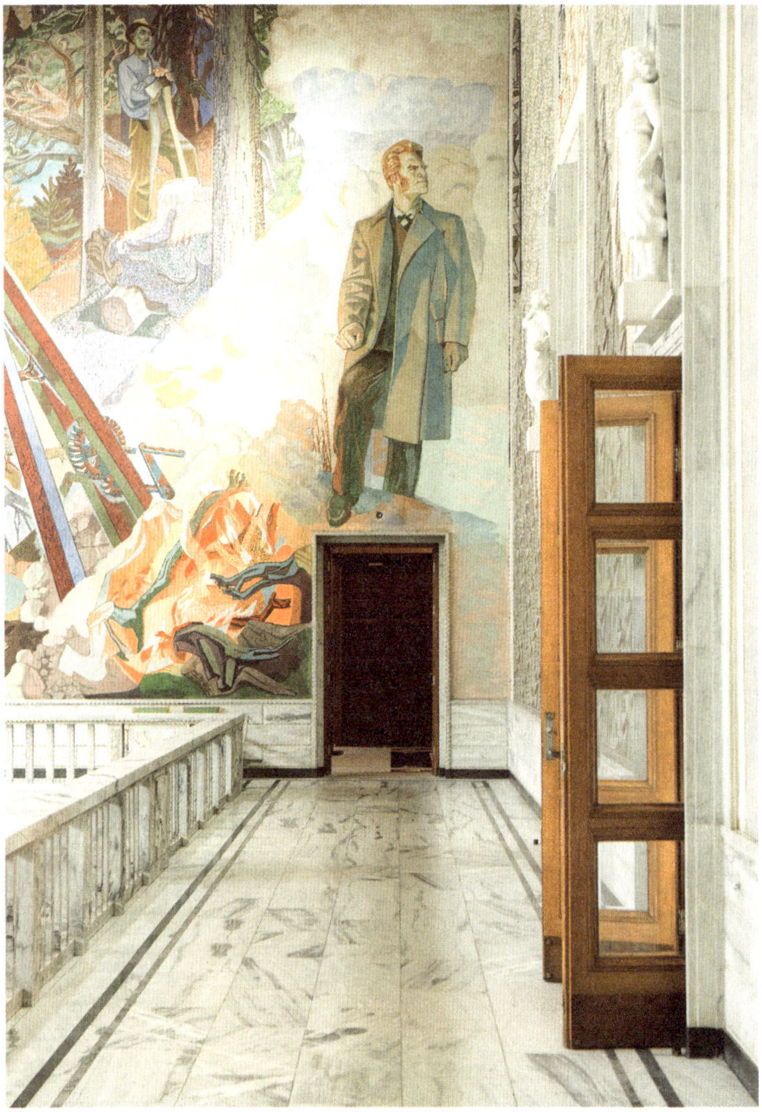

ABOVE

Extensive murals inside Oslo City Hall show scenes from the daily lives of the Norwegian people.

OPPOSITE

This mural depicts the legend of St Hallvard, the patron saint of the city of Oslo.

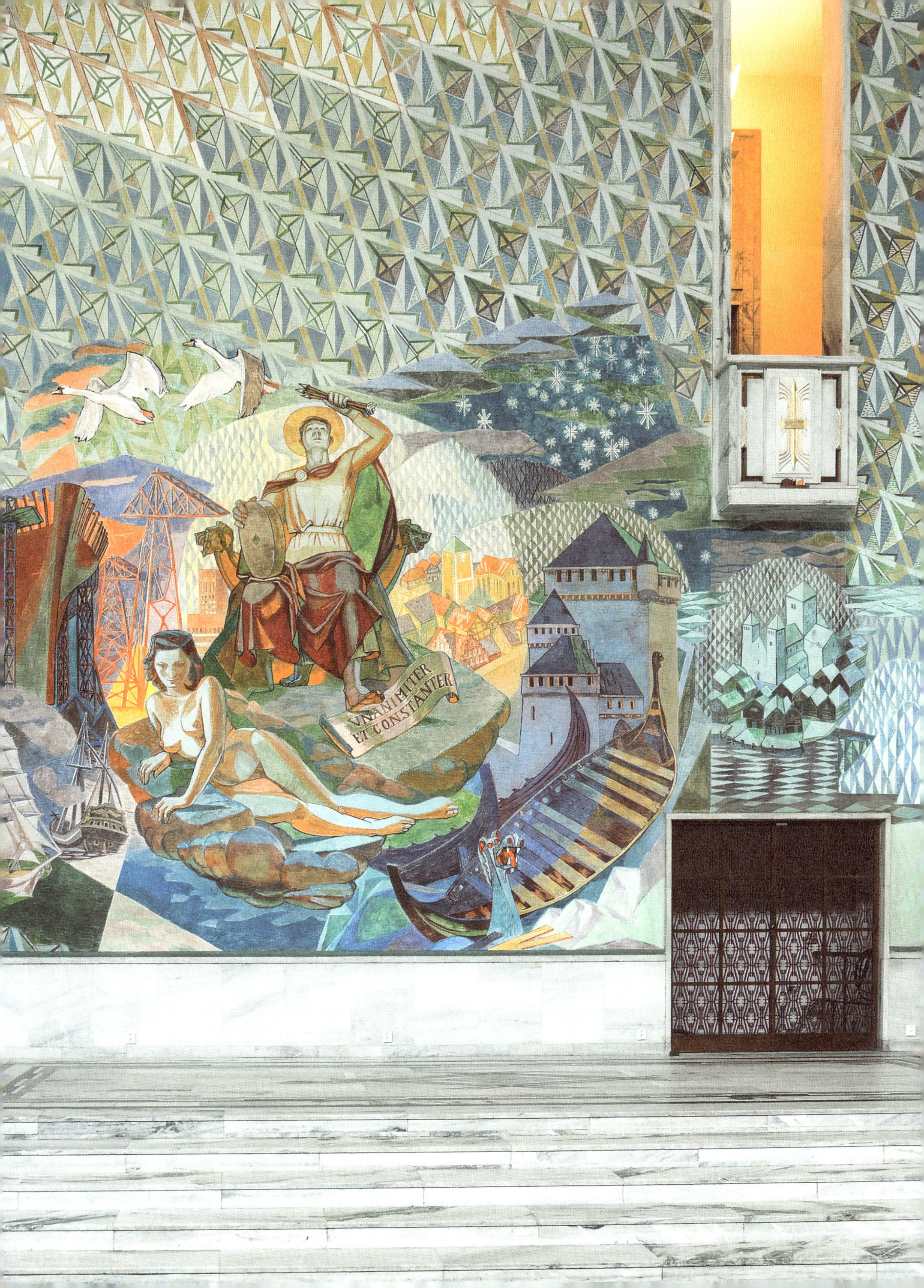
VNANIMITER
ET CONSTANTER

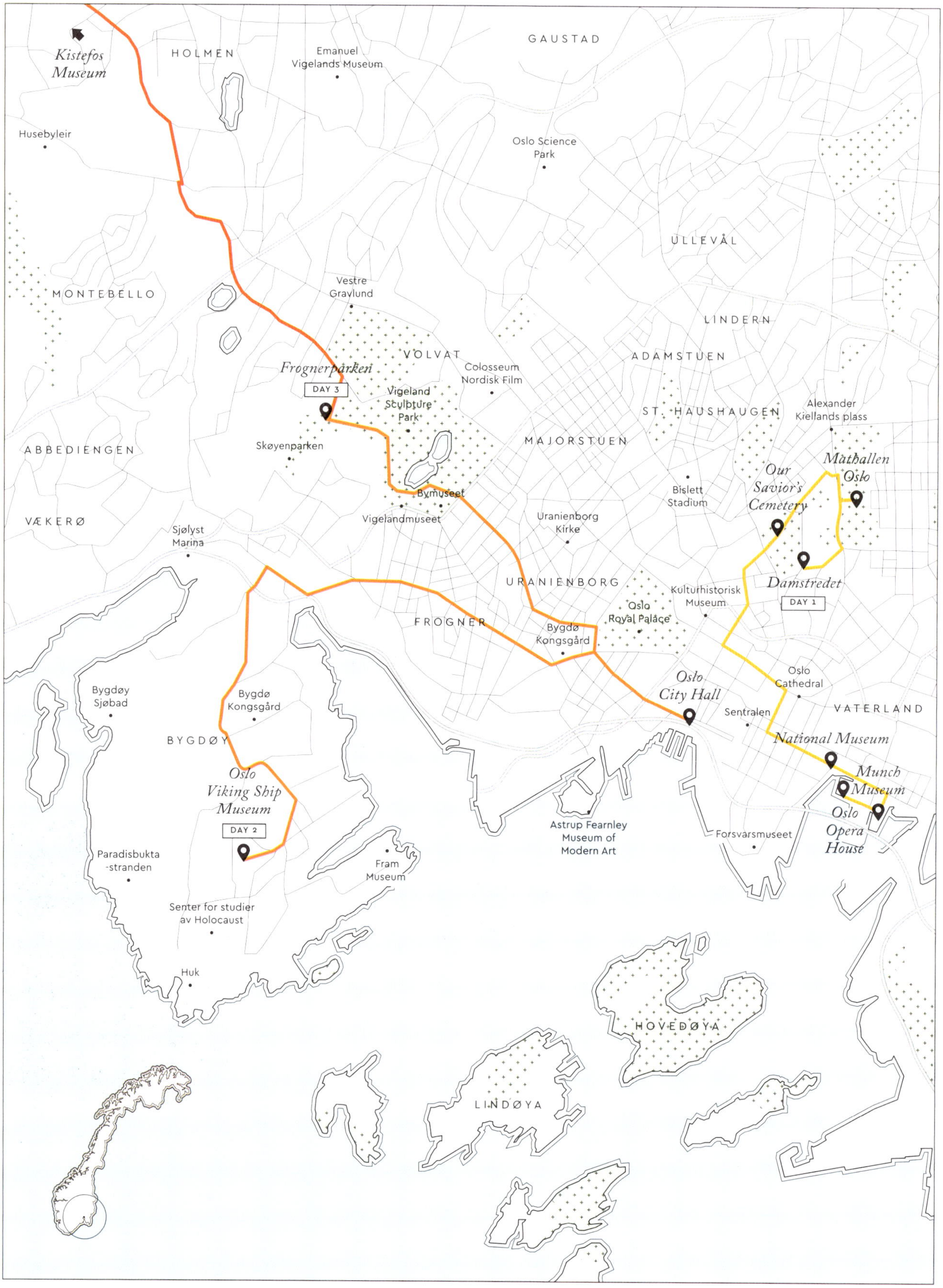
Kistefos Museum
HOLMEN
Emanuel Vigelands Museum
GAUSTAD
Husebyleir
Oslo Science Park
ULLEVÅL
MONTEBELLO
Vestre Gravlund
LINDERN
VOLVAT
ADAMSTUEN
Frognerparken
DAY 3
Colosseum Nordisk Film
Vigeland Sculpture Park
ST. HAUSHAUGEN
Alexander Kiellands plass
ABBEDIENGEN
Skøyenparken
MAJORSTUEN
Mathallen Oslo
Our Savior's Cemetery
Bymuseet
Bislett Stadium
VÆKERØ
Vigelandmuseet
Uranienborg Kirke
Sjølyst Marina
Damstredet
DAY 1
URANIENBORG
Kulturhistorisk Museum
Oslo Royal Palace
FROGNER
Bygdø Kongsgård
Oslo City Hall
Oslo Cathedral
Bygdøy Sjøbad
Bygdø Kongsgård
Sentralen
VATERLAND
BYGDØY
National Museum
Oslo Viking Ship Museum
Munch Museum
DAY 2
Oslo Opera House
Astrup Fearnley Museum of Modern Art
Forsvarsmuseet
Paradisbukta -stranden
Fram Museum
Senter for studier av Holocaust
Huk
HOVEDØYA
LINDØYA

ITINERARY

THREE DAYS IN OSLO

The only way to explore the center of Oslo is on foot or by bike, but this is no great hardship as the city is just the place for a pleasant stroll. This charming and lively capital is surrounded by hills, lakes, and forests, as if to remind us that the natural world is never far away, even in Norway's largest city.

DAY 1: DAMSTREDET TO THE OPERA HOUSE

Enjoy a peaceful morning's stroll along Damstredet, a small street reminiscent of Montmartre in Paris, before visiting the market at Mathallen. This unique food hall is a good place to buy some artisanal Norwegian produce and grab something quick for lunch. Edvard Munch's grave is to be found just around the corner and will serve as a good prelude to visiting the National Museum. This gallery opened in 2022 and features canvases by the greatest Norwegian painters, while the nearby Munch Museum concentrates on the work of this Norwegian pioneer of Expressionism. The long summer evenings are a perfect opportunity to round off the day. Soak up the city's atmosphere with a stroll along the waterfront beside the Opera House, before settling down on the promenade to enjoy the timeless joys of the sunset. The evening could then finish with a sauna, before diving straight into the Oslo Fjord.

DAY 2: CITY HALL TO FROGNERPARKEN

After being fortified with a hearty Scandinavian breakfast, head to the Viking Ship Museum to admire the Oseberg ship, a longship perfectly preserved in a burial mound that was discovered south of Oslo by a farmer in 1903. After this journey through time, head back to the city center to visit City Hall with its spectacular murals. The Nobel Peace Prize is awarded here every year on December 10, the anniversary of the death of Alfred Nobel. Enjoy a waffle and a coffee on the terrace before making your way to Frognerparken, for a stroll and to enjoy the evening illuminations. Vigeland sculpture park lies at the entrance, with two hundred and fourteen strange and amusing sculptures, all created by the Norwegian artist Gustav Vigeland.

DAY 3: THE KISTEFOS MUSEUM TO HOLMENKOLLEN

Get out of the city for the morning and visit the Kistefos Museum, an hour away from Oslo. This open-air museum of contemporary art on the site of an old paper mill also features the Twist, a spectacular gallery straight out of a science fiction film. On the way back to Oslo, don't forget to stop off in the district of Holmenkollen to climb the hill where the ski jump for the 1952 Winter Olympics was erected and from where there's an exceptional panoramic view of the city.

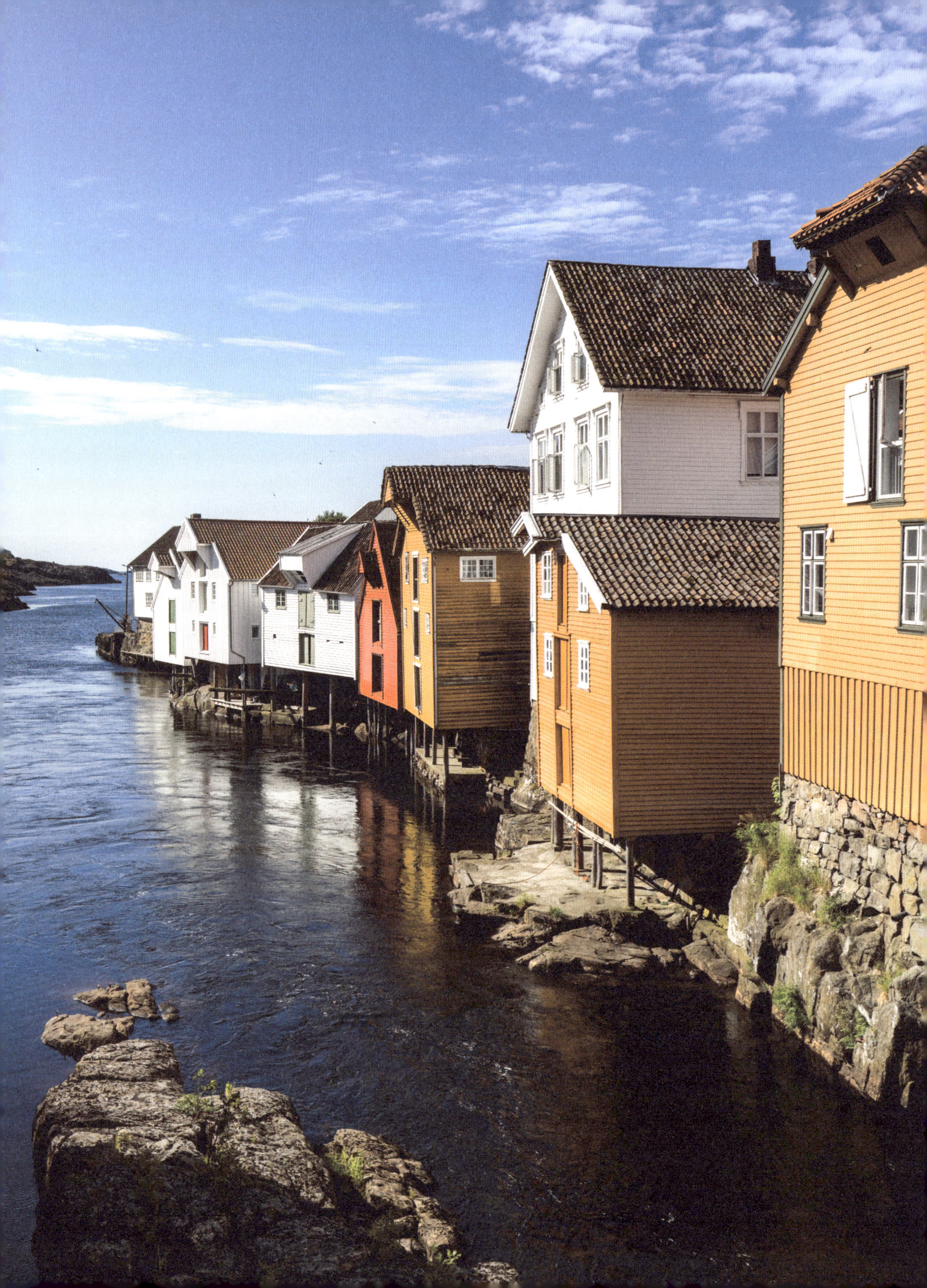

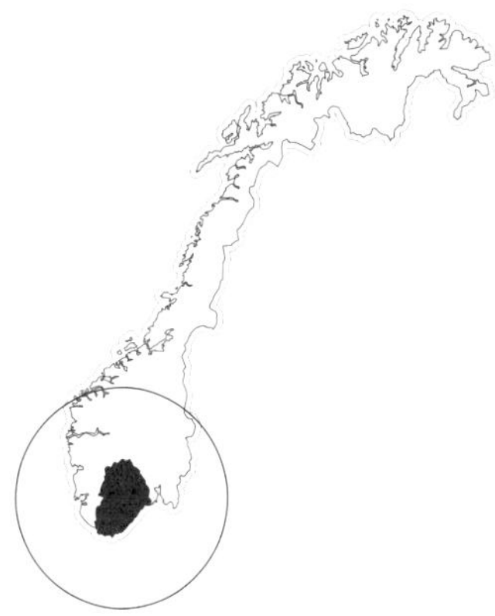

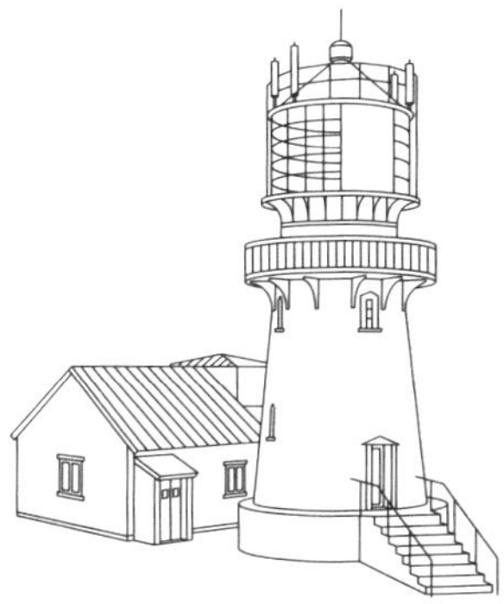

PICTURESQUE VILLAGES

THE SOUTH

SØRLANDET AND TELEMARK

Many Norwegians in search of a little peace and quiet seek out the tranquil and intimate atmosphere of this region to spend their family holidays far from the bustling crowds.

P.40

The picturesque wooden houses in the village of Sogndalstrand date back to the eighteenth and nineteenth centuries. The Sokna river running through the village is famed for its wild salmon.

OPPOSITE

The charming small village of Sogndalstrand has become one of the most popular tourist destinations in the area.

Each summer the small islands off the coast of Southern Norway, with their beautiful beaches of white sand, are the ideal place for watersports and hikes along coastal paths. The long sunny days of this season are also a perfect opportunity for an in-depth exploration of the tiny towns and villages along the coast, with their many whitewashed wooden houses.

The provinces are still deeply rooted in tradition. The countryside, a riot of bucolic scenery in a thousand different shades of green, is scattered with farmsteads and houses painted red, an effect only enhanced by the traditional wooden storehouses known as *stabbur* that are found throughout the region. These structures, raised up on stilts, were once used to store grain, preserved meat, and provisions for the winter.

When not shrouded in cloud, the famous peak of Gaustatoppen, looking out over the area north of Telemark, is a perfect vantage point for spectacular views across the south of the country. A few scattered snowfields survive on its uplands until the end of summer, a reminder of the harshness of winter in the areas further inland.

The small town of Rjukan witnessed one of the most daring sabotage missions of the Second World War, when, in 1943, a squad of Norwegian commandos who had been hiding out in the forest for days laid explosive charges to knock out the Vermork power station (which had been occupied by German soldiers), thus paralyzing Nazi Germany's nuclear program.

Last but not least, the stave church in Heddal (the largest in the country) and its counterpart nestling in the hills of Eidsborg form an essential part of the timeless charms of a region that is often overlooked. This well-kept secret is a wonderful place from which to begin exploring the country.

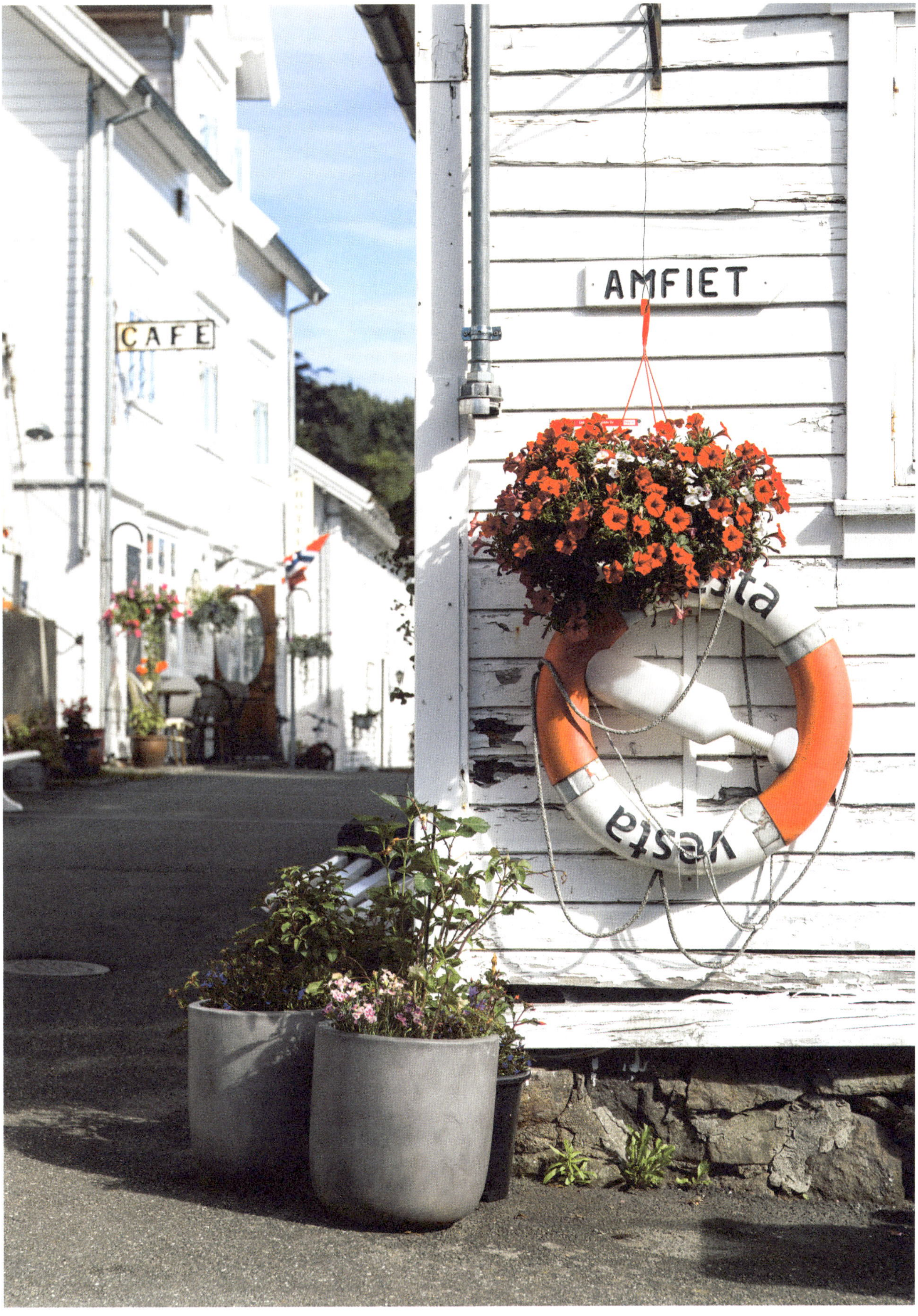
CAFE
AMFIET
vesta

THE ESSENTIALS

08

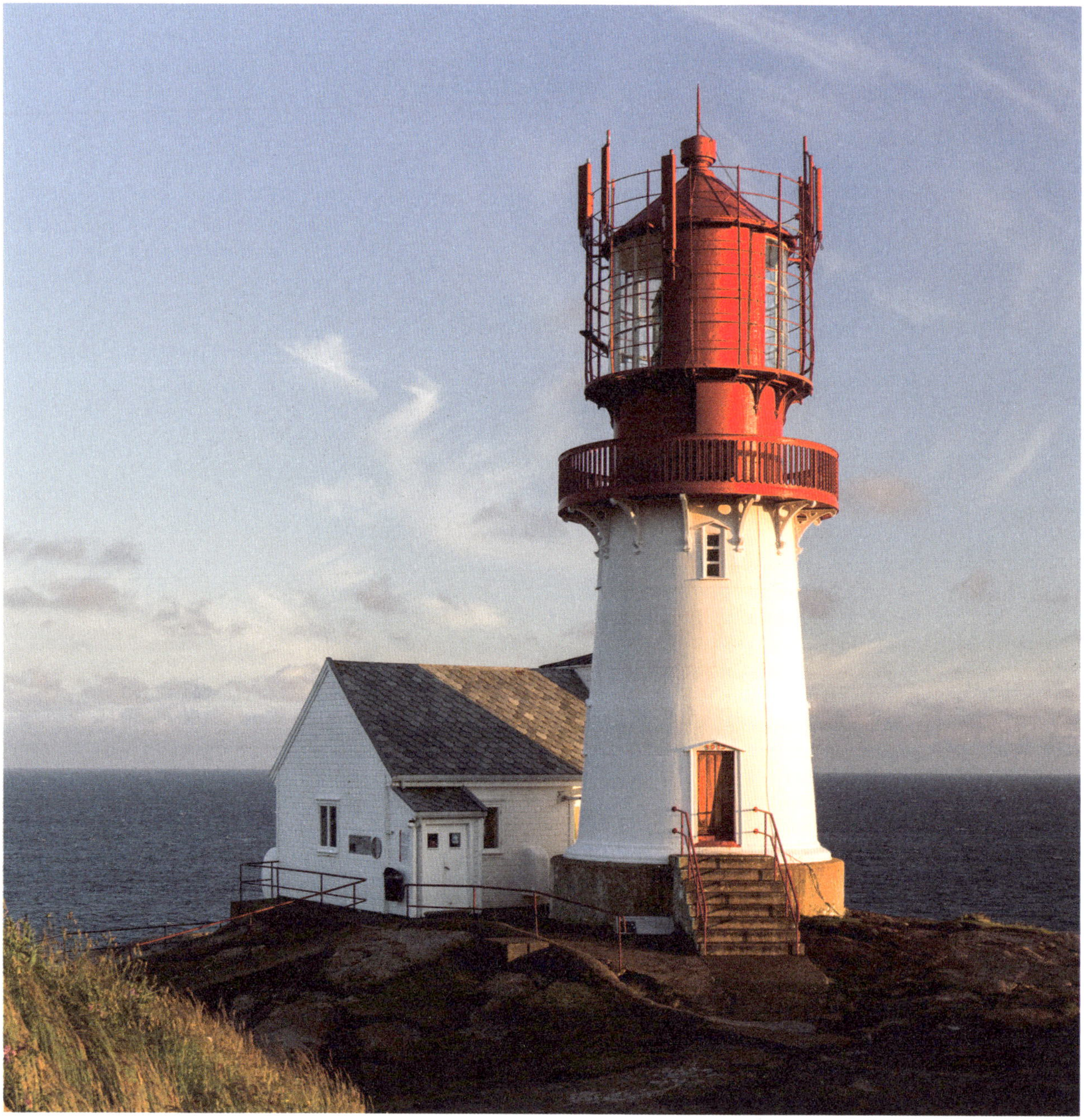

LINDESNES LIGHTHOUSE

Lindesnes Lighthouse stands proudly at the southernmost tip of Norway. It was built in 1655 and is the oldest lighthouse in the country.

09

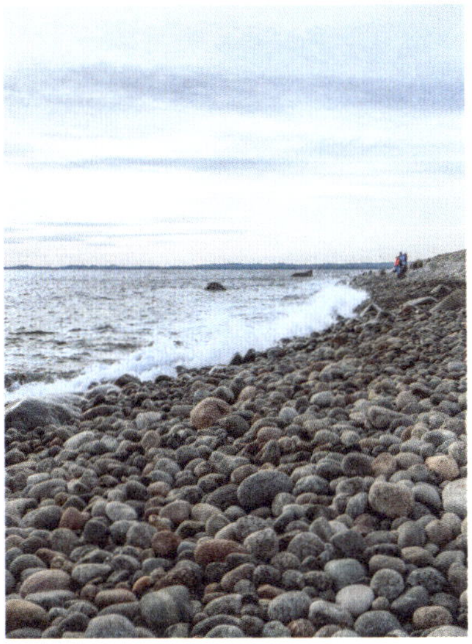

MØLEN

The beach at Mølen features funerary cairns dating back to the Iron Age that are now under UNESCO protection.

10

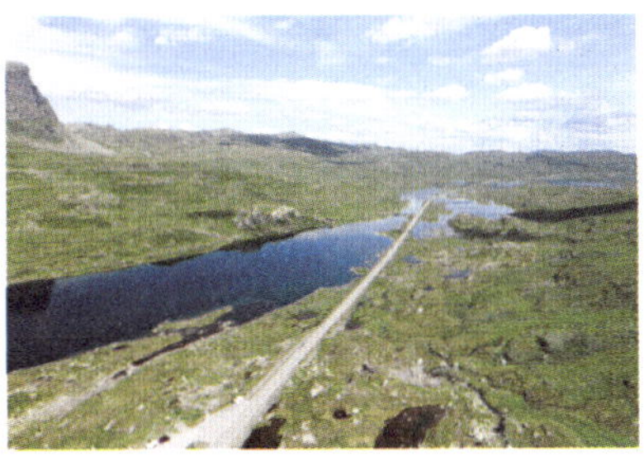

HARDANGERVIDDA

This magnificent desert plateau is home to Europe's largest herd of wild reindeer.

11

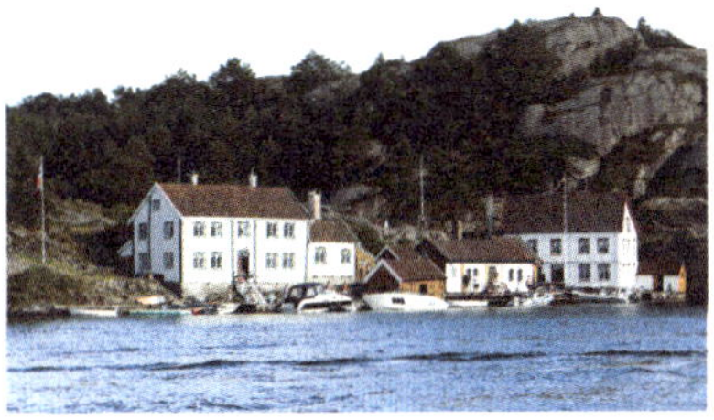

NY-HELLESUND

An intimate and cozy village tucked away on an archipelago that is truly a haven of peace. Norwegians love coming here to soak up the sun.

12

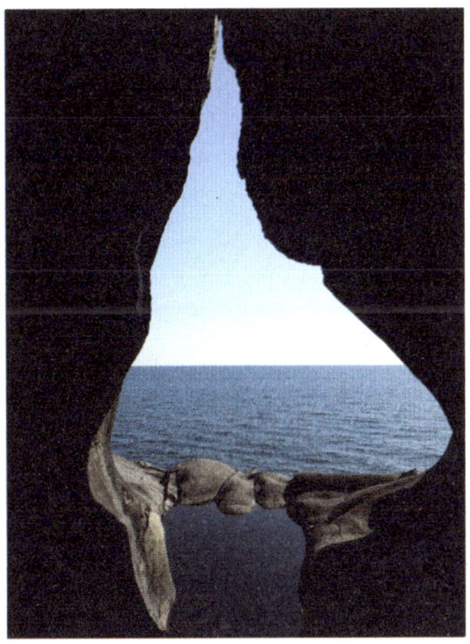

BRUFJELL

The Brufjell potholes are caves carved out 20,000 years ago during the last Ice Age, providing spectacular sea views.

13

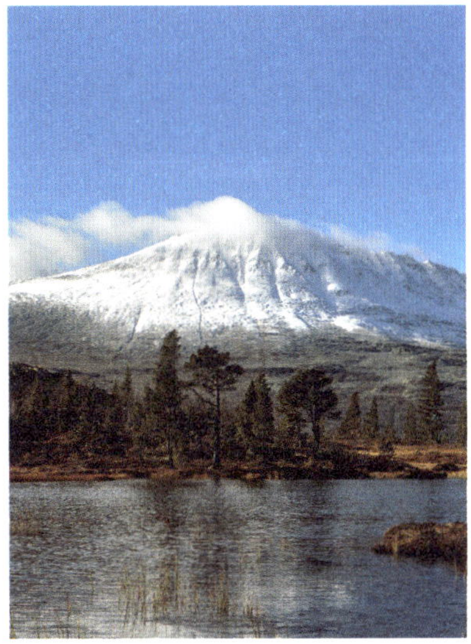

GAUSTATOPPEN

One of Southern Norway's highest peaks (6,178 ft/1,883 m).

14

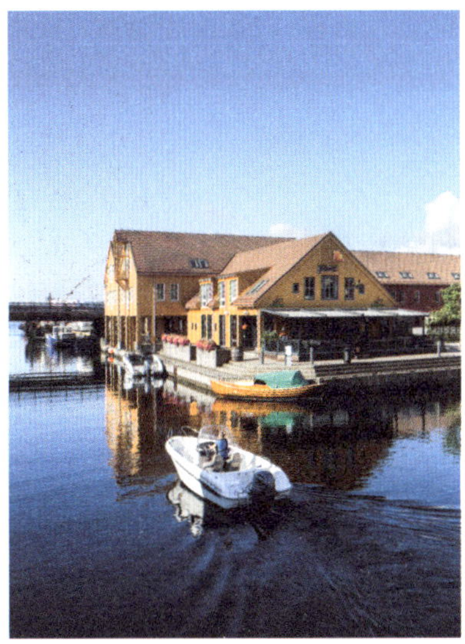

KRISTIANSAND

A pretty town full of flowers where it is pleasant to walk in summer.

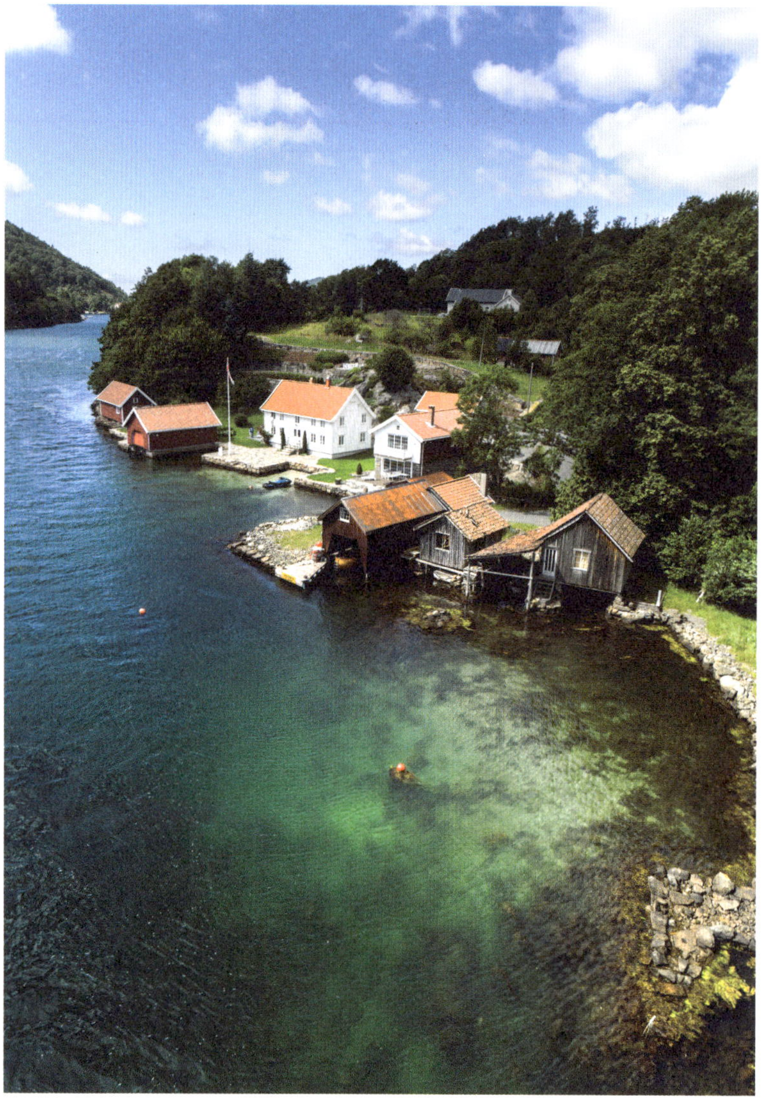

ABOVE

Southern Norway is a temperate zone in which temperatures can rise to 86°F (30°C) in summer.

OPPOSITE

Swimmers can expect crystal-clear water at Lista's famous beaches.

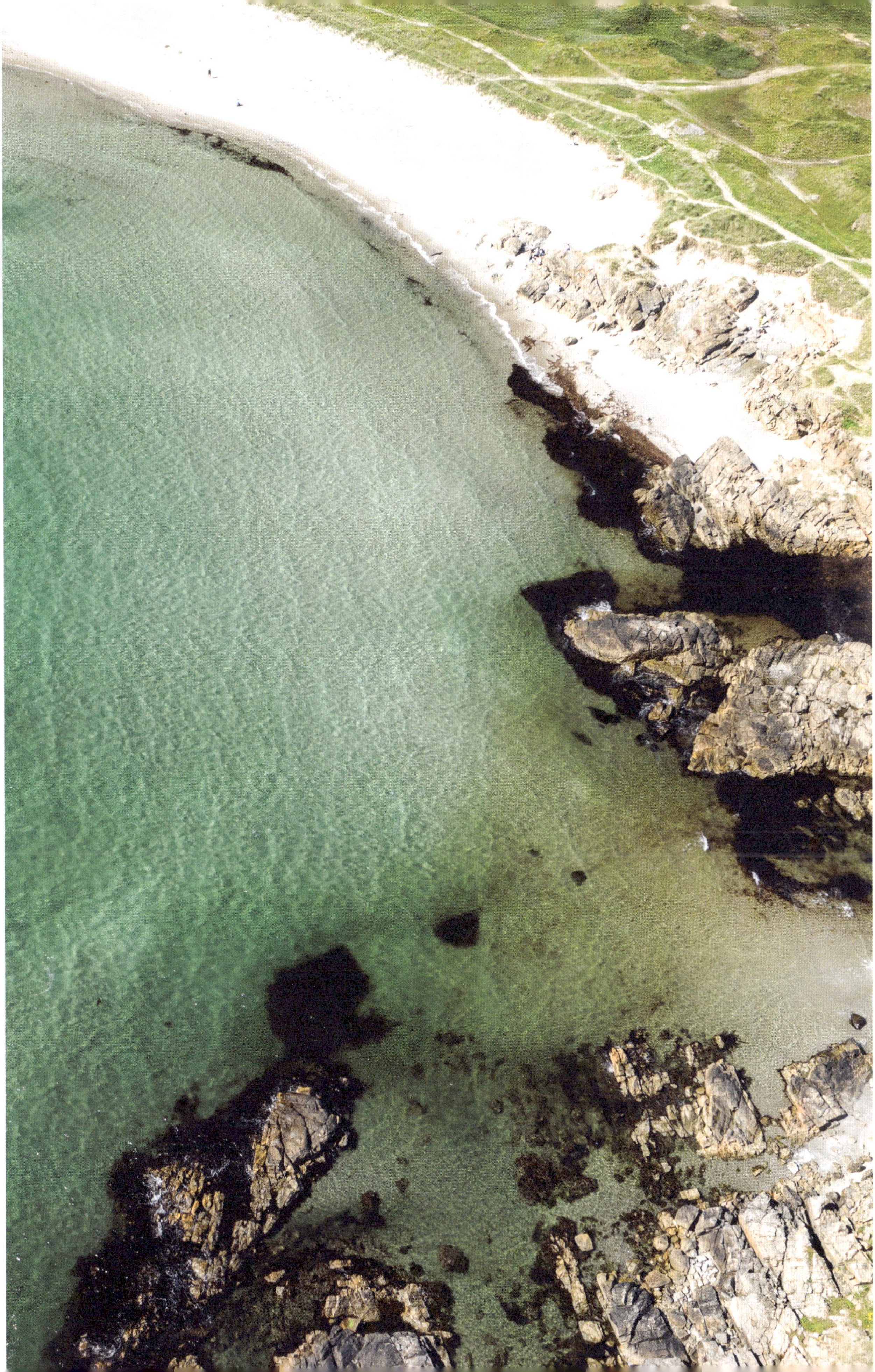

ART

THE PAINTERS

Although Norwegian artists have long drawn inspiration from the light and landscapes of their homeland, a truly Norwegian school of painting did not emerge until the nineteenth century.

Edvard Munch, the most famous Norwegian artist of them all, painted *The Scream* in 1893 after witnessing a spectacular and yet ominous sunset during a stroll through Ekeberg, a neighborhood looking out over Oslo Fjord. He painted five versions of this work that, many years after his death, would go on to break auction house records. One of these versions can now be seen in the new Munch Museum, which opened its doors in Oslo in late 2021.

Among the artists who have shaped Norwegian painting, Johan Christian Dahl was the first to depict the country's wide open spaces, including the Sognefjord and Nigardsbreen, an arm of the Jostedalsbreen glacier. He conjured a bucolic vision of a mountain farmstead that was later engulfed by the glacier's unanticipated advance (although the ice was eventually to retreat).

Amaldus Nielsen is considered Norway's first naturalist painter, creating a host of landscapes of the south and west of the country, in particular the beaches at Lista and Farsund and the tiny archipelago of Ny-Hellesund, which for a long time welcomed painters seeking tranquility during the mild weather of the summer months. *Morning in Ny-Hellesund* has now become one of his most famous canvases.

The spectacular fjords of Western Norway inspired the likes of Adolph Tidemand and his collaborator Hans Gude to paint the *Bridal Procession on the Hardangerfjord* and *Night Spear Fishing on the Krøderen Lake*, the latter a nocturnal scene of striking realism. The joint and respective works by these two artists profoundly influenced the development of Norwegian painting as part of Norway's Romantic Nationalism movement, a trend in art, literature, and popular culture between 1840 and 1867 that sought to emphasize the particularities and unique nature of Norwegian identity. This was an attempt to reassert a national identity that had been considerably diluted by Danish influence and dependence on Denmark during the centuries following the Black Death. The movement was characterized by a nostalgic aspect and has been the subject of numerous studies and extensive debate.

Although Harald Sohlberg painted many studies of the mining town of Røros, it is his *Winter Night in the Mountains* that is now considered among his masterpieces. In 2006 this was to result in the opening of the Sohlbergplassen viewpoint, an exposed concrete construction created by Carl-Viggo Hølmebakk from which visitors can admire the spectacular peaks of the Rondane mountains, the very scenery that inspired Harald Sohlberg's nocturnal work.

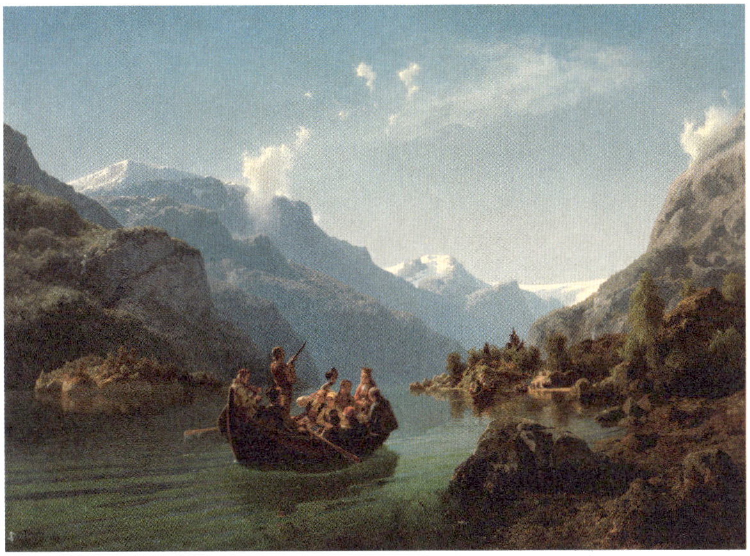

BRIDAL PROCESSION ON THE HARDANGERFJORD

This image painted by Hans Gude and Adolph Tidemand in 1848 has become one of the most famous in Norway. It can be seen at the Nasjonalmuseet in Oslo.

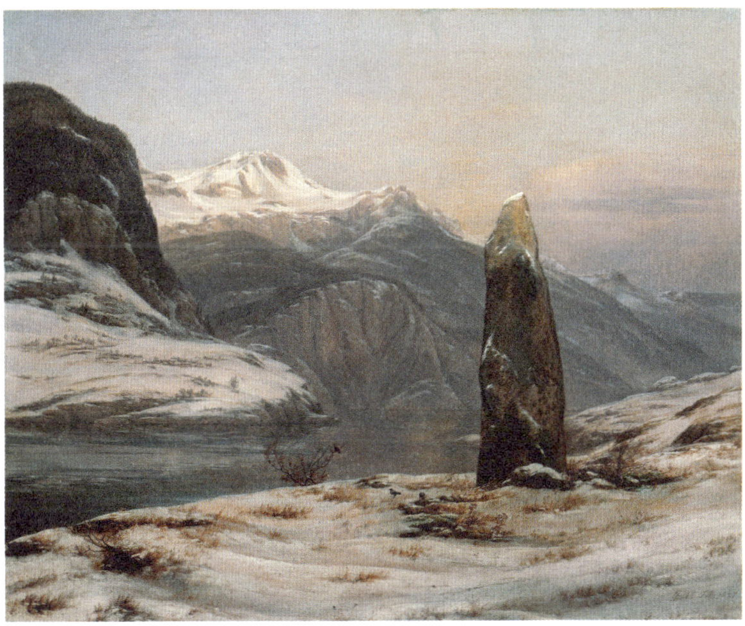

WINTER AT SOGNEFJORD

An oil painting on canvas created by Johan Christian Dahl in 1827 in tribute to Norway's natural surroundings.

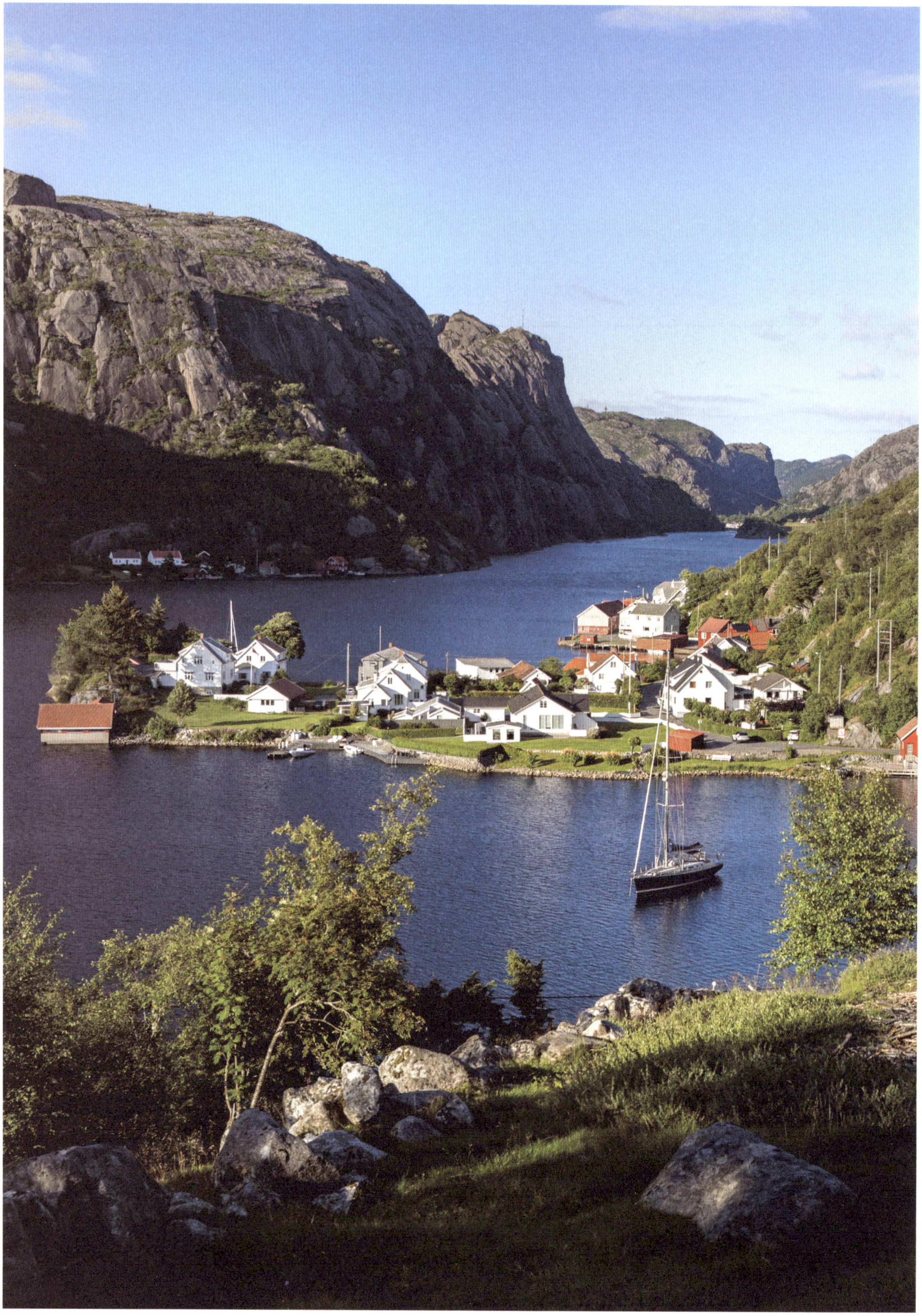

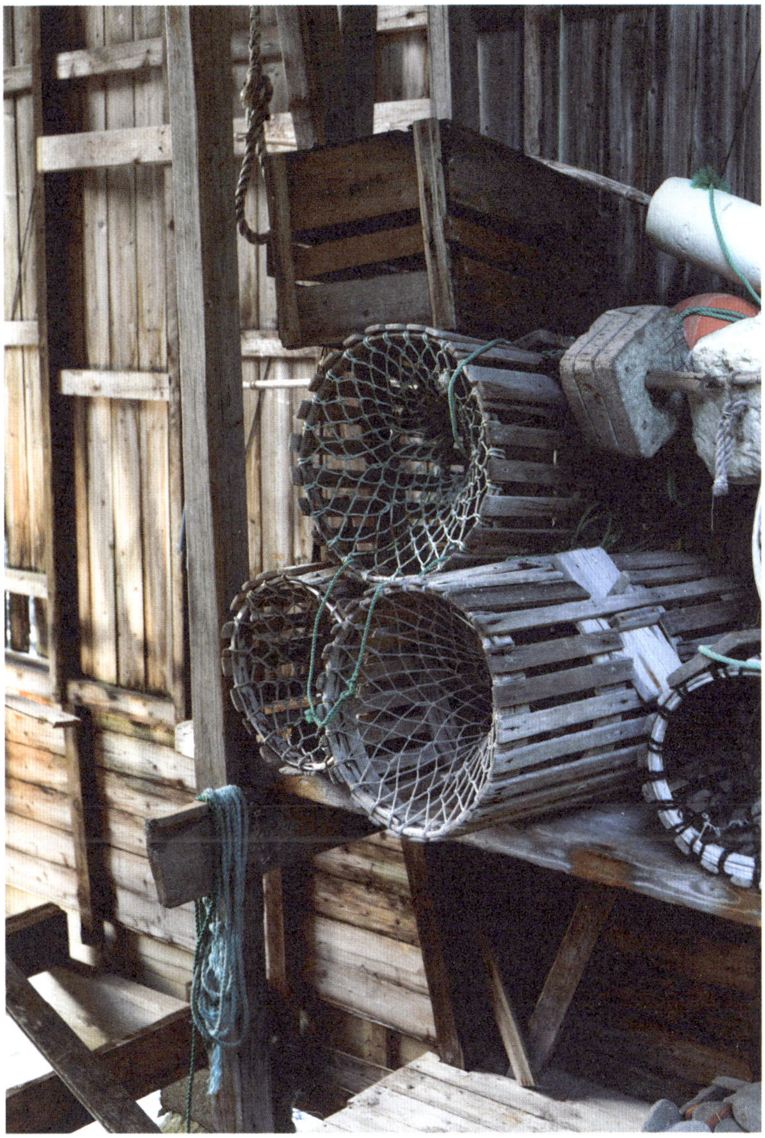

ABOVE

Traps used for fishing in storage in a boathouse.

OPPOSITE

Enjoy the views of the small village of Stornes on a walk to see the Brufjell potholes.

DEEP DIVE

NORWAY AND PETROLEUM

The discovery of oilfields off its coastline has made Norway one of the world's richest nations.

Norway was no more than a small fishing nation until the late 1960s, at which point it experienced an explosion in income and standards of living upon the discovery of vast oilfields in its coastal waters. This oil bounty has since propelled one of the poorest nations in Europe to become one of the richest countries on the planet.

Ekofisk, Norway's first oilfield, was discovered south-west of Stavanger in 1969, with many further deposits being found over the following years, first in the North Sea, then all along the Norwegian coast to the Barents Sea off the Russian coast.

Only the region around the Lofoten Islands, Vesterålen, and Senja has so far been spared from oil exploration, although the issue could one day resurface despite strong local opposition.

Aware that fossil fuel reserves cannot be exploited indefinitely, the Norwegian government created a petroleum sovereign wealth fund in the 1990s, to be managed by Norway's central bank. All state revenue generated from fossil fuel extraction is diverted to this fund, which invests to put the money to work. It is now the largest sovereign wealth fund in the world, with interests in nearly nine thousand companies across the globe that were worth in excess of €1,100 billion at the start of 2022.

It is also thanks to this sovereign wealth fund that the Norwegian state boasts one of the most comprehensive welfare systems in the world, funding pensions, unemployment benefits, education, and healthcare that is free for all. Norway is now in pole position on the Human Development Index and is considered the most egalitarian social democracy in Western Europe. These resources have also allowed it to take up a prominent position on the international stage relative to its population size and to punch above its weight in political and diplomatic terms.

Despite the role fossil fuel plays in the Norwegian economy, all the political parties have now come out in favor of phasing it out in response to the emergent challenge of climate change, although opinion is still split on the timeline. The Norwegian Petroleum Museum in Stavanger (which is part-funded by oil companies) contains an exhibition dedicated to human impact on the climate which concludes with the statement: "Global net carbon emissions must be reduced to zero by 2050. Norway cannot be an exception."

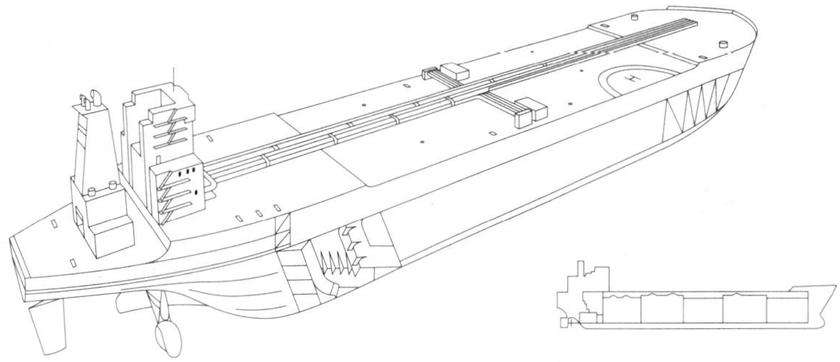

OIL TANKER STRUCTURE

There are two types of oil tanker: those with single hulls and those with double hulls. The inner hull of the latter insulates the tanker from contact with the sea, so double hulls are considered safer since oil can drain into the space between the two hulls in the event of an accident.

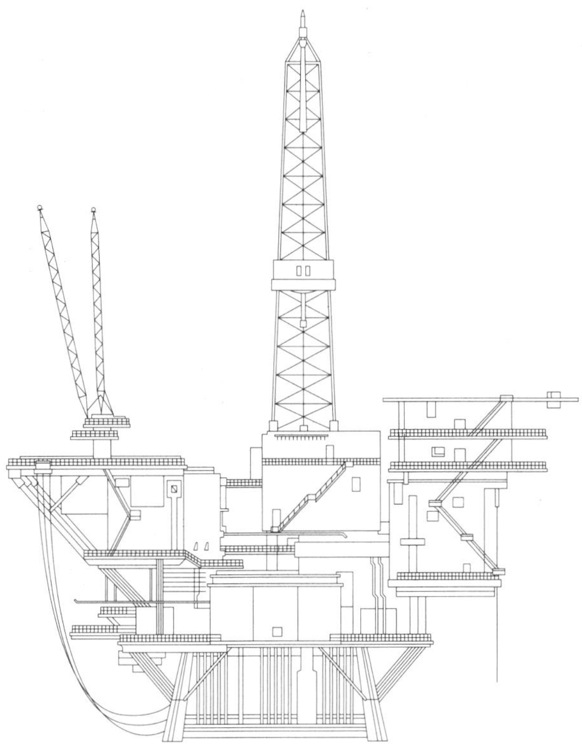

OIL RIGS

The unpredictability of their marine environments (tides, storms, currents) entails greater wear and corrosion than usual on oil rigs. Their design must therefore take all these parameters into account and adapt appropriately.

ABOVE

These ornamental woodcarvings decorate one of the doors of the Heddal Stave Church. Look for the fire-breathing dragon.

OPPOSITE

The church in Heddal was built around 1250 and is the largest stave church in the country.

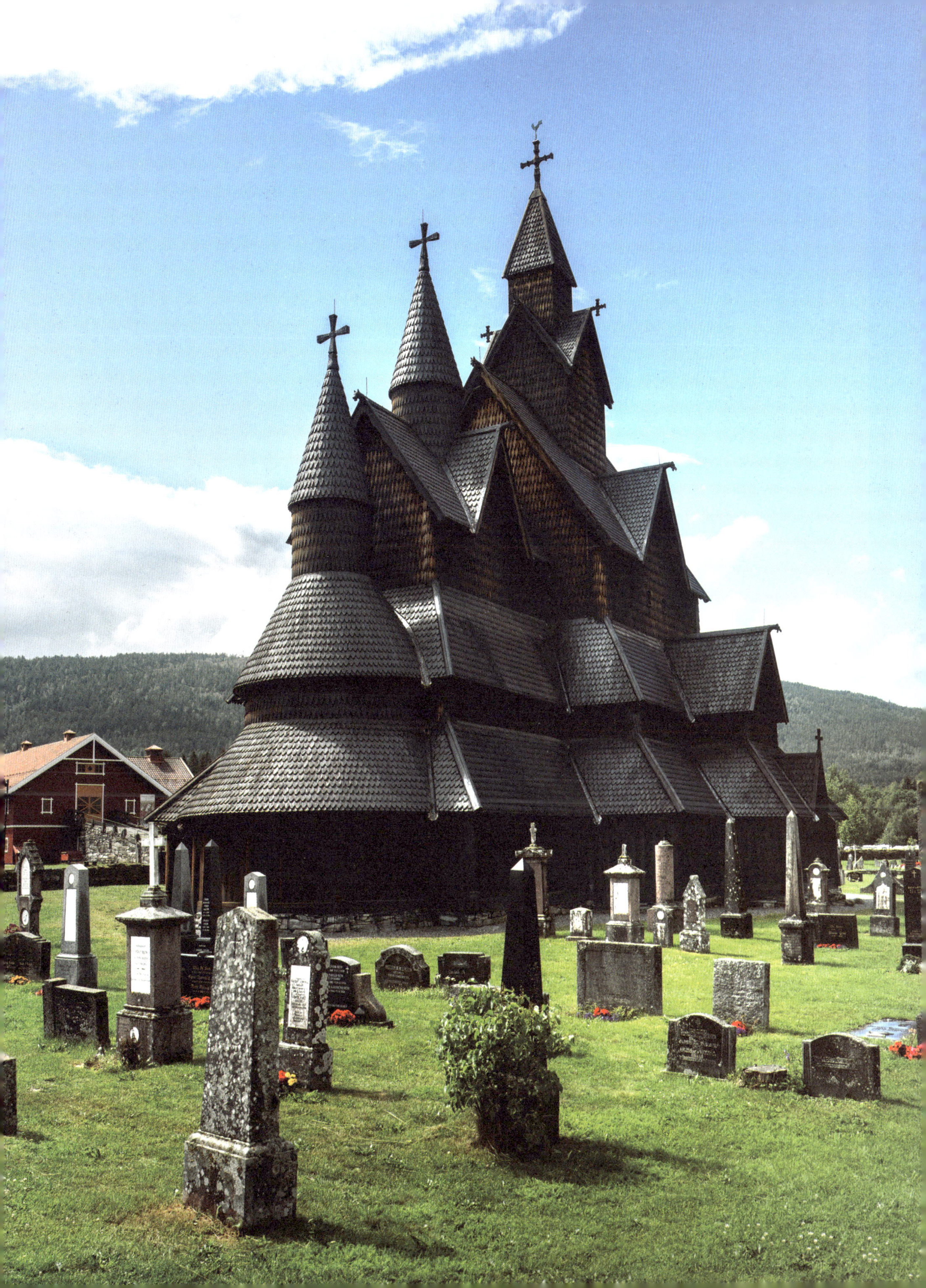

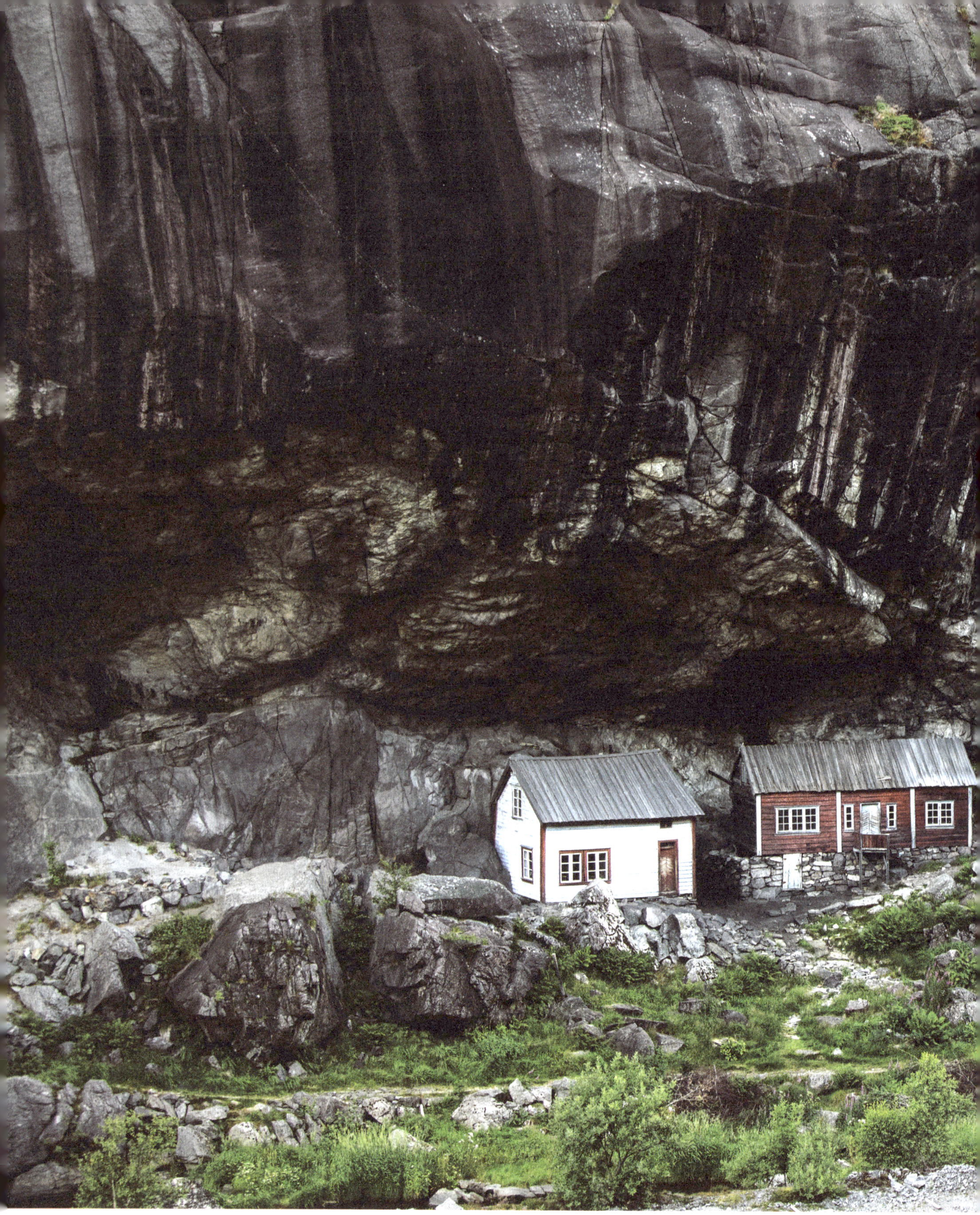

These two wooden houses dating from the nineteenth century are protected in the lee of a rocky overhang known as Helleren.

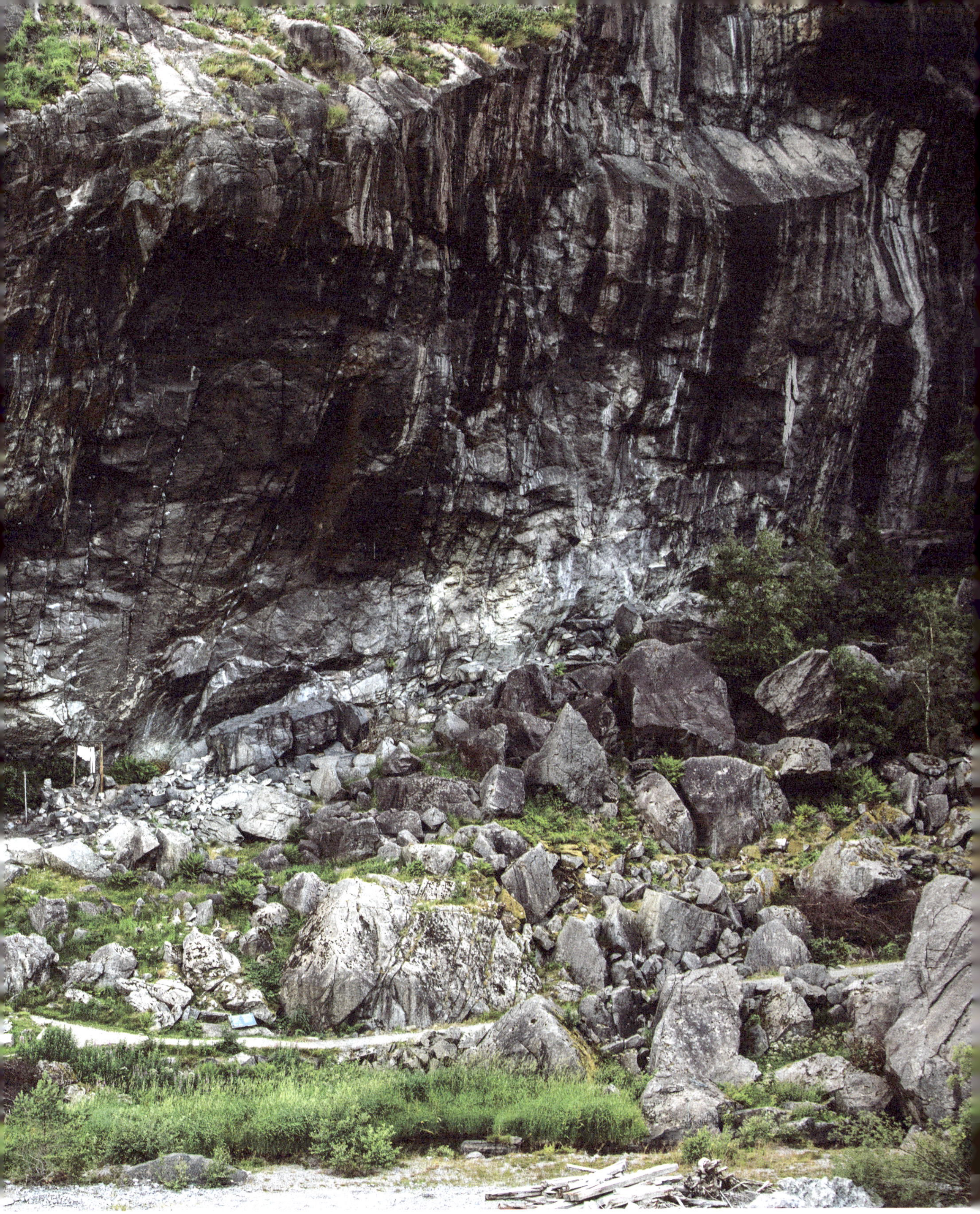

LIFESTYLE

NORWEGIAN SAUNAS

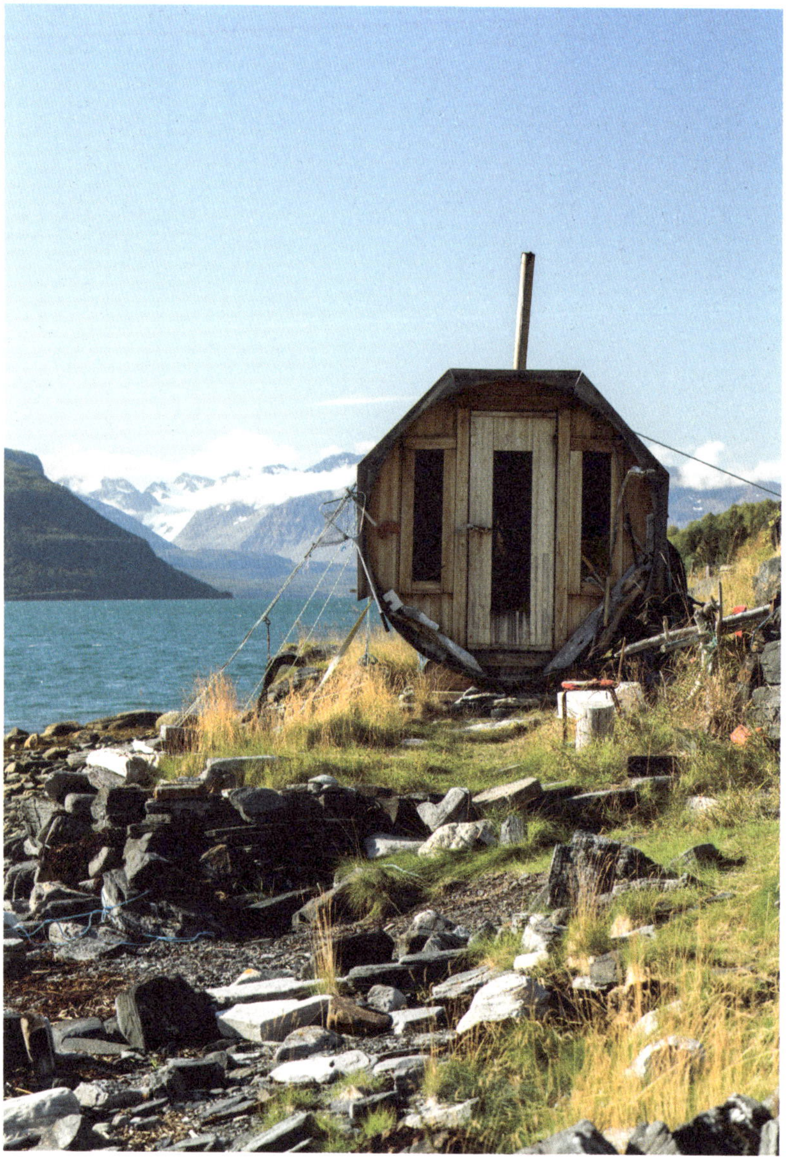

THE LYNGEN ALPS

This private sauna has been firmly tied down to withstand storms. Visitors can enjoy a moment of rest, relaxation, and warmth here during the long winter months.

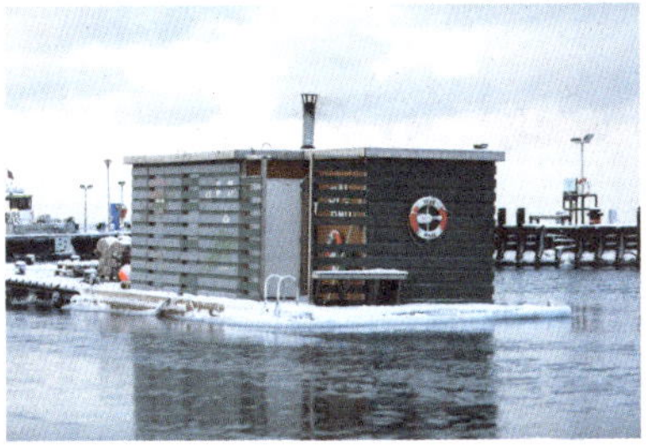

SVALBARD

The chilly waters of Svalbard are the ideal place for a dip among the ice floes.

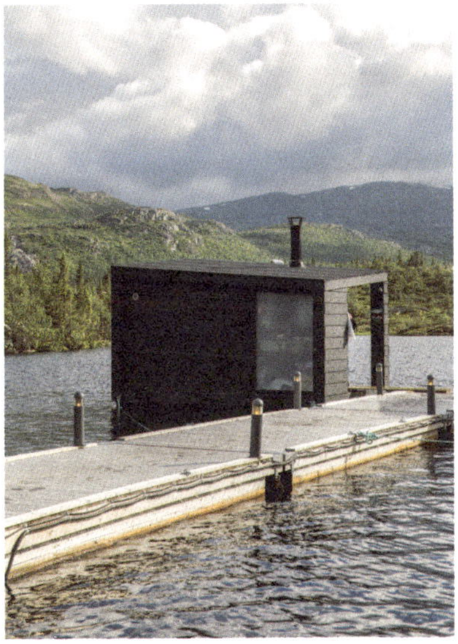

GAUSTABLIKK

Enjoy mountain views from this sauna floating at the foot of Gaustatoppen.

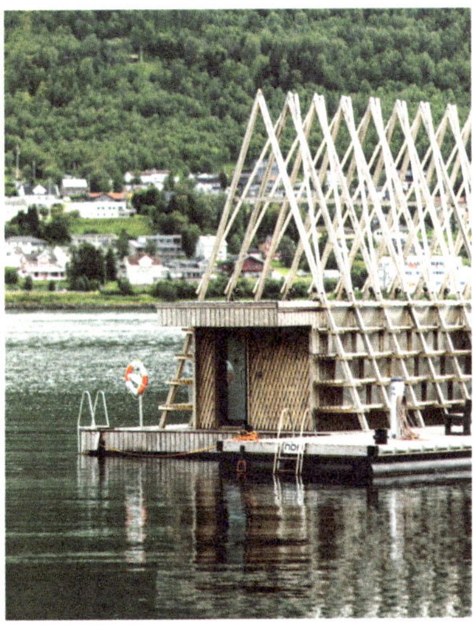

PUST TROMSØ

The structure of this sauna was inspired by racks that dry cod.

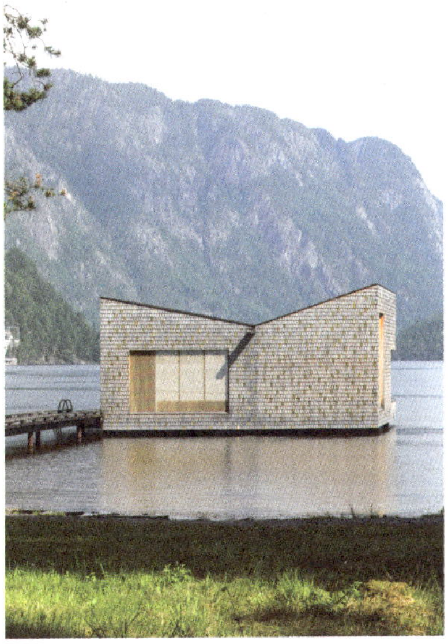

SORIA MORIA SAUNA

The shape of this sauna in Telemark is a free interpretation of the surrounding scenery.

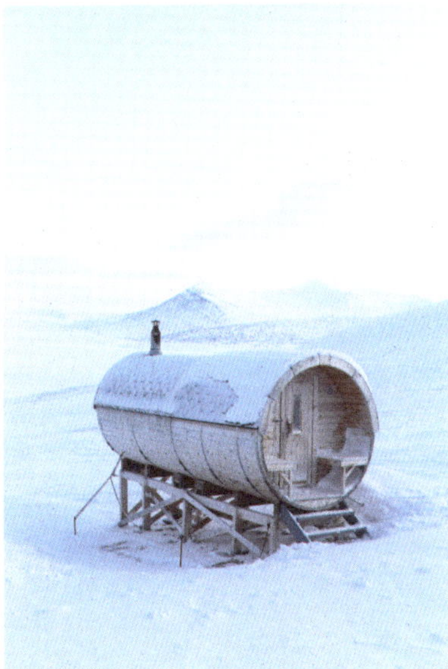

JUVA CABIN

The Juva Cabin sauna in Svalbard is the perfect place for a moment of rest and relaxation after a hard day spent dog sledding.

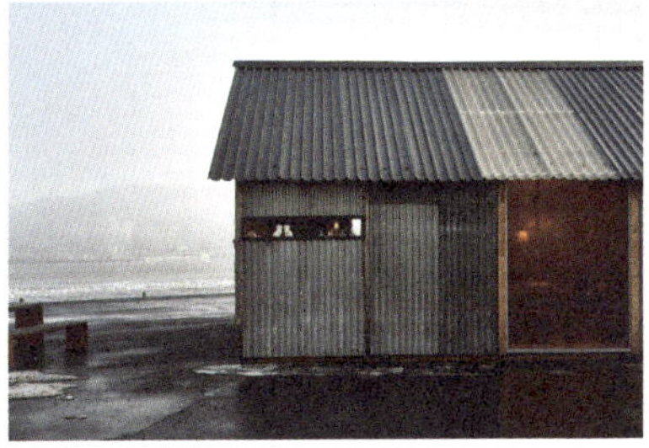

SALT OSLO

This sauna is in a cultural center that stages concerts and plays.

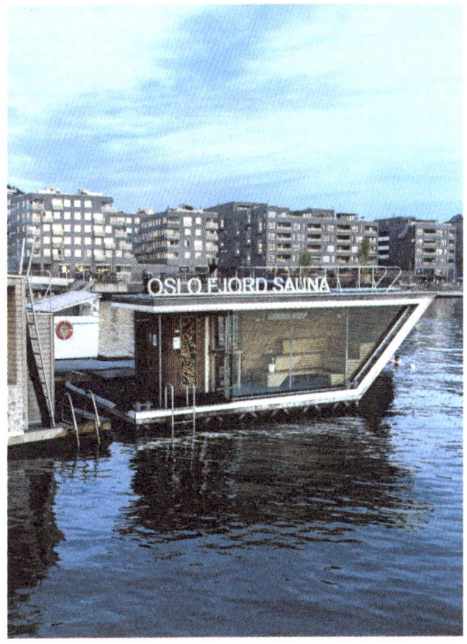

OSLO FJORD SAUNA

This sauna was made from driftwood and recycled materials.

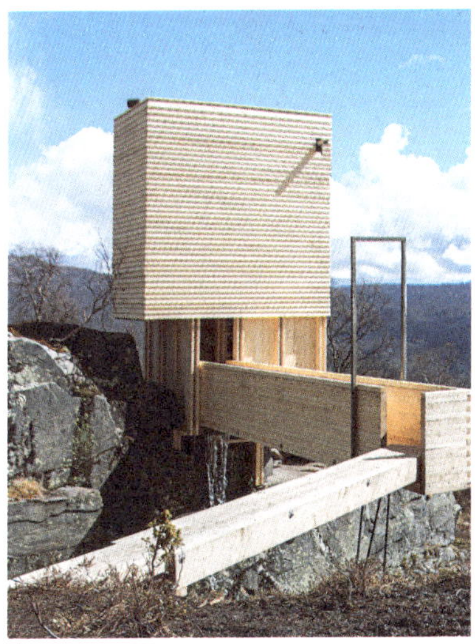

ELDMØLLA

A sauna based on the *kvernhus*, a kind of small Norwegian watermill.

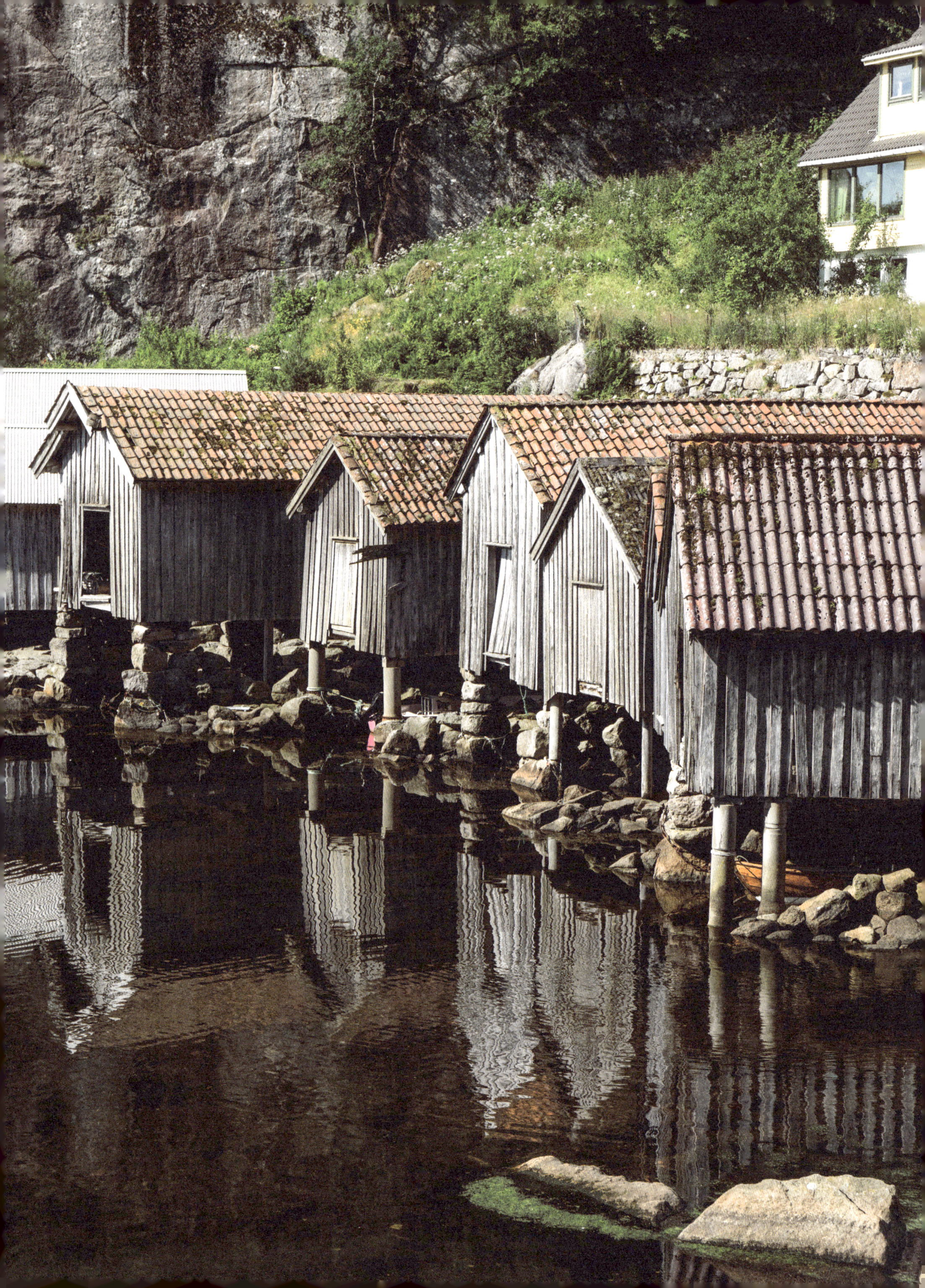

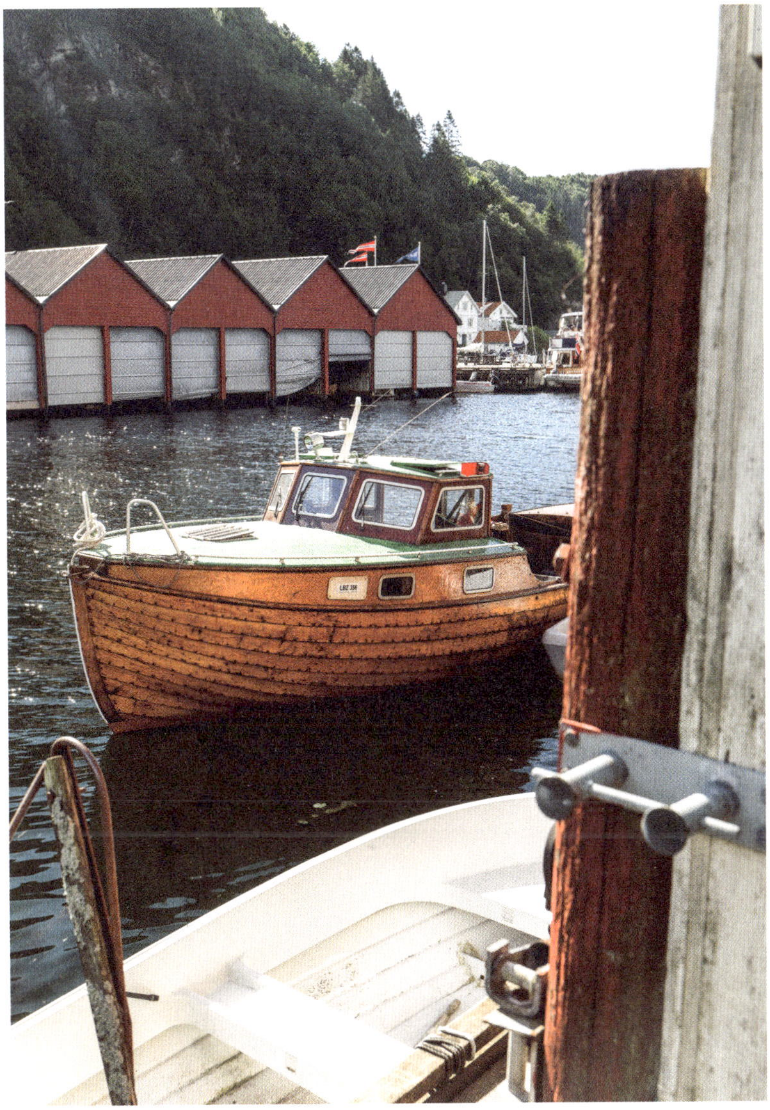

ABOVE

A wooden boat is moored to the dock while the owner gets their fishing tackle ready nearby.

OPPOSITE

A fleet of small boats is used to transport passengers and freight around the region. Specially designed boathouses protect them from the elements.

EXCURSION

UNDER

DINING BENEATH THE WAVES

The first subaquatic restaurant in Europe, Under serves gourmet food accompanied by extraordinary views beneath the waves across the seabed—an experience not to be forgotten.

At first sight, Under could be taken for the remnants of a maritime disaster where it seems a building has collapsed into the water in the wake of a powerful storm that has left part of the structure resting on the bottom of the sea. And yet it is nothing of the sort. This amazing monolithic construction, 112 ft (34 m) long, has been meticulously designed by Snøhetta, the renowned firm of Norwegian architects, to give visitors an experience that is entirely out of the ordinary.

"Under is a natural extension of the way we are pushing boundaries," explains architect Kjetil Trædal Thorsen, the founder of Snøhetta. The aim of this incredible architectural feat is to "provide new perspectives and ways of seeing the world, both above and below the surface of the water."

The part of the concrete structure that remains exposed has been designed to blend into the natural environment over the the years and is intended to serve as a habitat for marine species, to be colonized like an artificial reef by algae and shellfish.

The stripped-back interior, with its sleek oak paneling, can accommodate up to forty diners at the closest of quarters with the sea. A balcony at the restaurant entrance offers a panoramic view of the dining room and a bar where cocktails can be sipped at sea level.

An undersea world dancing to the slow rhythm of waves and currents can be glimpsed through the wall of thick glass. The fish in the dull blue of the bay swim idly around among the seaweed and rocks, occasionally eyeing diners with curiosity. Every now and again, harp seals or eider ducks come to hunt, diving right in front of the patrons in an unforgettable spectacle.

While the view may change with the weather and the seasons, the massive concrete walls—which are 20 in (50 cm) thick—promise to withstand even the fiercest winter blast, ensuring that diners can enjoy the underwater scenery in complete tranquility.

In addition to the architectural experience, the aim is to create a gourmet journey of discovery using locally sourced wild produce, including fish, shellfish, seaweed, berries, mushrooms, and game. Under's Michelin-starred chef and his brigade have an abundance of ingredients at their disposal with which to be creative and experiment throughout the year.

It is no coincidence that in Norwegian the word *under* means both "beneath" and "miracle," and here, 16 ft (5 m) below the surface, the phrase "sea view" takes on a whole new meaning.

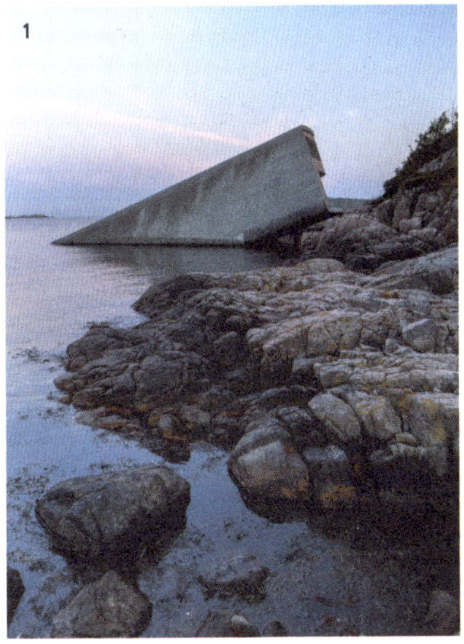

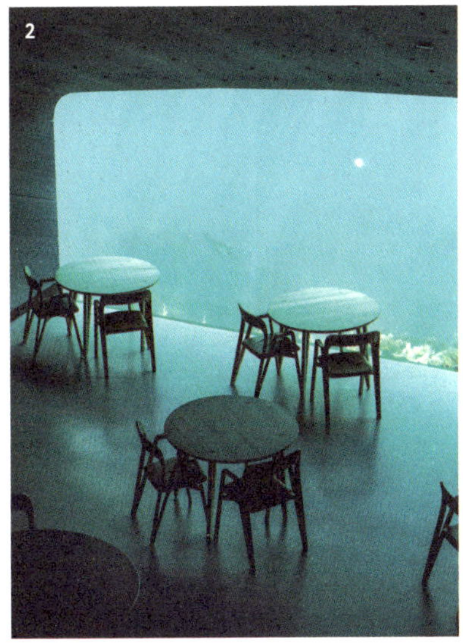

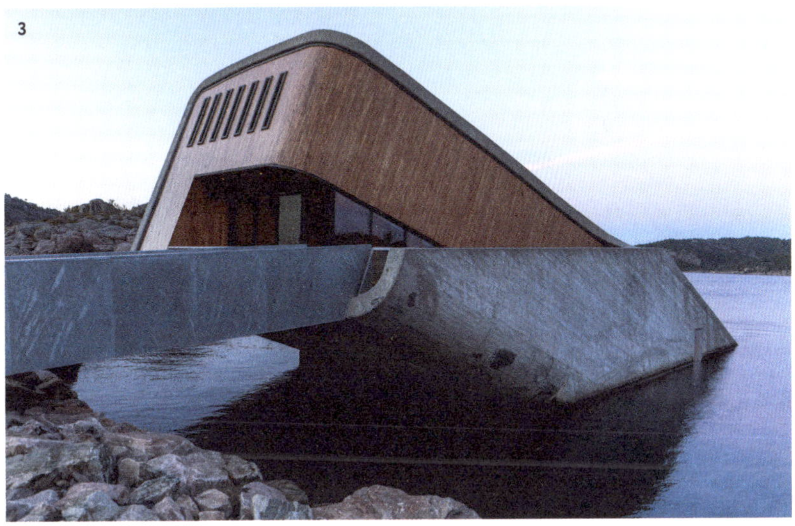

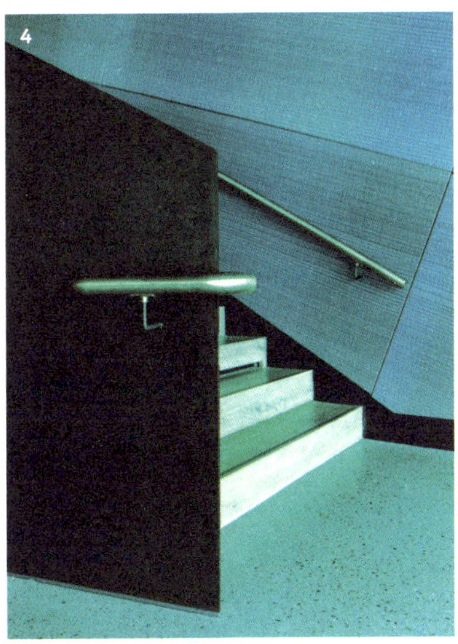

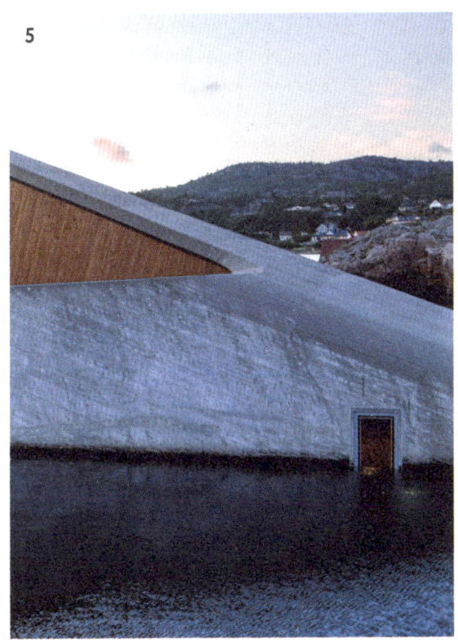

1/ MONOLITHIC

The restaurant's imposing structure is in sharp contrast with the coastal scenery.

2/ 20,000 LEAGUES UNDER THE SEA

Visitors can directly observe passing fish and the seabed through two picture windows.

3/ WELCOME ABOARD

Crossing the walkway is a little like boarding a ship as diners get ready to brave the Norwegian waters.

4/ DECOR

The fixtures and fittings were also designed by the Snøhetta architecture firm in collaboration with local carpenters.

5/ OBSERVATION

Beneath the water the exterior surface of the building is gradually transforming into a reef to be colonized by marine flora and fauna.

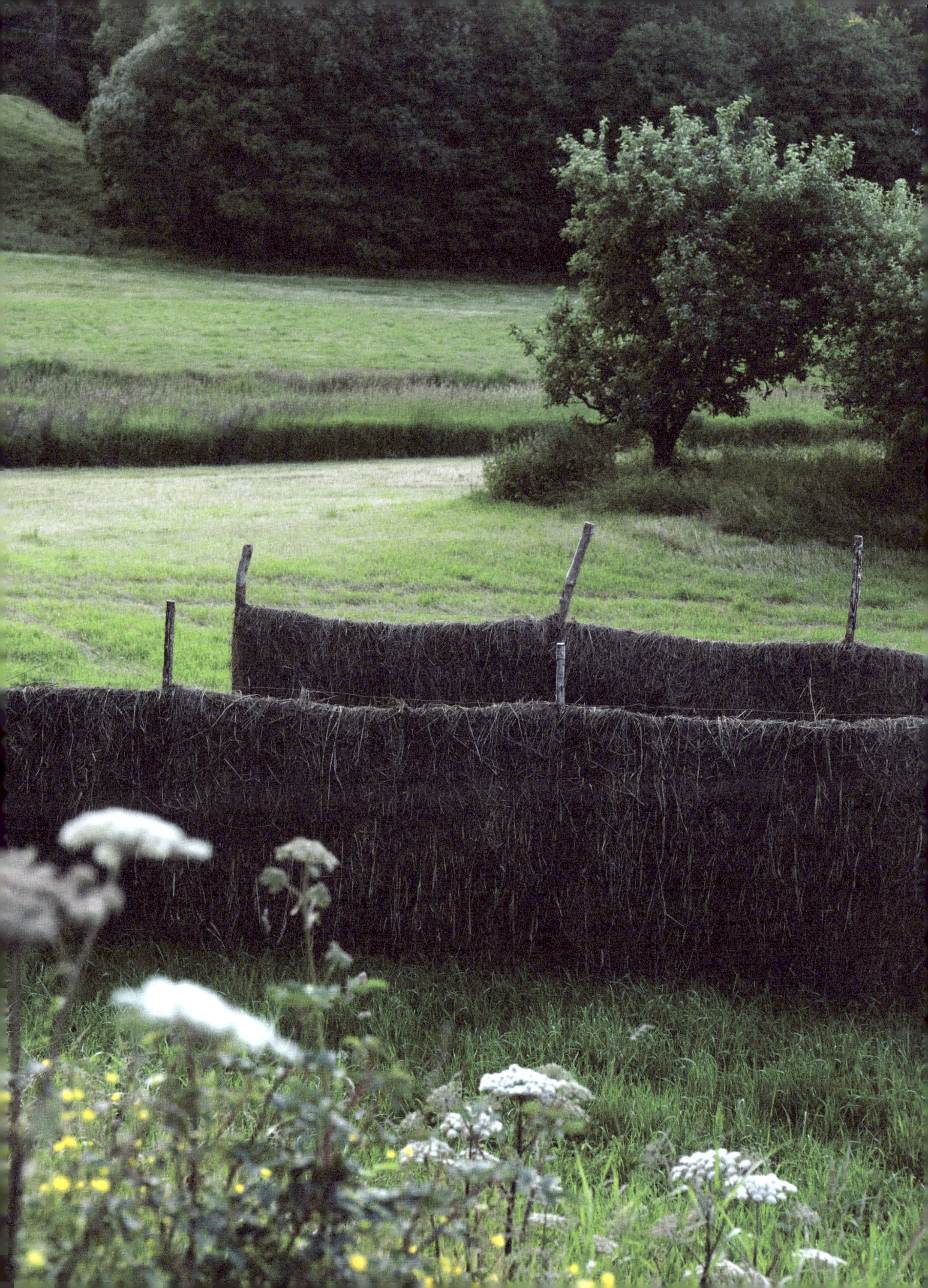

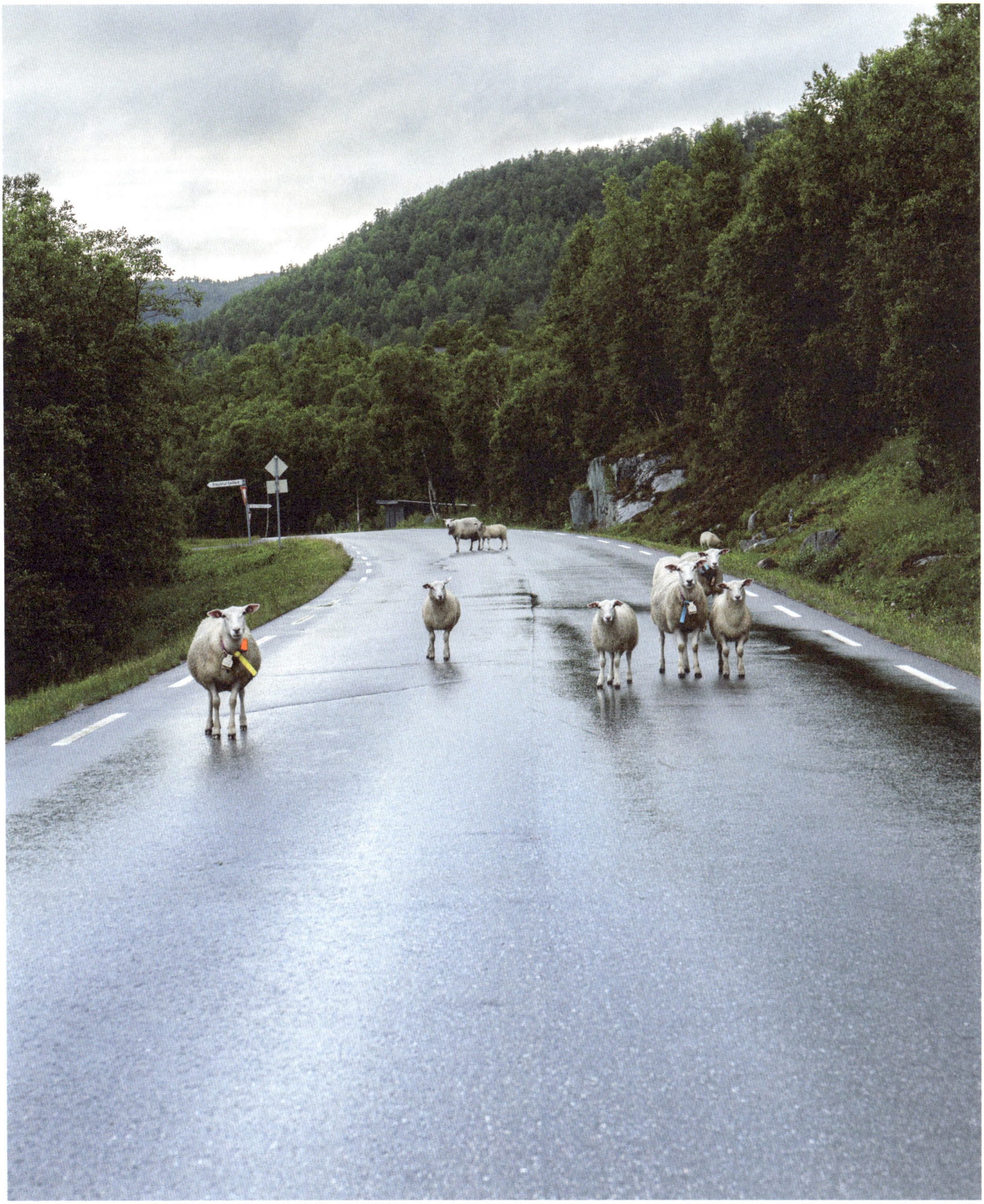

ABOVE

It is best to keep an eye out; you never know who you'll run into on the road.

OPPOSITE

Animal fodder laid out on traditional drying racks in the Setesdal valley.

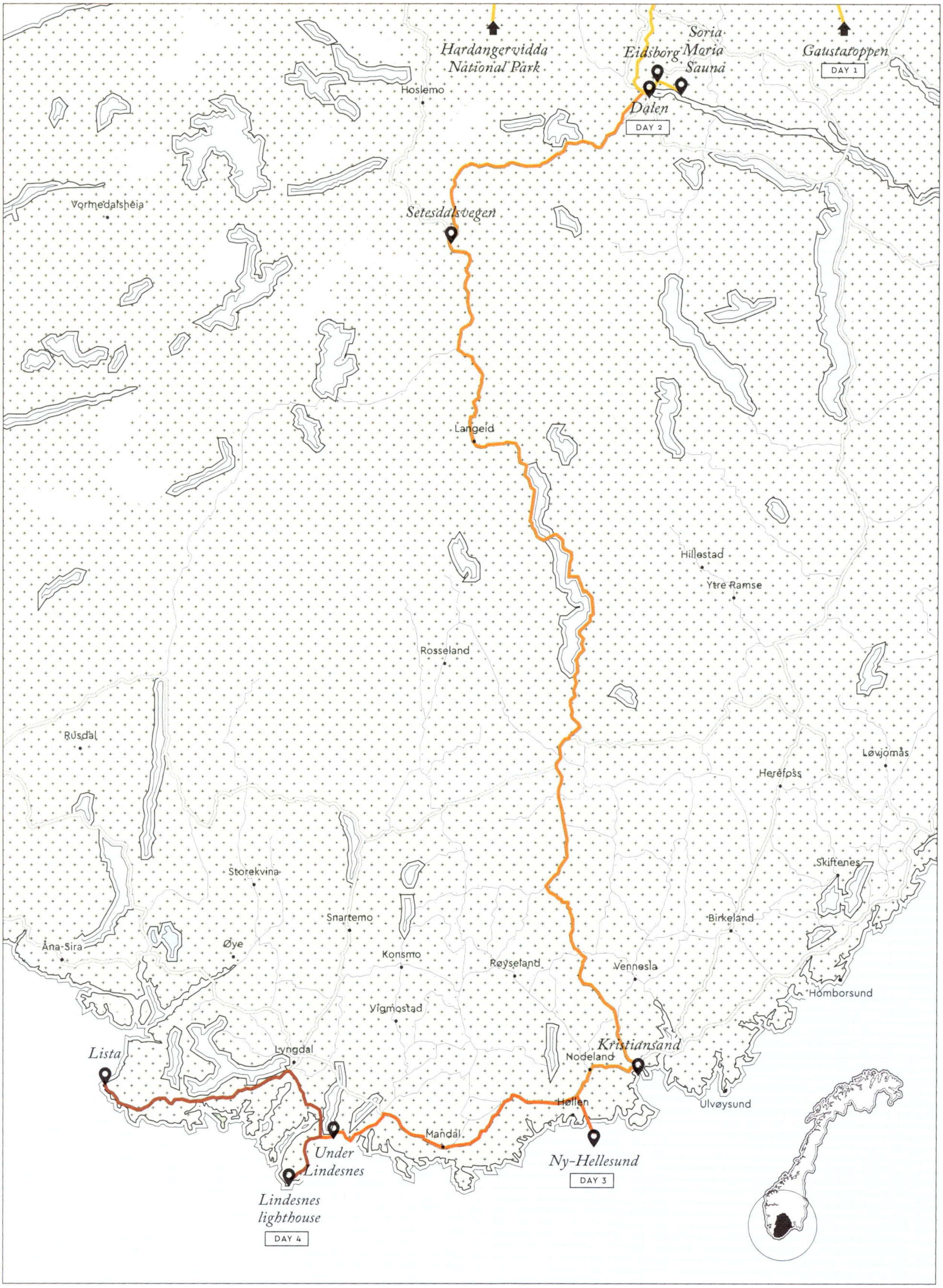
Hardangervidda National Park
Eidsborg
Soria Moria Sauna
Gaustatoppen
DAY 1
Hoslemo
Dalen
DAY 2
Vormedalsheia
Setesdalsvegen
Langeid
Hillestad
Ytre Ramse
Rosseland
Rusdal
Løvjomås
Herefoss
Skiftenes
Storekvina
Snartemo
Birkeland
Åna-Sira
Øye
Konsmo
Røyseland
Vennesla
Homborsund
Vigmostad
Lista
Lyngdal
Kristiansand
Nodeland
Hollen
Ulvøysund
Mandal
Under Lindesnes
Ny-Hellesund
DAY 3
Lindesnes lighthouse
DAY 4

GAUSTATOPPEN TO THE BEACHES OF THE SOUTH

This region, nicknamed Little Norway, is often overlooked by tourists, but it has all kinds of iconic Norwegian scenery to offer the visitor.

DAY 1: GAUSTATOPPEN TO DALEN

A mountain with a difference. During the Cold War, rock was blasted out to install a funicular railway within Gaustatoppen in a truly extravagant but impressive feat of engineering. It is now possible to hitch a ride to the top to find one of the most beautiful outlooks in Southern Norway. Continue toward the south-west and Hardangervidda will slowly reveal itself, a superb plateau of tundra scenery. Every winter this is a destination for adventurers in training for polar expeditions. Stop off at the stave church in Eidsborg before heading for Dalen to try the Soria Moria Sauna and then plunge straight into the icy waters of the lake.

DAY 2: ALONG THE SETESDAL VALLEY TOWARD KRISTIANSAND

The Setesdal valley was isolated for a considerable period of time, which served to preserve its folklore and regional identity. It also ensured the valley's inhabitants maintained a very specific diet and dialect and an almost medieval way of life. The journey between Dalen and Kristiansand takes a couple of hours and is a perfect opportunity to enjoy the charming scenery of this traditional valley on the way down to the coast. Kristiansand itself is a charming, flower-filled town, with numerous wooden houses, and cafés and restaurants with terraces.

DAY 3: A VISIT TO NY-HELLESUND

With its air of tranquility, friendliness, and slow pace of life, Ny-Hellesund epitomizes the ambience of the south. There are no motor vehicles here and just fifteen permanent residents (bolstered by more in the summer months) enjoying a lifestyle cut off from the rest of the world. There are no roads, only hiking trails that crisscross the islands. Everyone knows everyone else on this small archipelago that has been a source of inspiration for a host of painters, in particular Amaldus Nielsen for his famous canvas *Morning in Ny-Hellesund*. This is one of Norway's best-kept secrets, and few foreign tourists are bold enough to venture this far.

DAY 4: LINDESNES LIGHTHOUSE TO LISTA BEACHES

What's not to like about a lighthouse that feels as though it has been built at the end of the earth? The light went on in Norway's first lighthouse at the southernmost tip of the country in 1655 and it remains in operation to this day. Lindesnes lighthouse stands on top of a windswept hill. Just around the corner is Under, the famous gourmet restaurant that provides the unusual opportunity of dining beneath the waves. It is a unique experience that would be the perfect way to either round off a trip or act as a prelude to continuing on to Lista and its endless beaches of white sand, some of the most beautiful in the country.

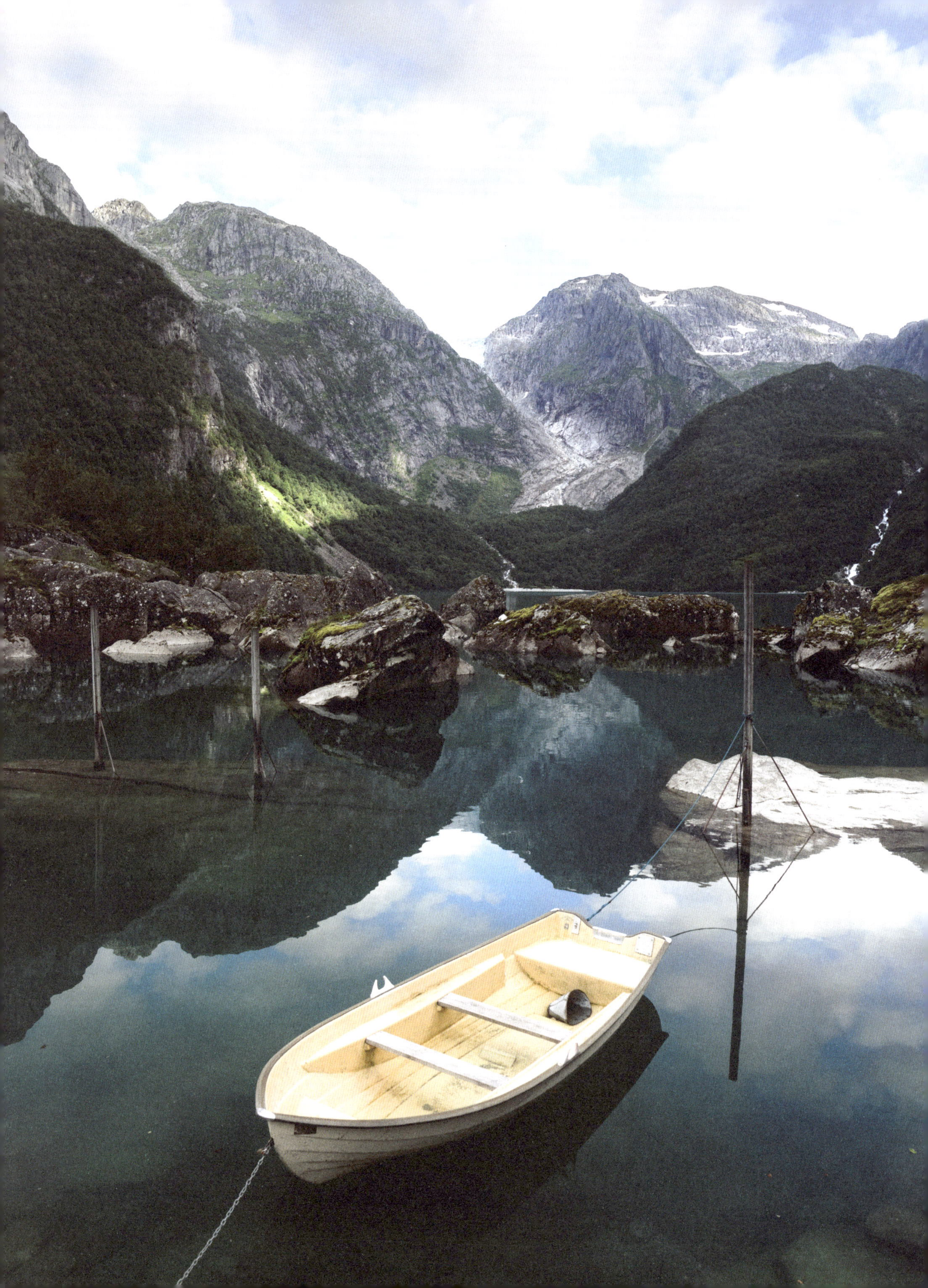

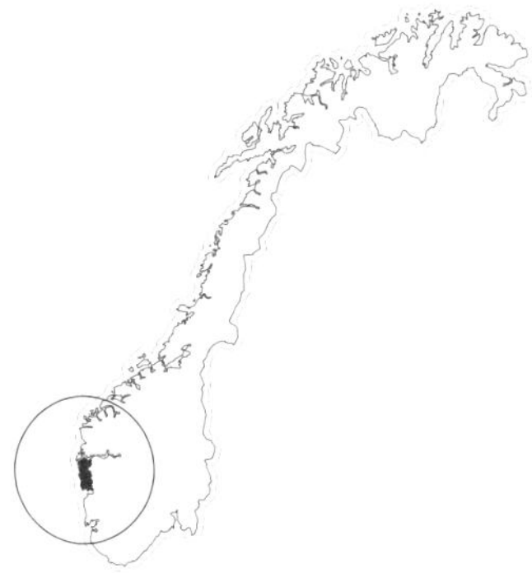

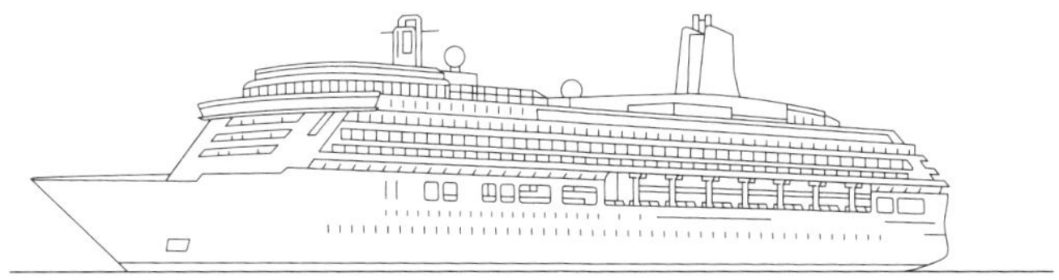

A KINGDOM OF FJORDS

BERGEN

AND THE FJORDS

The scenery for which Norway is most famous lies in a region that has been carved and shaped by glaciers over millennia.

P.68

The turquoise lakewater of Bondhusvatnet flows down from the Folgefonna glacier.

OPPOSITE

Preikestolen, or Pulpit Rock, plunges vertiginously into the waters of Lysefjord 1,982 ft (604 m) below. The views from the clifftop are simply amazing.

Some of the country's most breathtaking scenery is to be found in Western Norway, with a riot of incredible views in this kingdom of fjords.

The spectacular wall of granite at Preikestolen is almost worth the trip alone, with the view looking down from the edge to the limpid waters of Lysefjord a dizzying 1,982 ft (604 m) below. The hike to Preikestolen could also serve as a taster for the trail to Trolltunga, another equally exceptional geological formation. This rocky outcrop (whose name literally means "the troll's tongue") juts out horizontally over the void, an unforgettable experience for those who make the trip to stand on it.

The amazing sights don't stop here, however. There are any number of waterfalls scattered across the landscape. Låtefossen is a particularly striking example of the power of water as it thunders down onto the Hardangervidda plateau. The many orchards of Hardangerfjord produce a delicious dry cider that goes perfectly with a traditional lunch, perhaps sampled in Agatunet, a tiny village (in)famous for having been home to one of Norway's last executioners.

A walk through the Bondhusdalen valley offers the perfect opportunity to see Folgefonna at close quarters, an immense glacier that can also be hiked across if equipped with crampons. Across the region are constant reminders of the ancient glaciers whose retreat has scoured the vertical walls of rock that plummet down from great heights to the turquoise waters of the fjords—on a geographical scale, a relatively recent development that explains the region's dramatic scenery.

The charming city of Bergen is typically Norwegian and leaves an indelible impression on those interested in its rich history (despite the annual two hundred and forty days of rain). It serves as an ideal base from which to explore the fjords, while the many students who call it home make for a party atmosphere in its bars and streets throughout the year. Bryggen, with its colorful wooden buildings, is a district of Bergen that dates back to medieval times and is most famous for having been a trading outpost of the Hanseatic League back in the day, not to mention for also surviving any number of fires over the centuries.

The railway line between Bergen and Flåm is renowned for the scenery through which it passes, making it the perfect way to continue a journey north toward magnificent Sognefjord, where a number of old farmsteads have been preserved. In the nineteenth century, English aristocrats would come to the neighboring village of Lærdal to fish for wild salmon, making these anglers the area's very first tourists!

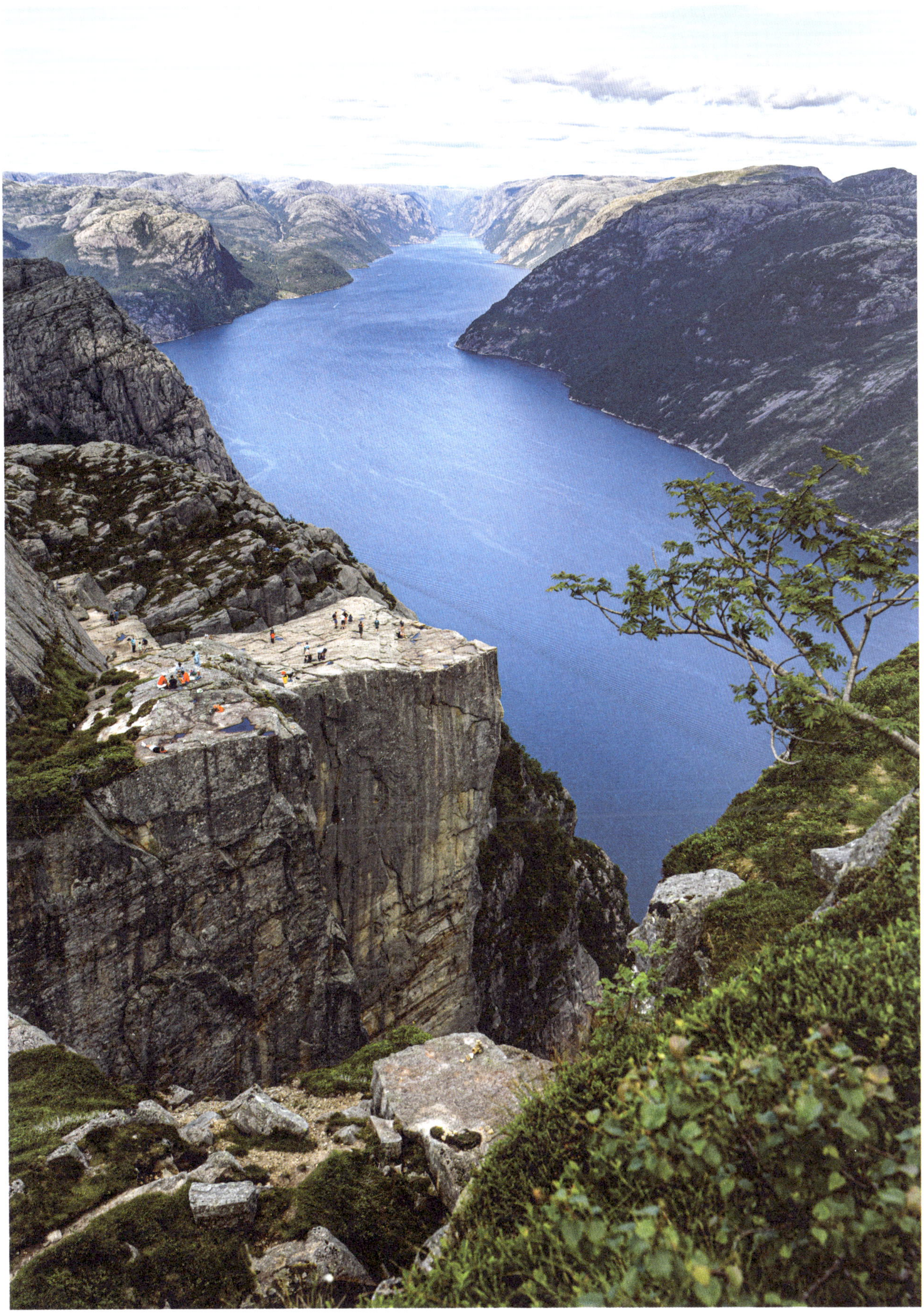

THE ESSENTIALS

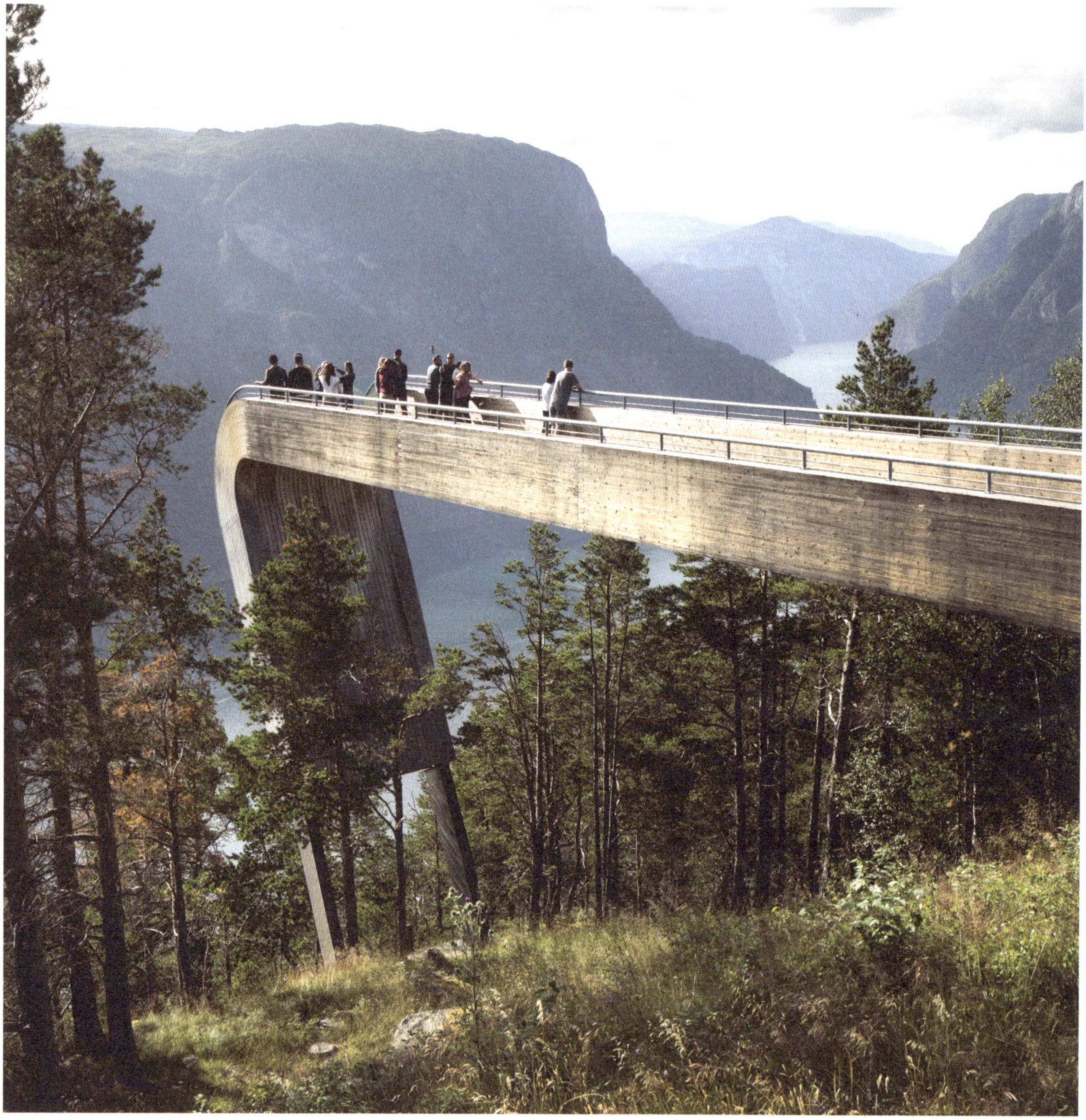

STEGASTEIN VIEWPOINT

This viewing platform of wood and steel is 100 ft (30 m) long and 13 ft (4 m) wide, and stands at an elevation of 2,130 ft (650 m). Its unusual architecture and breathtaking views over Aurlandsfjord make it an unmissable stop.

16

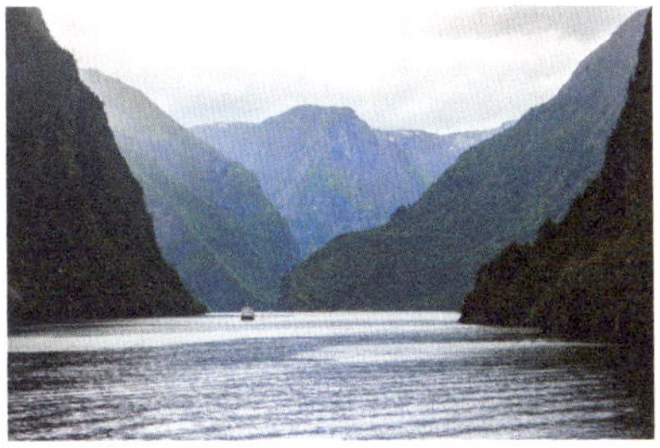

SOGNEFJORD

The deepest (4,290 ft/1,308 m) and the second-longest fjord in the country, extends no less than 127 miles (204 km) inland. Its banks are dotted with small villages and their orchards.

17

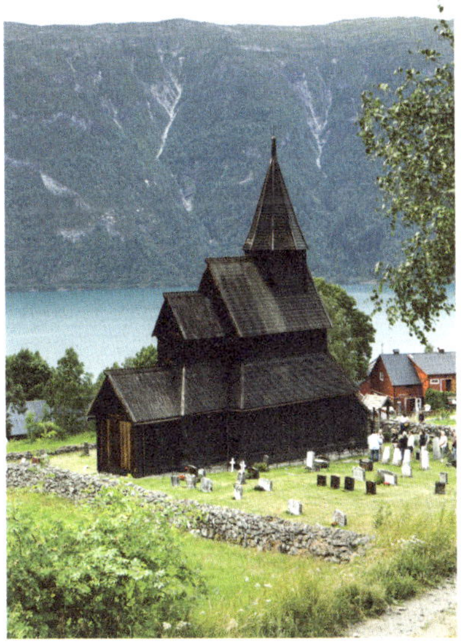

URNES STAVKIRKE

Urnes Stave Church was built on the banks of Sognefjord in 1130 and is the oldest of its kind in the country.

18

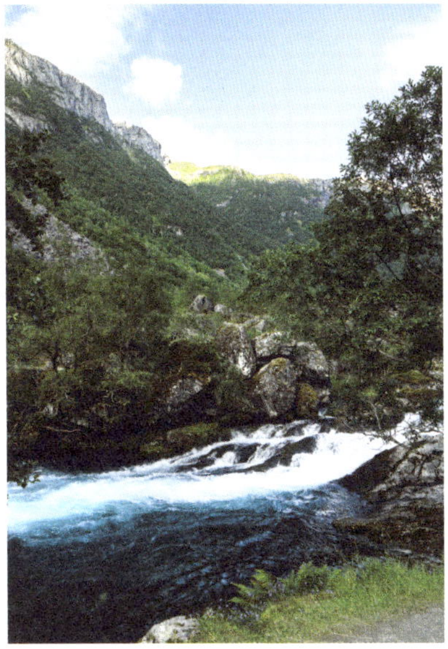

BONDHUSVATNET

The road that leads from the glacial lake at Bondhusvatnet was built in 1863 to transport ice to the fjord for export.

19

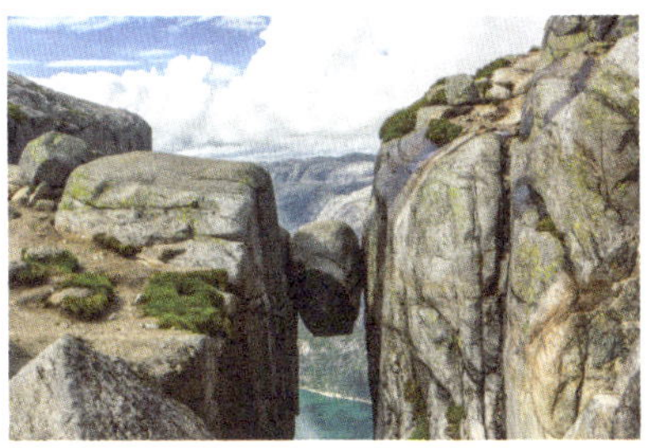

KJERAGBOLTEN

A trek of three hours is required to get here, but the reward will be some stunning photos—this boulder, wedged between two sheer walls of rock at a height of 3,230 ft (984 m), was deposited here by retreating glaciers.

20

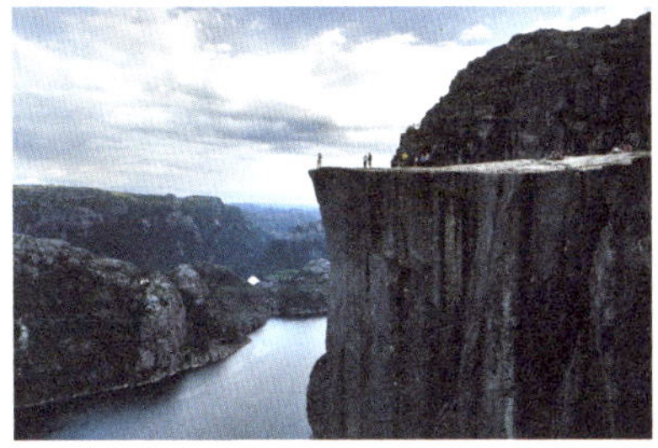

PREIKESTOLEN

The view from the flat top of this imposing cliff, from which visitors can stare into the abyss, is stunning. It is one of the most popular tourist sites in the country.

21

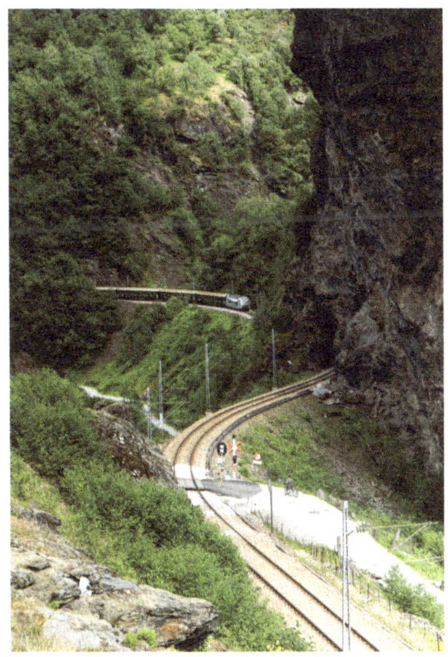

THE TRAIN TO FLÅM

The railway line between Flåm and Myrdal enjoys magnificent scenic views of Western Norway.

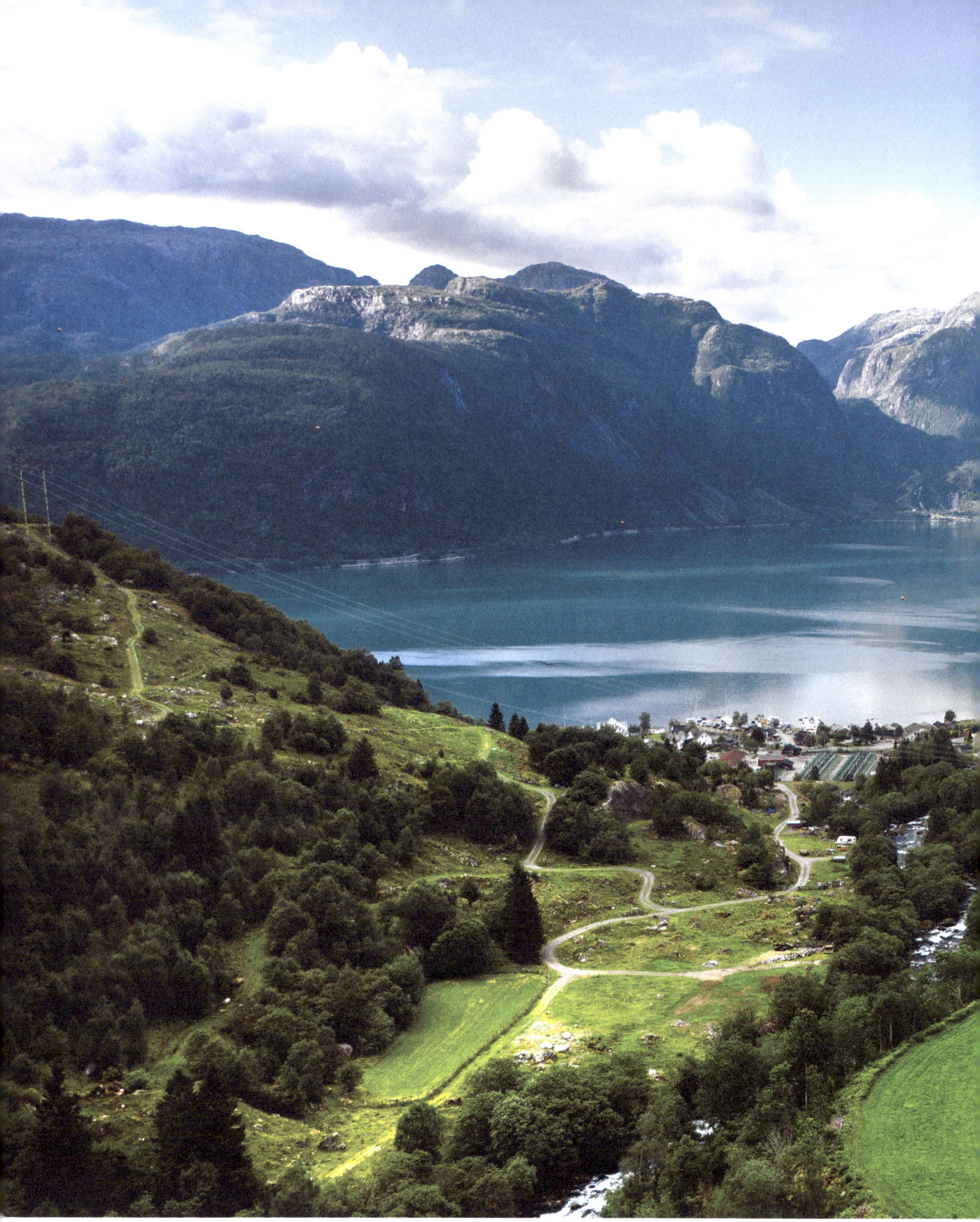

The village of Bondhus lies on the banks of one of Hardangerfjord's many arms. The turquoise waters of the fjord reflect the landscape's myriad shades of green.

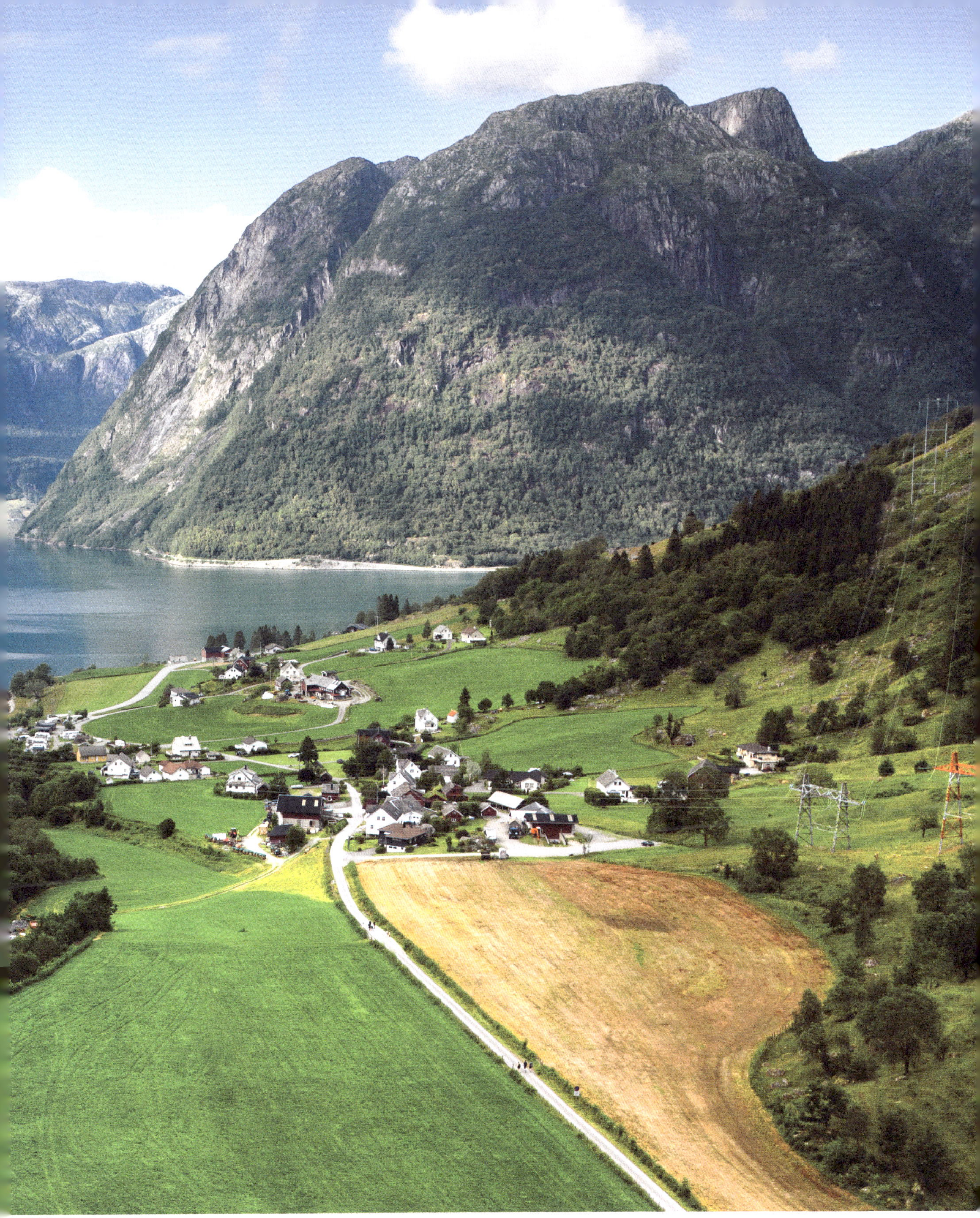

FOOD AND DRINK

AGA SIDERI HARDANGERFJORD

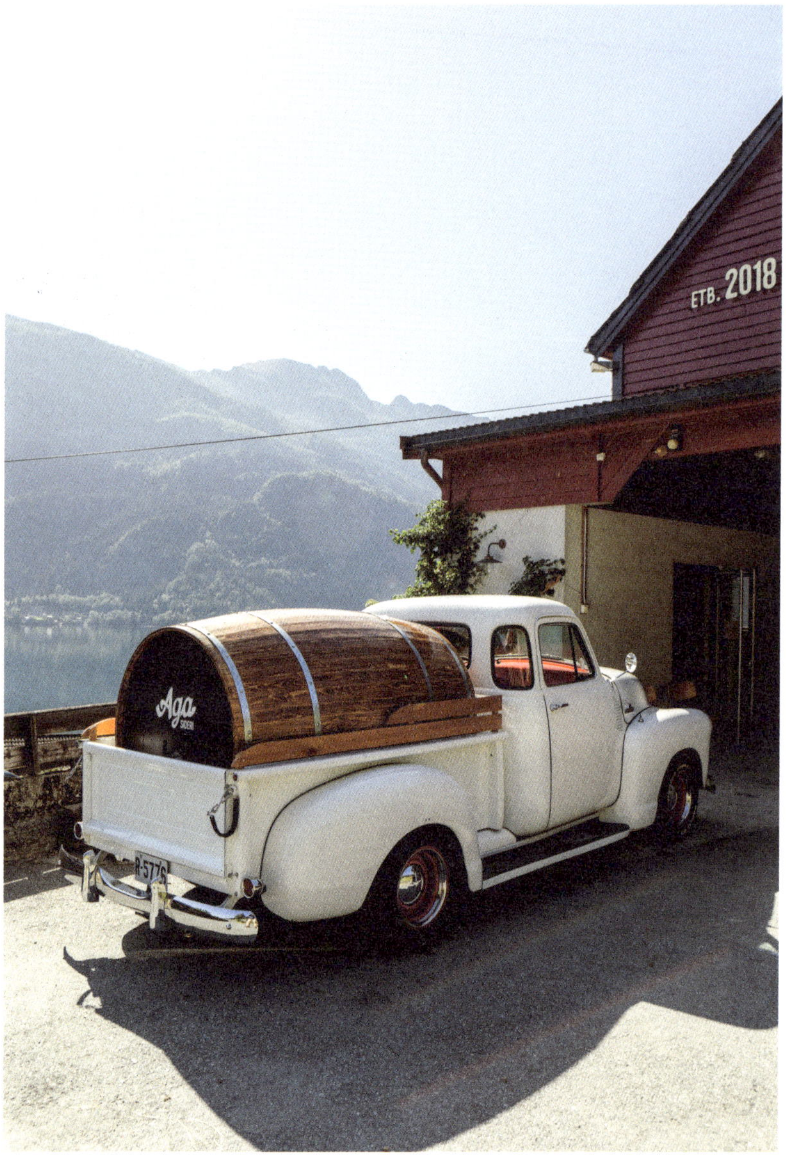

A PLEASANT CLIMATE

Aga cider mill is ideally located on the sunny banks of Sørfjorden, one of the arms of Hardangerfjord, which enjoys a mild and temperate climate.

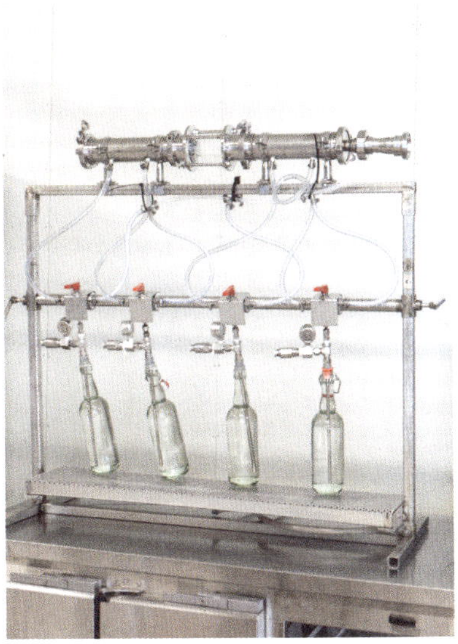

ARTISAN PRODUCTION

The cider mill produces 13,000 gallons (50,000 liters) of artisan cider per year.

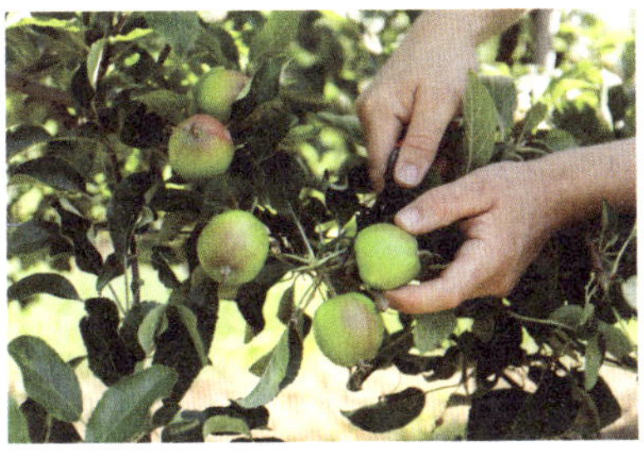

A COUNTRY APPLE

Sweet and acidic, the apples used by Joar have been growing here for generations.

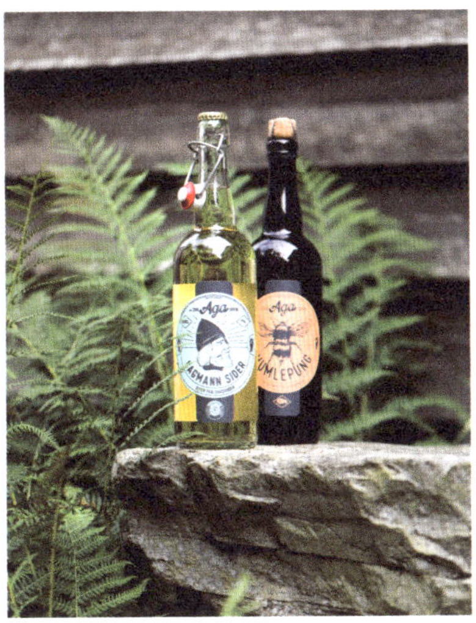

LAGMANN AND HUMLEPUNG

The two most popular ciders produced here are dry and best served chilled.

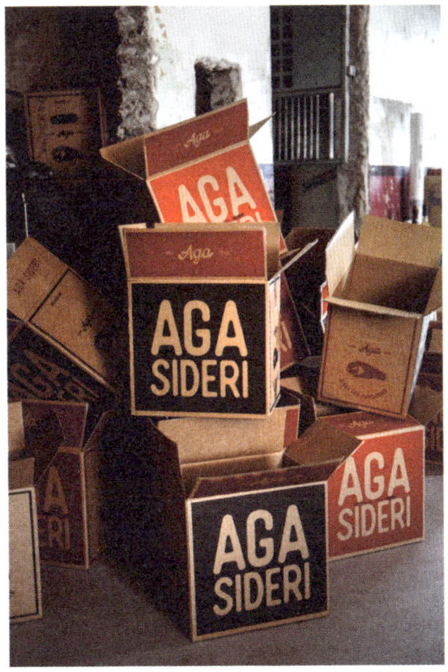

AGA SIDERI

Following university studies in Bergen, Joar Aga decided to go green and buy his uncle's farm.

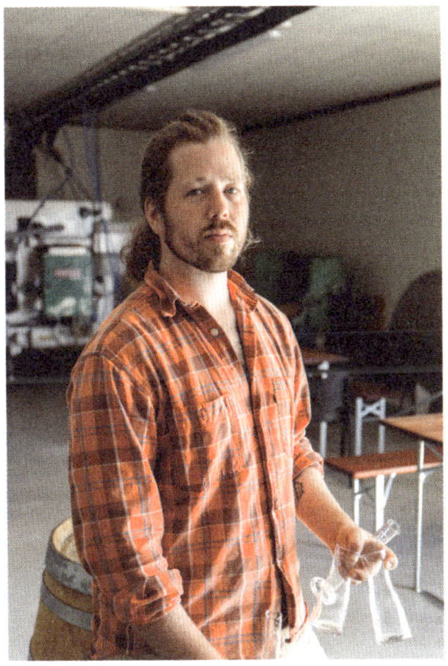

CIRCULAR TOUR

Joar welcomes visitors in his store, but they can also take part in a tasting at the cider mill.

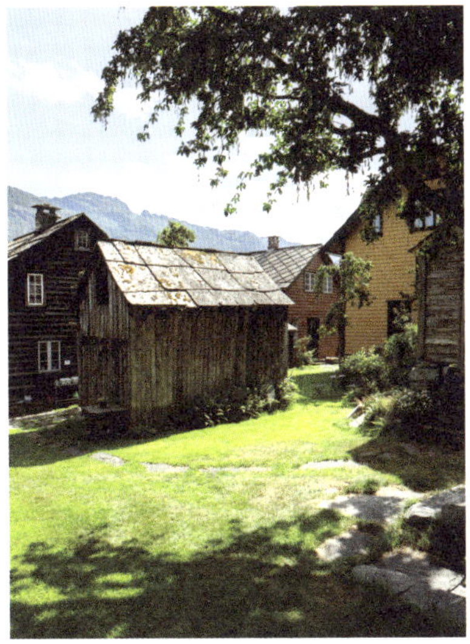

AGATUNET

The thirteenth-century hamlet of Agatunet is surrounded by orchards.

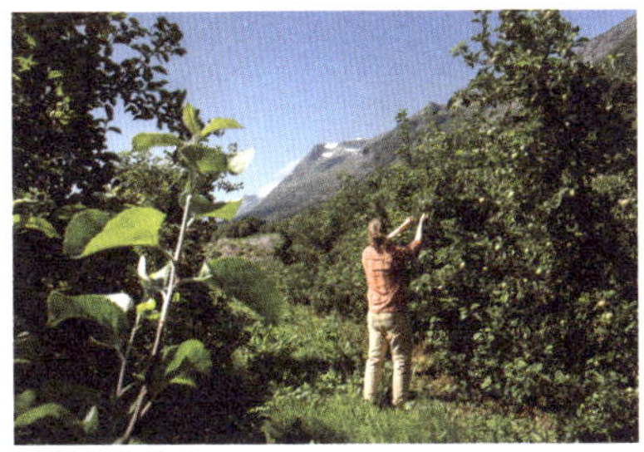

AT THE FOOT OF THE GLACIER

Folgefonna glacier overlooks the valley where the apple trees grow.

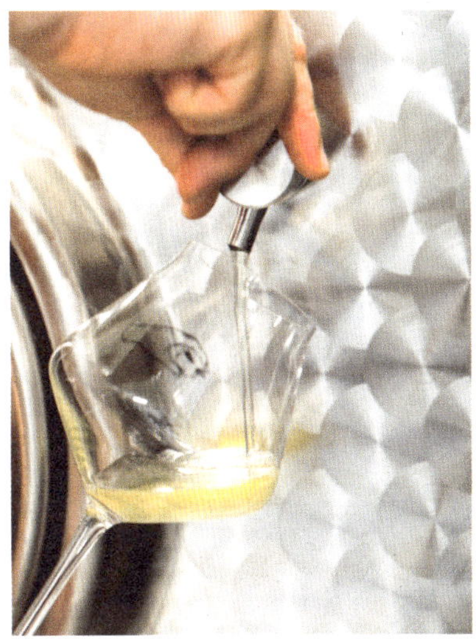

QUALITY

Joar's cider is very popular in Norway and has won numerous awards.

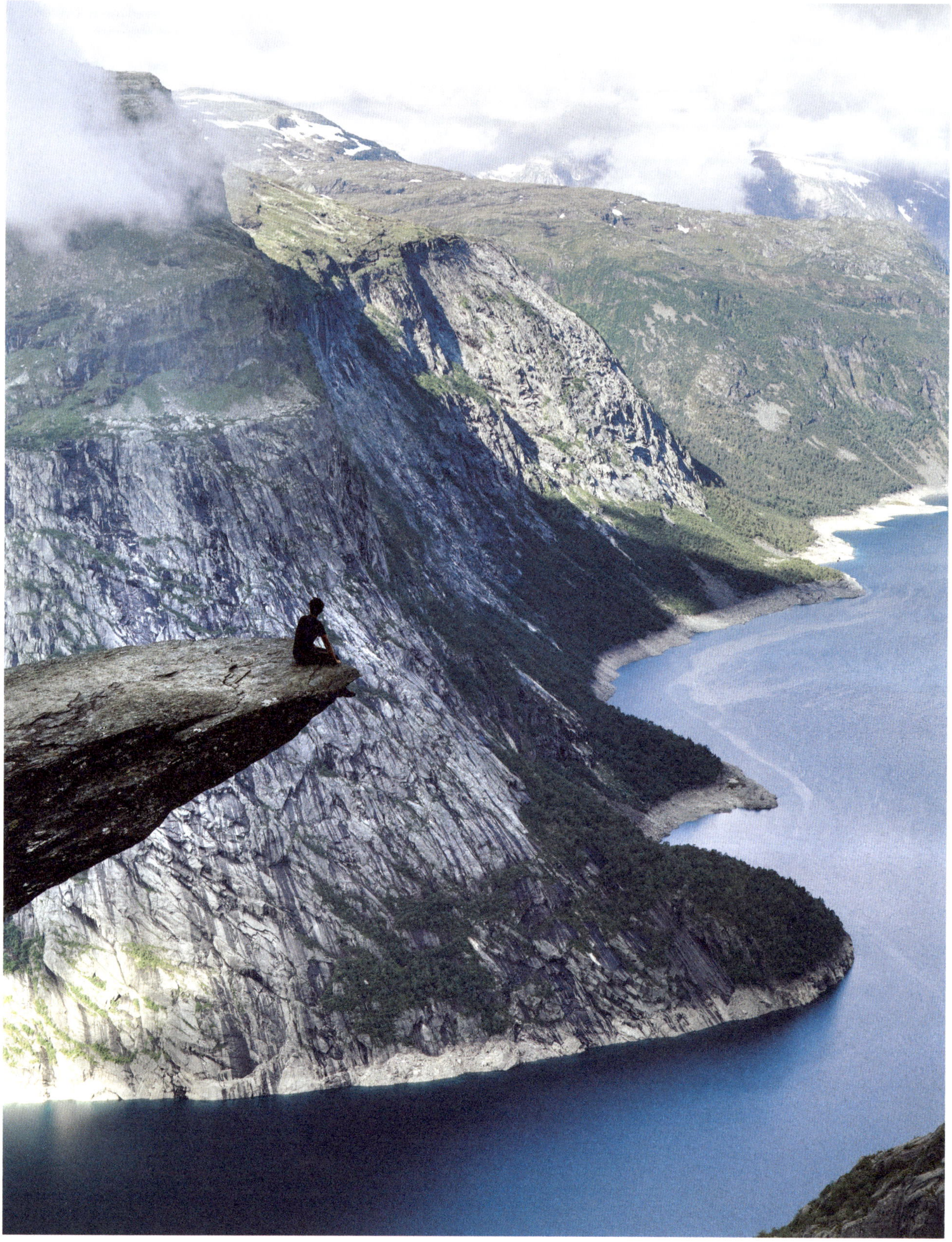

Lovers of spectacular scenery should not miss the hiking trail to Trolltunga (literally, the "troll's tongue").

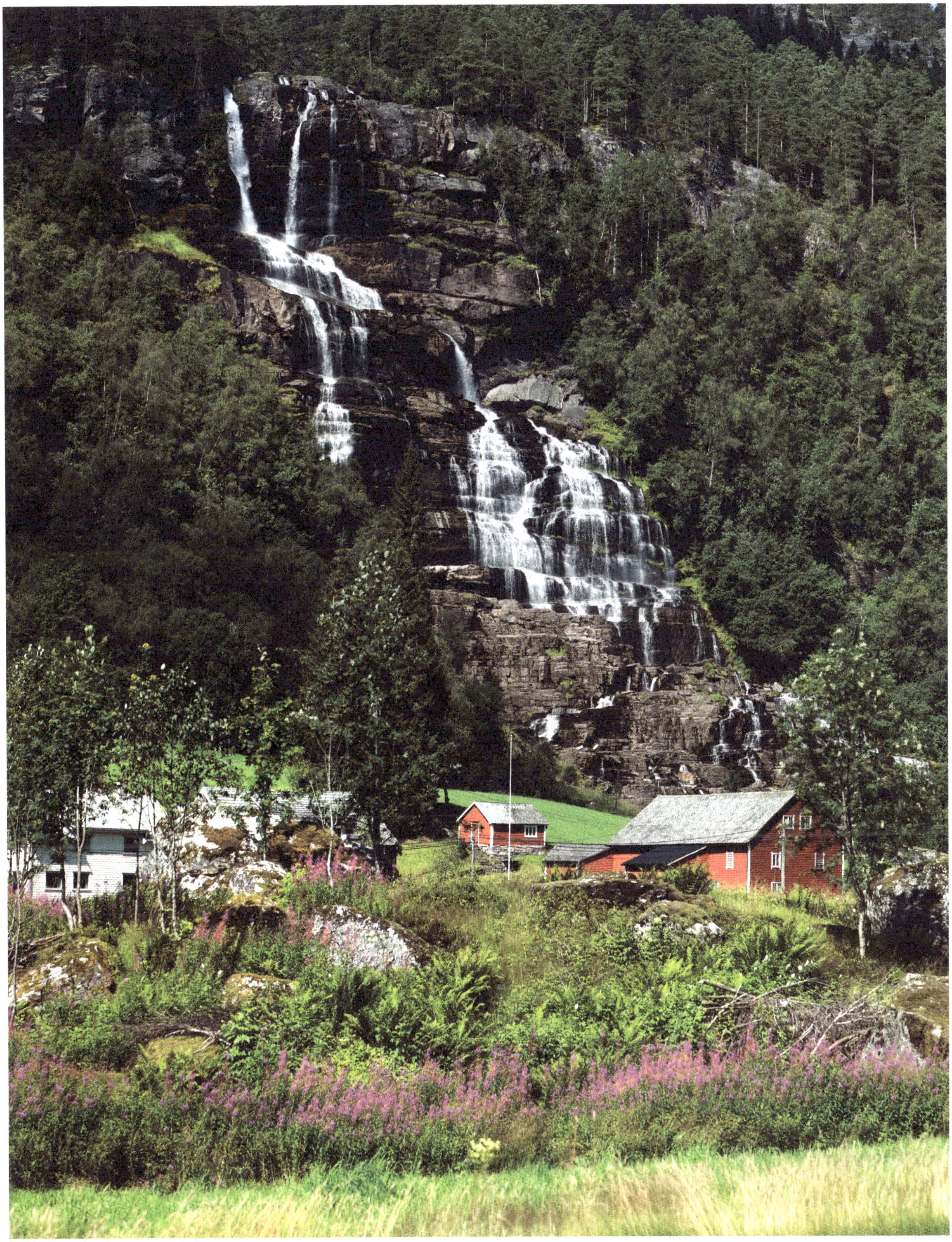

Many of the waterfalls scattered among the hills and mountains of the region can be seen from the roads.

HISTORY

HURTIGRUTEN

THE ROAD TO THE FAR NORTH

Hurtigruten (Norwegian for "express route") is a ferry and cruise line operating between Bergen and Kirkenes and is popular with tourists wishing to explore Norway's coastline from the sea.

Until the mid-twentieth century, Norway's road and rail infrastructure was so underdeveloped that the north of the country was entirely cut off during the winter, enduring almost total isolation for months on end. News would only reach the small towns near the Arctic Circle with the arrival of spring. All this was to change on July 2, 1893, however, when the DS *Vesteraalen*, the Hurtigruten line's first steamer, made her maiden voyage from Trondheim to Hammerfest. The route was later extended south to include Bergen and by 1908 boats were traveling as far as Kirkenes, the last town to the north before the Russian border.

This heavily subsidized new sea route long remained a vital link for the villages on the coast, ensuring they were supplied with provisions, mail, other necessities, and of course the latest news from the rest of the country.

Freight traffic declined with the development of road and air networks in the wake of the Second World War, but in the 1990s the Hurtigruten line responded by reorienting its services toward tourism, upgrading levels of comfort to meet the expectations of visitors from overseas. This strategy proved a winner for the company over the long term as customer numbers rose and now fluctuate between 450,000 and 550,000 passengers per year (70 percent of whom are tourists).

Nowadays, the ships put in to no less than thirty-four different ports along the 1,700 miles (2,700 km) between Bergen and Kirkenes, with a full round trip taking eleven days of sailing. In 2011 NRK (Norway's state television channel) televised the voyage of one hundred and thirty-four hours from Bergen to Kirkenes from aboard MS *Nordnorge*, setting a world record for the longest uninterrupted live television broadcast.

Every day, at the same time, a ship leaves port at Bergen and returns twelve days later. The arrival of the costal express in ports en route is the high point of the day for many Norwegians. During these stopovers, locals will often come aboard for a coffee and a catch-up on the latest news before disembarking, earning the nickname *Kaffegjengen* ("the coffee gang" in Norwegian).

Geirangerfjord, the Lofoten Islands, and the North Cape are just some of the spectacular landscapes that can be explored via the Hurtigruten line. Norway's stunning coastline is undoubtedly a prime factor in explaining the route's increasing popularity with visitors from overseas. The option of traveling to the far north for a glimpse of the Northern Lights or midnight sun has also helped to make Hurtigruten one of the most popular cruise lines in the world.

THE HURTIGRUTEN

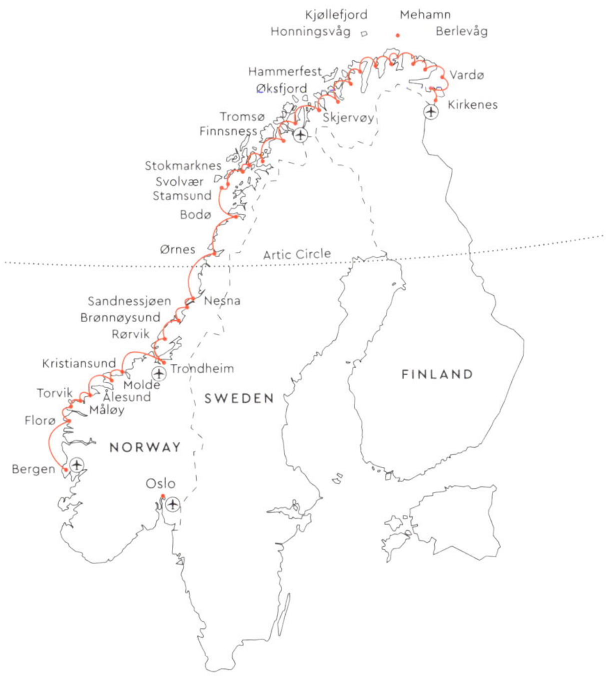

HURTIGRUTEN'S PORTS OF CALL

The coastal express serves thirty-four ports. Although a good proportion of those on board are now tourists, it still transports freight and carries passengers commercially.

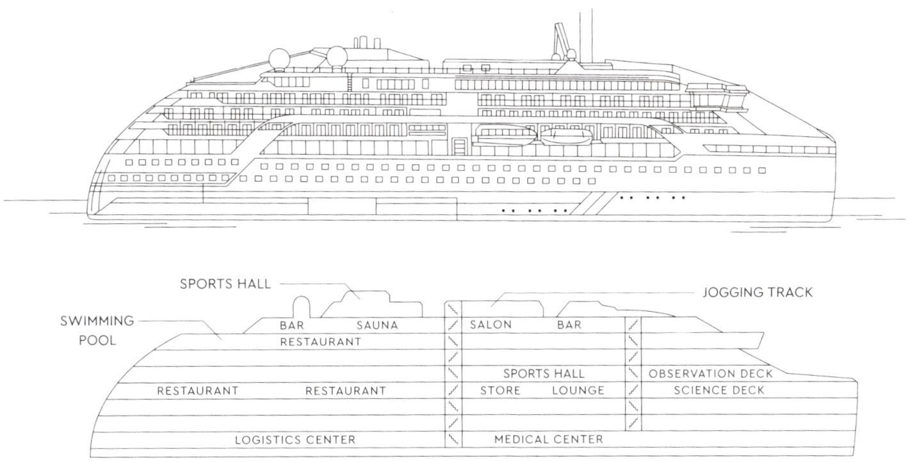

CROSS-SECTION OF A HURTIGRUTEN FERRY

Depending on the model, Hurtigruten ships can accommodate between 120 and 650 passengers. Each ship is designed to meet its occupants' every need.

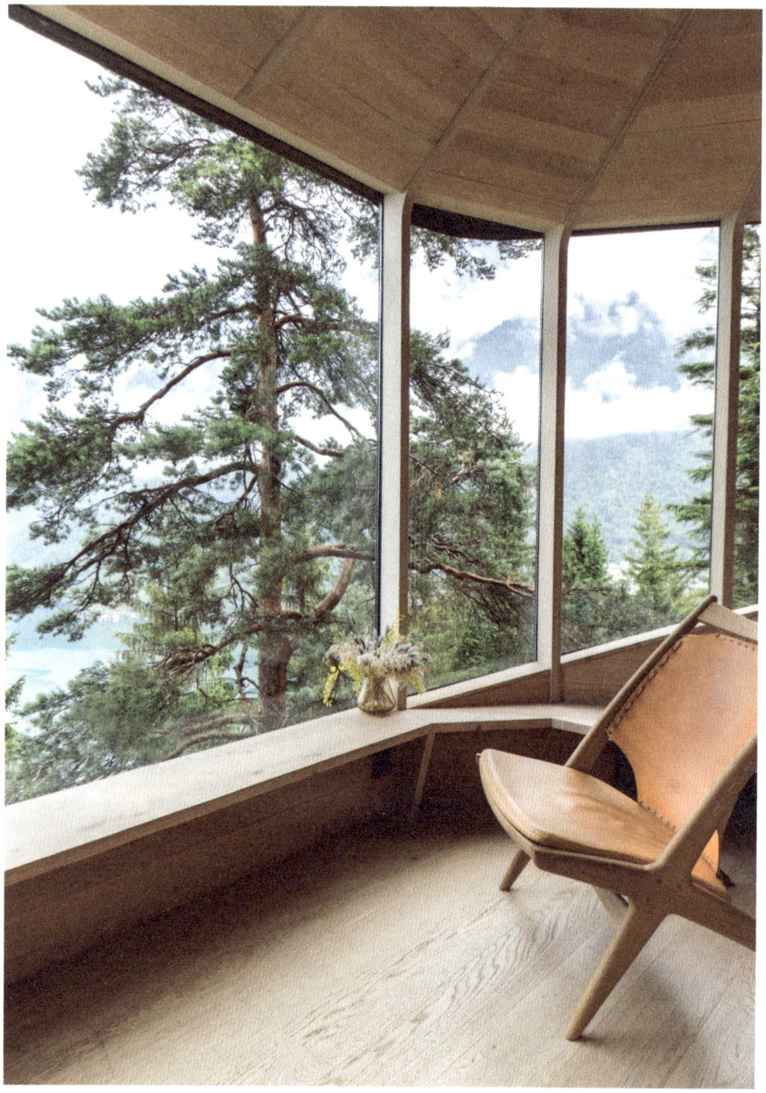

ABOVE

A breathtaking view of the fjord.

OPPOSITE

Woodnest is a treehouse perched among the pines high above the village of Odda.

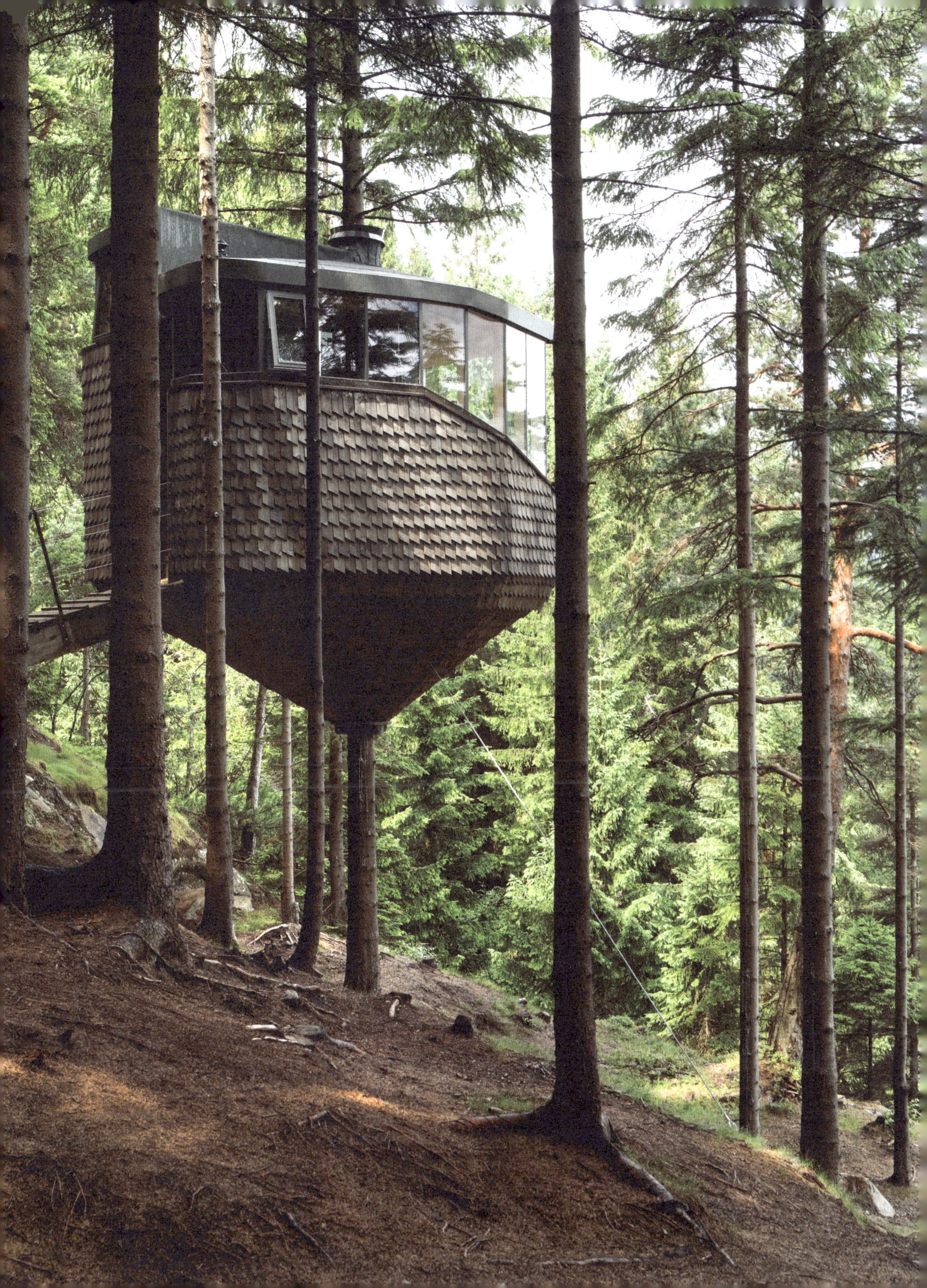

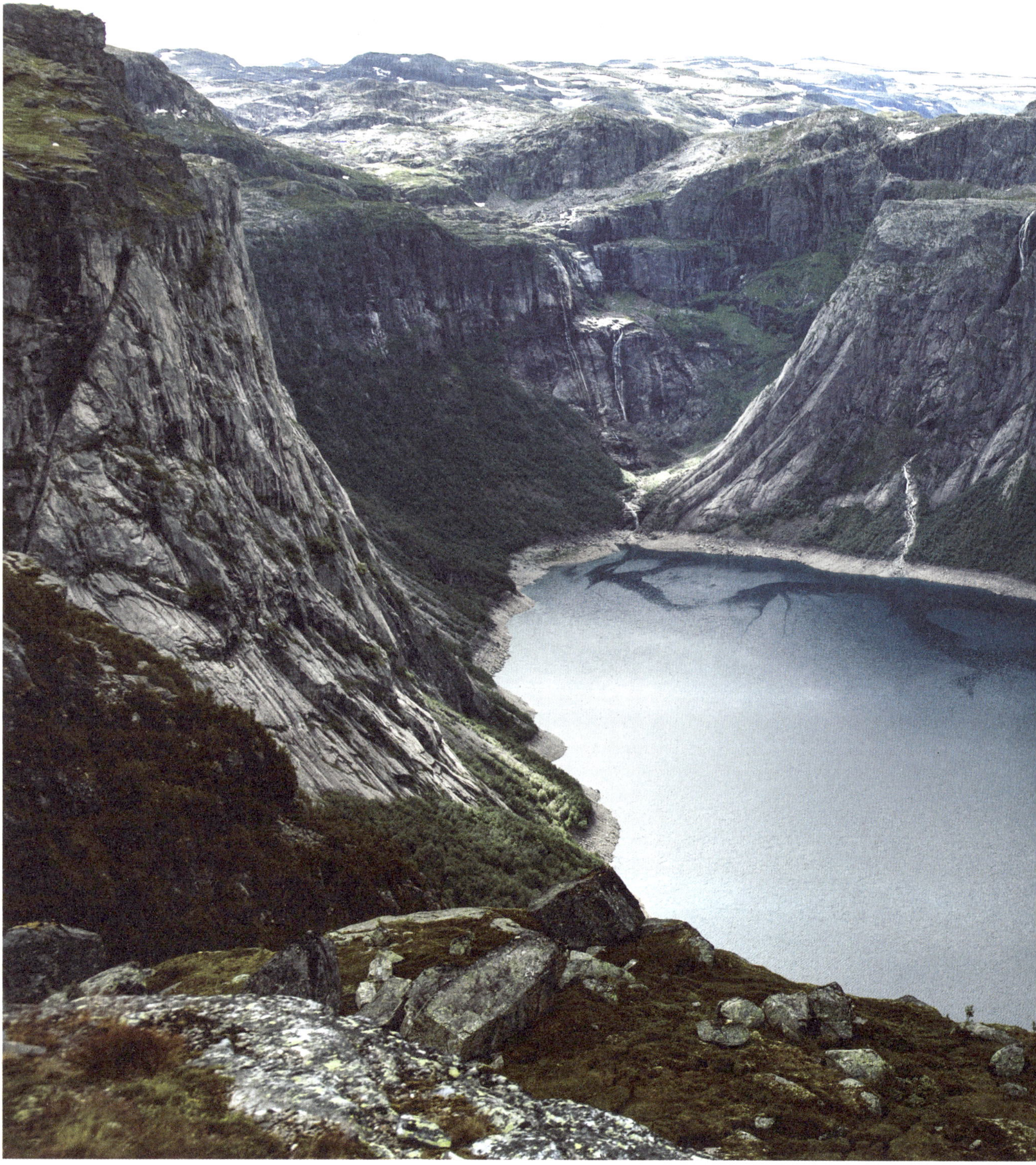

Follow the hiking trail to Trolltunga for a dizzying view out over the lake at Ringedalsvatnet and the surrounding cliffs carved out by glaciers and the passage of time.

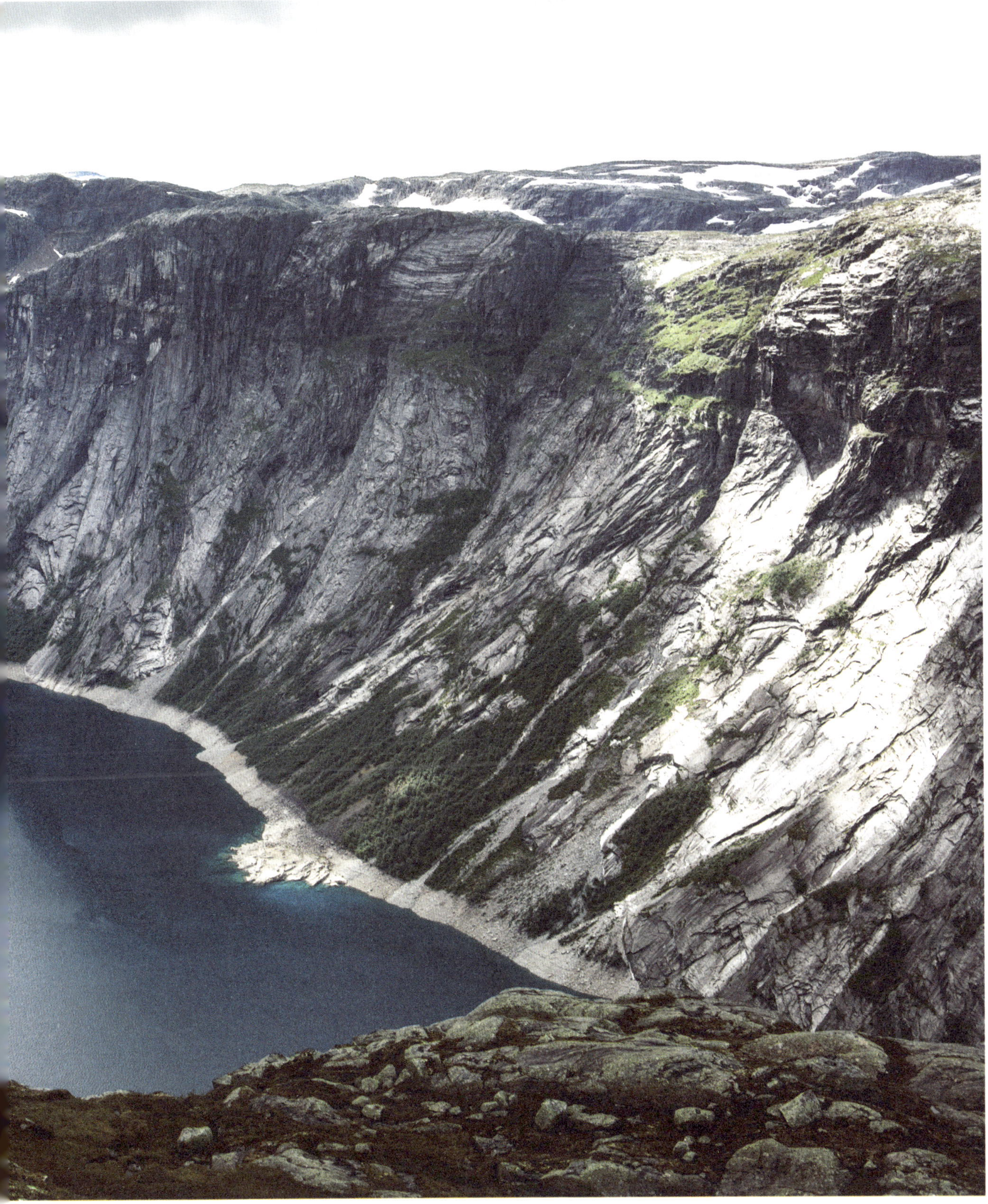

CULTURE

NORWEGIAN CUISINE

THE FLAVORS OF THE GREAT OUTDOORS

Norwegian cuisine is rich and diverse reflecting the country's climate and geography.

In a country bounded by the sea and dominated by mountains, it seems quite natural that meat and fish should be ingredients of choice in Norway's cuisine. The Sami people living in Norway's far north raise reindeer prized for their lean and tasty meat, which is usually grilled or stewed on special occasions. Among the many lamb-based dishes is one that is rather surprising—*smalahove*, a sheep's head that is salted, smoked, and then steamed, before being served with mashed potatoes and swede. Despite its unusual appearance, *smalahove* is said to be delicious.

In terms of seafood, the renowned Norwegian salmon vies with king crab, shrimp, mackerel, and herring for a place on fishermen's stalls. These fish are usually smoked to preserve them for eating later in the season, but for a real treat, they can also be grilled and enjoyed fresh.

The cod fished in the Lofoten Islands at the end of winter is hung to dry slowly in the fresh breezes of the Arctic. In Norway it is usually either cooked fresh or rehydrated after drying—as *lutefisk*, for example, a cod-based delicacy eaten at Christmas with sides of bacon, split peas, and potatoes.

Norway's fruit harvest includes wild berries that grow in abundance throughout the country and are picked in summer. The Norwegians gather large amounts of blueberries, cranberries, gooseberries, cloudberries, strawberries, and raspberries which are transformed into jams and jellies in preparation for winter. The berries are rich in flavor and can be used to make delicious desserts or as a garnish for meat and fish.

Norwegians typically start the day with a hearty breakfast of bread with cheese, cucumber, tomato, and marinated fish, all washed down with generous helpings of coffee. It may come as some surprise to learn that Norway is the world's second-largest consumer of coffee after Finland, with an average daily intake of three cups per inhabitant.

Lunch might involve a sandwich of cheese, shrimp, egg, and mayonnaise, but Norwegians like nothing better than settling down at the end of the day to a hot meal of meat or fish with a vegetable side, a moment of conviviality that is often rounded off with a glass of aquavit, a smoky spirit flavored with dill.

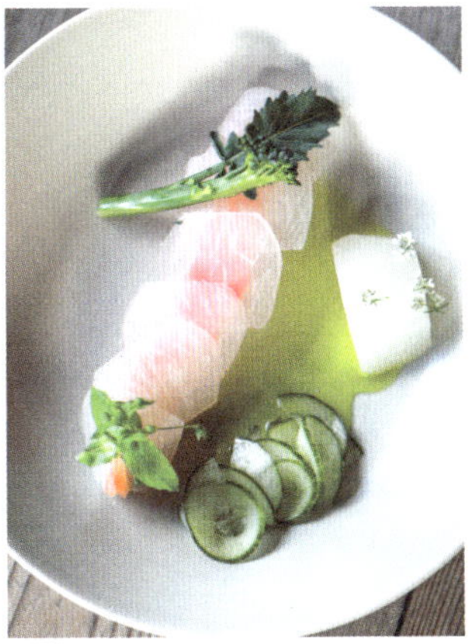

Chris Schønefeld, chef at the Juvet Landscape Hotel, expertly prepares fermented vegetables.

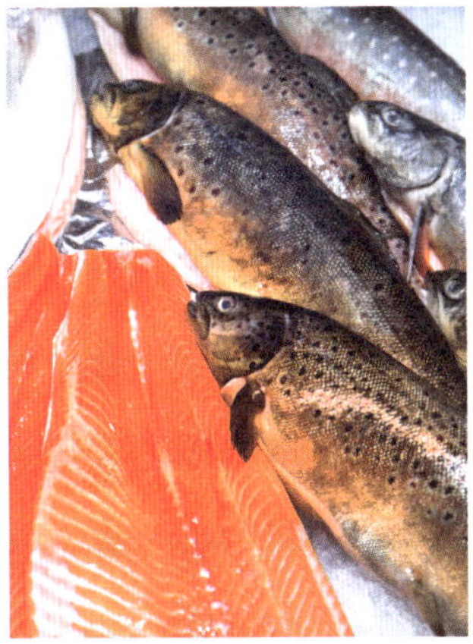

Smoked trout is extremely popular and is even beginning to supplant salmon in some dishes.

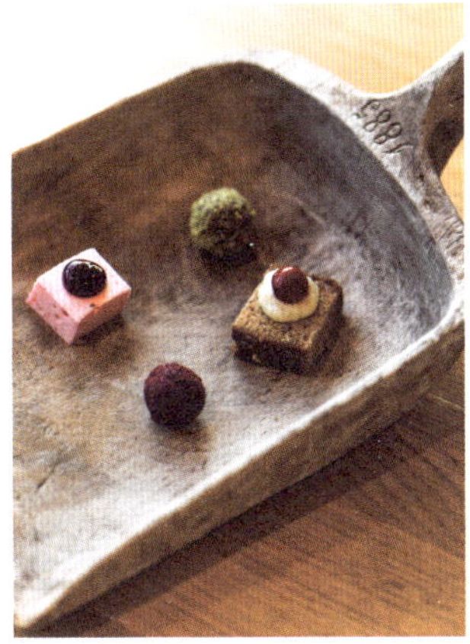

Elegant desserts made with seasonal berries and are delicately sweetened.

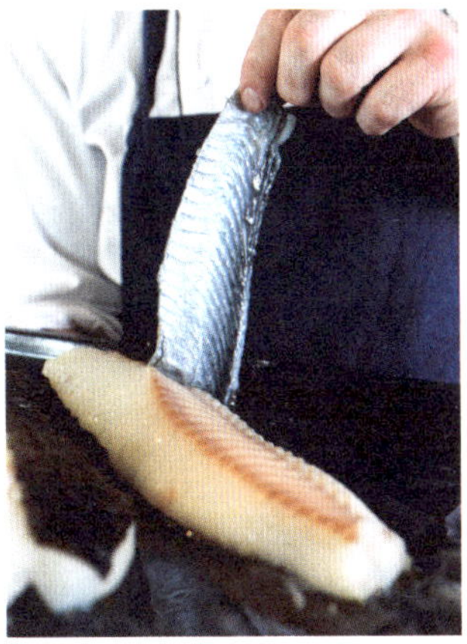

Cod is a classic ingredient in Norwegian cuisine.

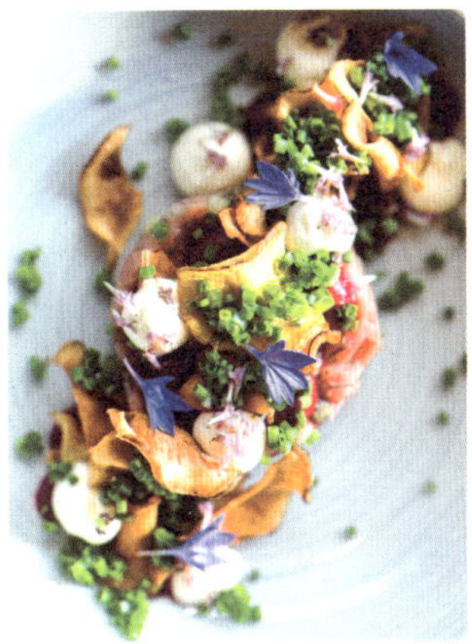

Try some veal tartare with creamed celery and potato chips at the BrimiBue Hotel.

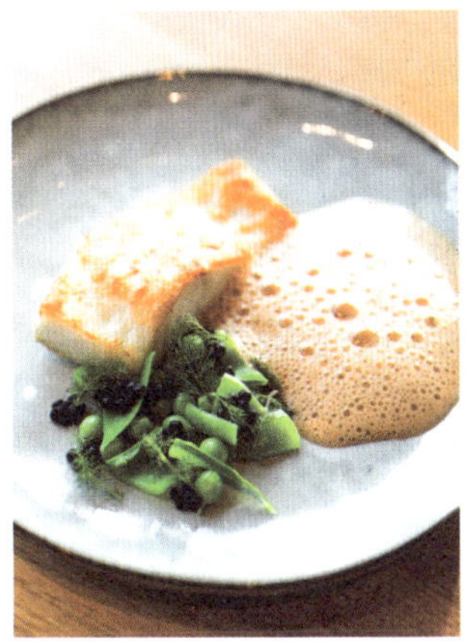

Turbot and crunchy vegetables with a crayfish sauce.

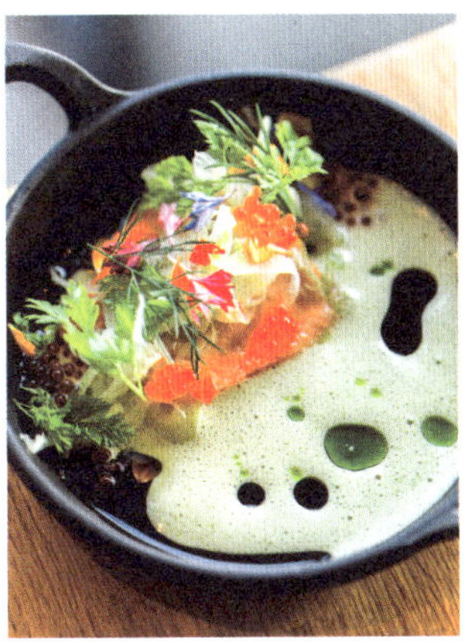

Top chefs often decorate their dishes with flowers during the summer season.

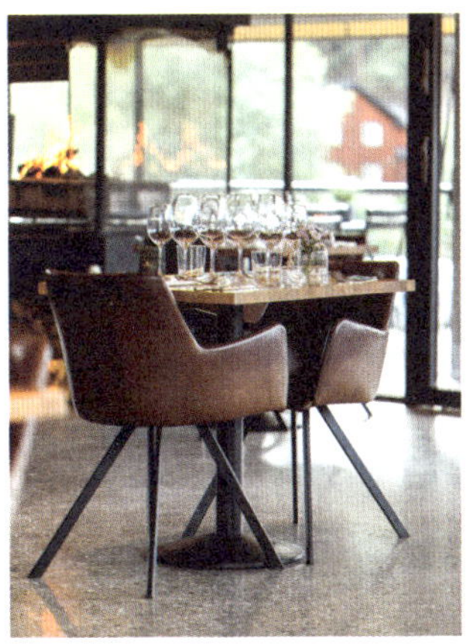

An open fire is just one part of the warm ambience in the BrimiBue dining room.

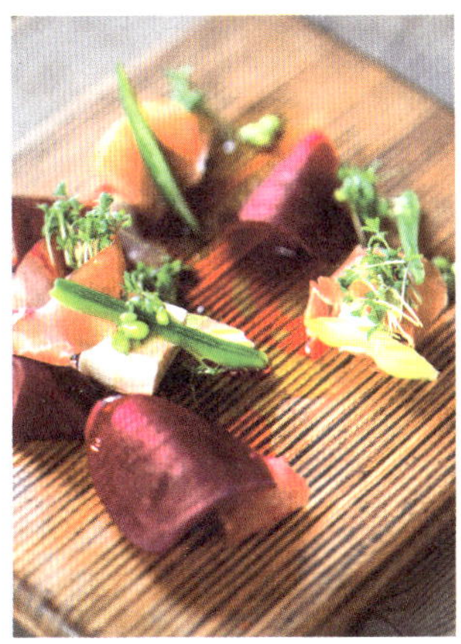

Dried reindeer meat with fermented beetroot and baby greens.

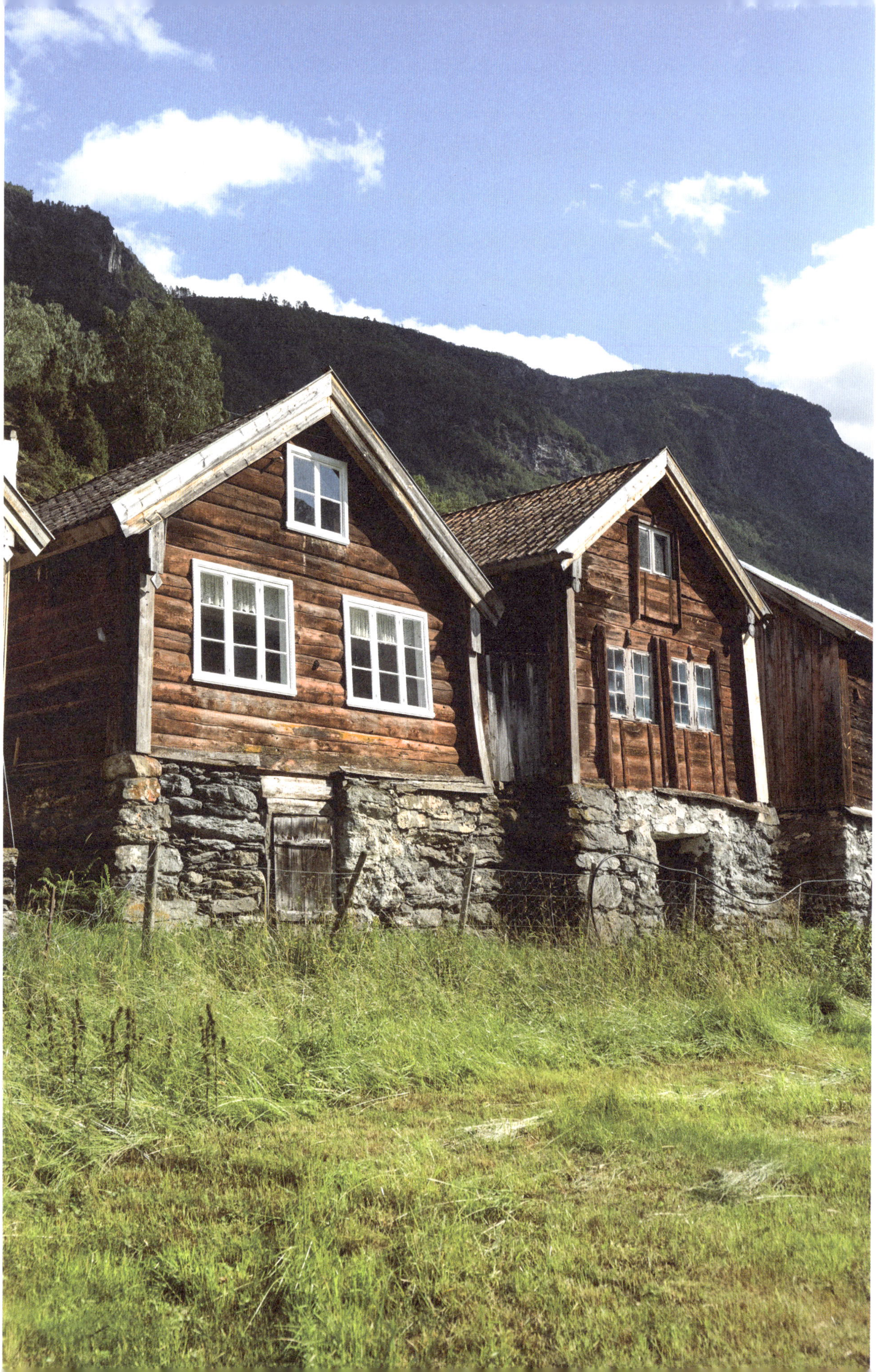

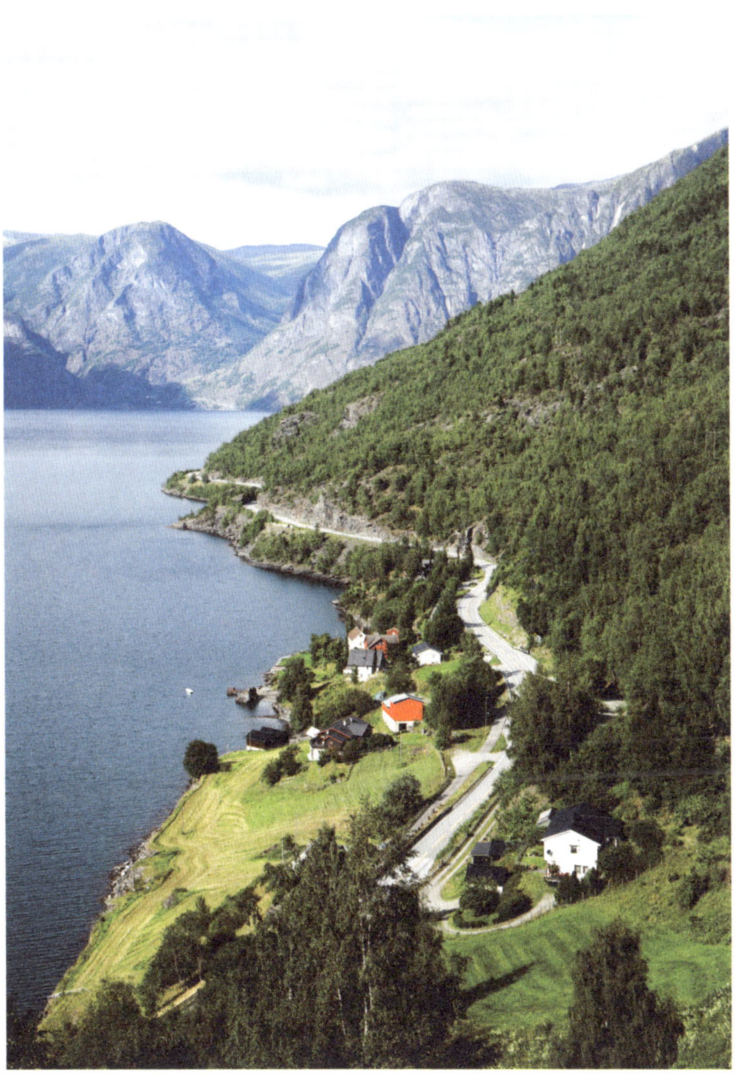

ABOVE

The view over Aurlandsfjord from Otternes Farmyard, near Flåm.

OPPOSITE

Otternes Farmyard is a cluster of twenty-seven buildings, the oldest dating back to the seventeenth century.

ARCHITECTURE

BRYGGEN

A HISTORIC AREA OF BERGEN

The harbor district of Bryggen represents a real link with the past, offering a fascinating glimpse of medieval Norway.

Bryggen (Norwegian for "wharf") is a historic waterfront area of Bergen. For centuries merchants flocked here, turning it into one of the most important trading ports in medieval Northern Europe. Cod was salted, dried, and exported to Europe in massive quantities, and in return, Norway received wheat, barley and malt, along with honey, beer, wine, and clothing.

The Hanseatic League set up one of its trading posts in the city in 1360. At its peak, this powerful export organization founded by the merchant cities of North Germany was represented in nearly two hundred cities and maintained a near-monopoly on trade between the western and eastern parts of Northern Europe. It therefore exerted a considerable influence on Bryggen for some four centuries, virtually turning it into a German colony with almost all the privileges of a free city.

Bryggen has been ravaged by fire on numerous occasions throughout its history (most notably in 1702 when the town was reduced to ashes), but each time has been rebuilt almost as an exact replica in accordance with the original twelfth-century plans. The iconic architecture of this medieval district features rows of timber-framed houses with gabled facades two or three stories high.

At the rear of each house is a small stone storehouse (*kjeller*) in which the most valuable goods would be protected from fire.

Bryggen was very nearly demolished to make way for modern buildings after the last major fire in 1955, but a thirteen-year program of archeological excavations helped to highlight the importance of preserving the site, with runic inscriptions, scraps of medieval clothing, and a host of ceramic objects (some originating from the Middle East) all confirming the significant role Bryggen had played during the Middle Ages. All these objects are now exhibited in the Bryggens Museum, which opened in 1976, and the entire area was inscribed on UNESCO's World Heritage List in 1979.

The area used to be slightly run down, but tucked in behind the restaurants and cafés, the neighborhood is now home to numerous boutiques and artists' studios. The two thousand merchants of the Hanseatic League have been replaced by a new and enthusiastic community of dynamic and creative innovators who continue to breathe new life into this iconic and unmissable part of Bergen.

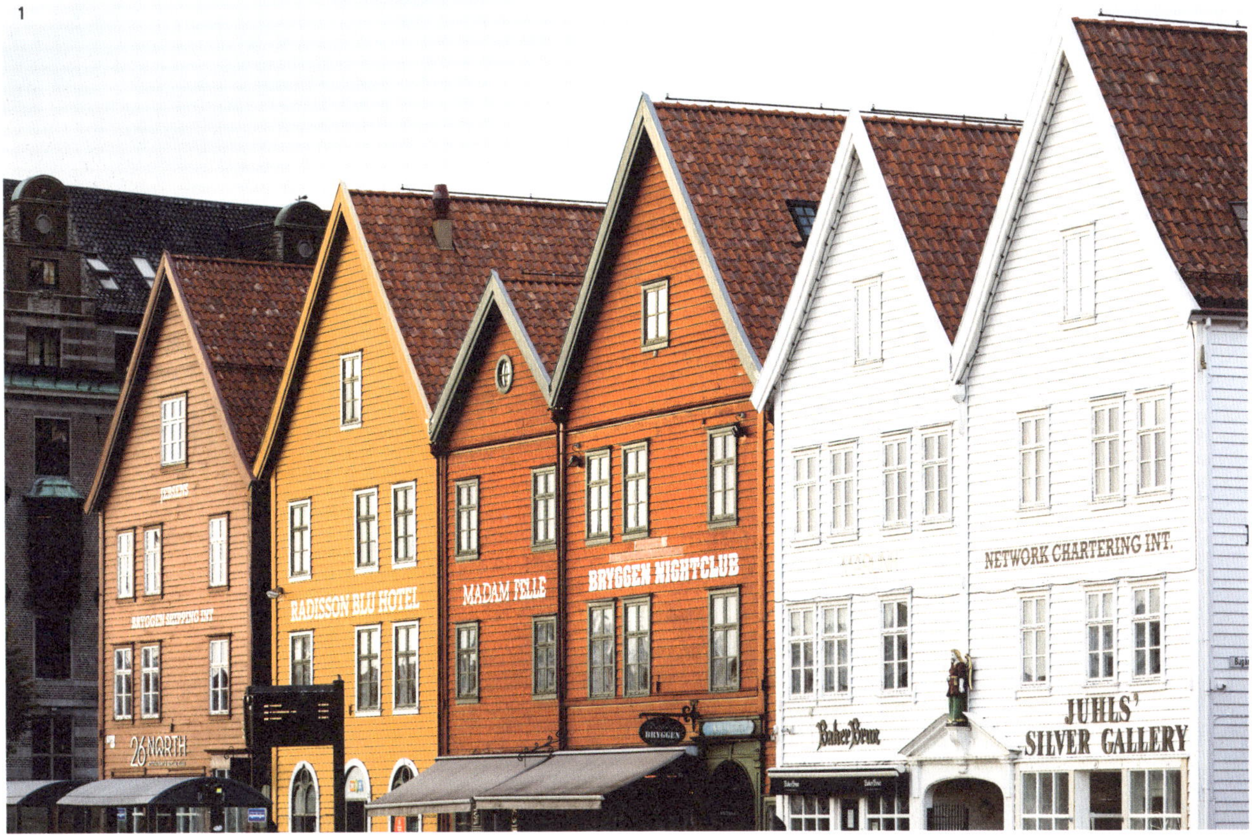

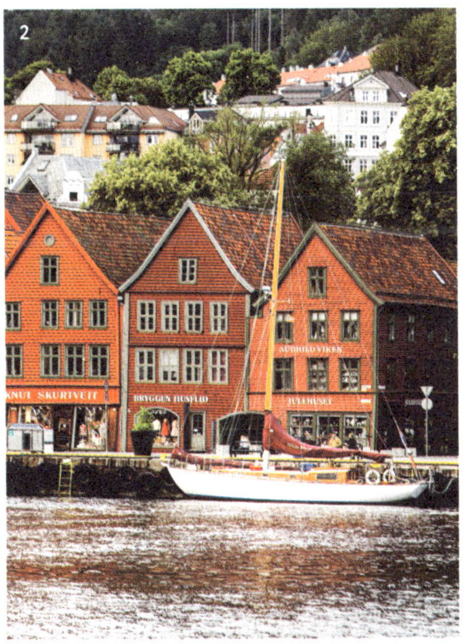

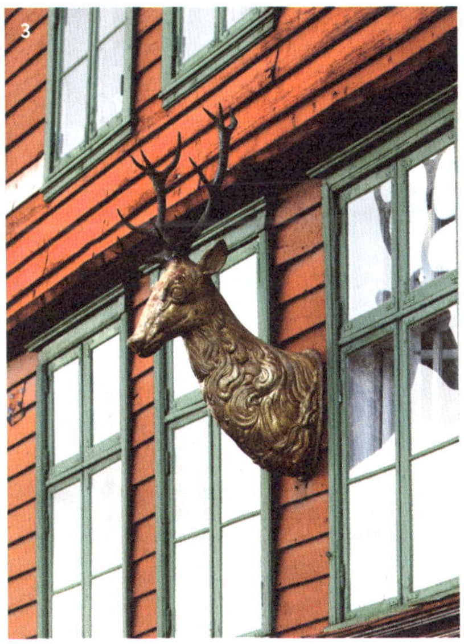

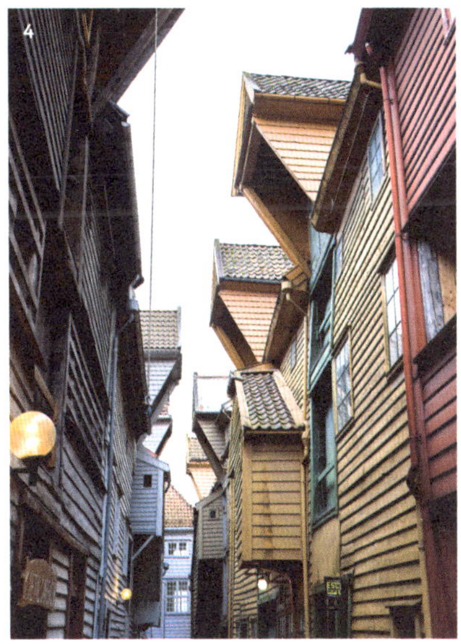

1 / UNIQUE BUILDINGS

The district of Bryggen is famous for its superb timber-framed buildings, which once served as merchants' homes or and storehouses.

2/ 3/ THE WHARF

After the Nazi occupation of Norway during the Second World War, the name (*Tyskebryggen*, or the German Wharf) that had been used since the time of the Hanseatic League was changed simply to *Bryggen* (the Wharf).

4 / THREAT OF FIRE

Some of the small alleyways in Bryggen are extremely narrow. After a fire in 1916, wider streets were built to serve as firebreaks in the event of a repeat event.

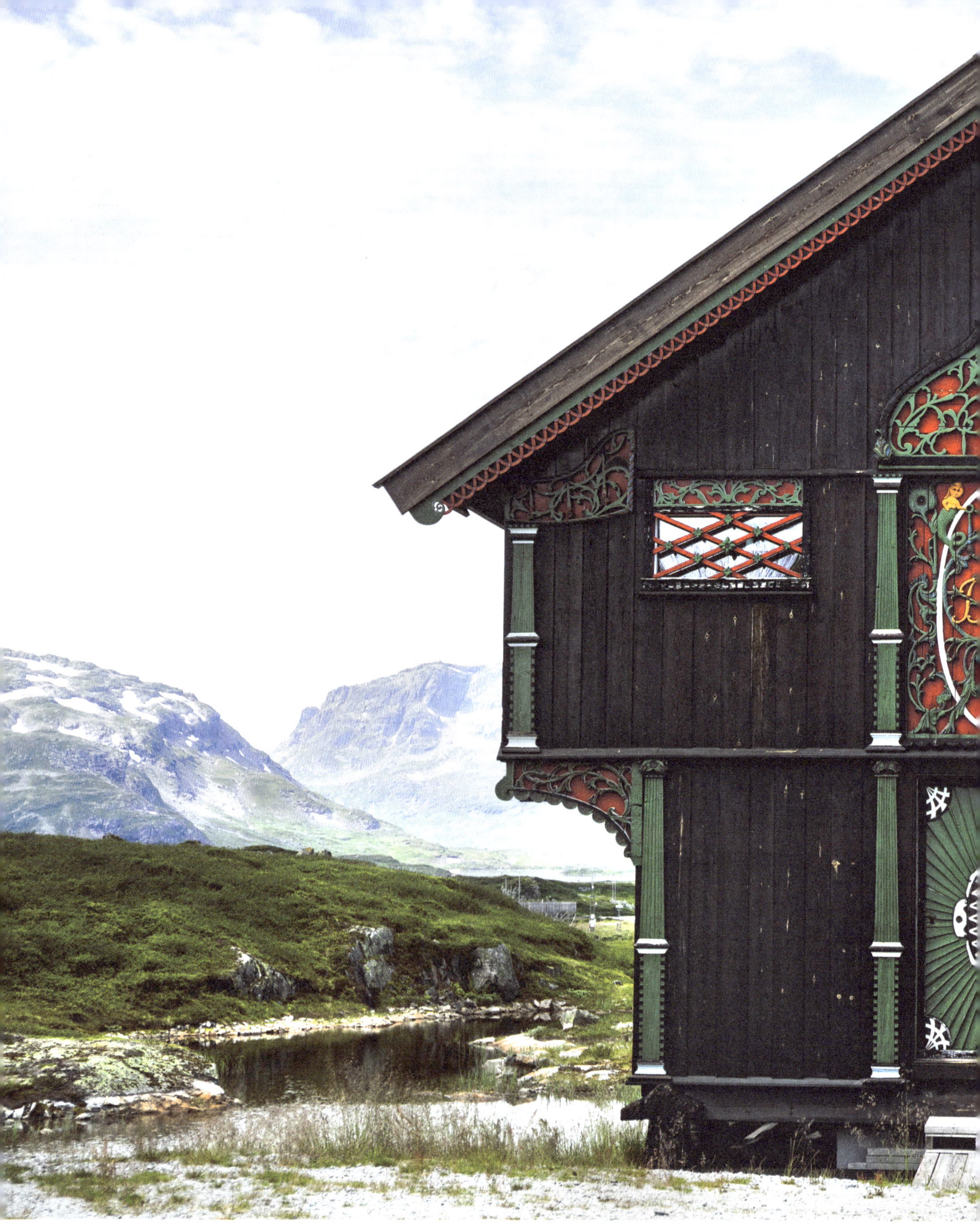

A richly decorated stabbur *(traditional Norwegian storehouse) in Hardangervidda.*

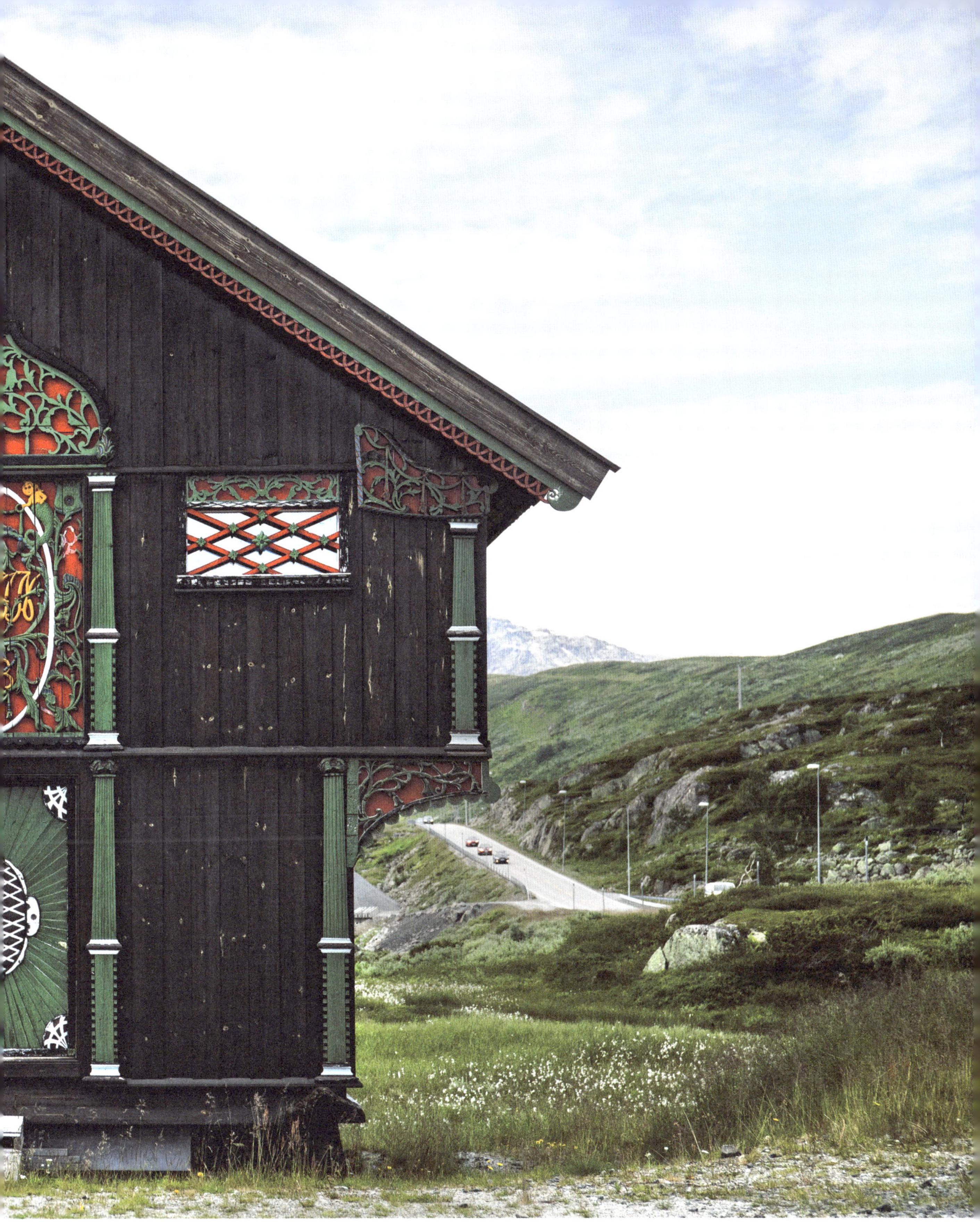

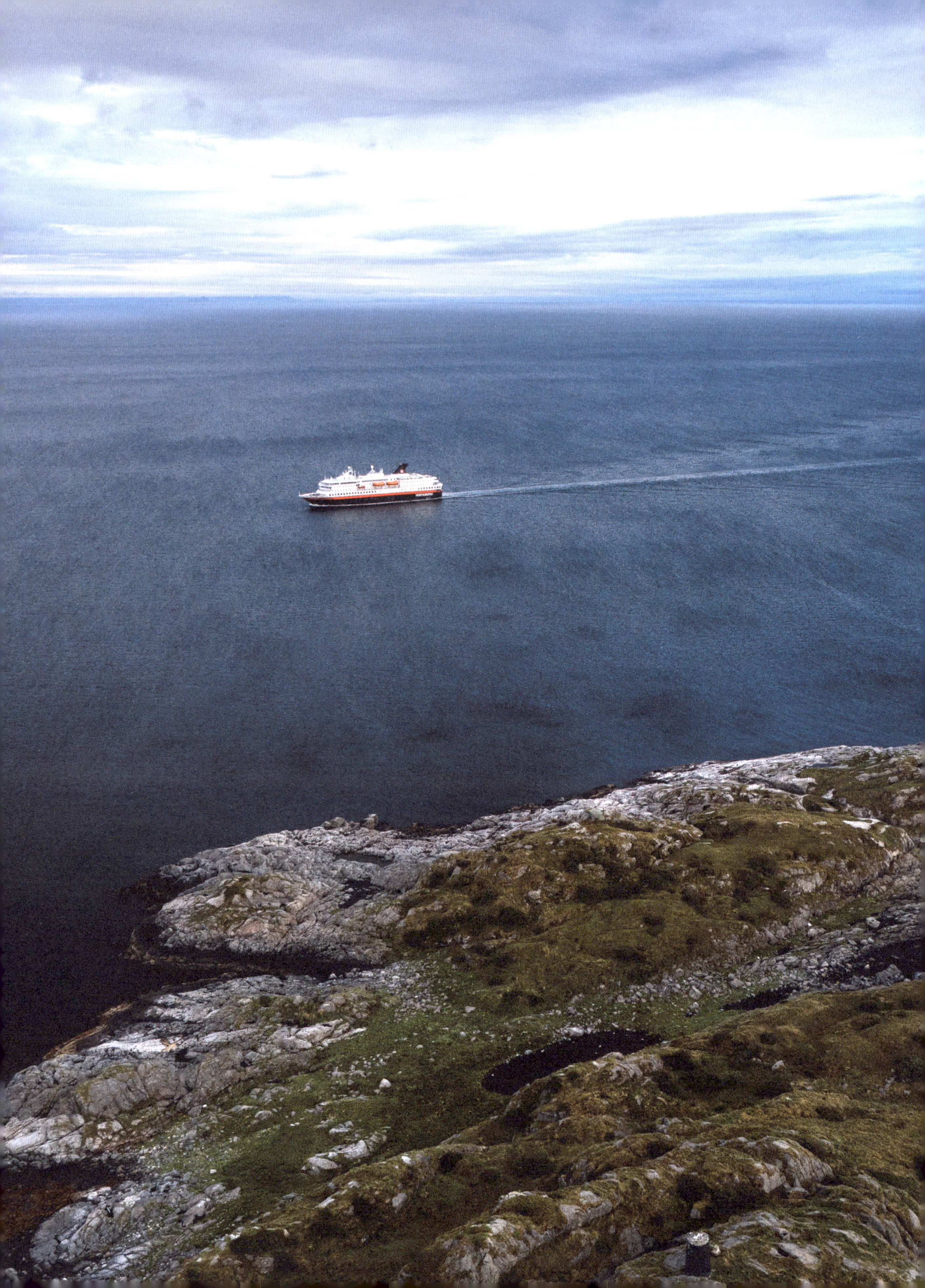

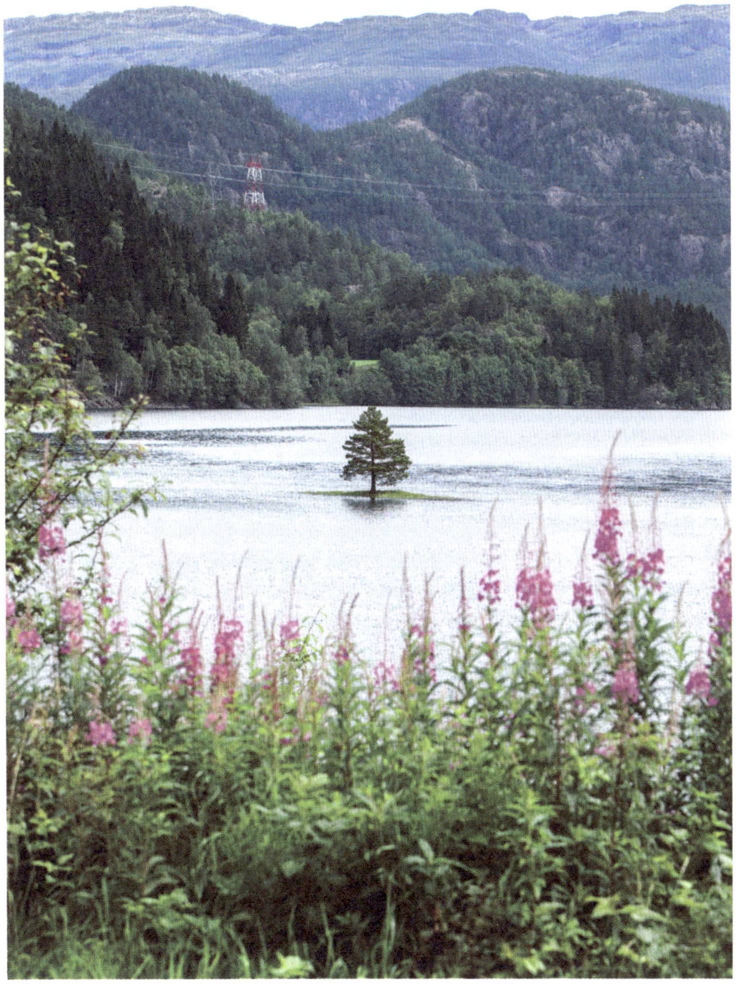

ABOVE

Norway takes advantage of its many lakes and rivers to generate electricity, with 95 percent of the country's power now being produced hydroelectrically.

OPPOSITE

The Hurtigruten Coastal Express plies the Norwegian seaboard between Bergen and the far north.

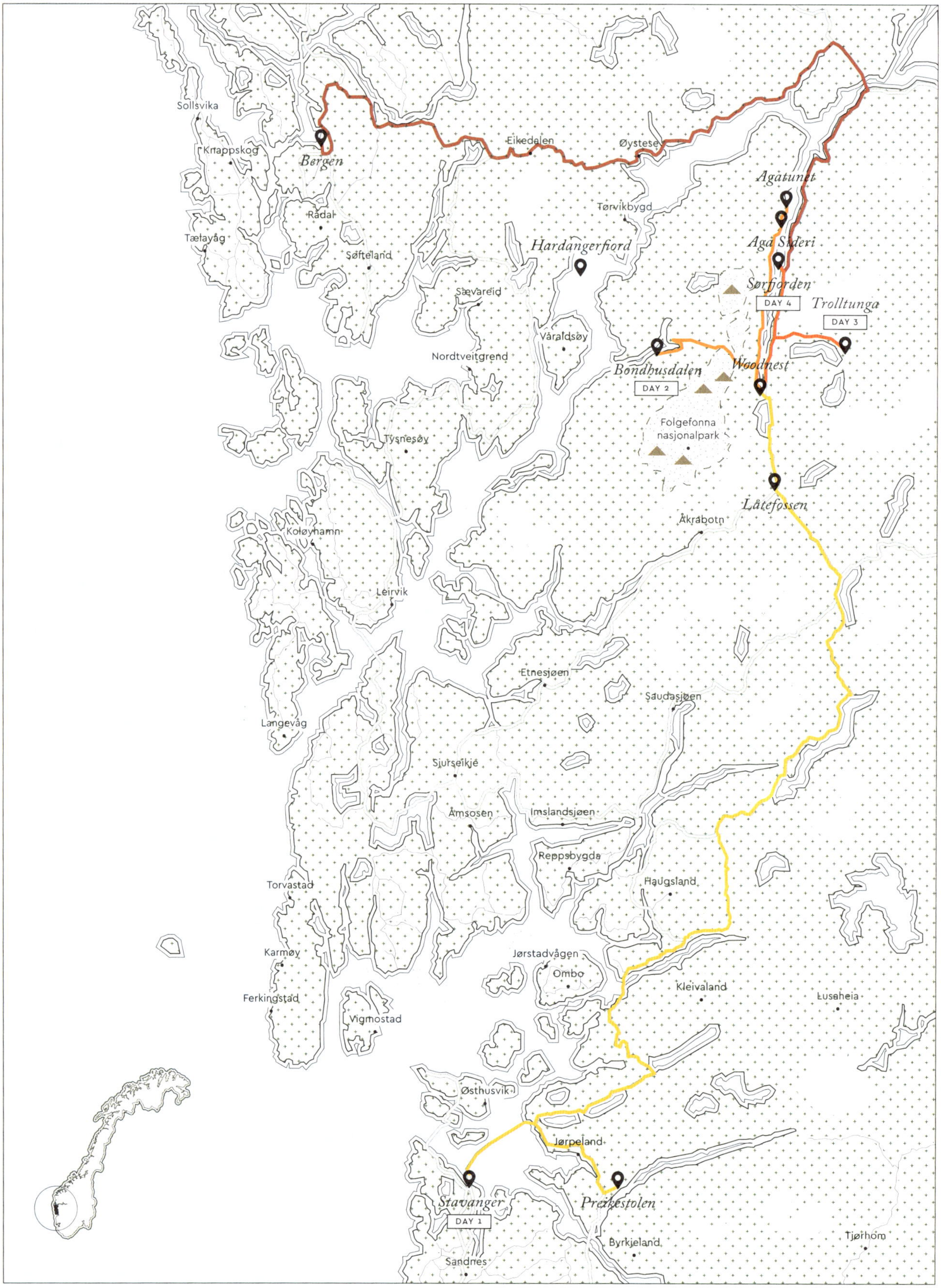

Sollsvika
Knappskog
Bergen
Rådal
Tælavåg
Søfteland
Eikedalen
Øystese
Tørvikbygd
Hardangerfiord
Sævareid
Nordtveitgrend
Våraldsøy
Agatunet
Aga Sideri
Sørfjorden
DAY 4
Trolltunga
DAY 3
Bondhusdalen
DAY 2
Woodnest
Folgefonna
nasjonalpark
Tysnesøy
Låtefossen
Åkrabotn
Koløyhamn
Leirvik
Etnesjøen
Saudasjøen
Langevåg
Sjurseikje
Åmsosen
Imslandsjøen
Reppsbygda
Haugsland
Torvastad
Karmøy
Jørstadvågen
Ombo
Kleivaland
Lusaheia
Ferkingstad
Vigmostad
Østhusvik
Jørpeland
Stavanger
DAY 1
Preikestolen
Byrkjeland
Tjørhom
Sandnes

ITINERARY

FOUR DAYS FROM STAVANGER TO BERGEN

This region boasts some of Norway's most famous sights and scenery, from Preikestolen to Trolltunga.

DAY 1: PREIKESTOLEN TO HARDANGERFJORD

Spend a night at Stavanger in preparation for hiking the path to the immense granite cliff at Preikestolen the next day. This is a magical spot from where the views are outstanding. Once you have managed to tear yourself away, head north to Hardangerfjord, making sure to stop off at Låtefossen on the way to admire the waterfall as it tumbles down from the heights of the Hardangervidda plateau. Those with the appetite for some more climbing can spend the night perched in a beautiful wooden cabin among the trees in the Woodnest, from where there are breathtaking views of Hardangerfjord.

DAY 2: THE CIDER MILLS OF HARDANGERFJORD

Numerous cider mills can be found scattered along the banks of Hardangerfjord, where the apple trees are a beautiful sight when in blossom in the spring. Stop off at Aga Sideri to taste Joar's delicious dry cider and explore the charming medieval hamlet of Agatunet. Finish the day with a short walk to the lake at Bondhusdalen along the well-made and easily accessible track that approaches very close to the Folgefonna glacier.

DAY 3: TROLLTUNGA

This famous hiking route is now often busy with tourists but is no less unforgettable for all that. While it is not really necessary, the keenest hikers can make an early start to reach Trolltunga before the crowds, with some even choosing to make camp here to enjoy the quiet solitude of dawn. A relaxing sauna at Heit Sørfjorden is a very pleasant way in which to end a day of hiking this beautiful trail.

DAY 4: BERGEN

In Bergen, known as the city of the Seven Mountains, take the cable car that leads to the top of one of these surrounding peaks to enjoy a panoramic view of the city from high above. However, if the weather is poor, there are any number of museums offering alternative entertainment, including the Bryggens Museum, with its displays of ceramics, runic inscriptions, and fragments of ancient clothing unearthed during excavations in the medieval district of Bryggen. The Hurtigruten Coastal Express ship casts off for Kirkenes from the neighboring quay; these legendary ships are a familiar sight at their moorings here. Once the capital of Norway, Bergen is a manageable size for visitors to explore and an excellent bookend for any excursion to Western Norway—it is no coincidence that it is known as the "gateway to the fjords."

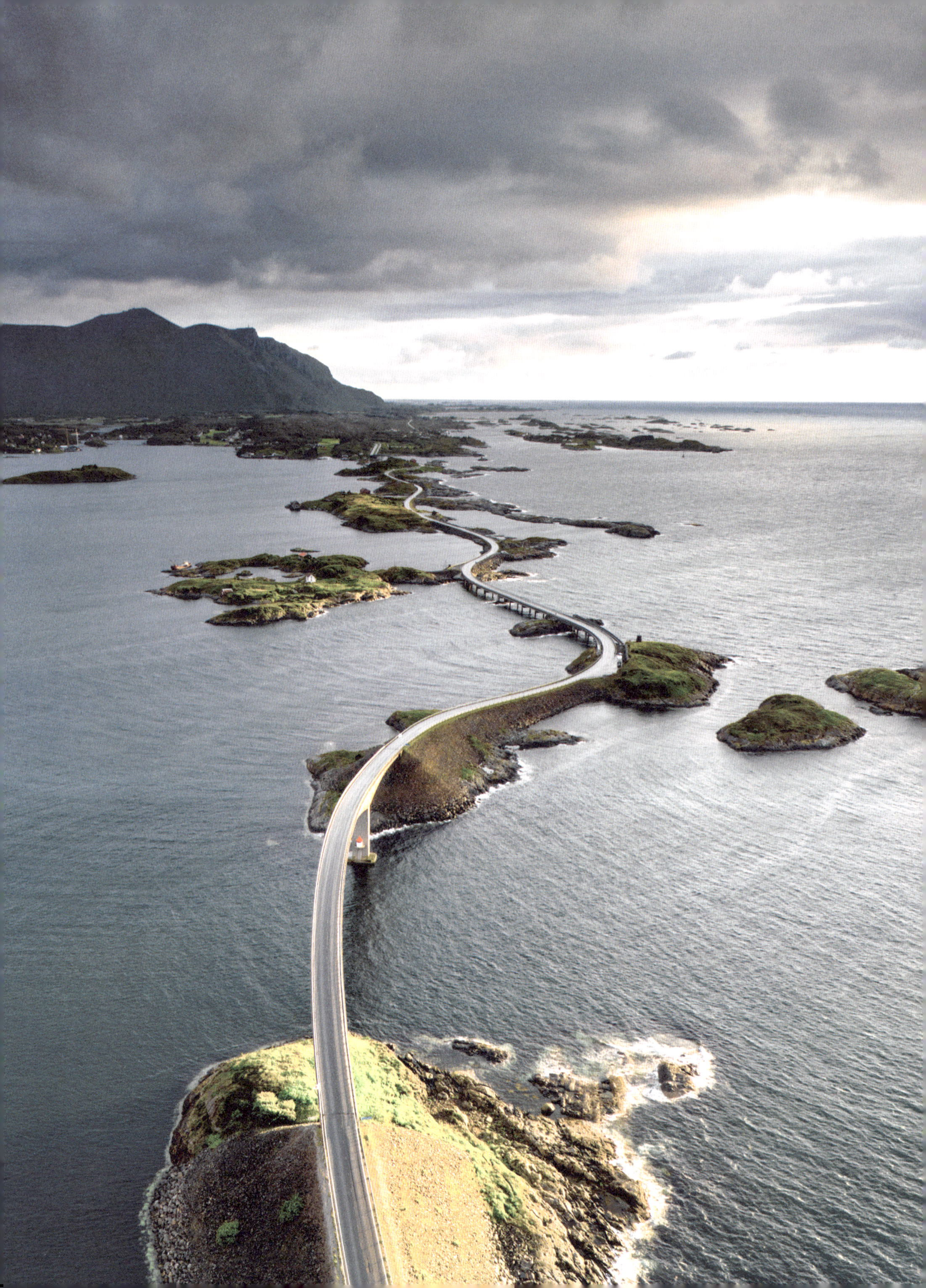

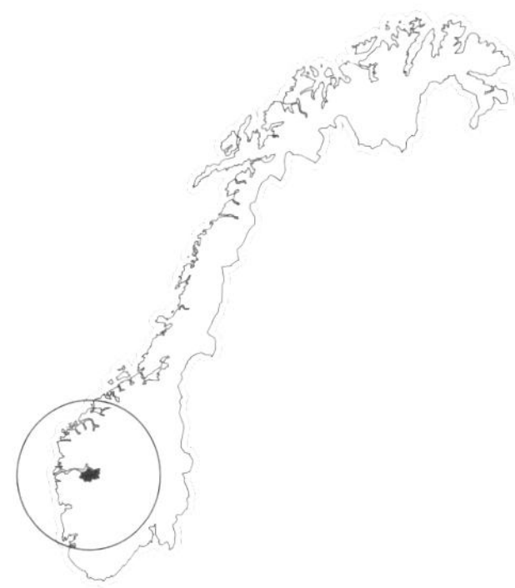

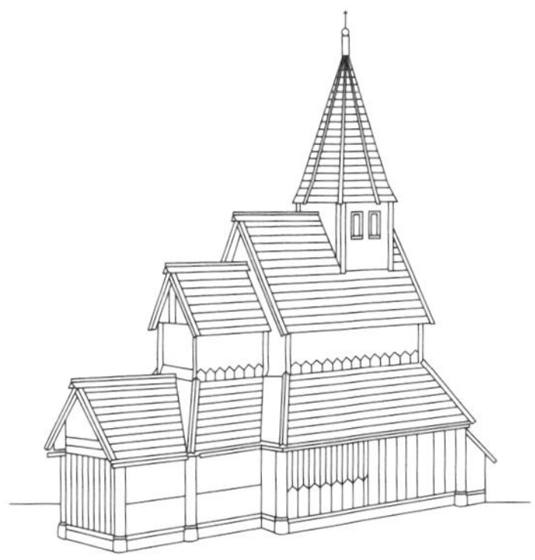

A LAND OF CONTRASTS

THE WESTERN FJORDS

The fjords of Western Norway, including the area around the famous Geirangerfjord, are some of the most popular tourist destinations on earth.

P.98

The Atlantic Road was opened in 1989 and stretches for some 5 miles (8 km). Connecting a host of small islands via eight bridges, it has become one of the most popular tourist routes in the country.

OPPOSITE

*Skageflå farm looks out over Geirangerfjord.
Although the buildings were abandoned in 1916, tourists can still visit here.*

The iconic scenery of Norway's fjords has been listed by UNESCO as a World Heritage Site, attracting visitors from all over the world. Many tourists choose to hop aboard the famous Hurtigruten Coastal Express that during the summer plies the route to the end of Geirangerfjord. From here they can explore spectacular waterfalls, leafy forests ringed by snow-capped peaks, and see the dizzying, sheer cliffs of the fjord, which rise to a height of 4,600 ft (1,400 m) above sea level.

The village of Geiranger can be found nestling at the far end of the fjord. This is where to join the hiking trail that climbs up to some very remote, tranquil farmsteads. The views are once again breathtaking and panoramic, this time of the glacial valley. At the very end of the trail is the old farmstead of Skageflå, from where there are views of all 1,350 ft (410 m) of the Seven Sisters waterfall. These few farms clinging to the hillside represent the last traces of the fjords' agricultural heritage and once provided shelter for farmers and their livestock during the summer. In the warmer months, the herds would be moved the short distance to these pastures on higher ground, where the meadows on the steep slopes would provide fresh grass for the animals until the arrival of the fall.

Glaciers may have shaped the region's landscape in the past, but they have not entirely disappeared from its present. It is still possible to observe the effects of ice on rock when exploring the glacier at Jostedal, an immense icefield that is the largest glacier in Continental Europe. Nigardsbreen, one of the glacier's arms, advanced down the valley at the turn of the eighteenth century, engulfing the farmstead of Nigard Njelvær, but when it retreated several years later, not a trace of the farm's buildings was to be seen. On still mornings, the turquoise waters of the glacial lake at the base of Nigardsbreen are transformed into a mirror dotted with ice floes.

Traveling by boat is a way of life here, with some ferries sailing throughout the night to bring locals and visitors to their destinations. The closer you are to the Atlantic coast, the more essential travel by water becomes to avoid long detours by road. The coastline is constantly battered by wind and storms and has a unique atmosphere, especially at Kråkenes Lighthouse and around the West Cape, perfect spots from which to admire views stretching out to the horizon. Runde Island has something of the feel of the Faroe Islands, and from mid-April to the beginning of August is also a great place to look for puffins—a truly unforgettable experience.

From the turquoise waters of the fjords to the salt-laden air at the coast, the Western Fjords and the surrounding area offer a tremendous diversity of landscape and spectacular, unspoiled nature.

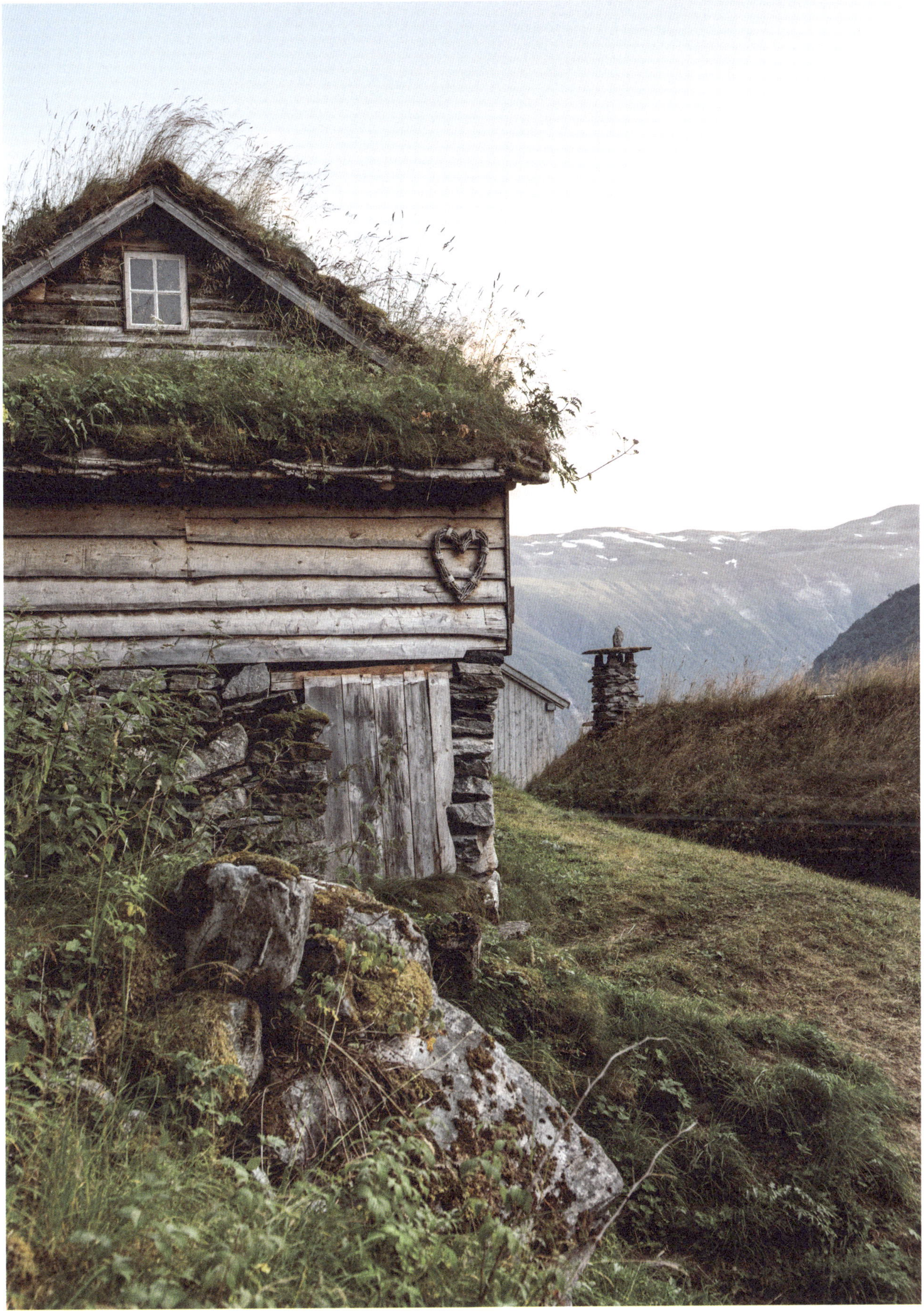

THE ESSENTIALS

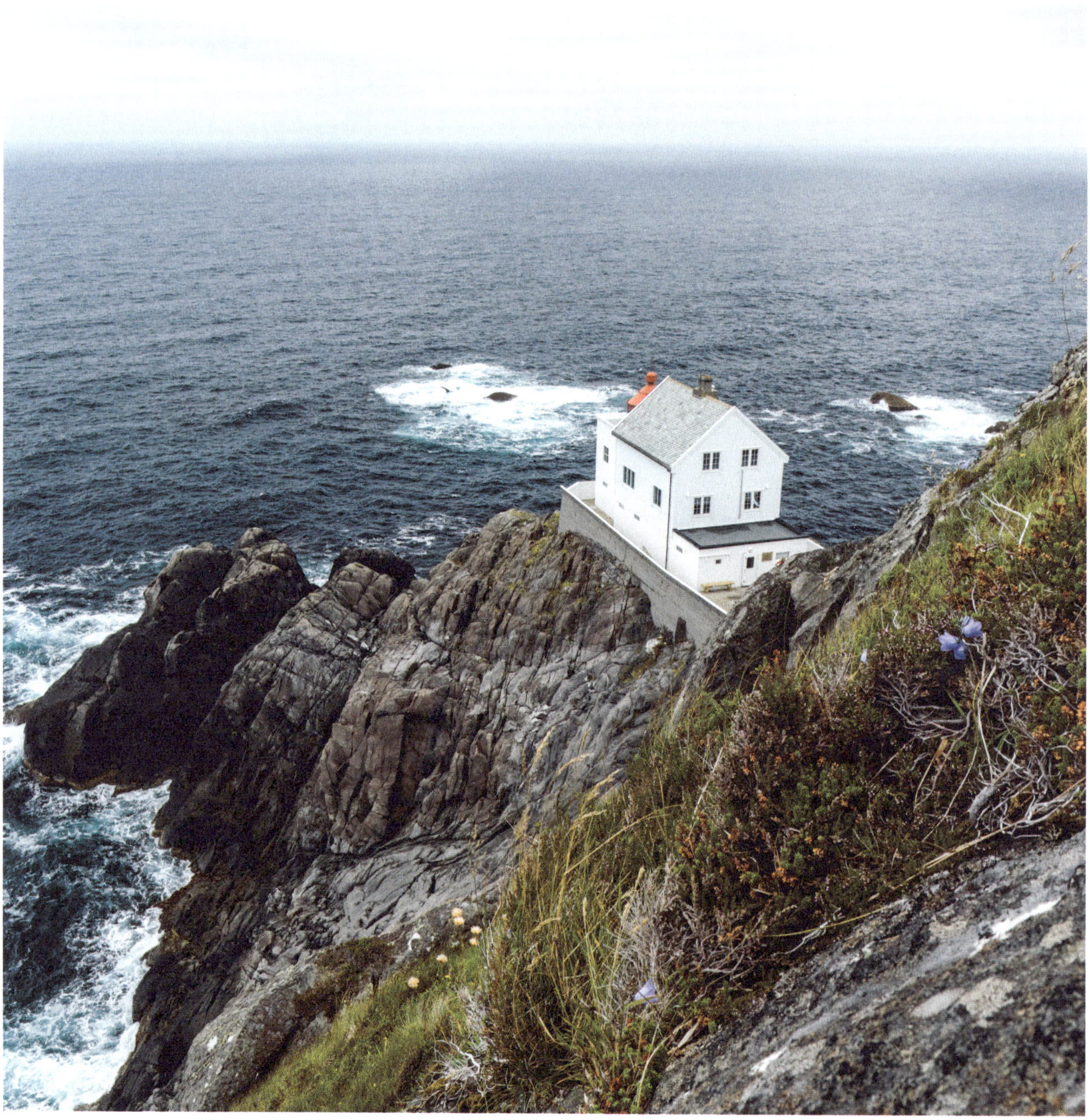

KRÅKENES FYR

Situated at one of the most westerly points of the Norwegian coast, Kråkenes Lighthouse was built in 1930. It is now possible to stay overnight in a small guesthouse next to the lighthouse.

23

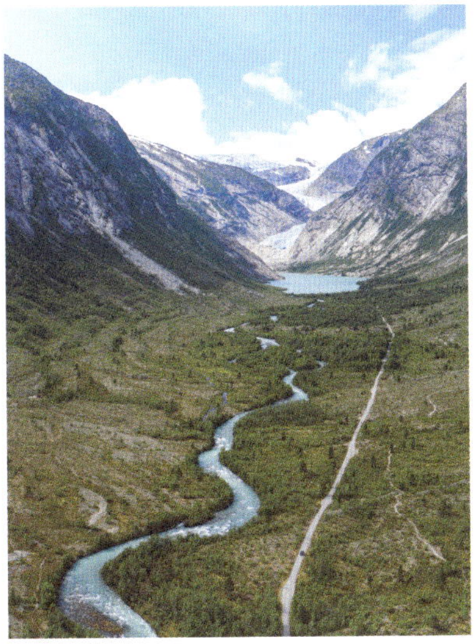

JOSTEDALSBREEN

With a surface area of 188 sq miles (486 km^2), Jostedalsbreen is the largest glacier in Norway.

24

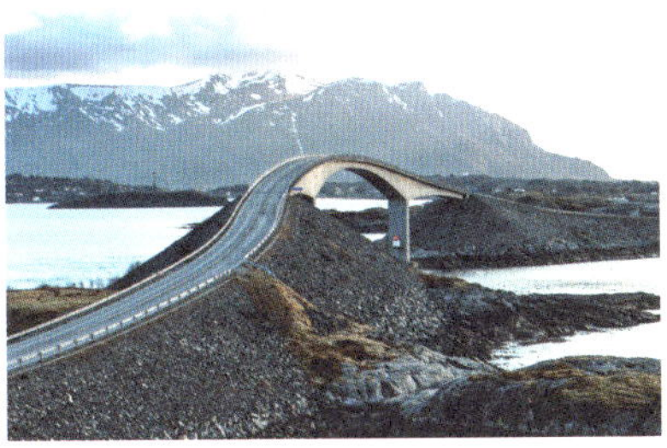

THE ATLANTIC ROAD

The road is undoubtedly at its most impressive when the winter swell breaks on the coast.

25

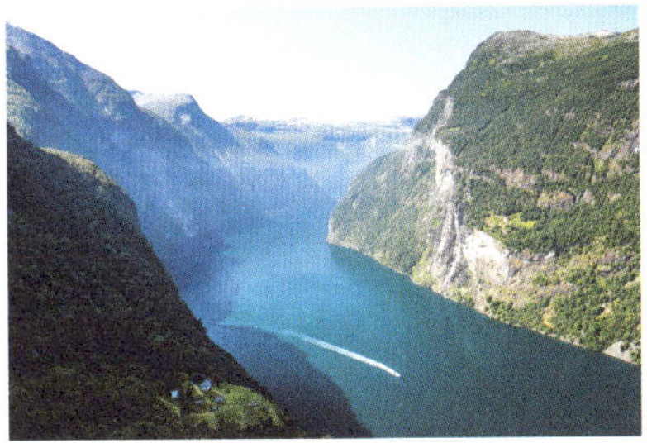

GEIRANGERFJORD

Some of the most impressive views in the country can be found here. The fjord is now listed as a UNESCO World Heritage Site.

26

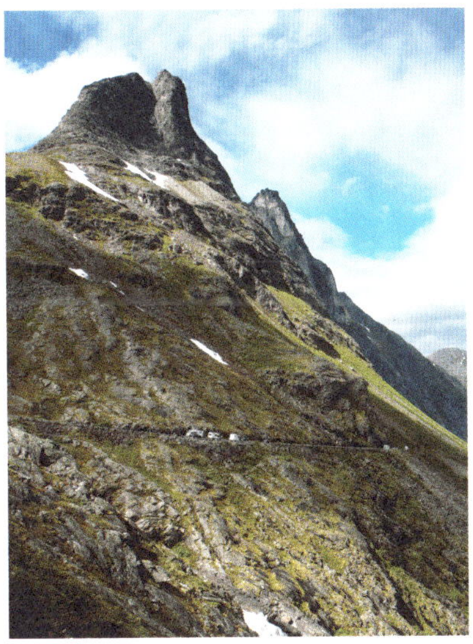

TROLLSTIGEN

The Trollstigen is a road along which there seems to be a spectacular panorama at every turn. Enjoy views over the valley from a multi-platform observation point.

27

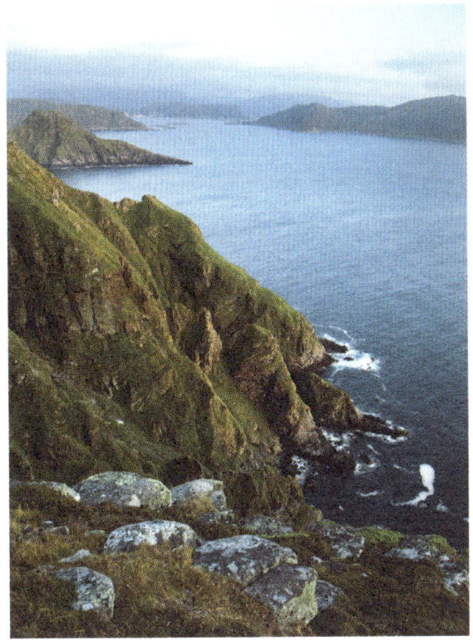

RUNDE ISLAND

The island's cliffs are populated by flocks of seabirds that come here to breed. Of these, the Atlantic puffin has a special place in Norwegian culture.

28

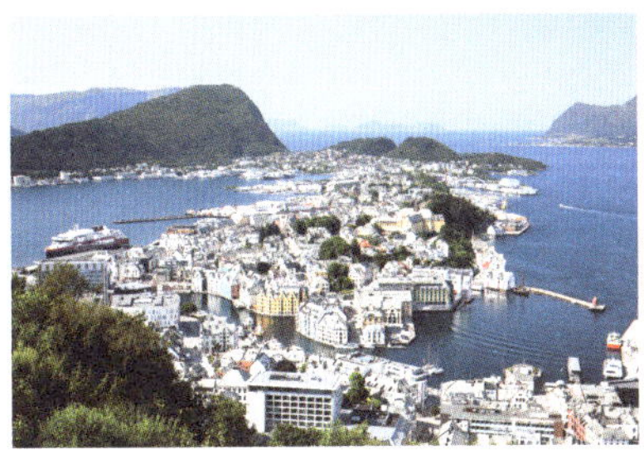

ÅLESUND

A port town renowned for its art nouveau architecture. The Hurtigruten Coastal Express stops here as it shuttles between Bergen and the north of the country.

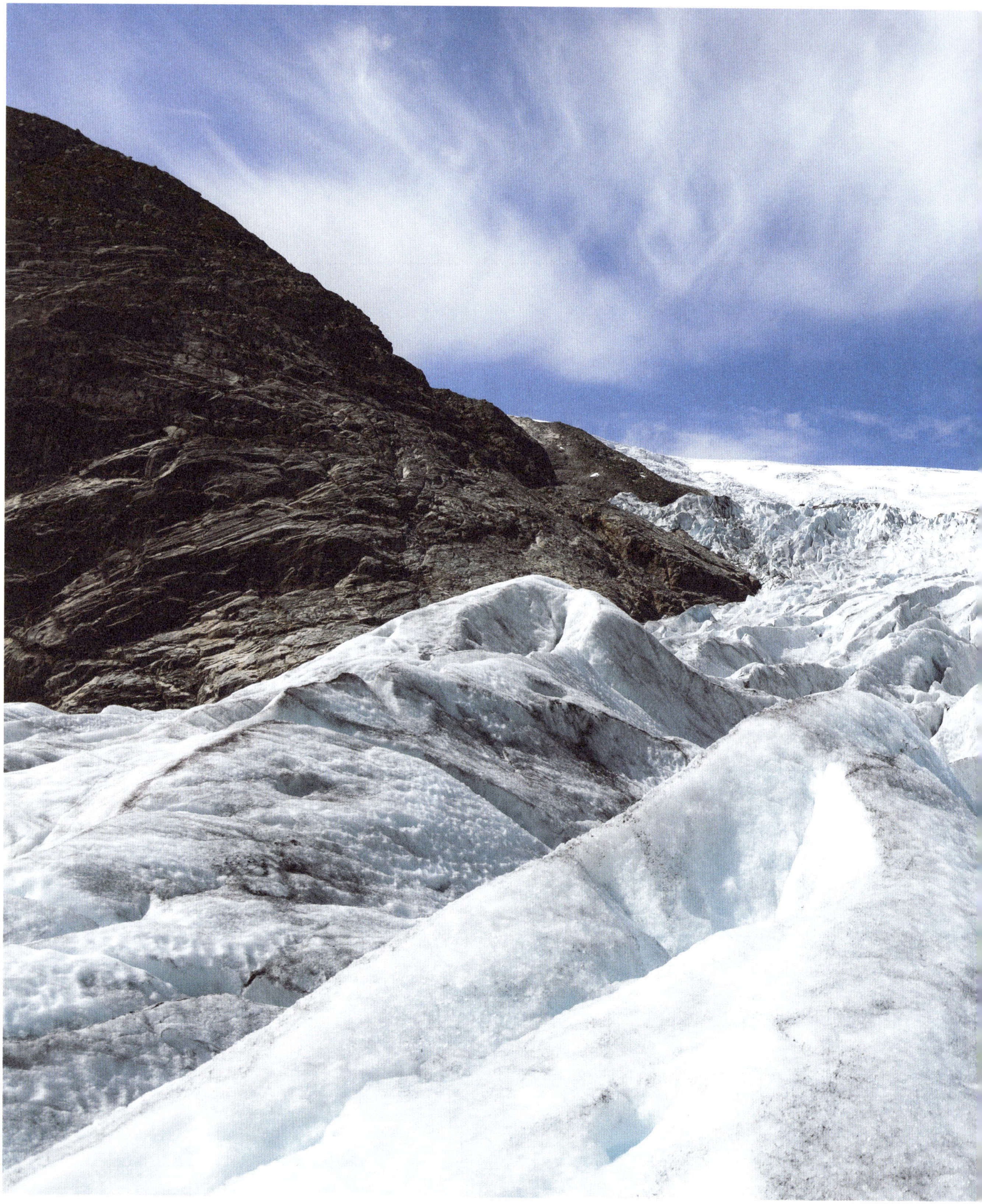

Walkers brave enough to venture out onto the glacier will find a sea of ice rising to a height of 6,420 ft (1,957 m) above sea level.

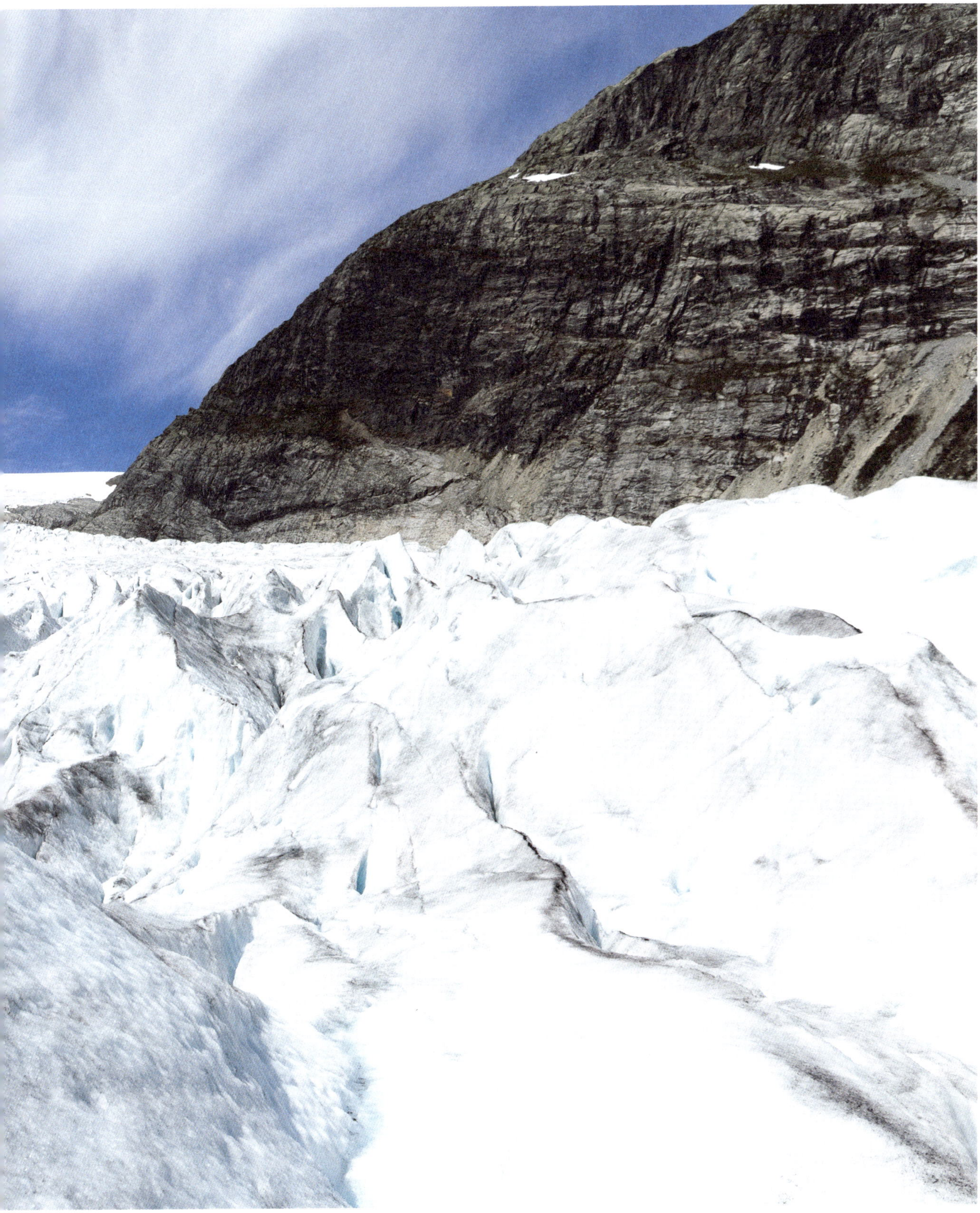

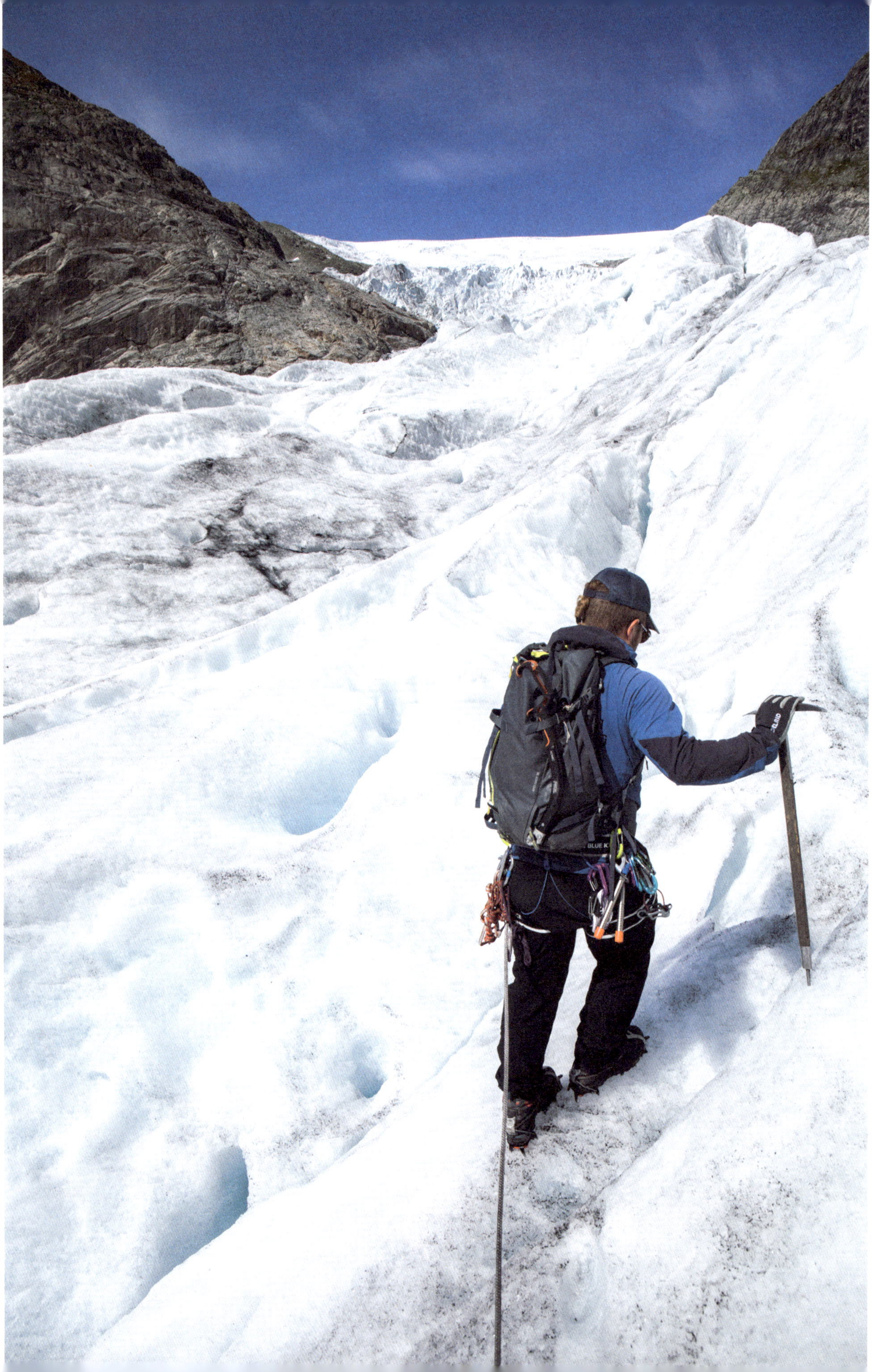

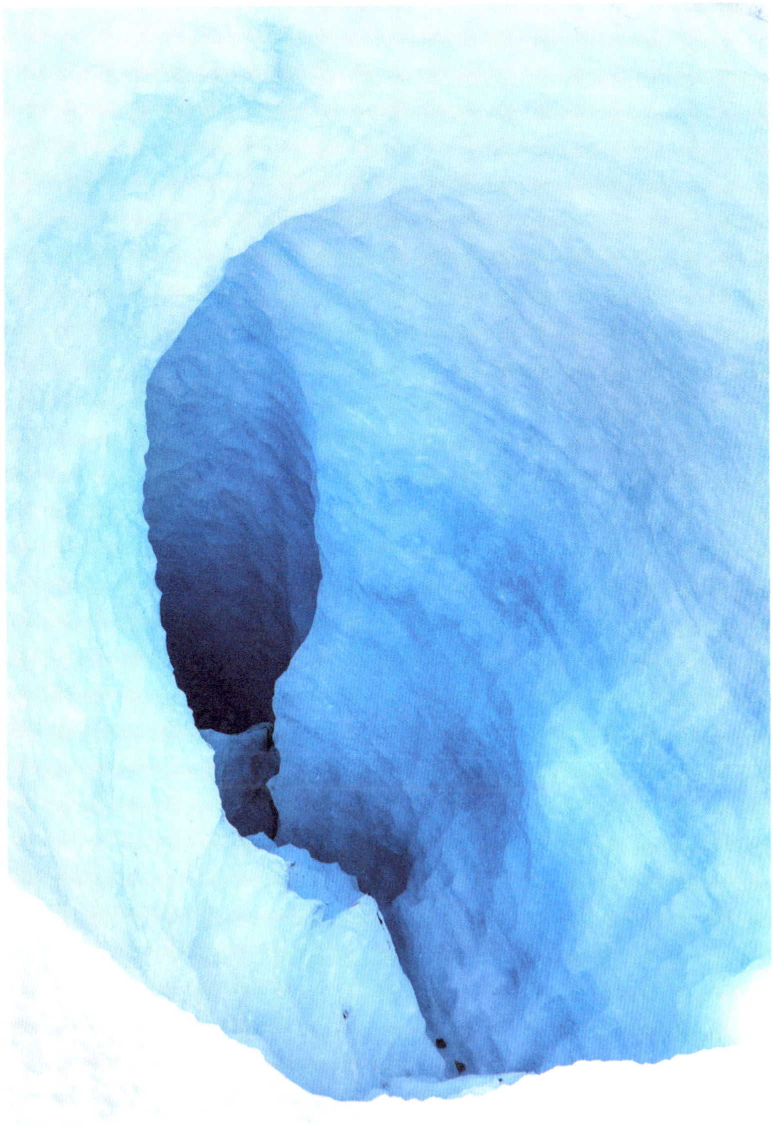

ABOVE

A moulim is a sinkhole carved into the ice by meltwater or rainwater. The structure and surface of the glacier are in a constant state of flux from day to day.

OPPOSITE

When stepping out onto the glacier, crampons, ropes, and ice axe are an absolute must.

DEEP DIVE

THE FJORDS

It took several million years for glaciers to shape the iconic landscape of Norway.

Although fjord is one of the few Norwegian words to have entered common usage, the geological formation itself can be found in many regions around the world, from Alaska and Iceland to Greenland, Chile, and Argentina.

The fjords scattered along Norway's western coastline are fine examples of recent glacial activity. They were formed three million years ago as the glaciers that covered the country slowly melted.

In geological terms, the fjords are located along the North Atlantic rifted margin. Uplift and tilting during the Tertiary era resulted in the formation of immense drainage systems that flowed west, while the monumental weight of the glaciers and the action of water on rock surfaces during the Pleistocene era (Ice Age) caused erosion that carved out valleys for miles on end. Seawater was later able to penetrate inland as the ice retreated. With the melting of the ice sheets, a phenomenon known as post-glacial rebound caused the land to rise up by well over 300 ft (92 ft), further deepening the fjords. The two hundred or so fjords of the western coast were all formed in this manner, creating some of the most magnificent and spellbinding scenery in the country.

The often-brackish waters of the fjords contain both seawater and fresh water carried down from lakes and melting glaciers, but these two waters of differing salinity mix very little: the fresh water floats to the surface while the denser, salty seawater remains in the depths. Low in oxygen, these calm waters encourage sedimentation.

The cliff walls of the fjords are impressive enough, but they plunge way below the surface of the water. The deepest point of famous Sognefjord is 4,290 ft (1,308 m) below the surface, and at 127 miles (204 km) in length, it is also the longest fjord in Northern Europe. Not every fjord is quite as spectacular, however: Oslo Fjord is a classic example of where the surrounding scenery can be quite flat.

The Western Fjords are also home to a particularly wide variety of wildlife, including the Arctic fox, four species of deer, and a host of marine mammals such as dolphins, orcas, and whales, not to mention Atlantic salmon and a hundred or so species of bird. Traces of human activity, particularly the farmsteads and pastureland between which livestock was shuttled, add a layer of recent history to the fjords, which has also helped to shape these unique landscapes.

HOW A FJORD IS FORMED

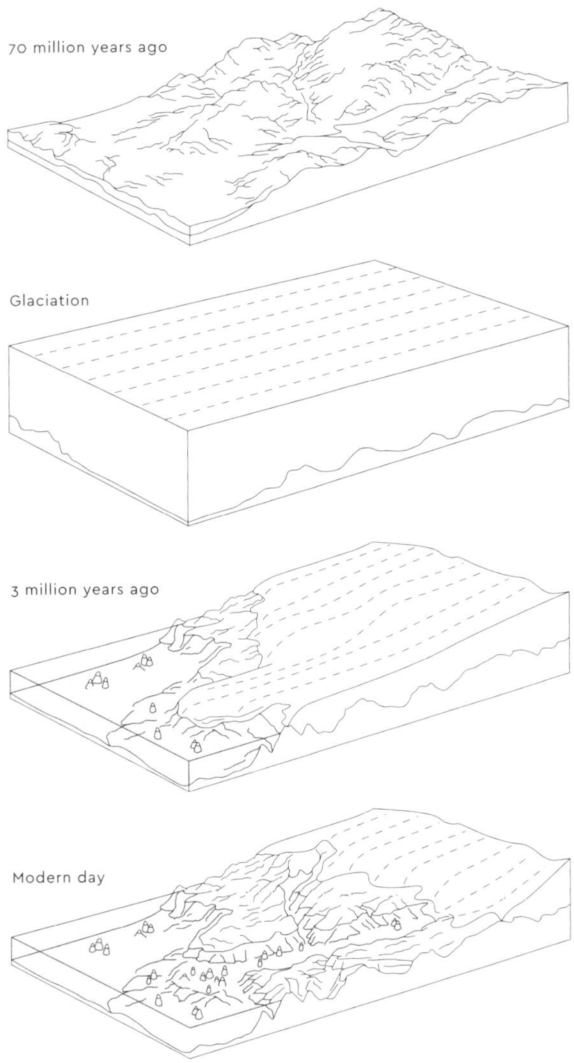

SOIL EROSION

A fjord is formed when ice covering a valley during a period of glaciation retreats to reveal the land that has been worn away by erosion, the lowest level of which is now below sea level.

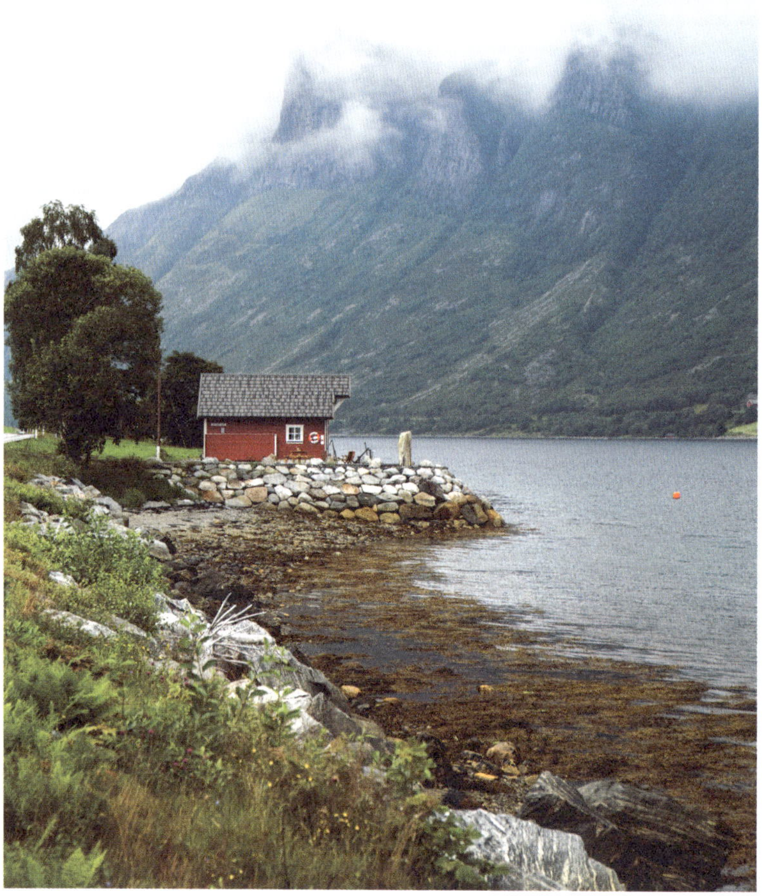

ABOVE

A fishing shack on the shores of the fjord is almost lost in the mist.

OPPOSITE

Skageflå farmstead is perched on the steep slopes above Geirangerfjord. In 1873 a landslide carried away most of the nearby arable land.

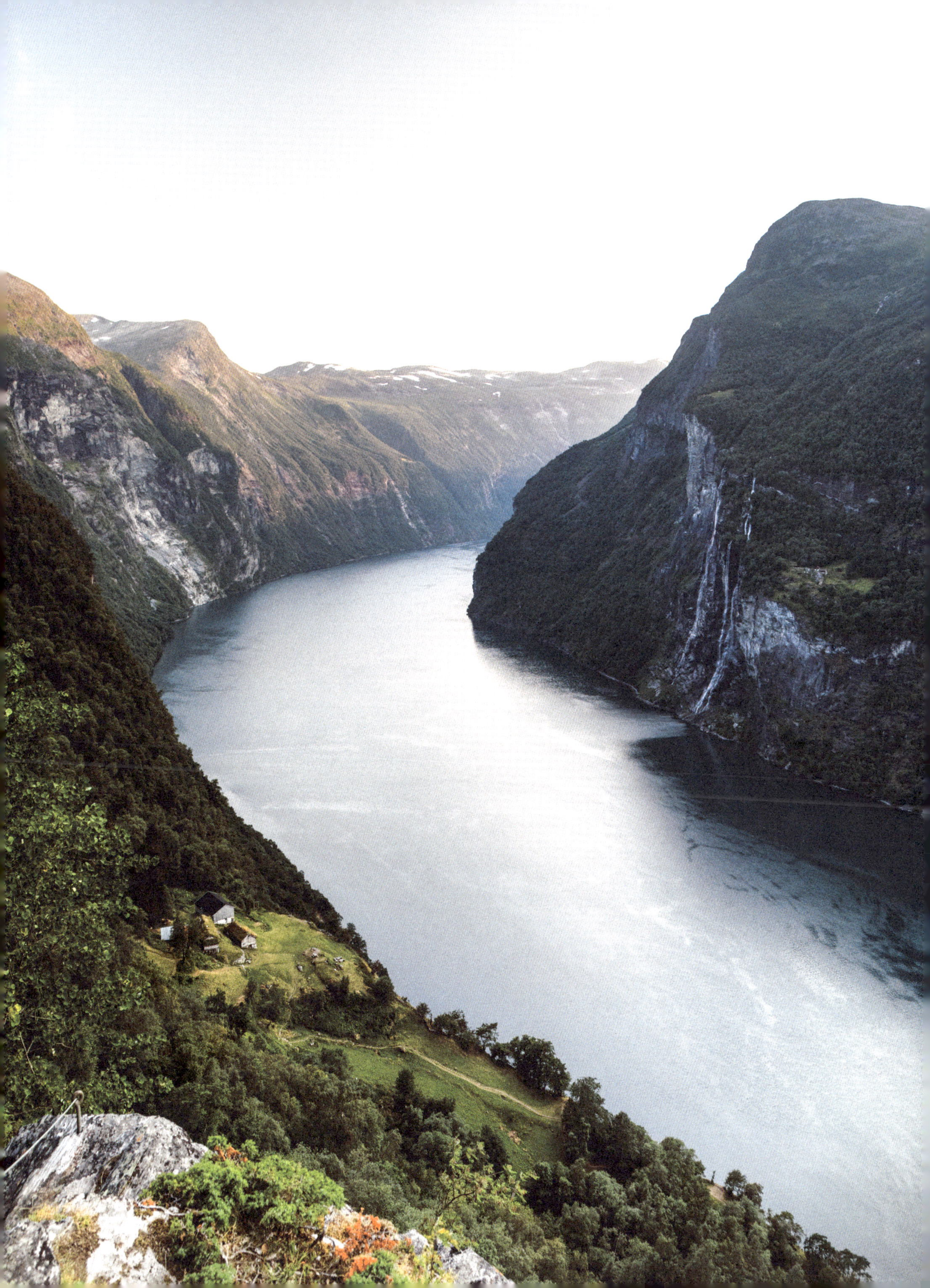

ARCHITECTURE

STAVE CHURCHES

Stave churches are true feats of architecture, constructed in the Middle Ages and directly inspired by Viking longships.

The medieval Norwegian churches known as *stavkirker* (stave churches) were built between 1150 and 1350. The name derives from the use of a framework of wooden posts lined with walls of wooden planks. In Norwegian, *stav* means stick or pole and *kirke* means church. These churches are true architectural masterpieces and rank among the most technically advanced wooden buildings of the Middle Ages. The oldest *stavkirke*, built at Urnes in 1130, was inscribed on the UNESCO World Heritage list in 1979.

Although a total of some one thousand *stavkirker* were built in Norway, there are now no more than twenty-eight left in the whole country. The remainder are thought to have been dismantled or left to decay (a by-product of Norway's growing disinterest in religion), although the Black Death was also a contributory factor, ravaging the country in 1349 and causing the death of a third of the population. Since a Norwegian satanist set fire to Fantoft church in Bergen in 1992, burning it down entirely, all such churches are now protected with security systems and fire alarms.

The architectural structure of these churches is highly distinctive and unlike any other, except perhaps for the design of Viking longships. Stave churches are built using *kne* (meaning elbow), wooden braces that connect crossbeams and posts, ensuring the structure will withstand storms. Not a single metal nail is used, and some churches, for example the one at Borgund, feature elements typical of Viking art, such as gable ends decorated with dragon heads.

Many of the carvings found on the wooden doors and roof ridges of the churches reproduce motifs inspired by both Christian lore and Scandinavian mythology, featuring a wealth of fantastical creatures. Although alterations have been made to the buildings over the centuries, the appearance of most of the churches is little changed from the original. Any additions to the fixtures and fittings or alterations to the space itself are also indications of shifts in religious practice and changes in the way society is organized over the generations.

The use of high-quality wood that has been dried slowly and then coated in a natural pitch made from pine resin (along with a preference for stone foundations) has ensured that the buildings have stood the test of time over the centuries. A new coat of pitch is applied every forty years or so to protect the wood from rain damage and the rigors of winter, and it is this coating, dark in color, that gives these medieval churches their mysterious aspect, as if they have leapt straight out of Norwegian legend.

1

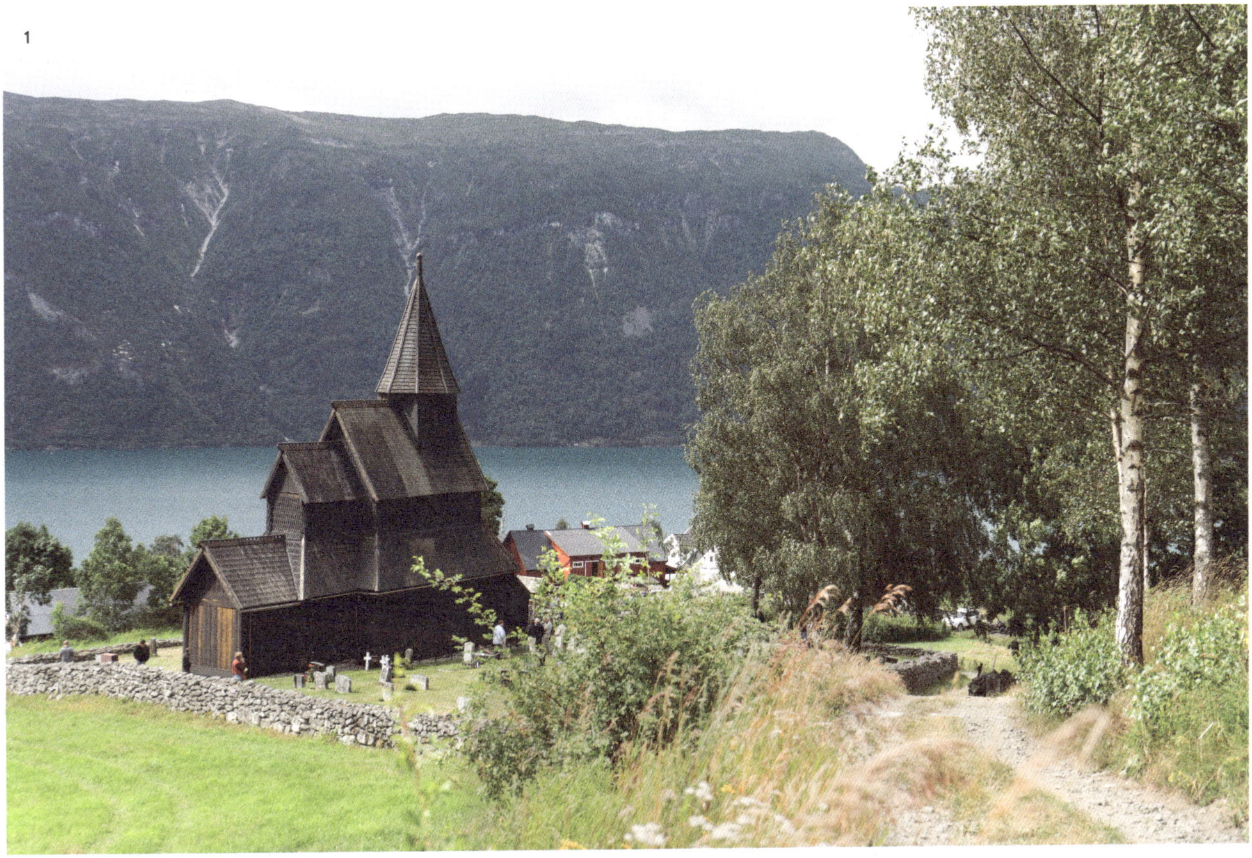

2

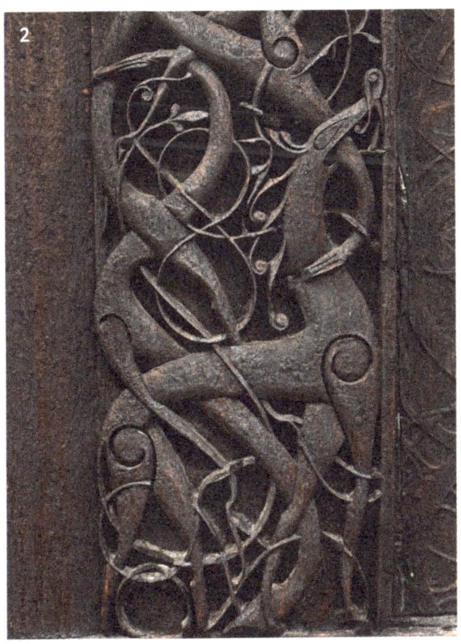

3

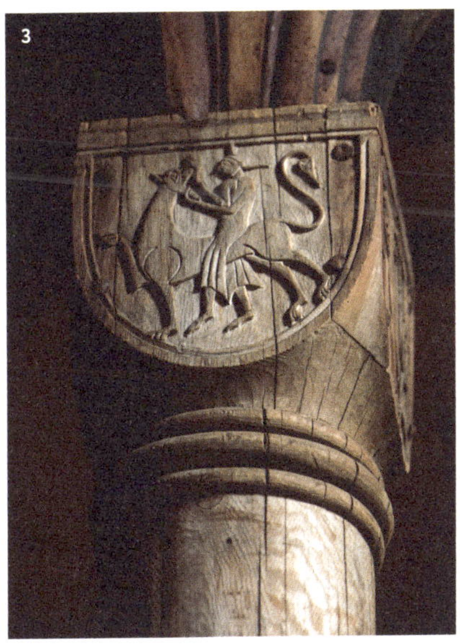

4

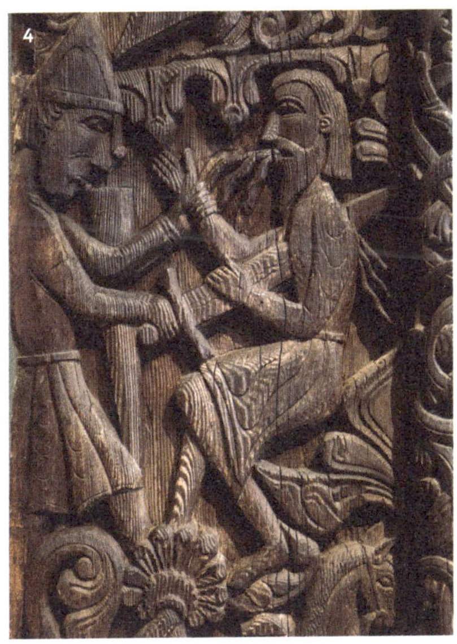

1/ 2/ URNES STAVKIRKE

The north face of the church features a portal and two side panels with intertwined decorative elements sourced from an eleventh-century building.

3/ CAPITALS

The pillars inside the church are topped with capitals featuring relief carvings depicting mythical figures and animals.

4/ A SLIGHT DISAGREEMENT

A portrayal of combat carved on a stave church portal now in Oslo's Museum of Cultural History.

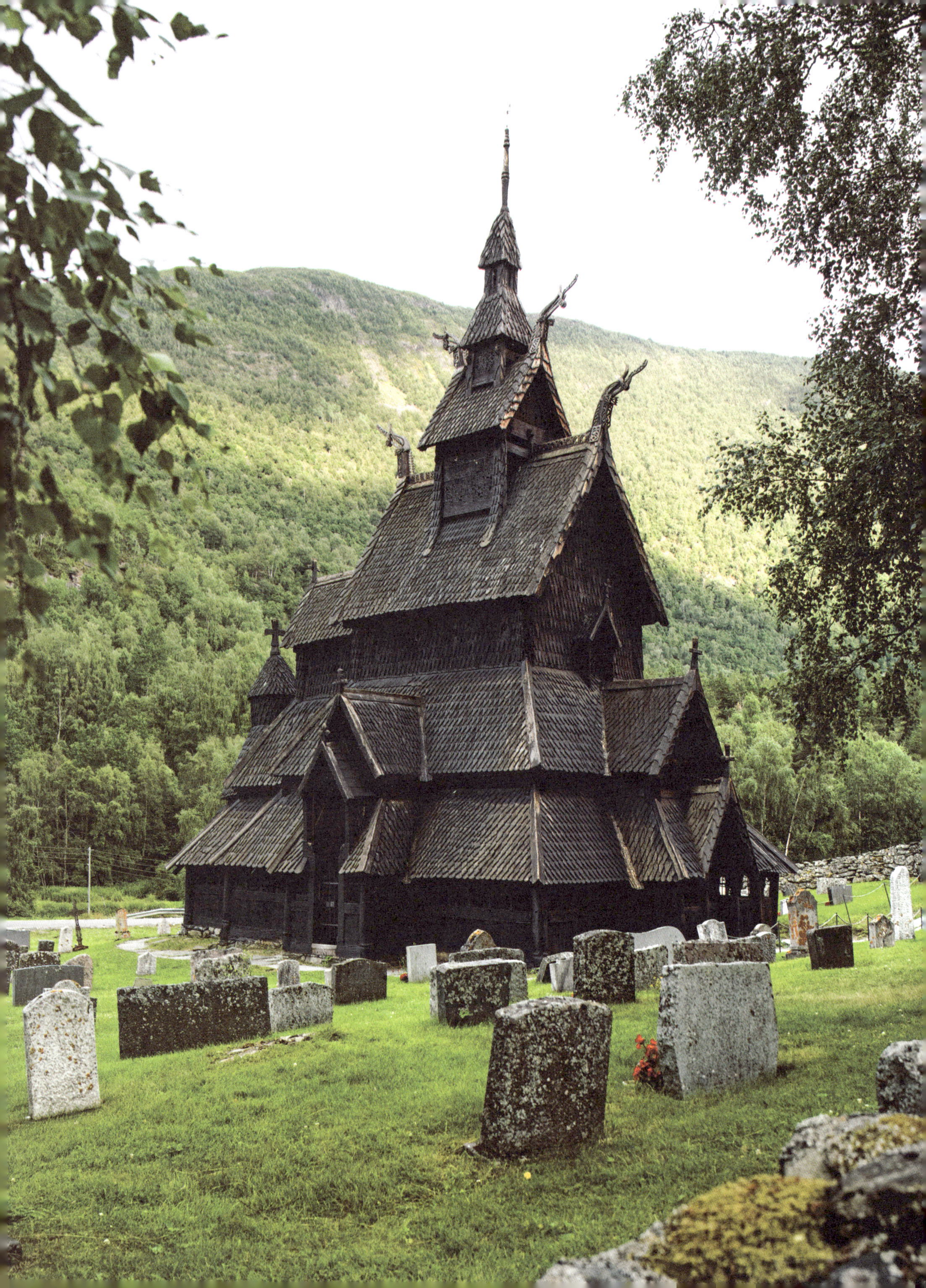

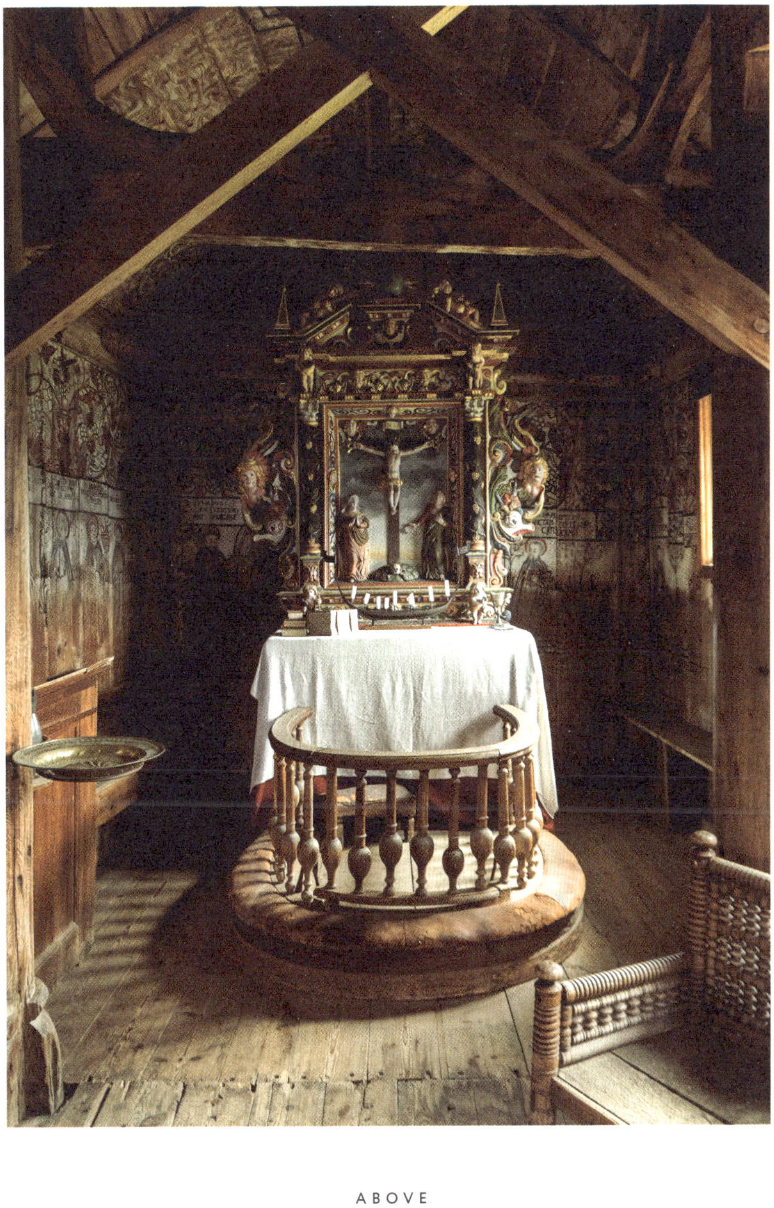

ABOVE

The bishop's throne (bottom right) and the candle holder shaped like a longship on the altar of Urnes stave church both date from the twelfth century.

OPPOSITE

The best-preserved stave church in the country is in Borgund. It was used as a model for the churches at Gol and Hopperstad when these were rebuilt.

EXCURSION

JUVET LANDSCAPE HOTEL

This hotel nestling in the Valldal valley is located in an incredible natural setting and is truly unique.

People come from far and wide to stay in this unique hotel with a reputation that extends far beyond Norway's borders, particularly among fans of unusual architecture and cinephiles who like to hunt down filming locations—it featured briefly in Alex Garland's film *Ex Machina*. Juvet Landscape Hotel is hidden away in a relatively isolated position, however—it is not the kind of place that people just stumble across.

It is fair to say that the hotel was always intended to be unique, designed by architects at Jensen & Skodvin to blend seamlessly into its setting and to leave no trace when it is time for it to be dismantled and the site cleared. The end goal of its designers was to imagine the hotel as no more than a guest in the natural cycle of the area and so to refrain from digging extensive foundations or using explosives in its construction.

As a result, the site is a collection of several ultra-modern and minimalist buildings that merge perfectly into the scenery. These are arranged to provide each guest with the privacy required to enjoy their stay, enabling them to immerse themselves in the natural world of Norway in all its rawness and authenticity. Nature is a presence in its own right here, and the wide picture windows are perfect for admiring the outside world while enjoying the pleasant sensation of being truly cocooned safe and warm inside. The hotel's character is further influenced by the neighboring glacier and the mountains that surround the site, which was constructed around an old wooden farmstead. Further upstream, water cascades energetically down the spectacular Gudbrandsjuvet waterfall before changing character to flow tranquilly as a river below the hotel. Guests can swim here in summer and even take a dip in winter, perhaps after a sauna in the hotel spa.

Summers are brief in Norway, so local produce is traditionally dried, salted, smoked, or fermented for storage. It therefore makes sense for the hotel restaurant to work with the local ingredients that include smoked fish, game, fresh and fermented vegetables, mushrooms, and wild berries. The result is food that is on a par with the architecture in terms of excellence. Some hotel guests find the whole experience so enchanting and enjoyable that they opt to extend their stay. One director of a large company notably decided to stay on for three weeks rather than the two days initially planned.

Not every traveler need follow suit, however. Even just a short stay can ensure an experience that the location and the warm welcome provided by the staff will make unforgettable.

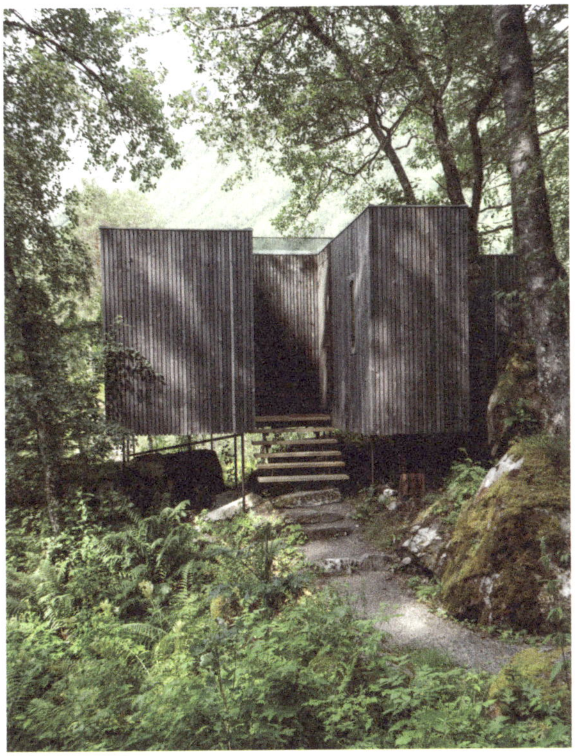

INTO THE WOODS

The large picture windows in each room make it easy to see nature in all its glory.

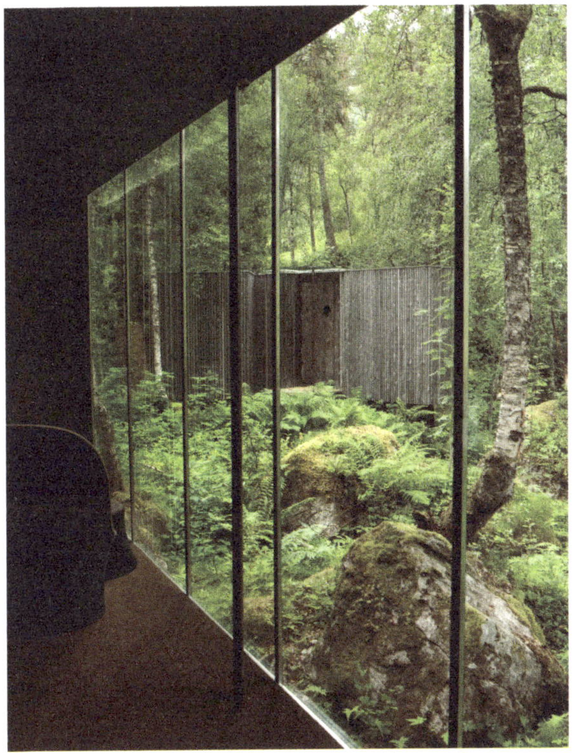

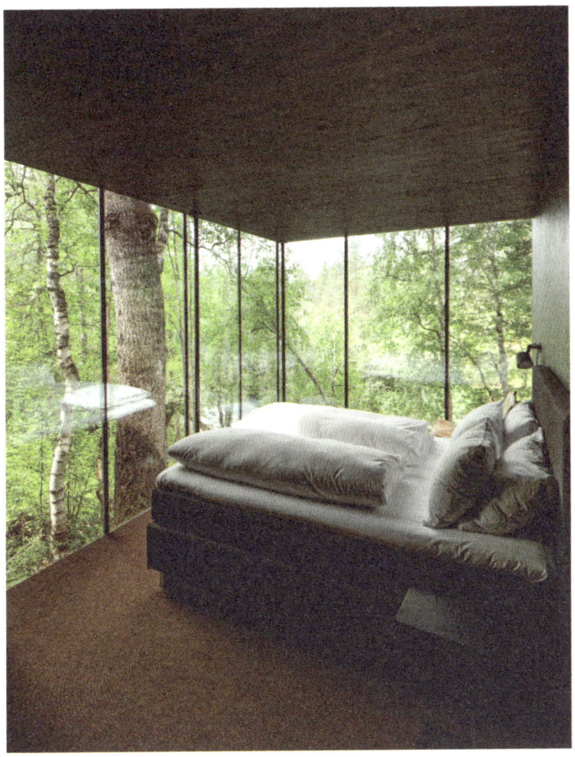

OUT IN NATURE

They may be cocooned deep in the comfort of a luxury hotel room, but guests are sleeping in the middle of the forest.

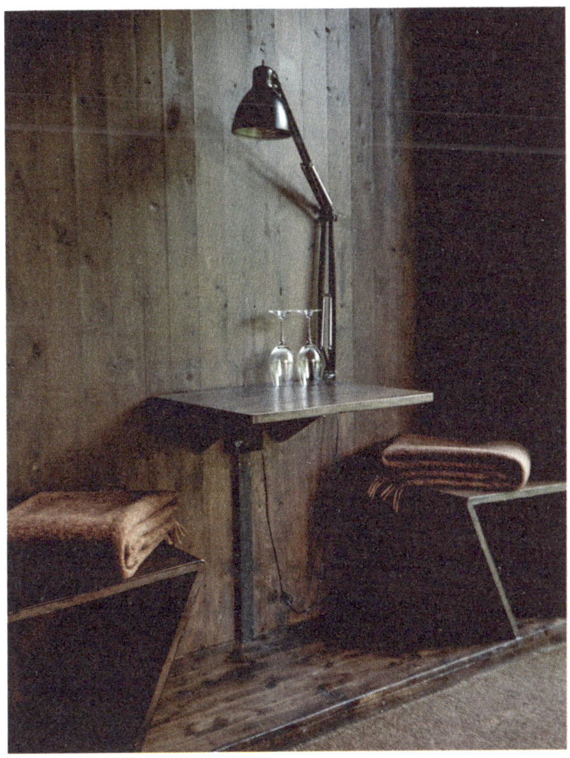

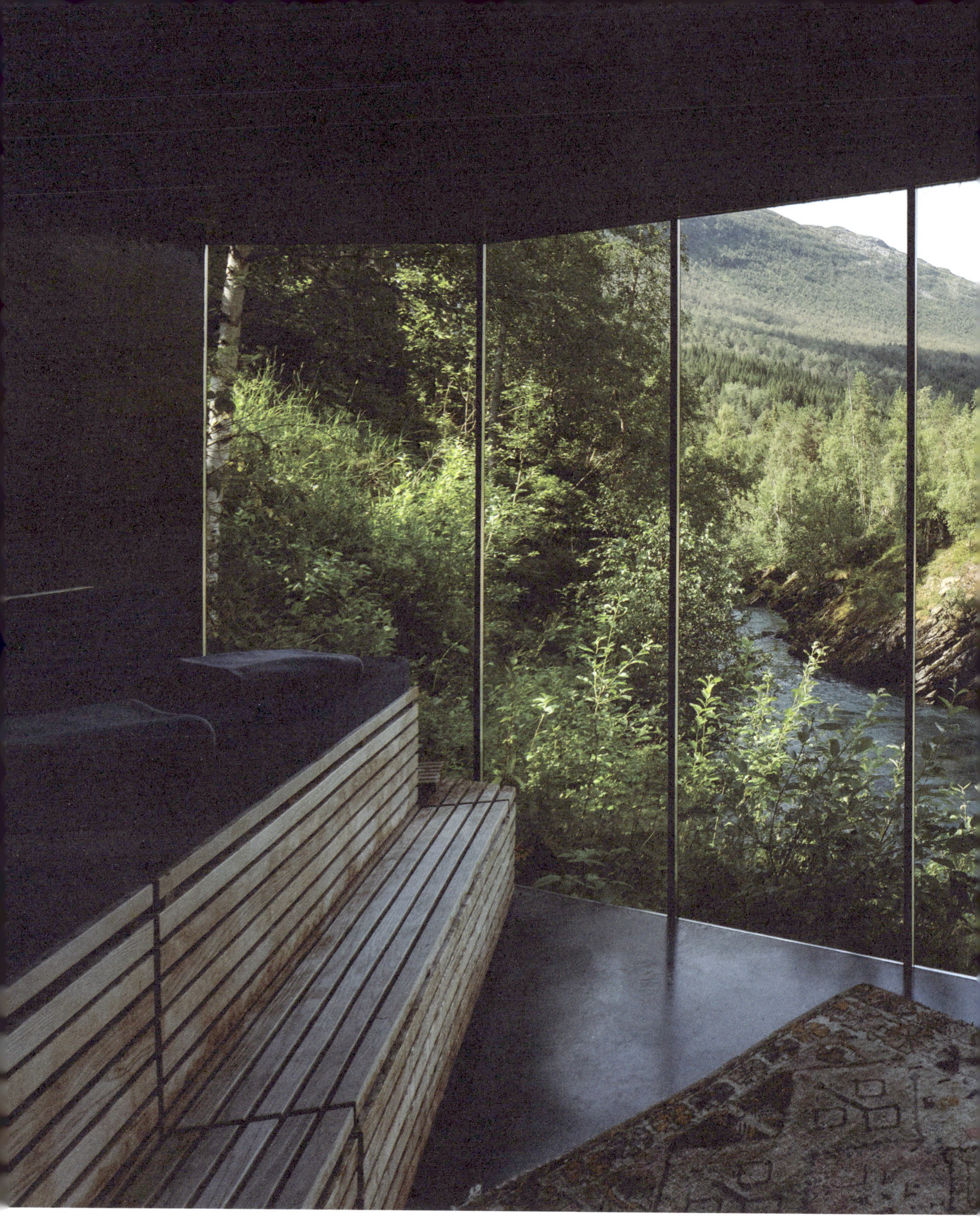

Guests can take time out for relaxation after a long day's hiking.

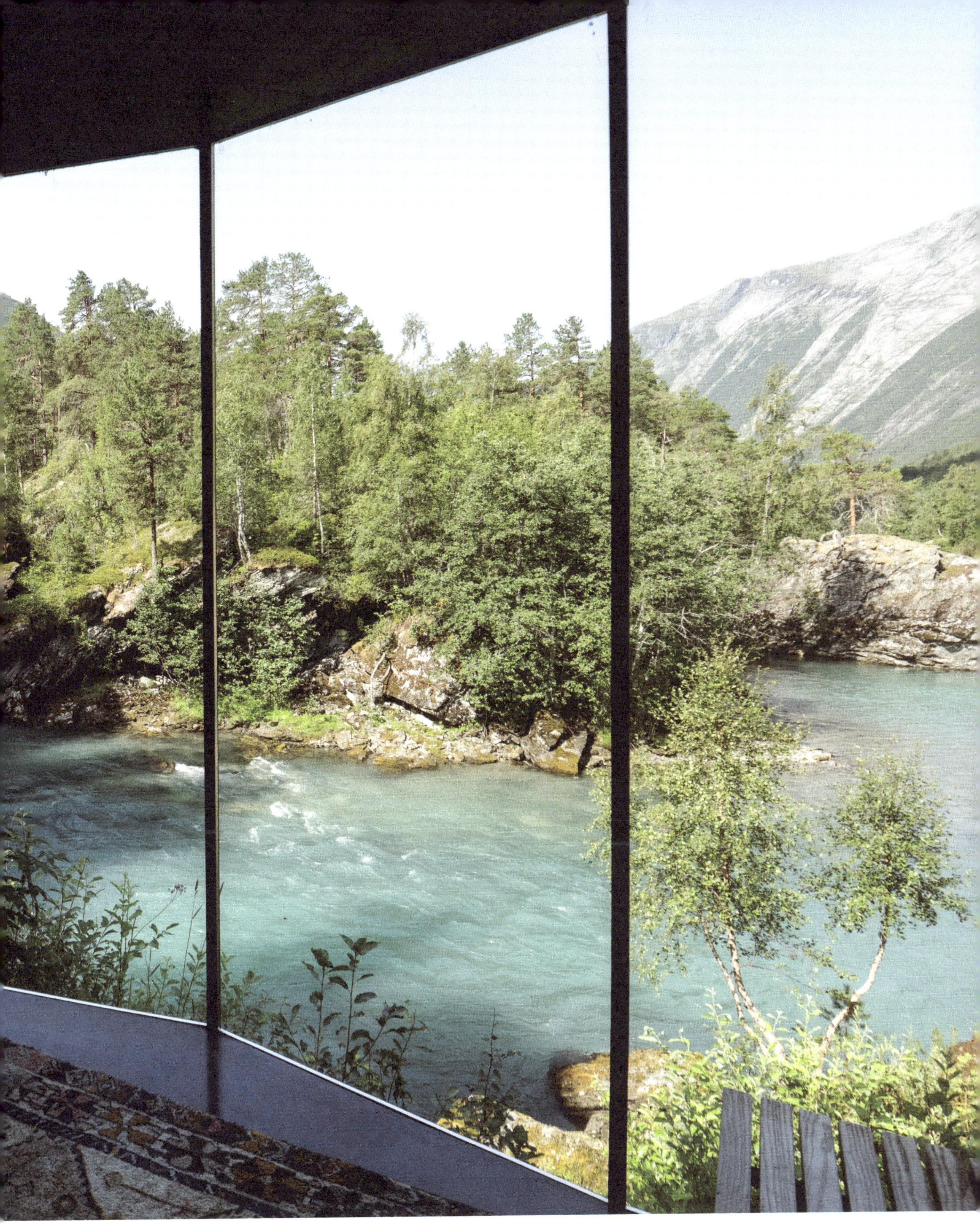

NATURE

NORWEGIAN PLANTS

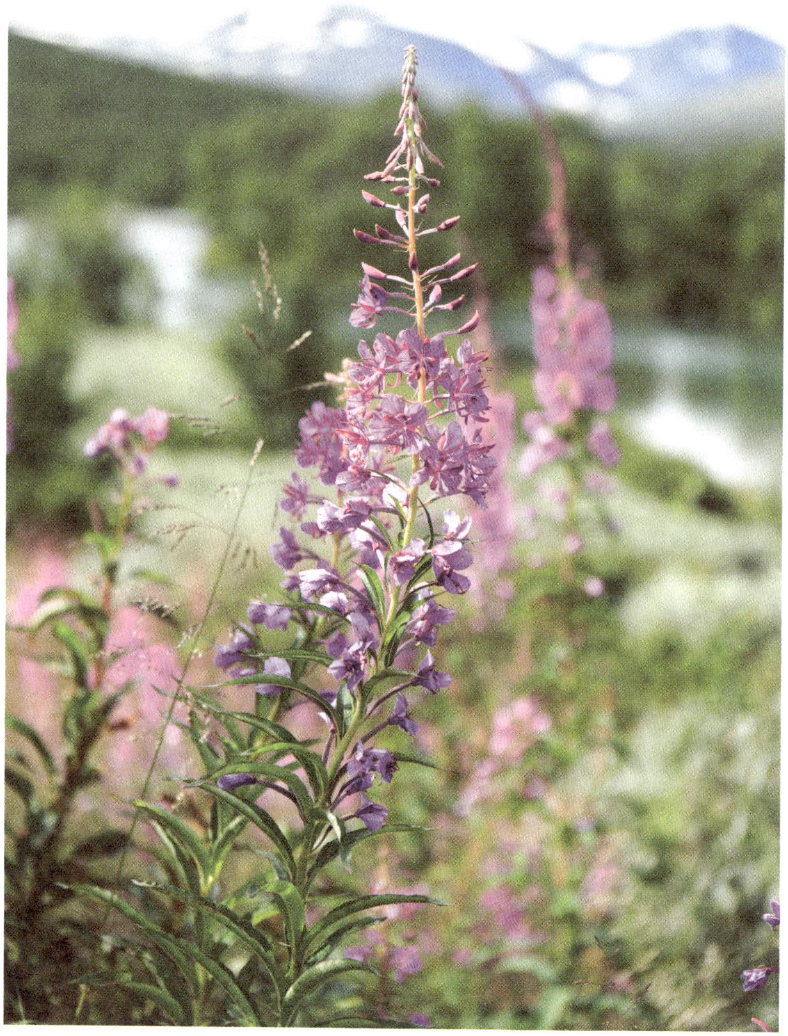

FIREWEED

This colorful perennial thrives in open woodland and semi-mountainous climates. It is almost ubiquitous in Norway.

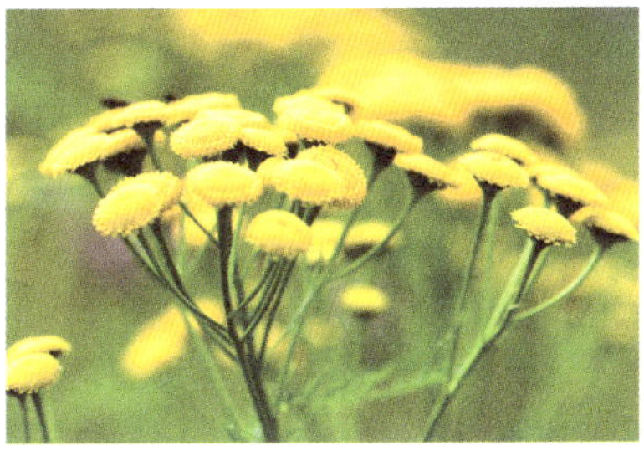

TANSY

This plant's essential oils release a strong odor when handled.

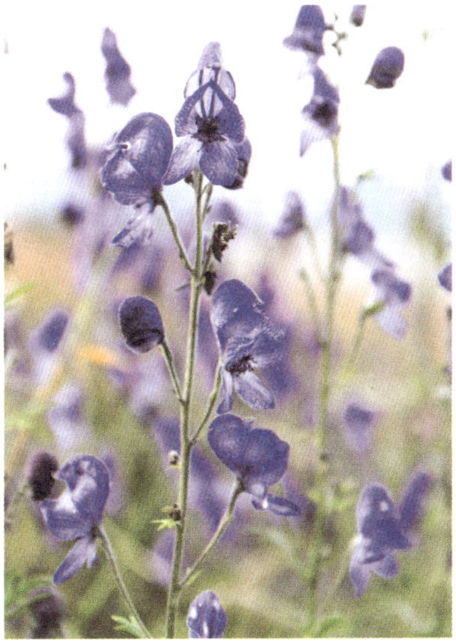

ACONITE

Also known as monkshood, due to its flowers which resemble a monk's cowl.

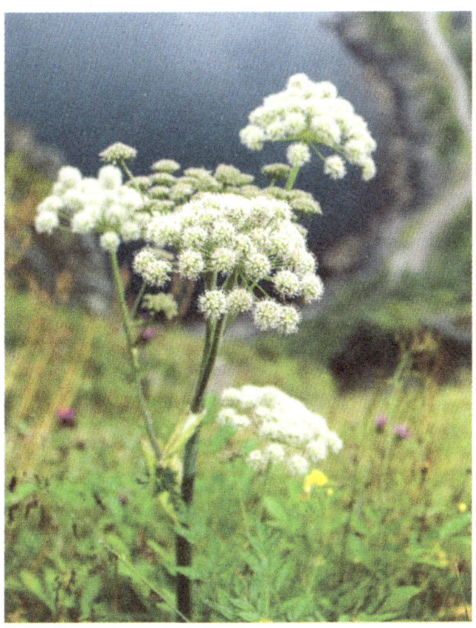

ANGELICA

This plant from Northern Europe has been used in herbal medicine for centuries.

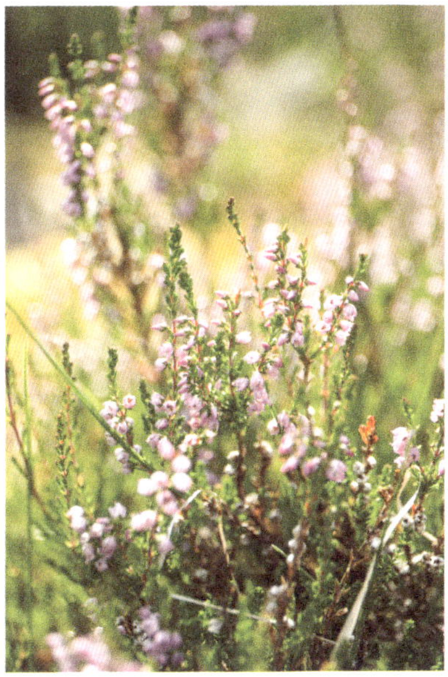

HEATHER

Heather is an important source of food for some animals when the landscape is blanketed in snow.

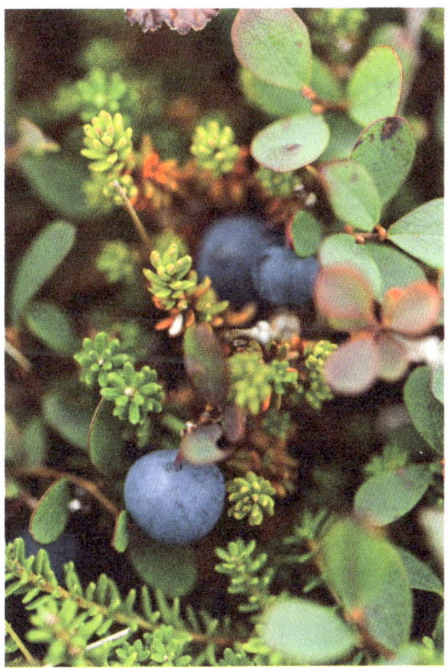

NORTHERN BILBERRY

Northern bilberries are often eaten fresh or may be turned into jelly. They are also served as an accompaniment to several dishes, particularly game.

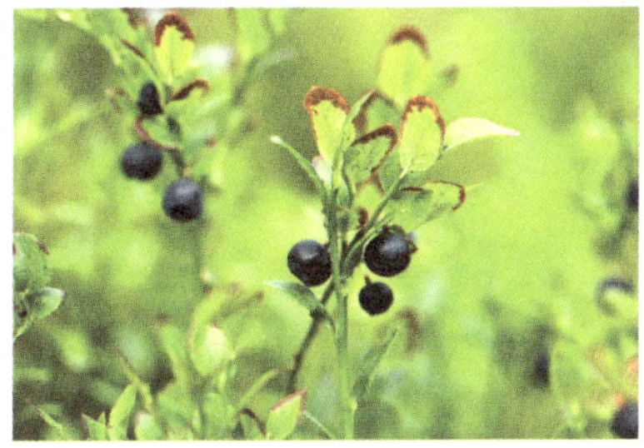

WILD BLUEBERRY

These blueberries are rich in antioxidants and grow abundantly throughout Norway.

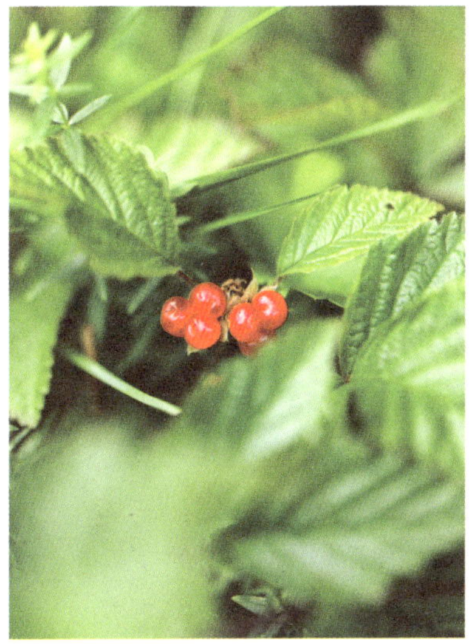

STONE BRAMBLE

An Arctic berry that is common in Russian cuisine.

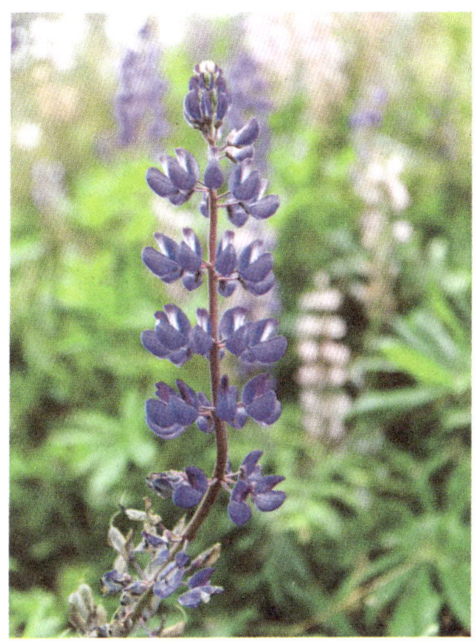

WILD LUPIN

This plant is found in a variety of colors and can reach a height of 5 ft (150 cm).

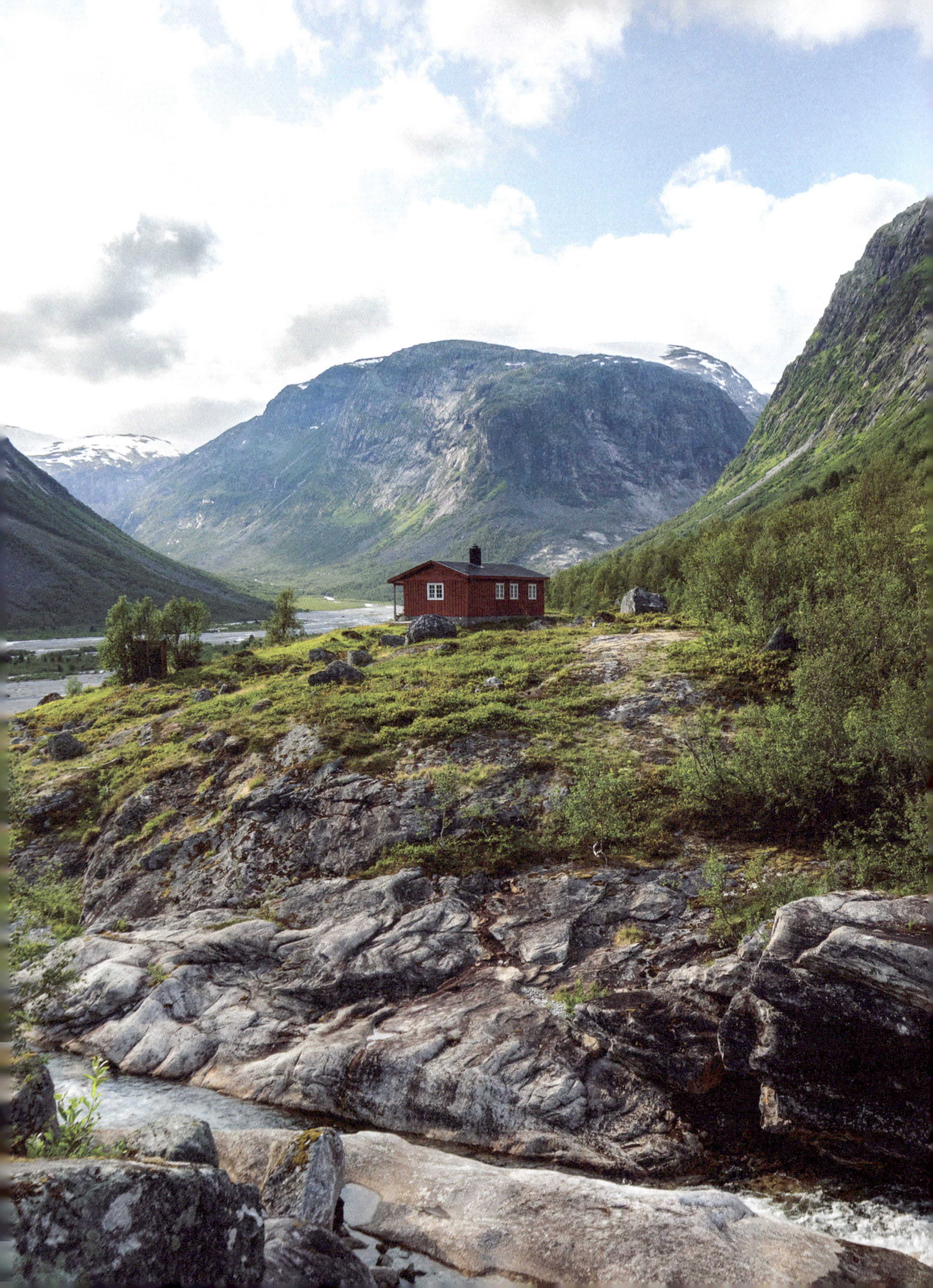

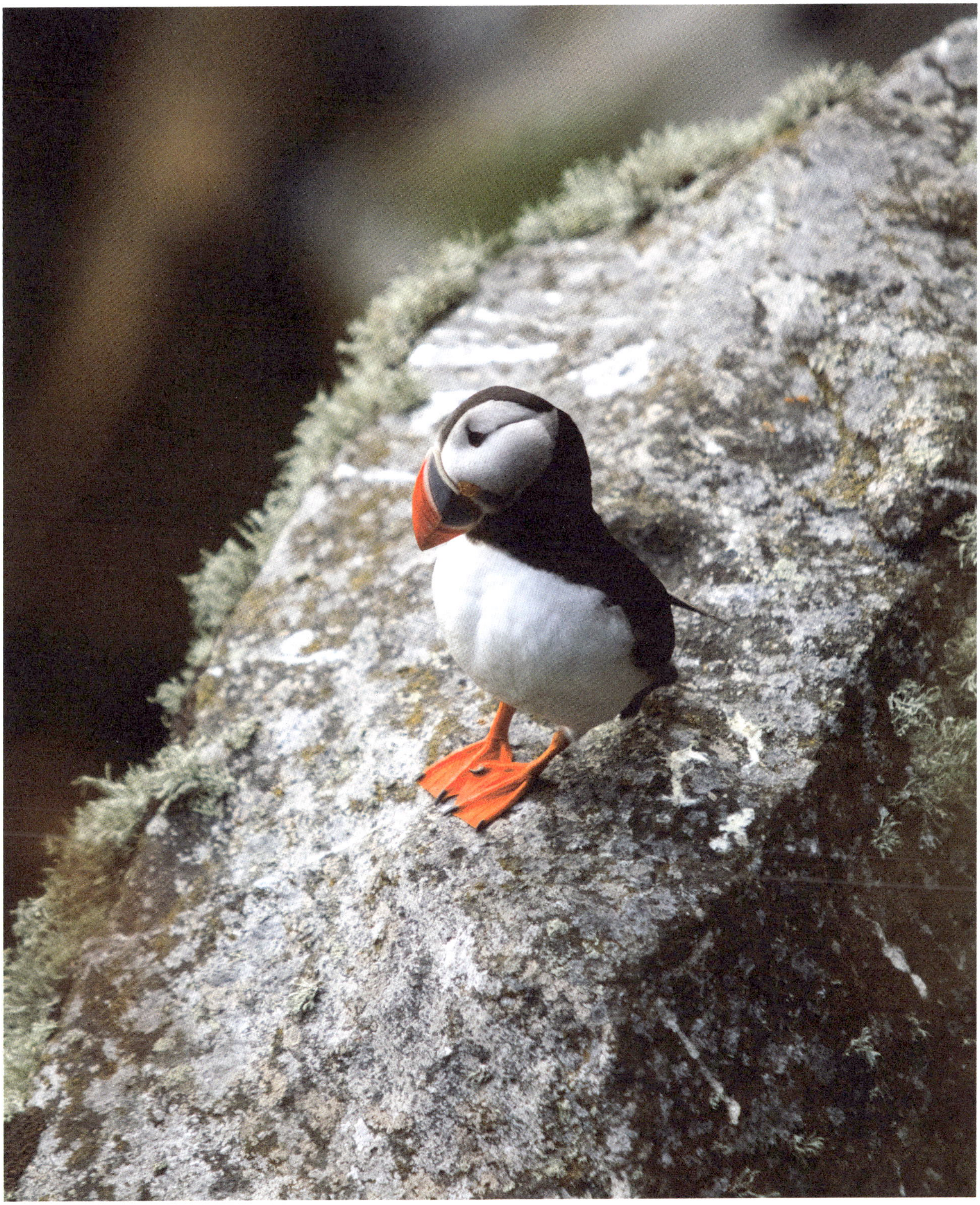

ABOVE

A puffin stands on a cliff at Runde Island. Thousands of birds return here every summer to breed.

OPPOSITE

This cabin nestling in the heart of the glacial valley below Jostedalsbreen seems to have been abandoned to nature.

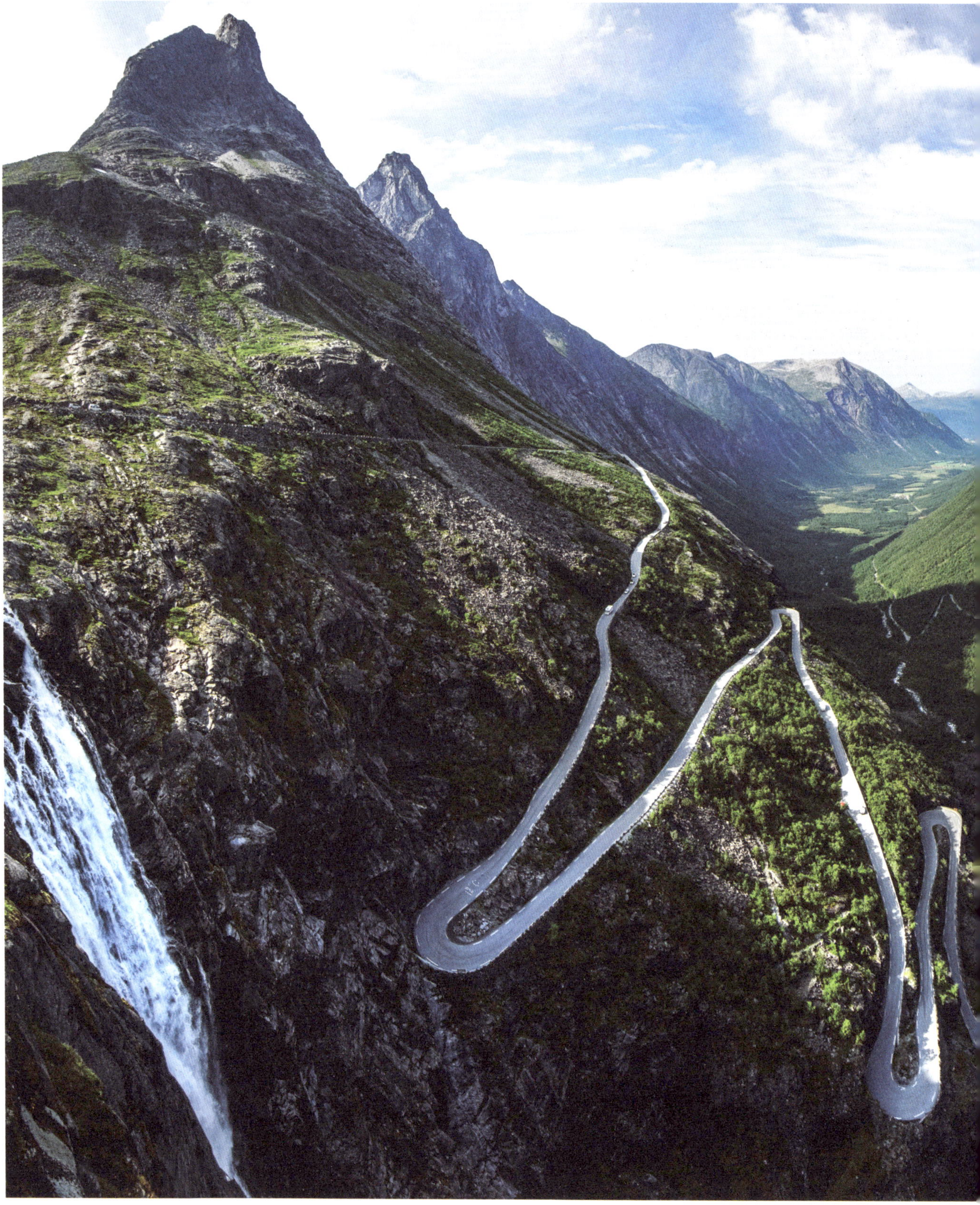

The Trollstigen is a scenic road with no less than eleven hairpin bends and gradients approaching 9 percent. It is impassable during the months of fall and winter.

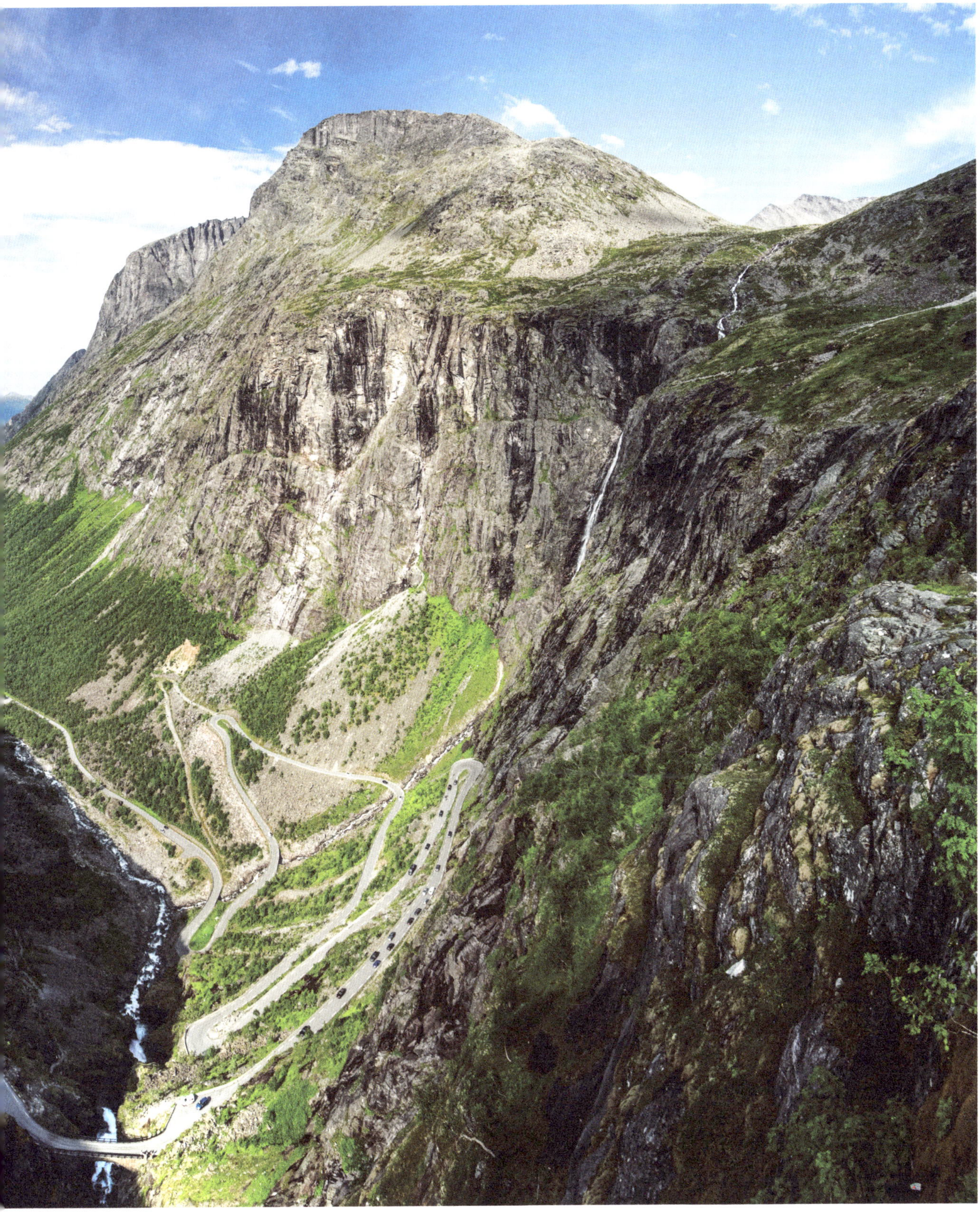

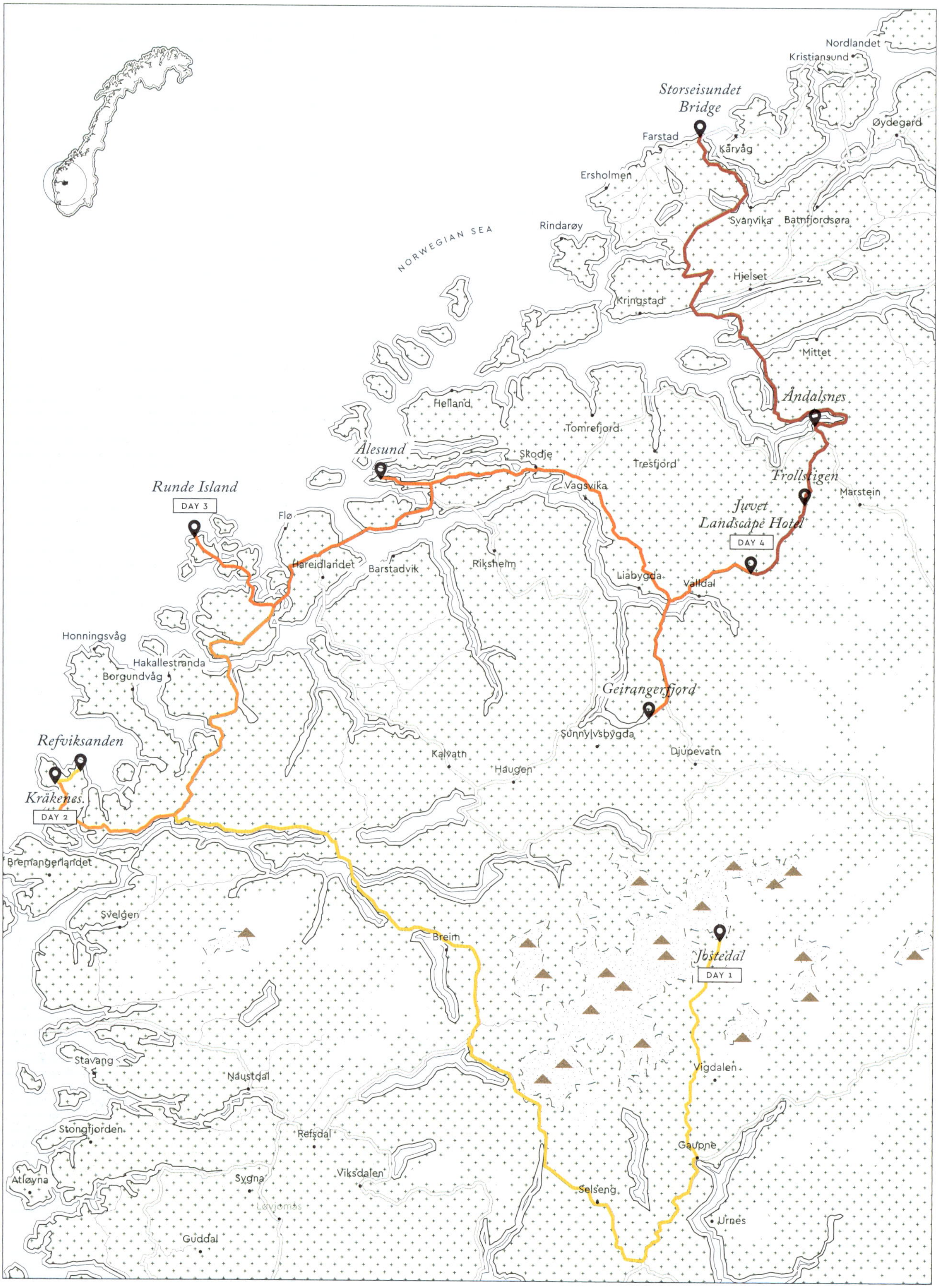
Nordlandet
Kristiansund
Storseisundet Bridge
Øydegard
Farstad
Kårvåg
Ersholmen
Svanvika
Batnfjordsøra
Rindarøy
NORWEGIAN SEA
Hjelset
Kringstad
Mittet
Åndalsnes
Helland
Tomrefjord
Ålesund
Skodje
Tresfjord
Frollstigen
Marstein
Vagsvika
Runde Island
DAY 3
Juvet Landscape Hotel
DAY 4
Flø
Hareidlandet
Barstadvik
Riksheim
Liabygda
Valldal
Honningsvåg
Hakallestranda
Borgundvåg
Geirangerfjord
Refviksanden
Sunnylvsbygda
Djupevatn
Kalvatn
Haugen
Kråkenes
DAY 2
Bremangerlandet
Svelgen
Breim
Jostedal
DAY 1
Stavang
Naustdal
Vigdalen
Stongfjorden
Refsdal
Gaupne
Atløyna
Sygna
Viksdalen
Selseng
Urnes
Gaddal

ITINERARY

FOUR DAYS ON THE WESTERN FJORDS

A trip along the Western Fjords promises majestic views, from Norway's spectacular coastline to the largest glacier in Continental Europe.

DAY 1: FROM JOSTEDALSBREEN GLACIER TO THE BEACHES OF REFVIKSANDEN

Jostedalsbreen, the largest glacier in Continental Europe, has several access points. Those wishing to make a hiking trip out on the ice, which is a thrilling experience, head to Nigardsbreen, one of the arms of the glacier, but if visiting in winter, a visit to an ice cave might be a good alternative. Judging from the gnarled trunks of the birch trees along the way, winters in the valley would seem to be pretty harsh. Head for Kråkenes, a few hours down the road, and spend a night beside the magnificent beaches of white sand at Refviksanden. If the weather takes a turn for the worse, the ambience around Kråkenes Lighthouse will be all the more dramatic.

DAY 2: FROM KRÅKENES TO RUNDE

The steep cliffs of the island of Runde are home to a large colony of seabirds, including the famous Atlantic puffins. These small birds, with their black backs and wings, white bodies, and distinctive, curved red and black bills, are most likely to be spotted at sunset between mid-April and the beginning of August. Lively (if slightly melancholy) cries herald their arrival and departure from the hundreds of nest sites on the cliff walls. Providing it can be observed without intruding, it is a fascinating spectacle, and a very special moment for any nature lover.

DAY 3: FROM ÅLESUND TO JUVET HOTEL

The port town of Ålesund is now one of the finest examples of art nouveau architectural style in Scandinavia, having been completely destroyed by fire in 1904. Surrounded by a string of islands, it is a perfect place to stop off on the way to the famous Geirangerfjord, which has been listed as a UNESCO World Heritage Site. Despite the ups and downs and changes in elevation, there is a splendid hiking trail to the farm at Skageflå, if calf muscles are up to it. Stop off at Juvet Landscape Hotel to take a look at architecture that has been perfectly integrated into its setting, or even stay overnight, comfortably cocooned in nature.

DAY 4: FROM TROLLSTIGEN TO KRISTIANSUND

Enjoy a hearty breakfast and then hit the road for Trollstigen, negotiating a splendid panoramic route to the viewing platform at the top, from where visitors can admire breathtaking views. The town of Åndalsnes below, surrounded by magnificent peaks, is another great place to stop off to recharge the batteries, but don't linger too long as there's still a way to go before reaching Storseisundet Bridge on the Atlantic Road just outside Kristiansund. The scenery is thrillingly spectacular on stormy days!

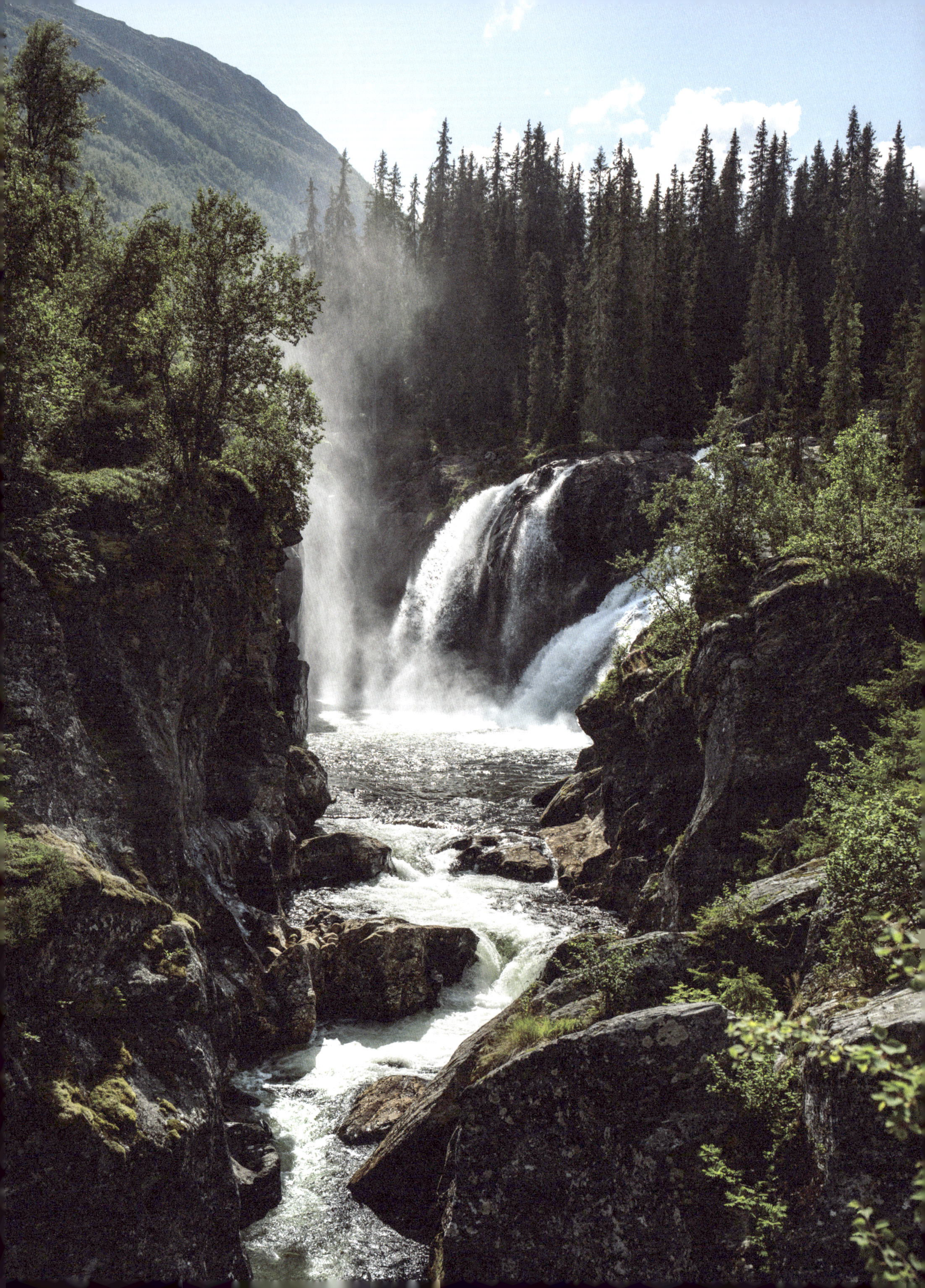

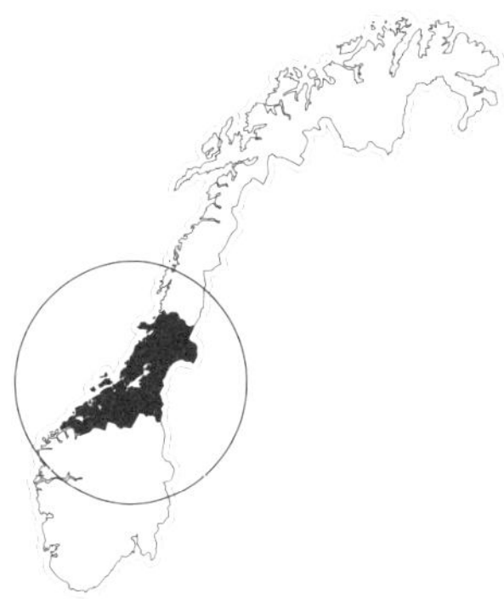

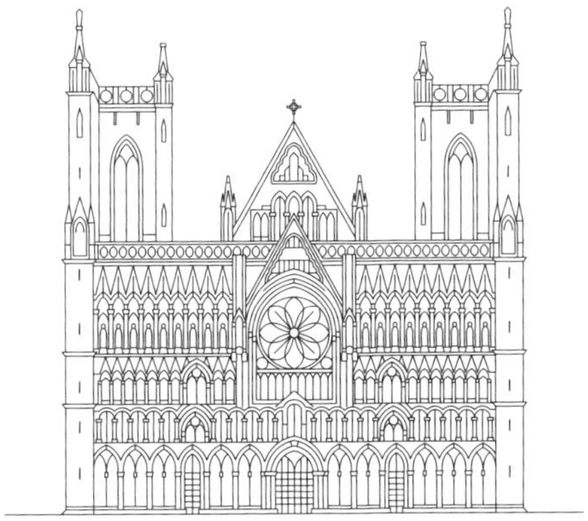

BETWEEN THE MOUNTAINS AND THE TUNDRA

CENTRAL NORWAY

AND TRONDHEIM

Central Norway has no reason to be ashamed of its lack of fjords —its many national parks offer a fascinating diversity of scenery that more than makes up for this.

P.128

With a drop of more than 60 ft (18 m), Rjukandefossen is simply one of the most beautiful waterfalls in the country.

OPPOSITE

For many Norwegians there is no better place than Jotunheimen National Park for a little freshwater fishing or hiking, and it might even be possible to catch a glimpse of lynx, wolverines, or wild reindeer here.

In Norwegian mythology, the trolls *(jotner)* chose to make their home in Jotunheimen ("land of the giants"), the name given to this vast area. While the jury is still out on the existence of trolls, it is indisputably the case that Galdhøpiggen (8,100 ft/2,469 m) and Glittertind (8,045 ft/2,452 m) are the highest peaks in all Scandinavia, which may go some way toward explaining Jotunheimen's popularity among Norwegians for its immense scale and unique scenery.

The Sognefjellet Scenic Route snakes along the northern border of Jotunheimen, with a pass at an altitude of 4,700 ft (1,434 m), offering breathtaking views of glaciers while enjoying one of the most beautiful mountain roads in the world. The area's talented chefs (and their kitchen brigades) work with local produce that includes mountain trout, reindeer, and other game, which are served with fresh or fermented vegetables, depending on the season. Some restaurants offer dishes that form a true voyage of local discovery, exploring the region's geography and climate.

For several decades the moose and wild reindeer of Dovrefjell-Sunndalsfjella National Park have shared their home with the musk ox, a large herbivore that had long been extinct there. When fossils of the species were discovered in the area, scientists decided to reintroduce the animal into its former habitat and, after several false starts, a last attempt made shortly after the Second World War proved successful. There are now thought to be more than two hundred and fifty musk oxen roaming wild in the park.

Rondane National Park nearby is a destination popular with hikers, who come to stay overnight in small mountain refuges. The road here passes the Sohlbergplassen viewpoint, from where there is a famous view of the mountain range. It was standing at this very point in 1913 that the artist Harald Sohlberg painted his work *Winter Night in the Mountains.*

Continue north to reach the city of Trondheim, which was founded by King Olav I Tryggvason in 997 and remained the capital of Norway until 1217. It is now the country's third-largest city by population and has become its technological capital. King Olav II played a crucial role in the spread of Christianity among his subjects and was subsequently canonized as Saint Olaf, becoming the patron saint of both Trondheim and Norway. Construction of Nidaros Cathedral began on the site of his tomb in 1070 and the building was to become the world's northernmost Gothic cathedral.

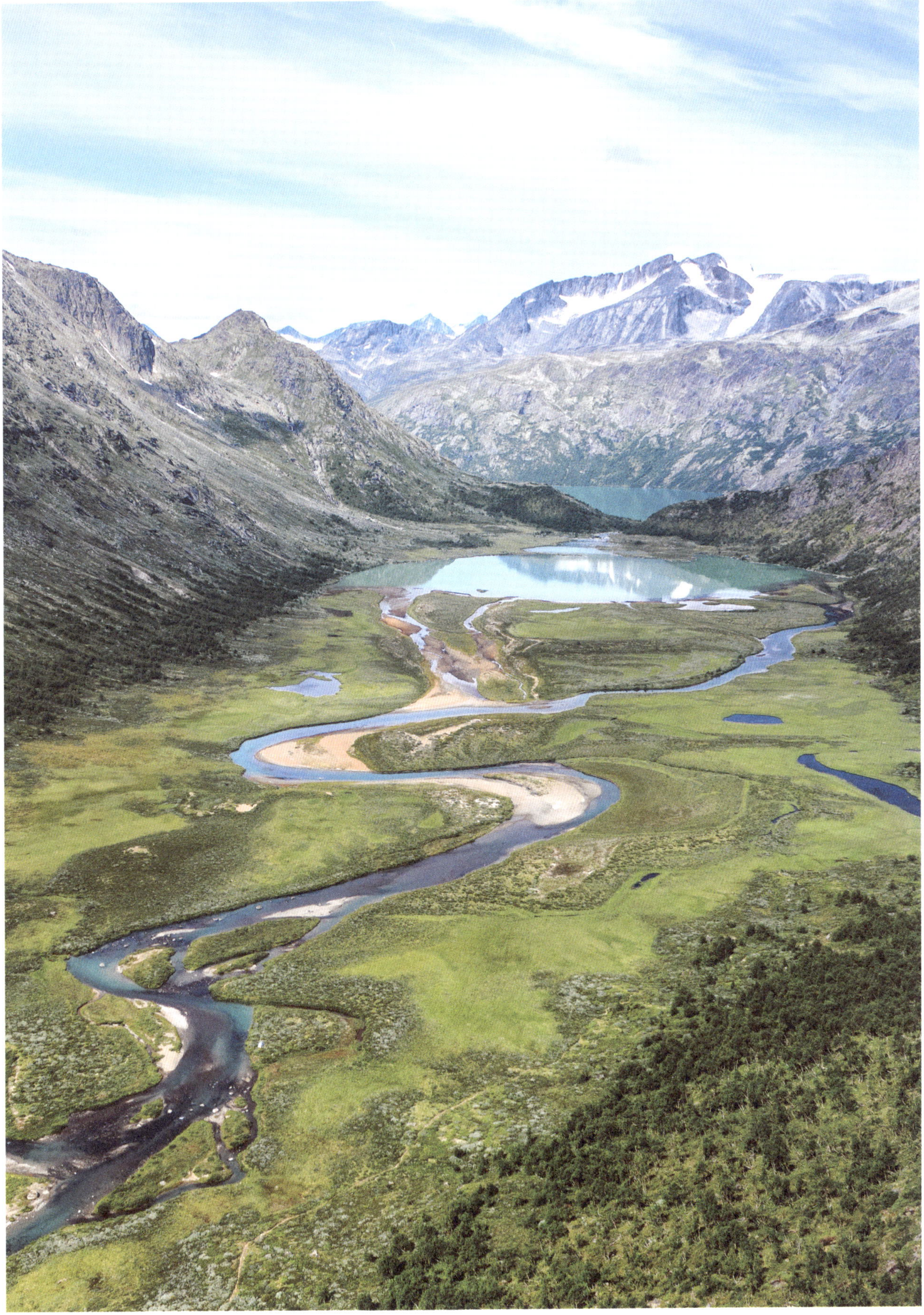

THE ESSENTIALS

29

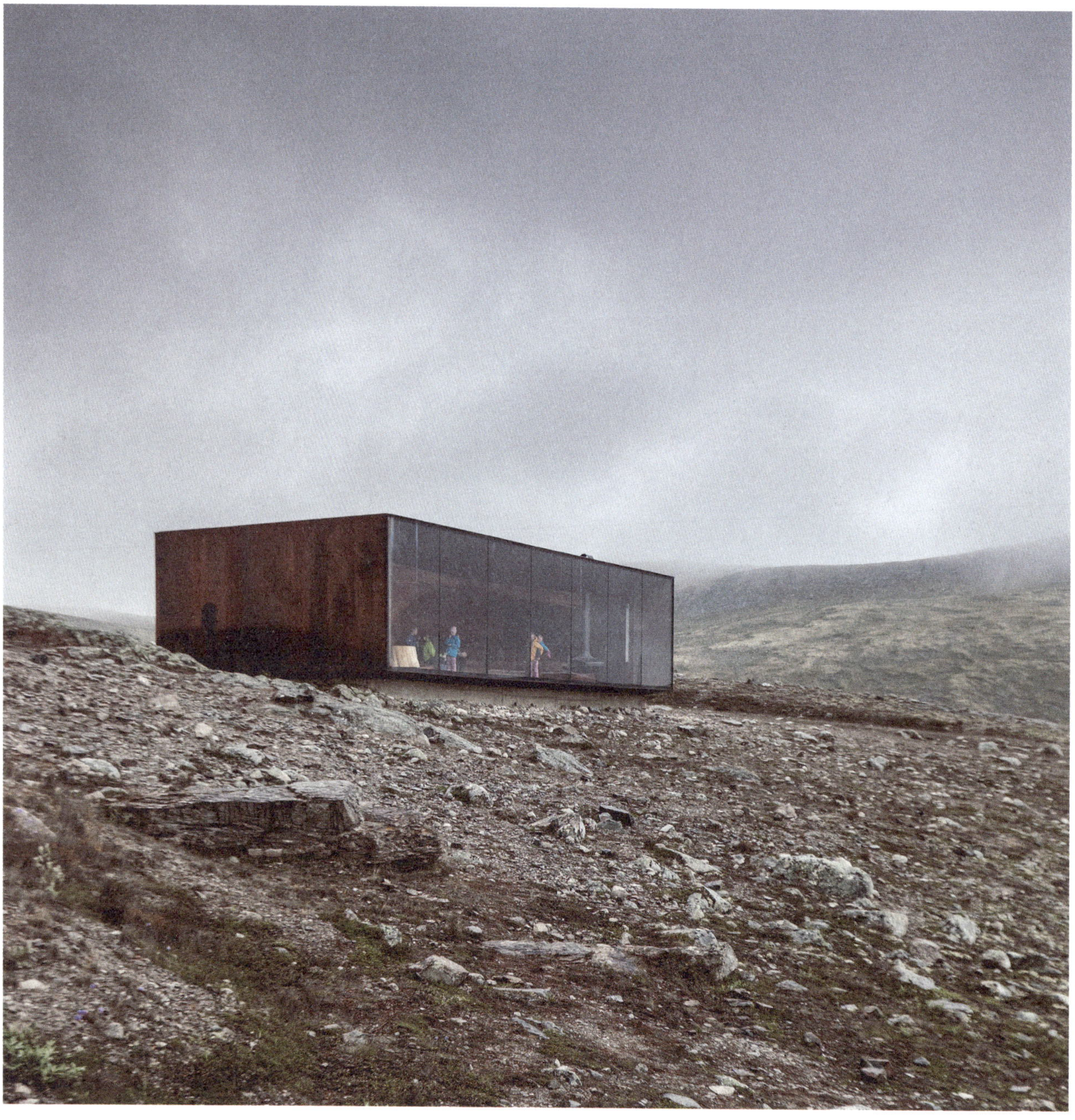

SNØHETTA VIEWPOINT

On a clear day, the view extends all the way to Snøhetta (7,500 ft/2,286 m), Dovrefjell's renowned highest peak. This viewpoint has won a host of prizes for its architecture, including the prestigious World's Best Display Building award in 2011.

30

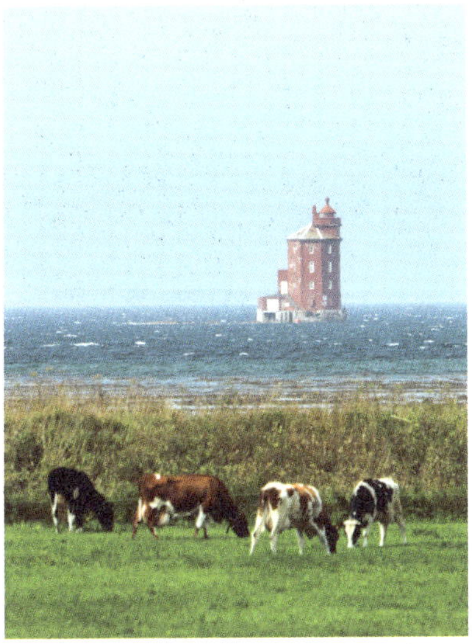

KJEUNGSKJÆR LIGHTHOUSE

The lighthouse was built in 1880 on a tiny rocky outcrop. It is possible to rent and stay overnight in the old lighthousekeeper's cottage here.

31

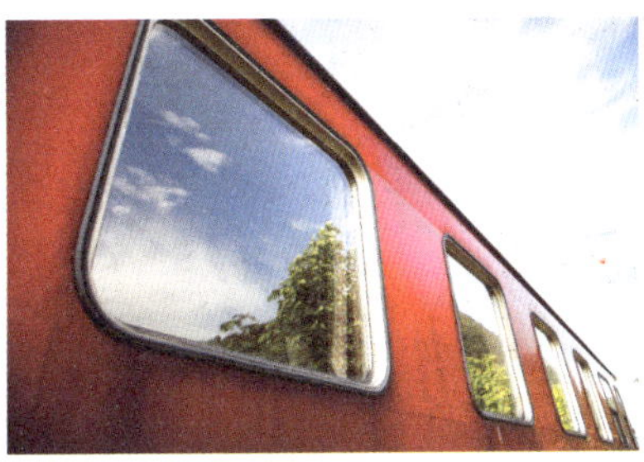

RAUMABANEN

The Raumabanen, which links the small towns of Dombås and Åndalsnes, has been called the prettiest railway line in Europe—the views are stunning.

32

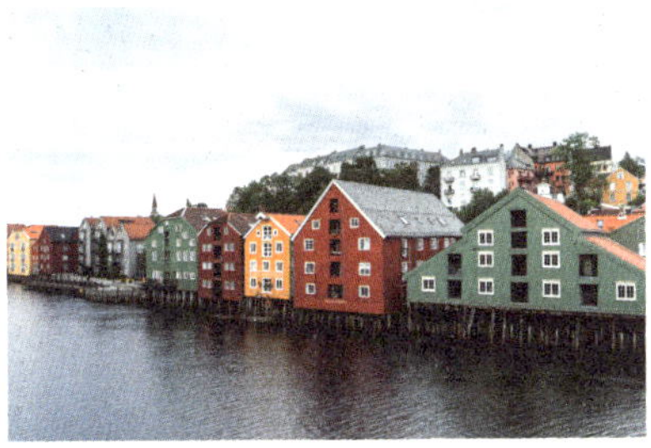

BAKKLANDET

These wooden buildings once housed humble laborers and manual workers, but this area of Trondheim has now become very fashionable

33

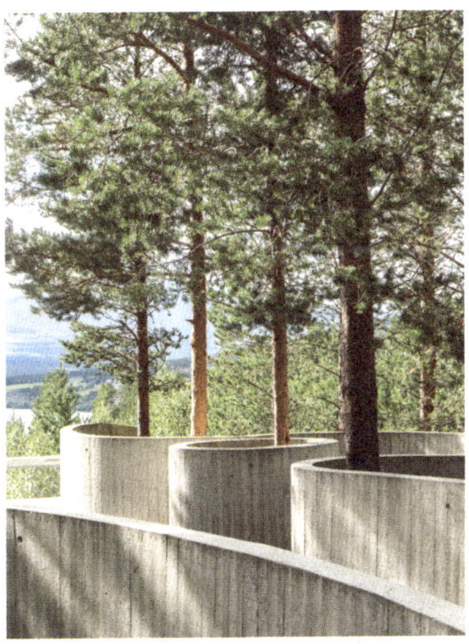

SOHLBERGPLASSEN VIEWPOINT

Come and enjoy the view that inspired Harald Sohlberg to paint his famous *Winter Night in the Mountains.*

34

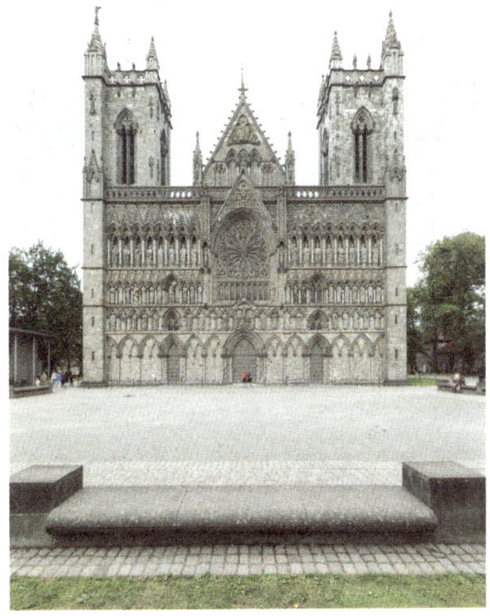

NIDAROS CATHEDRAL

The cathedral was built on the site of St Olaf's tomb. Norway's monarchs have been crowned here since 1814.

35

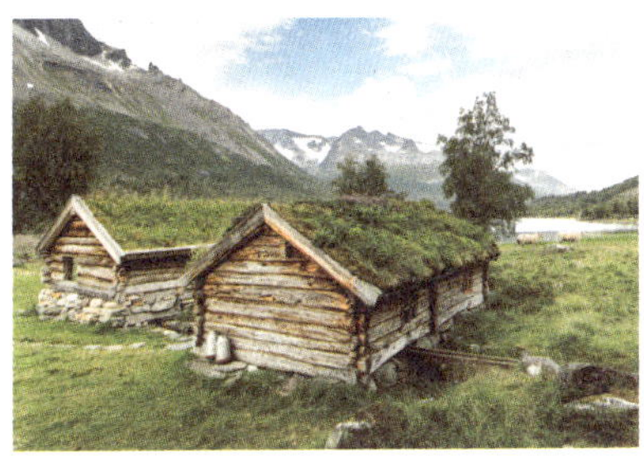

INNERDALEN

The pyramid-shaped mountain known as Innerdalstårnet looks out over a sublimely beautiful valley that is somewhat reminiscent of an American national park.

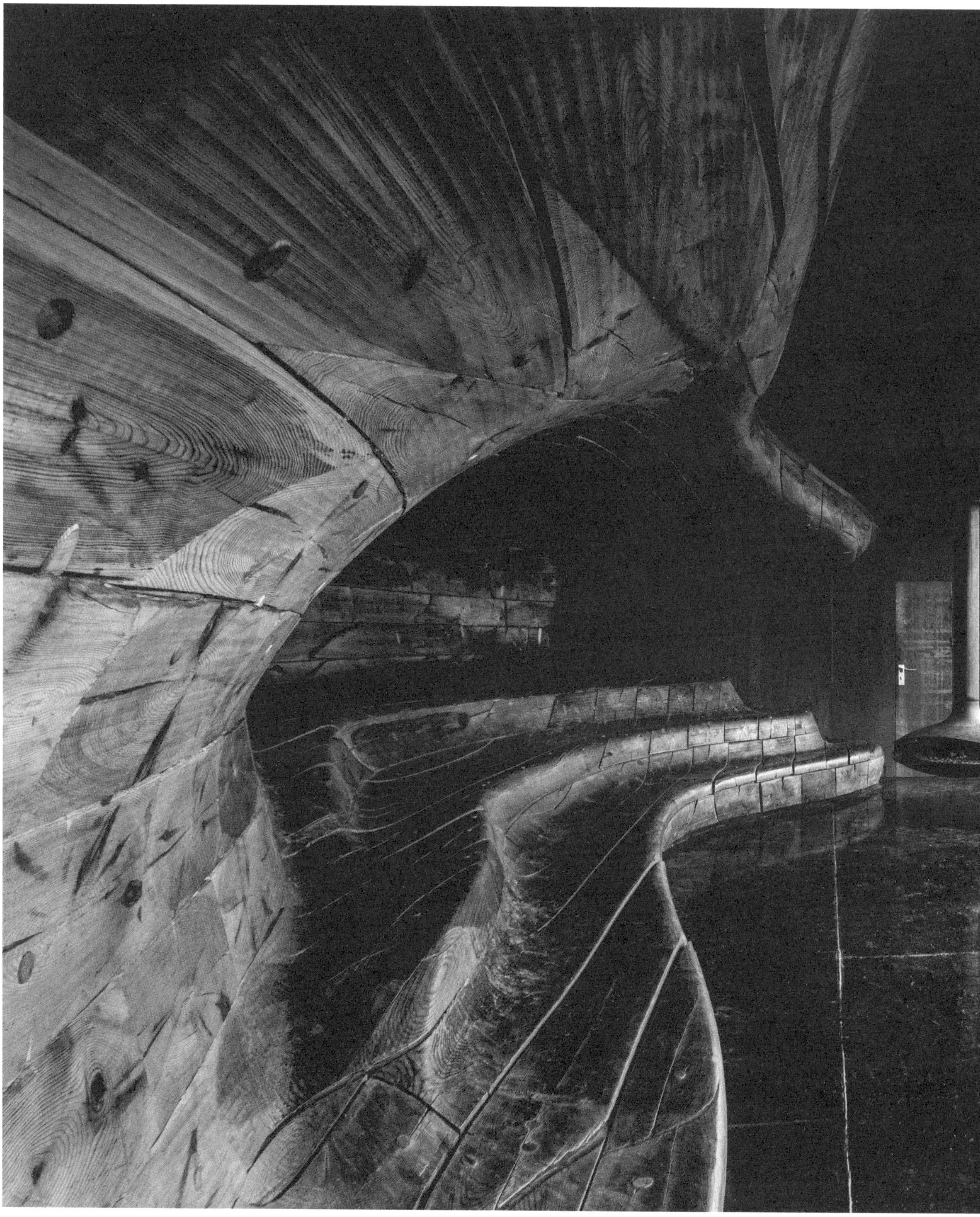

The steel frame of the Snøhetta Viewpoint is fitted with a picture window looking to the north, while the wooden exterior faces south.

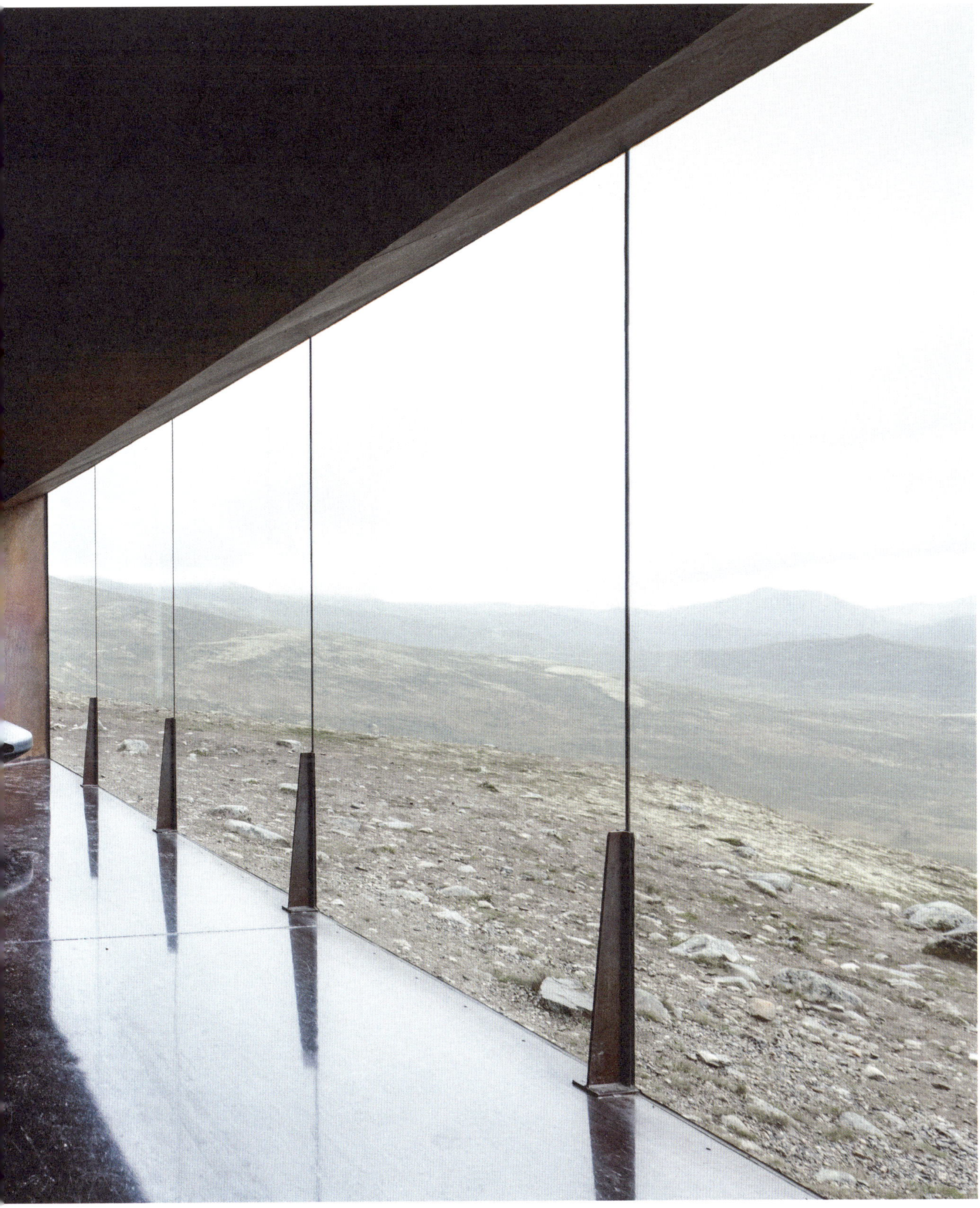

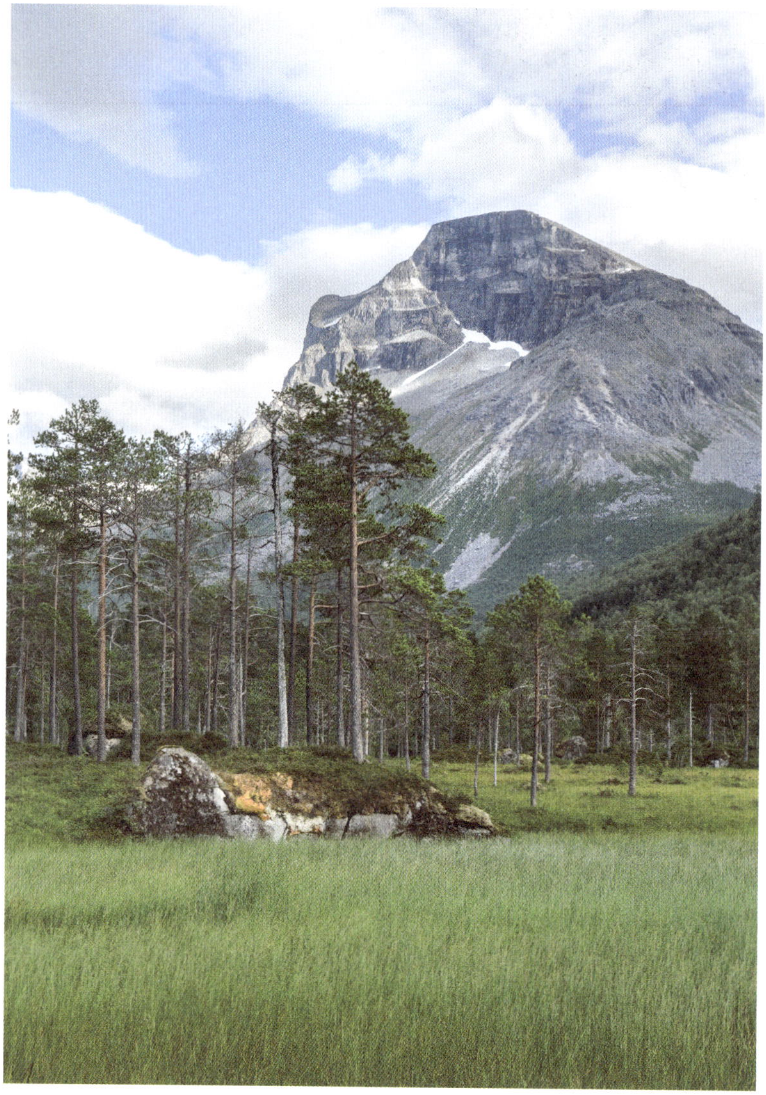

ABOVE

The valley of Innerdalen in the Trollheimen mountain range became the country's first nature reserve in 1967.

OPPOSITE

The scenery in the valley is a patchwork of old farmsteads and summer pastureland, creating a very pleasant, bucolic ambience.

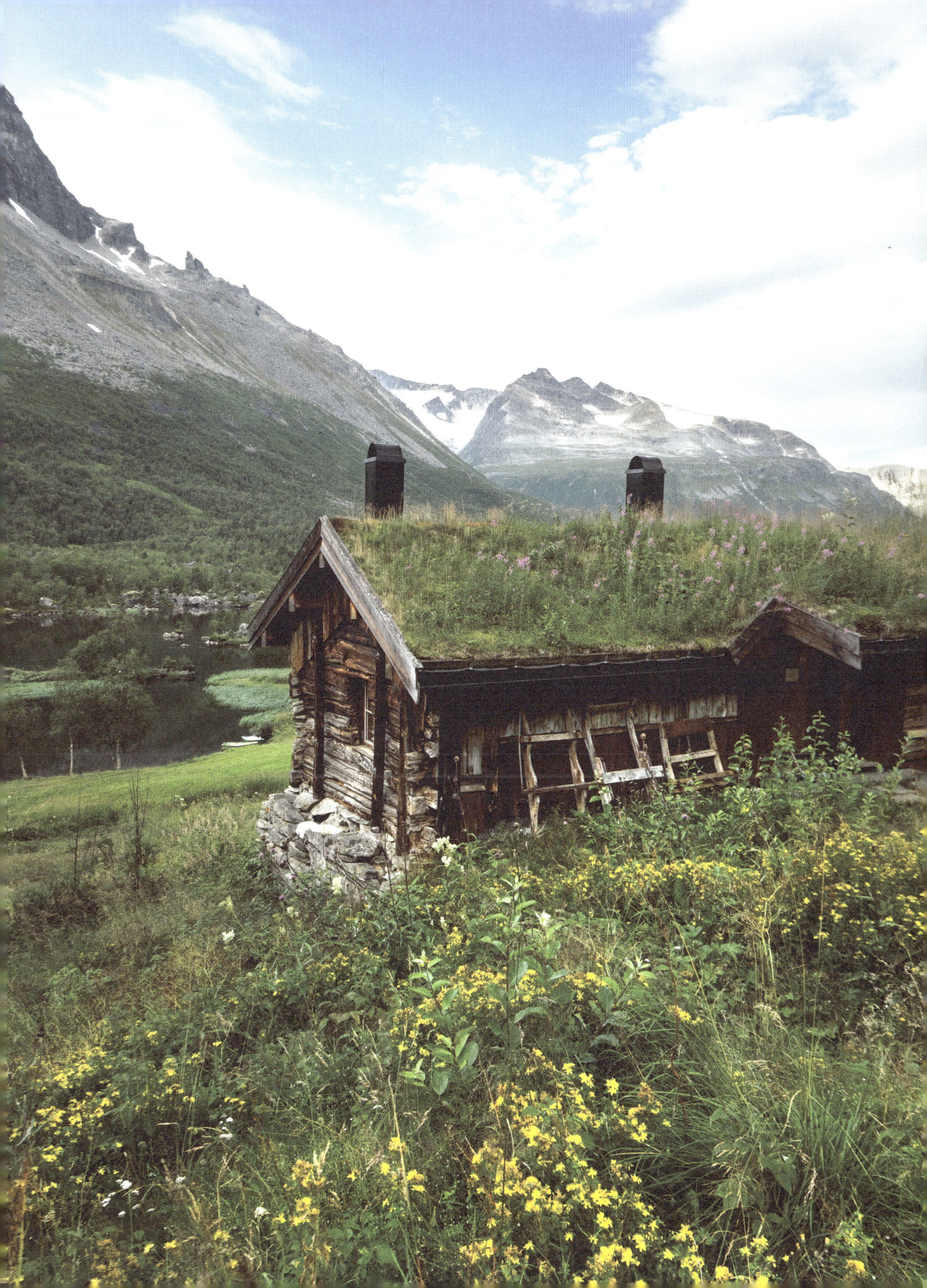

NATURE

MUSK OXEN IN DOVREFJELL

With its population of musk oxen, the Dovrefjell-Sunndalsfjella National Park is the only place in Europe where it is possible to catch a glimpse of this almost prehistoric-looking animal.

During construction of the Dombås railway line in 1913, workers discovered musk ox fossils dating back to the Pleistocene era, prompting a decision to reintroduce this legendary animal to the area. A dozen animals imported from Greenland were released in the region during the 1930s, followed by more in 1947. There are now around two hundred and fifty musk oxen living wild in the Dovrefjell-Sunndalsfjella National Park.

These powerful animals are covered in a thick, woolly coat that is eight times warmer than a sheep's fleece and perfectly adapted to the freezing temperatures of the Arctic winter. The musk ox is a herbivore, eating shrubs, grasses, lichen, and moss, and climbs up to the hilltops of Dovrefjell every winter in search of food. The windswept snow is at its thinnest here and so food is easier to find; the oxen scratch at the ground with their hooves to uncover it.

Herds are typically made up of fifteen to twenty individuals that live for around twenty years. Musk oxen are also found in other Arctic regions, in particular in Canada and Greenland. Genetically, they are actually closer to goats than cattle. The rutting season begins at the end of summer, at which point an army of wildlife photographers descend on the National Park to document the clashes between the males. Two candidates will fight it out during these spectacular encounters until one gives up and, after a gestation period of eight or nine months, females give birth in the spring to a single calf that is already kitted out in its woolly coat.

Visitors generally keep at a distance of about 660 ft (200 m) when observing musk oxen. Although the animal is generally placid, it is capable of choosing fight over flight and will confront threats head-on. Despite its massive body size (weighing up to 880 lb/400 kg), it is a nimble runner capable of charging at lightning speeds of up to 40 mph (60 km/h), so discretion is the better part of valor for the inexperienced observer.

The 7,500-ft (2,286-m) peak of Snøhetta, a mountain that features in many Norwegian legends, looks out over the 650 square miles (1,700 km^2) of the Dovrefjell-Sunndalsfjella National Park. This unspoilt setting is a Mecca for hikers in both summer and winter. Visitors come to roam and observe the wildlife, as the musk ox is not the only animal to be seen in the park. Exercise a little patience and it is possible to catch a glimpse of wild reindeer, moose, and Arctic foxes, not to mention willow ptarmigans, great gray owls, golden eagles, and peregrine falcons—all the more reason to visit this small corner of paradise.

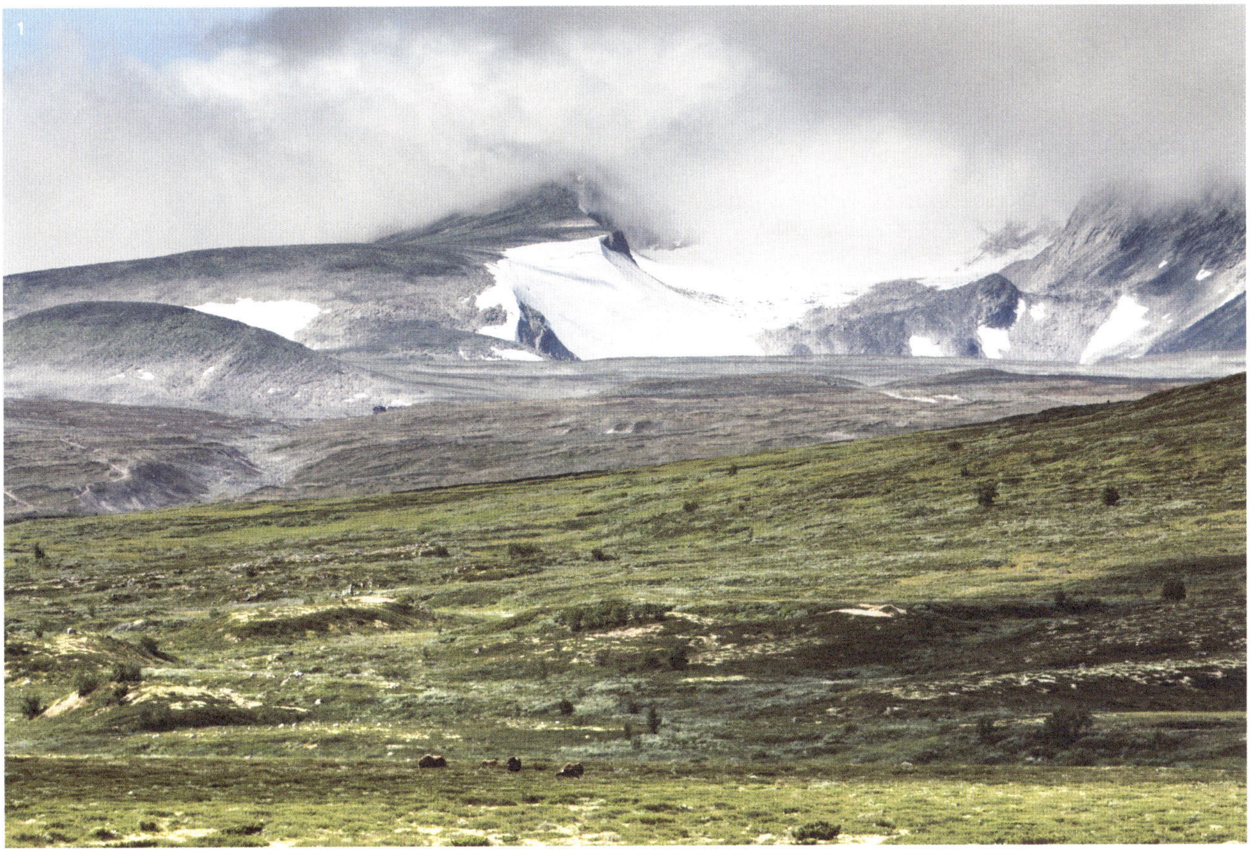

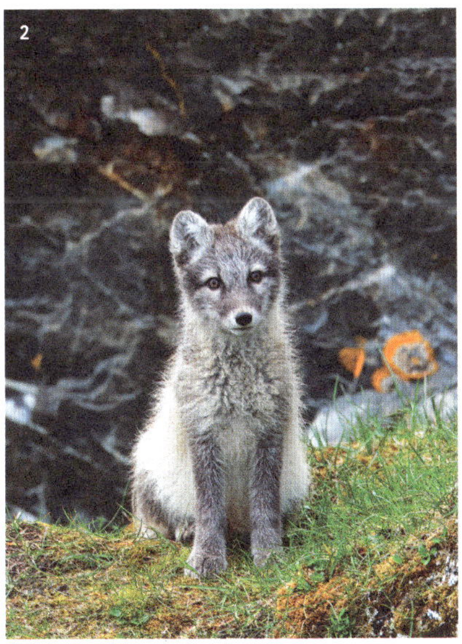

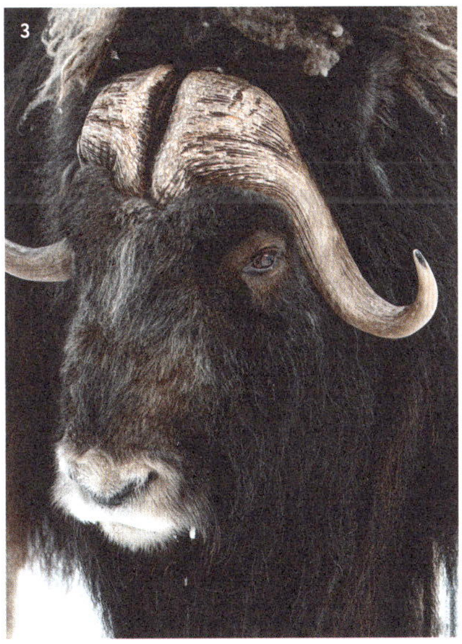

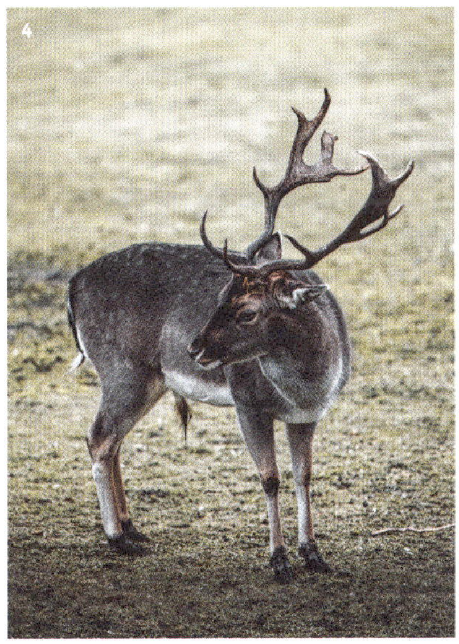

2 / CHANGING COLORS

Each fall, the fur of the Arctic fox changes from chestnut brown via gray to white, allowing it to camouflage itself effortlessly against the snow.

1 / 3 / MUSKY ODOR

The males produce musk, a strong-smelling substance, from glands near their eyes.

4 / A CROSS-BRED POPULATION

Unlike those found in Dovrefjell, reindeer found elsewhere in Norway are either of European origin or are crossbreeds.

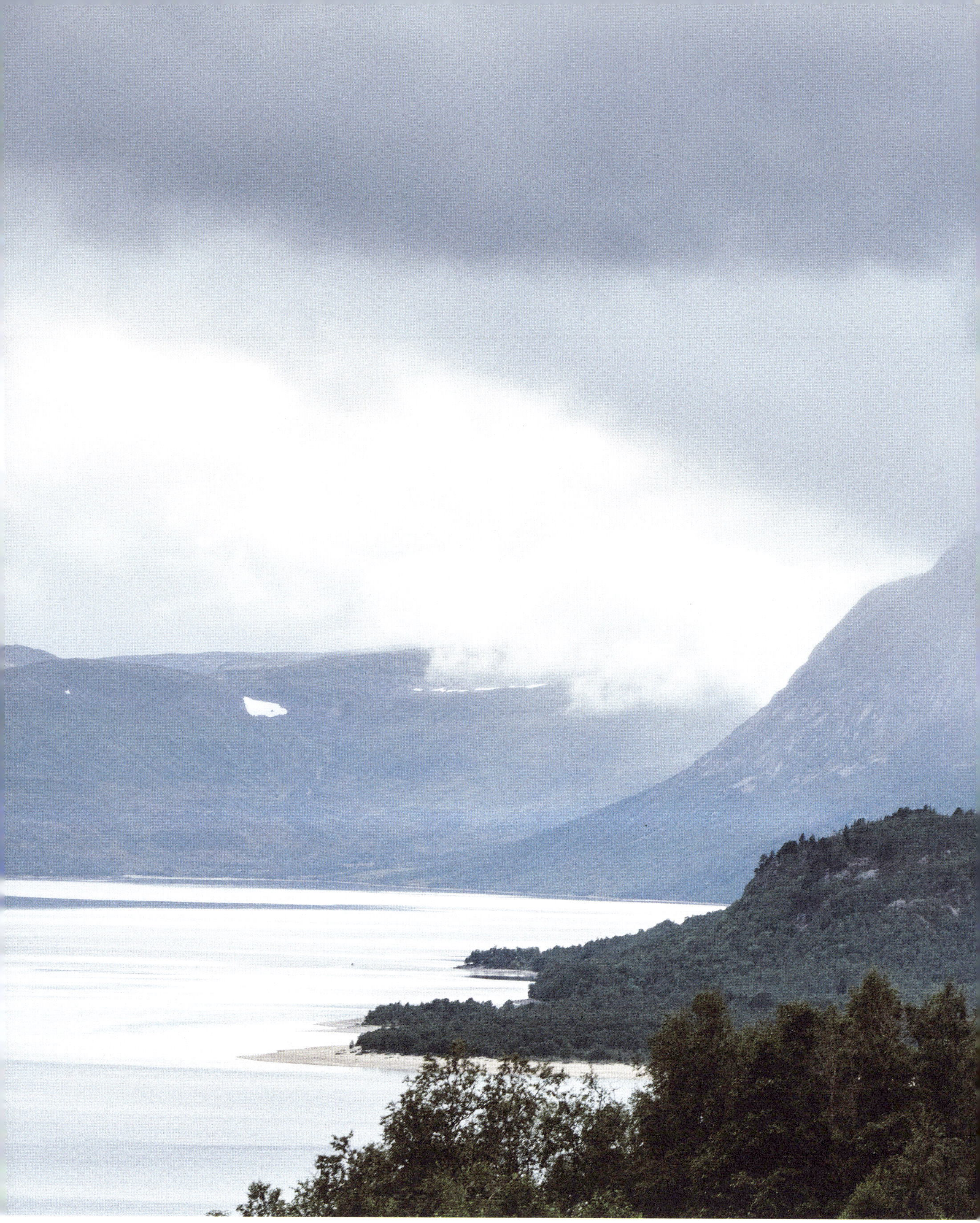

The Trollheimen mountains look out over the lake at Gjevillvatnet. A large number of arrowheads and other Stone Age artifacts have been unearthed in the region.

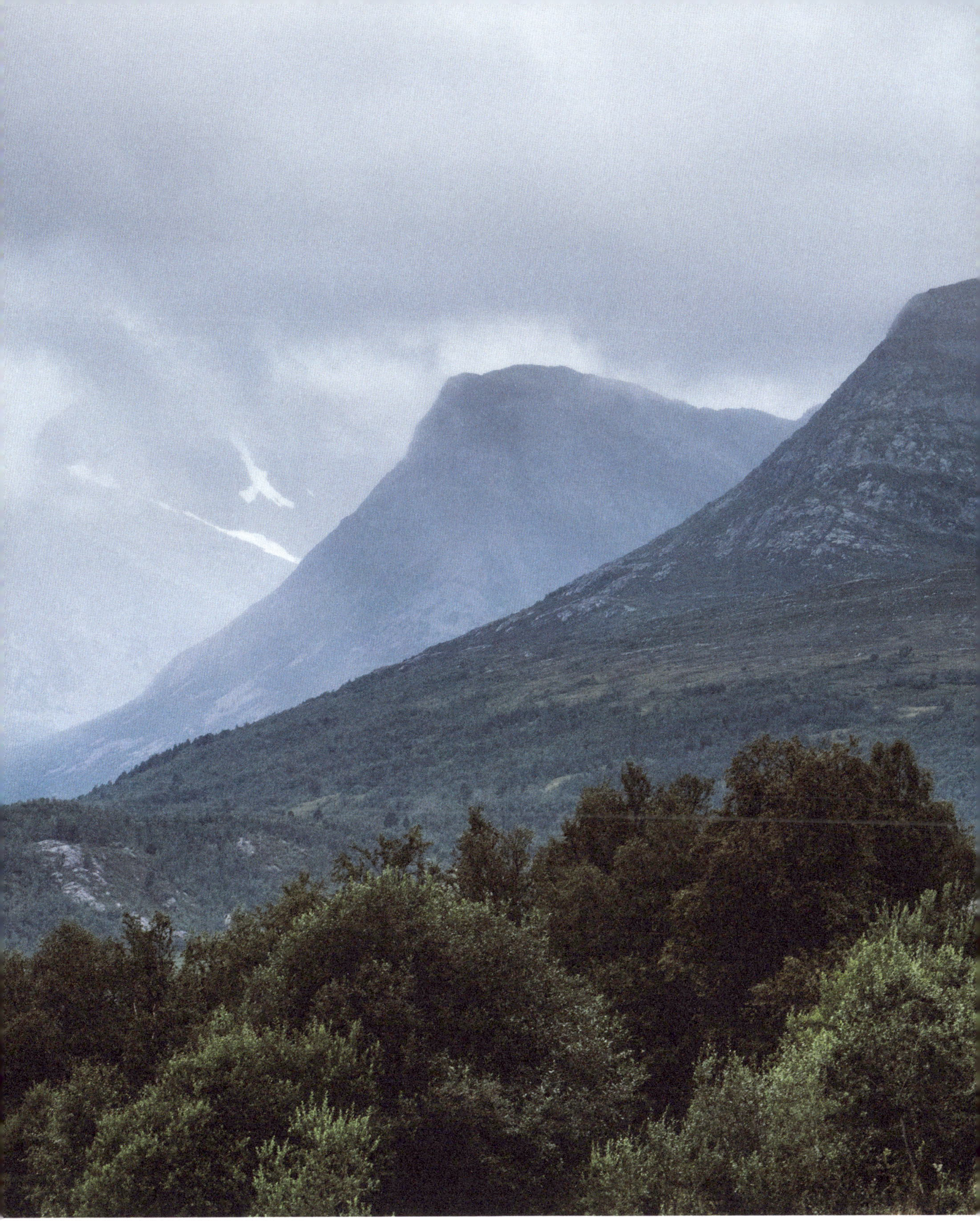

EXCURSION

THE SOGNEFJELLET SCENIC ROUTE

ON THE ROOF OF THE WORLD

The views of the Jotunheimen glaciers from the highest mountain road in Northern Europe are stunning.

The Sognefjellet Scenic Route is considered one of the most beautiful highways in the world and was designated Norway's first official panoramic route in 1997. The country now has eighteen *Nasjonale Turistveger* in a program aimed at showcasing the country's unique and picturesque scenery from a national network of tourist routes.

The route was opened in 1938 and extends for 68 miles (110 km) along Route 55 between Lom and Gaupne. It passes by Jotunheimen and Breheimen, two national parks with immense glaciers. The road is open from May to November but closes in winter as heavy snowfalls and extreme weather conditions make it dangerous and therefore impassable. When the route reopens in spring, both sides of the road are often lined with towering snowdrifts—an imposing sight.

The Sognefjellet Scenic Route begins in the small village of Lom, which is not much more than a crossroads but boasts a beautiful stave church and excellent restaurants, including BrimiBue. The road zig-zags along between lowland farms that give way to mountains covered in year-round snow. One of these crags, rising 8,100 ft (2,469 m) into the air, is none other than Galdhøpiggen, Norway's highest peak. The upland plateau of Sognefjellet is a wild and unspoiled spectacle of nature ringed by glaciers. There is no point in rushing; it is far better to take your time and to stop off to admire the scenery. There are a number of hiking trails that begin at the roadside and viewpoints offering stunning panoramic views of glaciers are within easy reach.

Previous inhabitants of the region did not have to wait for the road to be constructed to cross the Sognefjellet plateau. A succession of cairns (piles of stones topped with wooden stakes) have been used as landmarks since time immemorial to ensure travelers don't stray off the path in snowy or foggy conditions.

Pause at the Mefjell rest stop to find an artwork by the sculptor Knut Wold. This much-praised piece takes the form of a frame carved into a solid block of stone through which the Smørstad glacier can be viewed.

Continuing west, the view opens up to encompass the jagged peaks of the Hurrungane mountain range, revealing an entirely new landscape. The turquoise waters of Sognefjord finally come into view on the last leg of the journey to the village of Gaupne. And if you have enjoyed this trip, why not take the same way back?

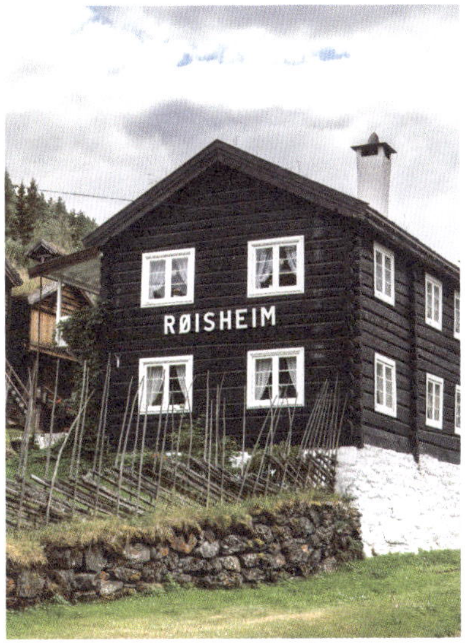

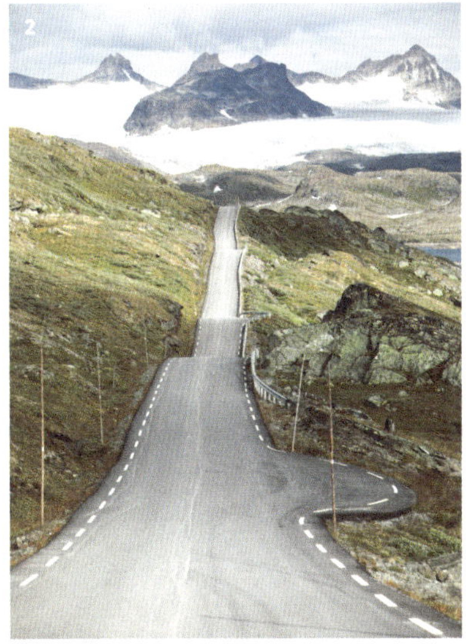

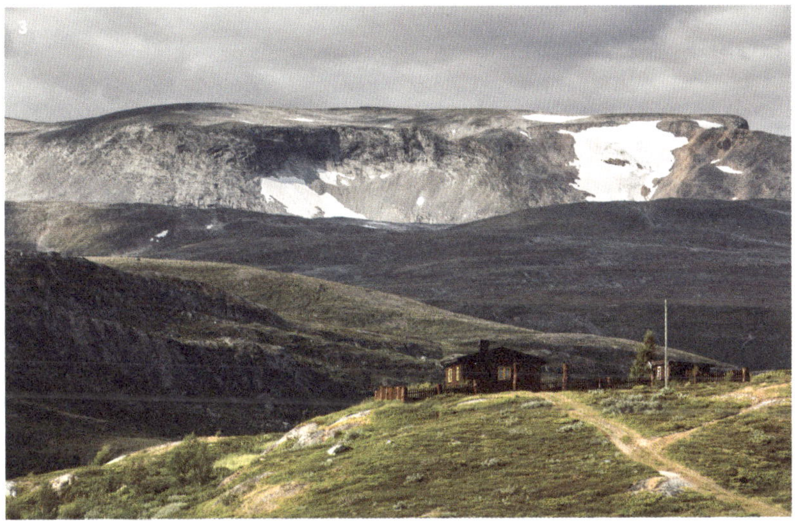

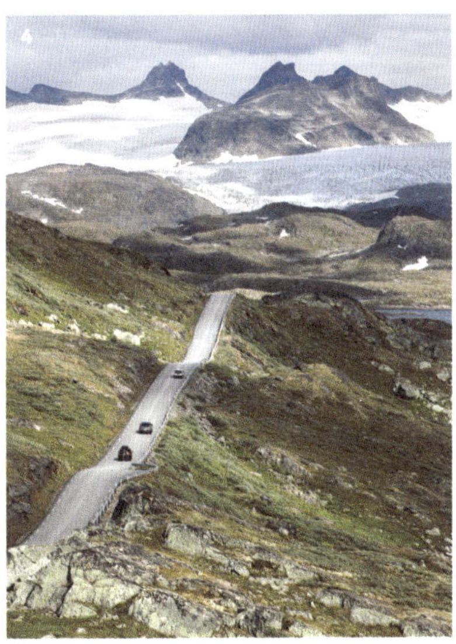

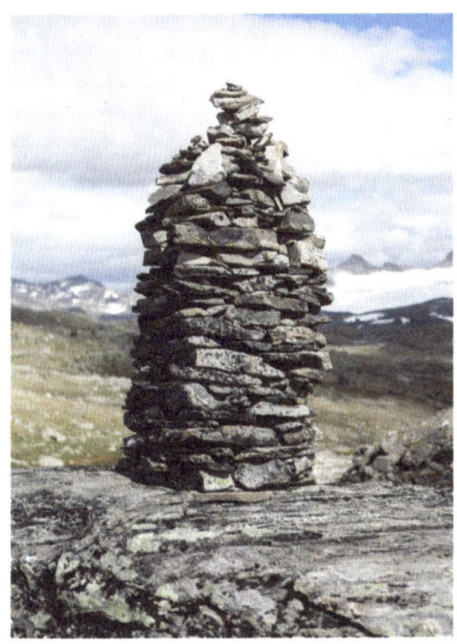

1/ RØISHEIM

This mountain hotel has become a real institution, frequented by travelers and mountain folk since 1858.

2/ A UNIQUE ROAD

The Sognefjellet Scenic Route skirts the national parks at Breheimen and Jotunheimen. The latter has twenty-four peaks that exceed 6,560 ft (2,000 m).

3/ HYTTE

Many Norwegian families possess a *hytte*, a small summerhouse, usually located out in the countryside.

4/ GLACIERS

The immense glaciers of Jotunheimen can be seen from Sognefjellet.

5/ CAIRNS

These stone cairns are several centuries old and are used as landmarks in the mountains during bad weather.

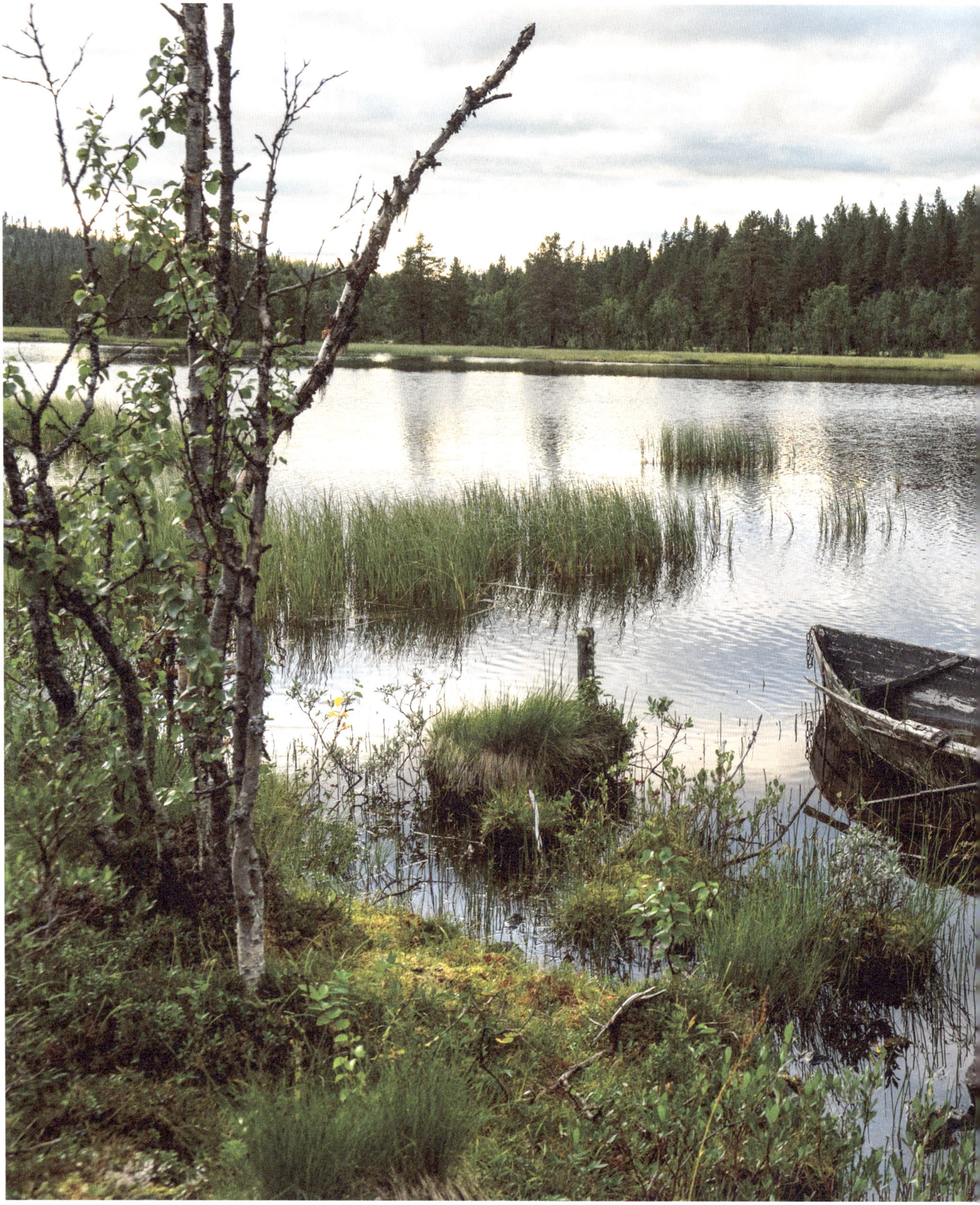

An abandoned dinghy patiently awaits the return of fishermen to a small lake near Oppdal.

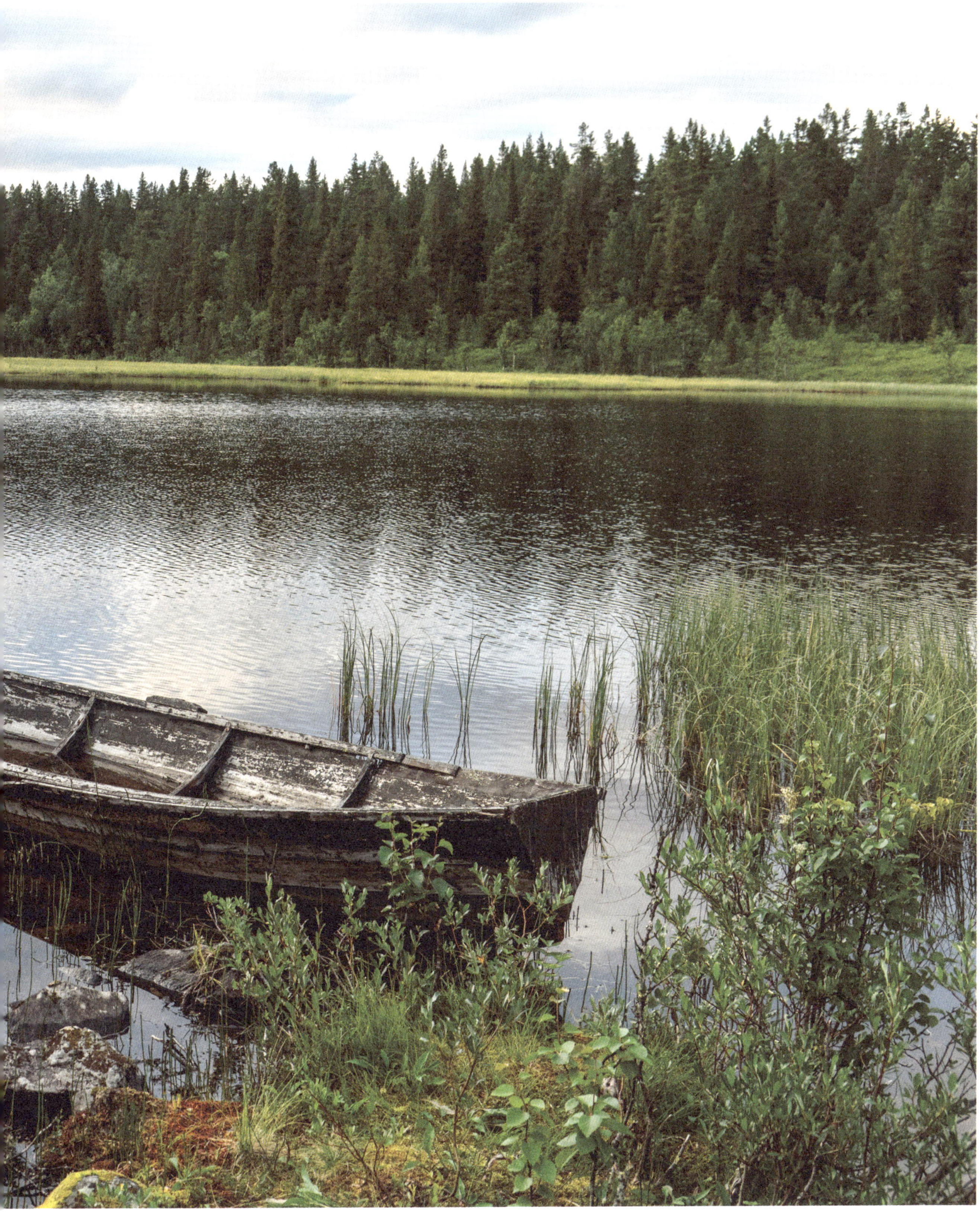

DEEP DIVE

PERMAFROST

Permafrost covers more than 15 percent of the land mass in the Northern Hemisphere; it is found mostly in the Arctic but also in some mountain ranges.

Permafrost is a geological term denoting soil that remains at a temperature below 32°F (0°C) for more than two consecutive years. It is primarily found in Arctic areas, in particular Greenland, Siberia, Alaska, and Svalbard.

Permafrost consists of three thermal layers, the uppermost of which is generally a few inches to a few feet thick and is known as the "active layer" as it melts in summer. The layer below this is permafrost in the strictest sense, with a temperature that consistently remains below freezing even though subject to seasonal variations. The third layer may be anything from several hundred feet to even as much as half a mile thick, as is the case in the Verkhoyansk mountain range in Eastern Siberia. Temperatures in this deepest layer gradually rise in lockstep with depth under the influence of geothermic heat flow, eventually reaching 32°F (0°C) at the lower boundary of the permafrost.

Intimately linked with climate change, permafrost has been closely monitored as an index of global warming by an international network of researchers. When permafrost thaws, it may release methane and carbon dioxide left over from the decomposition of plants and animals that have been trapped in the ice for millennia. The permafrost of the Arctic is estimated to contain some 1,500 billion tons of CO_2. By comparison, in 2019 human activity accounted for the emission of 43 billion tons of CO_2 equivalent.

The thawing of permafrost is already having consequences for those living in Arctic territories. Some buildings constructed directly on the ground in Siberia have had to be abandoned as the ice has rendered them too unstable. The majority of the buildings in Longyearbyen in Svalbard have been built on piles driven deep into the soil and rock, but structures supporting overground water and gas pipes may sometimes become victim to the thawing of the permafrost that takes place in summer. Pockets of water have been forming on the tundra in Lapland, making grazing difficult for reindeer.

Over recent years, this melting of the permafrost has also been uncovering relics from the last Ice Age. Archeologists have discovered arrowheads used by hunters several millennia ago, along with animal remains left frozen in the ice, sometimes in exceptional states of preservation, such as woolly mammoths found on the shores of the Laptev Sea in Eastern Siberia. Russians spend the summer months prospecting for their tusks, the ivory of which is greatly prized by Chinese collectors. Other animals—including lion cubs, a juvenile woolly rhinoceros, and a cave bear no less than twenty-five thousand years old—have emerged from the ground in Siberia.

PERMAFROST

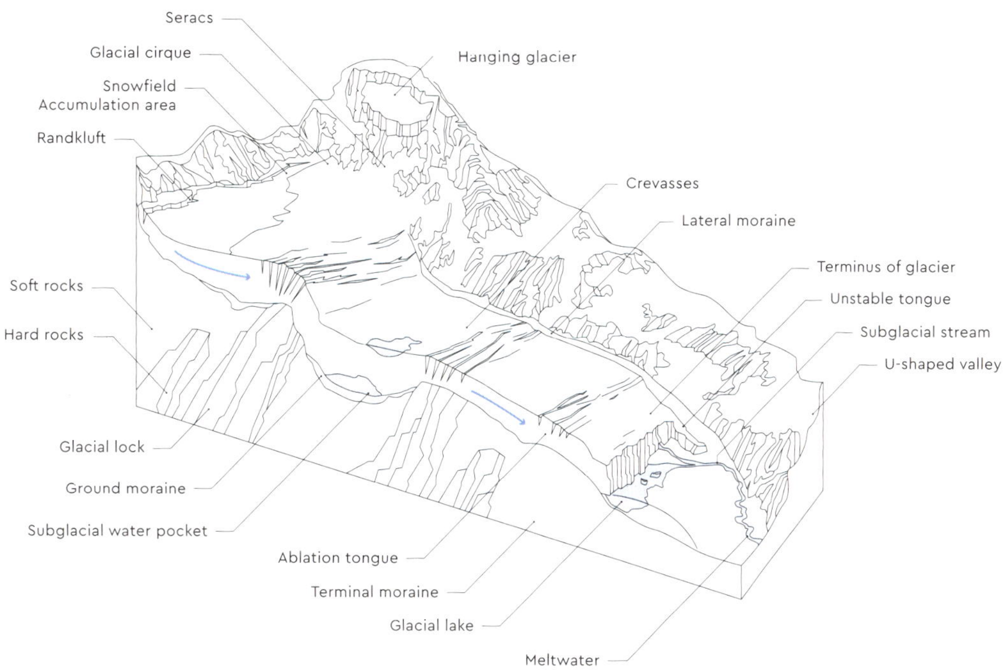

PERMAFROST AND ROCK GLACIERS

Rock glaciers are an indicator of a special kind of permafrost; their very distinctive morphology is the result of a mixture of rock debris and ice.

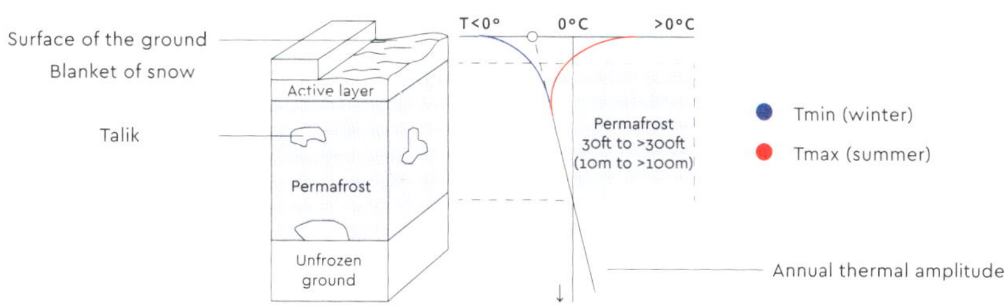

THE FUNCTION OF PERMAFROST

The formation and depth of permafrost is dependent on the climate in which it is located, and in particular on the annual temperature range of its immediate environment. The active layer is the surface layer, which achieves a temperature higher than freezing point during summer, unlike the permafrost, which never thaws.

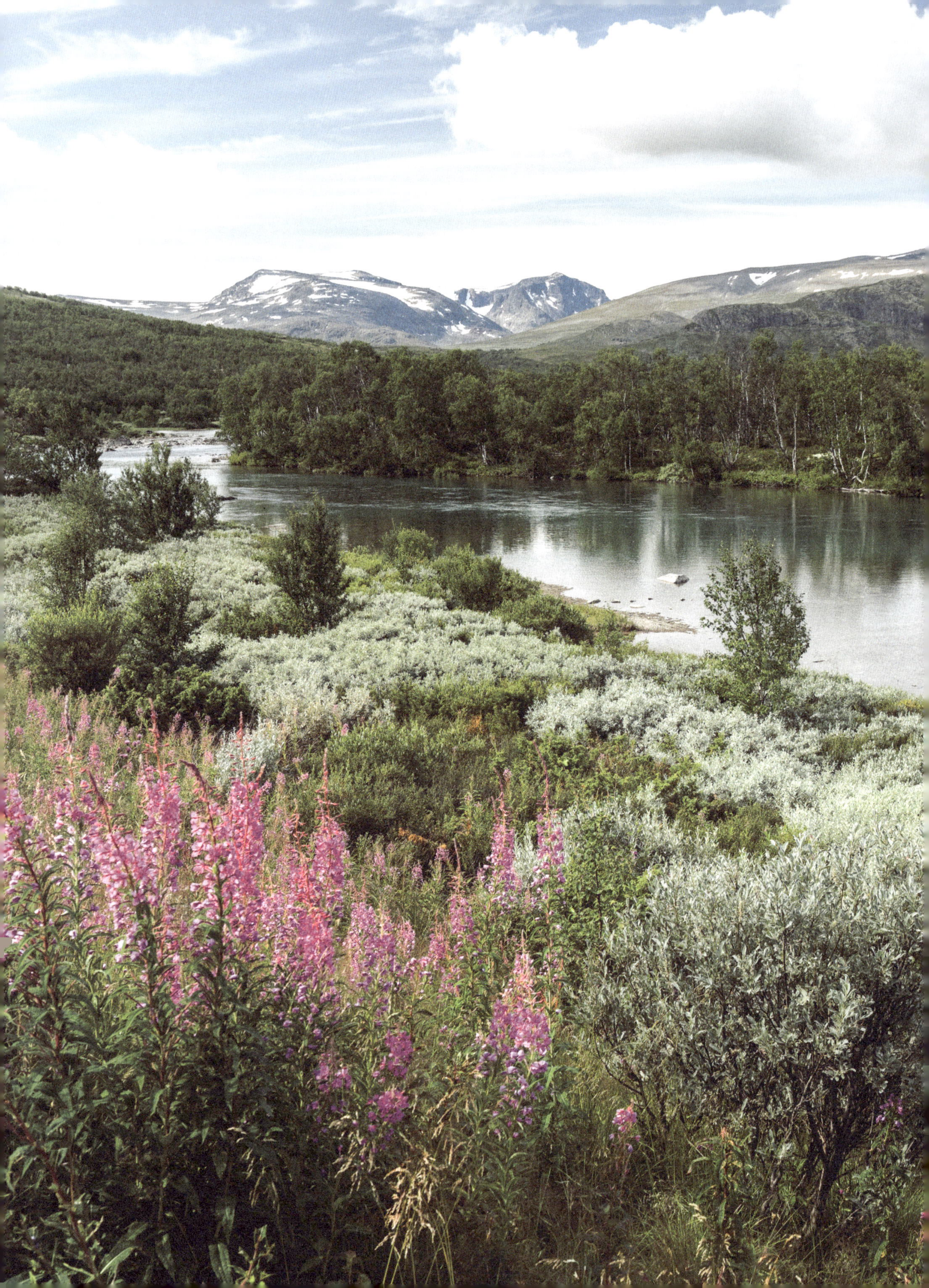

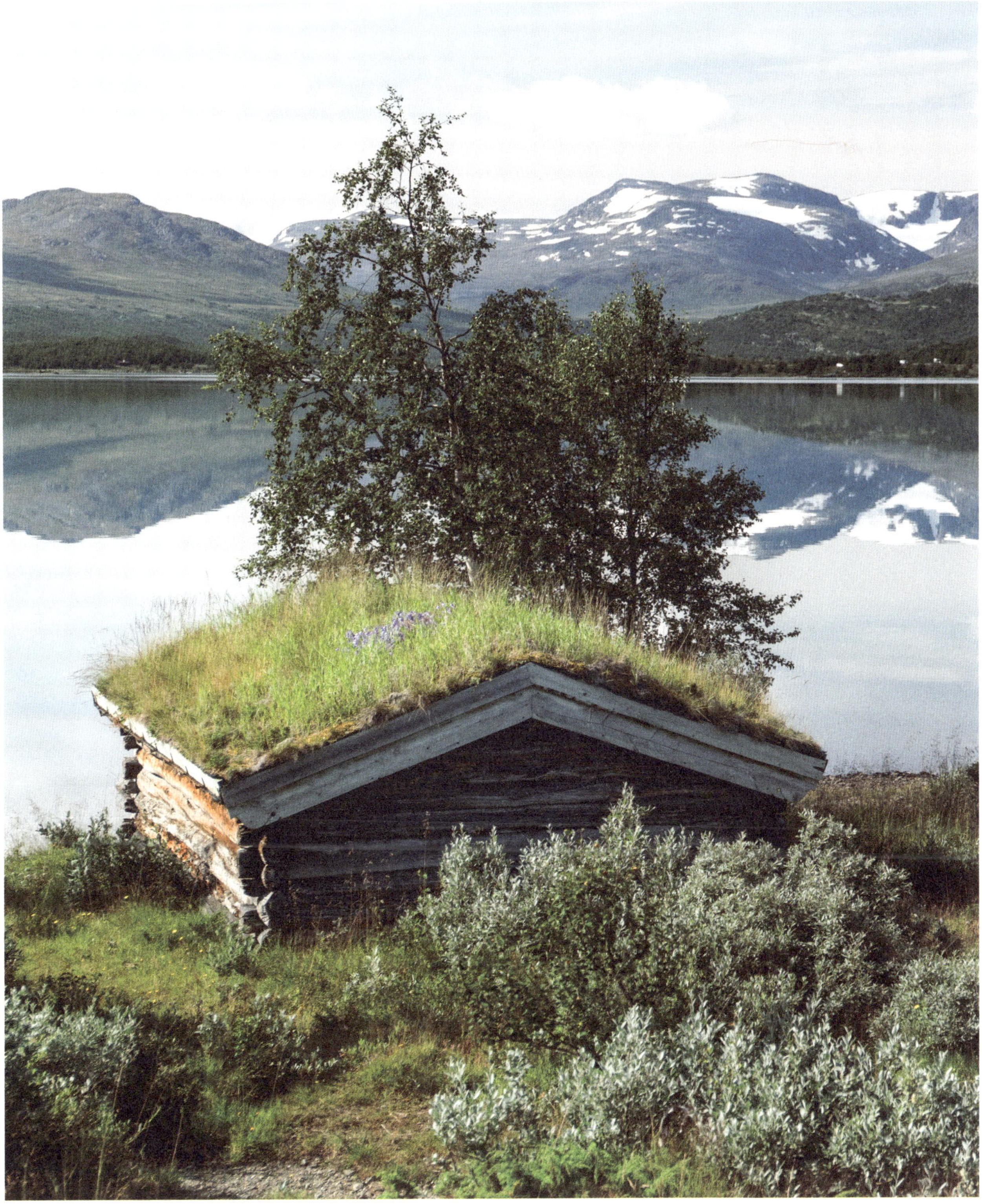

ABOVE

The scenery of Jotunheimen is reflected in the calm waters of this lake.

OPPOSITE

Fireweed grows on the shores of this river, which is very popular for wild bathing.

NATURE

FLY FISHING

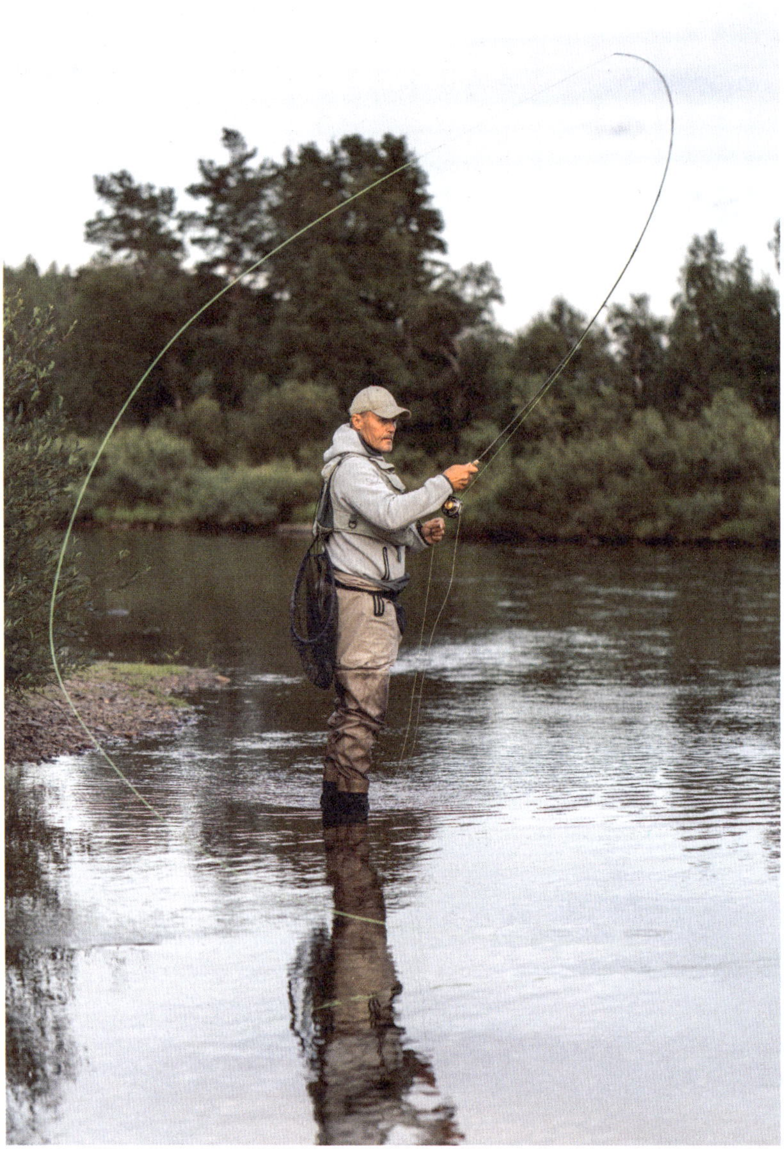

IT'S ALL IN THE WRIST

To cast the bait, the angler whips the rod through the air while simultaneously releasing the line, allowing it to be cast several dozen yards.

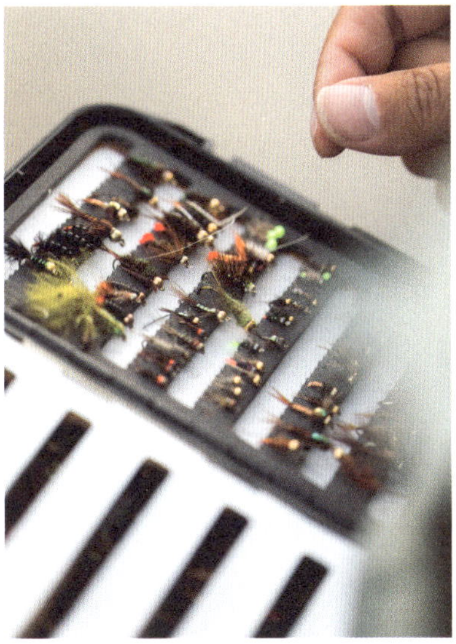

A COLLECTION

Various kinds of flies are used, depending on the location and season.

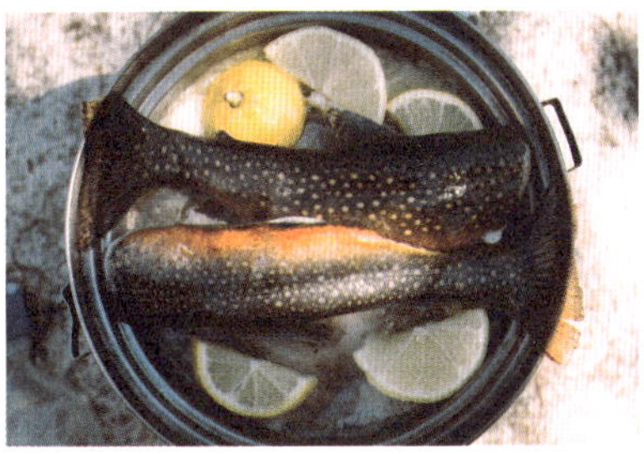

LUNCH IN THE FIELD

Well-prepared anglers have everything to hand to serve up the catch of the day.

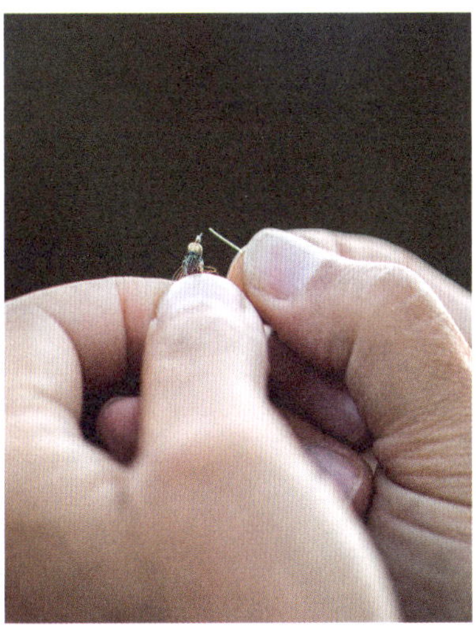

FEATHERWEIGHT

The fly is as light as a feather. Indeed, feathers are often used to tie them.

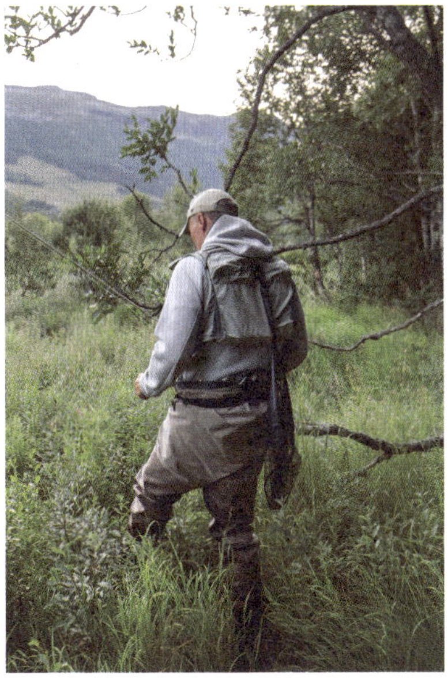

EXPLORER

It is sometimes necessary to venture into the tall grass to find the best fishing spots.

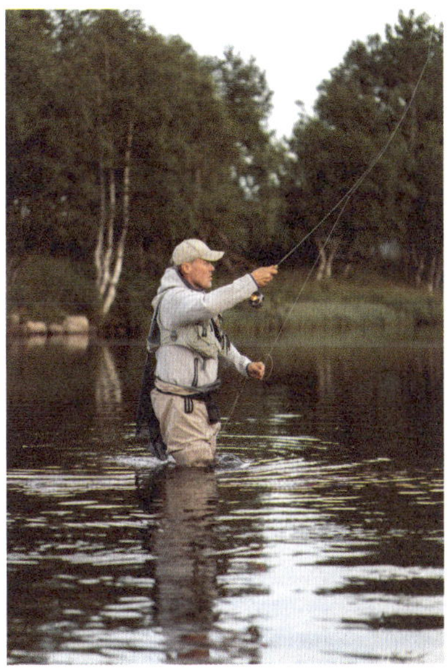

A PLAYGROUND

Norway's many lakes and rivers make it a real paradise for fly fishing enthusiasts from all over the world.

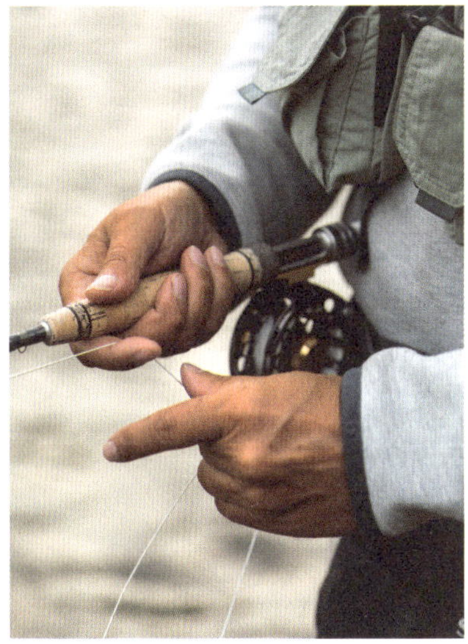

SLOW DOWN

Take your time and immerse yourself in the natural world.

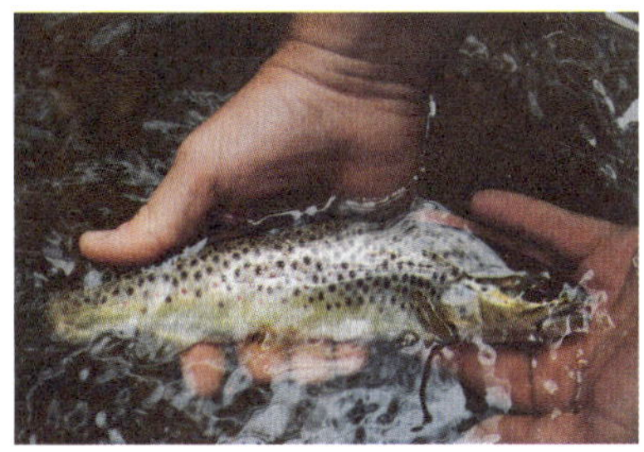

IT WAS THIS BIG

There are sizeable fish to be caught in the Hemsila trout stream.

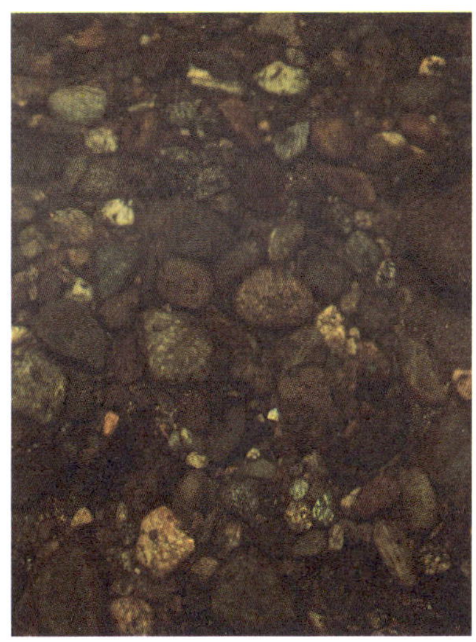

WATERS OF LIFE

The river water is rich in nutrients and can look a little peaty.

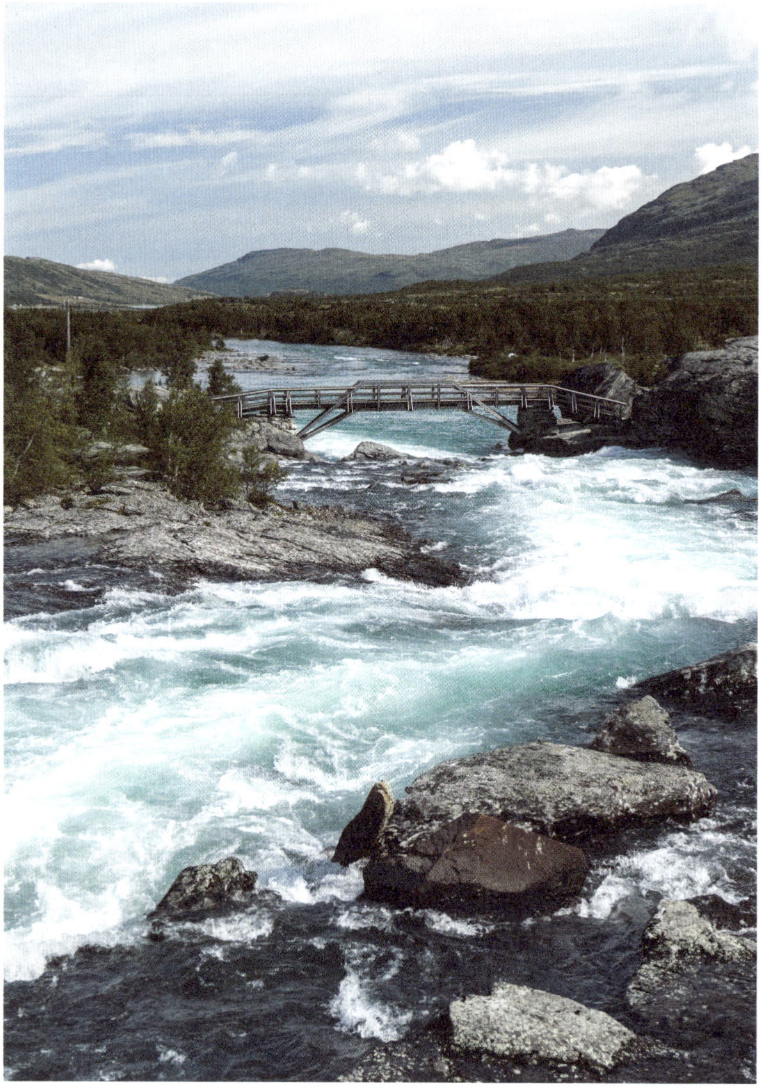

ABOVE

Glacial meltwater gives the mountain streams a unique color.

OPPOSITE

The forest floor is carpeted with lichen in an area untroubled by human activity, much to the delight of reindeer and moose.

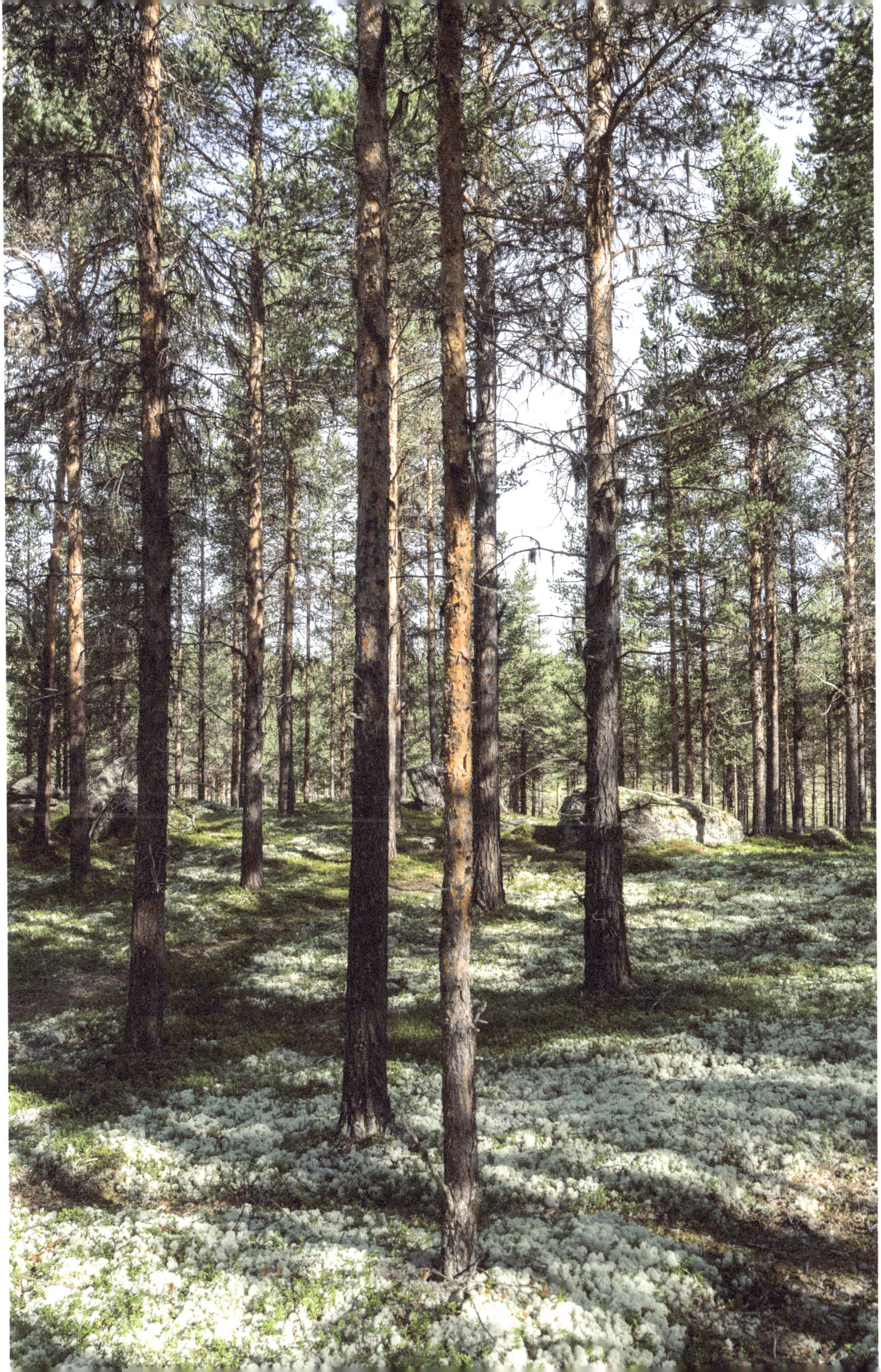

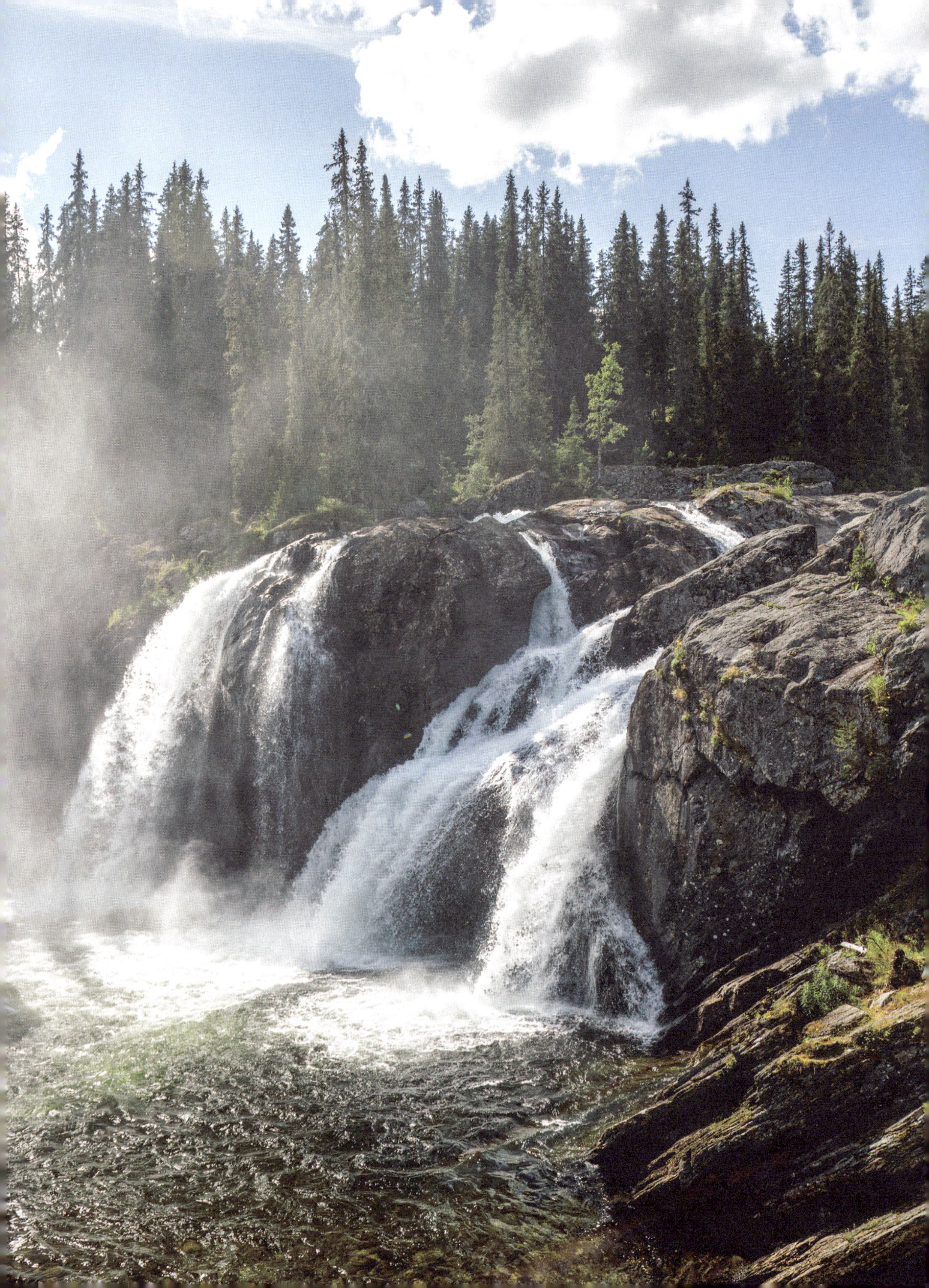

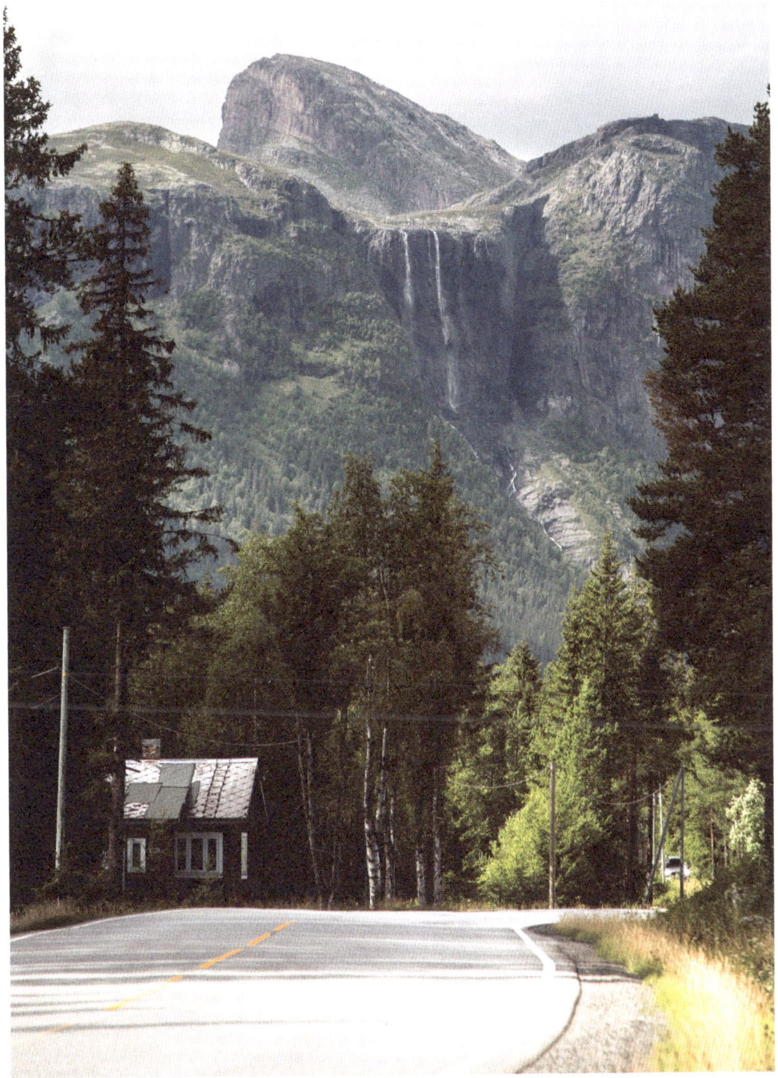

ABOVE

Hydnefossen waterfall has a drop of 500 ft (155 m), dominating the landscape on the way to Hemsedal along Route 55.

OPPOSITE

Rjukandefossen waterfall is a great place for a swim—flow of water and weather permitting.

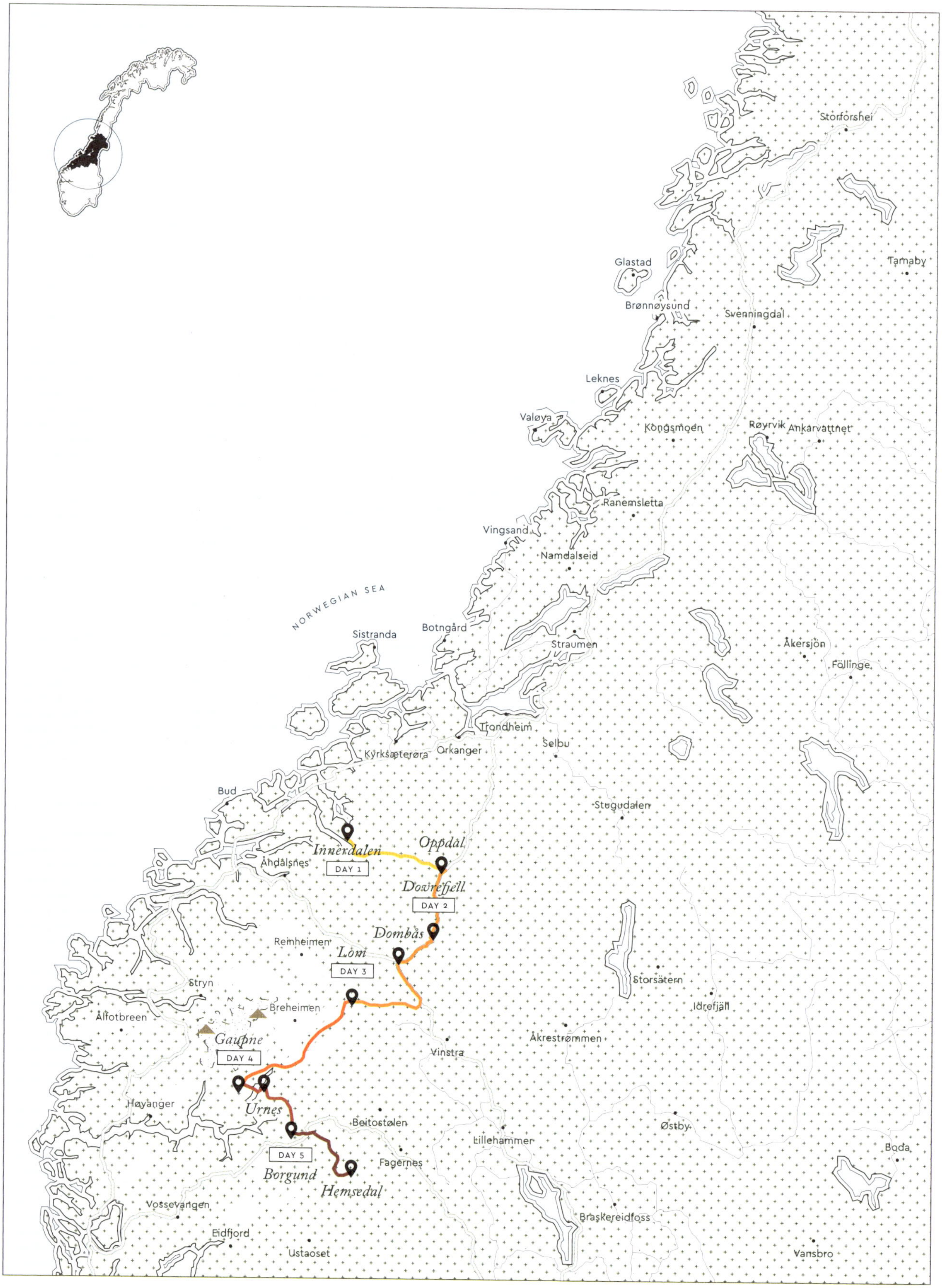
Storforshei
Tärnaby
Glastad
Brønnøysund
Svenningdal
Leknes
Valøya
Kongsmoen
Røyrvik
Ankarvattnet
Ranemsletta
Vingsand
Namdalseid
NORWEGIAN SEA
Sistranda
Botngård
Straumen
Åkersjön
Föllinge
Trondheim
Selbu
Kyrksæterøra
Orkanger
Bud
Stugudalen
Innerdalen
Oppdal
Åndalsnes
DAY 1
Dovrefjell
DAY 2
Dombås
Reinheimen
Lom
DAY 3
Stryn
Breheimen
Ålfotbreen
Gaupne
DAY 4
Storsätern
Idrefjäll
Åkrestrømmen
Vinstra
Høyanger
Urnes
Beitostølen
Lillehammer
Østby
DAY 5
Fagernes
Borgund
Hemsedal
Boda
Vossevangen
Eidfjord
Ustaoset
Braskereidfoss
Vansbro

FIVE DAYS EXPLORING CENTRAL NORWAY

There's more to Norway than fjords! The heart of the country is packed with unforgettable scenery, from Dovrefjell-Sunndalsfjella National Park to Hemsedal.

DAY 1: FROM INNERDALEN VALLEY TO OPPDAL

This valley was designated Norway's first nature reserve in 1967 and now has something of the feel of an American national park. It holds a special place in the hearts of Norwegians but is cheerfully overlooked by most tourists. Spend a night in a mountain refuge and then set off to conquer Innerdalstårnet, a mountain shaped like a pyramid, with a summit rising to 4,764 ft (1,452 m). On the return leg of this lovely hiking trip, don't forget to call in at Renndølsetra farm to try one of their famous waffles before continuing to Oppdal.

DAY 2: DOVREFJELL-SUNNDALSFJELLA NATIONAL PARK, FROM HJERKINN TO DOMBÅS

Follow the E6 south to the Snøhetta viewpoint and shelter from the elements in this unique structure while looking out over Dovrefjell-Sunndalsfjella National Park. If lucky, you might catch a glimpse of wild reindeer or musk oxen, but the park rangers are also adept at helping visitors to get a closer look at these massive beasts. All the same, it is best to keep a safe distance. Musk oxen can behave unpredictably and are able to reach speeds approaching 40 mph (60 km/h).

DAY 3: FROM LOM TO GAUPNE

Sognefjellet Scenic Route, Northern Europe's highest mountain road, is also one of the most beautiful highways in the world, climbing to a height of 4,700 ft (1,434 m) as it skirts Jotunheimen National Park, with breathtaking views of immense glaciers. Keen walkers may like to make a detour to Gjendesheim to hike the Besseggen Ridge trail. Once at the summit, it is clear why Jotunheimen is nicknamed the "land of the giants." The trail ends in Gaupne, just by Jostedalsbreen National Park.

DAY 4: FROM URNES TO BORGUND

Make an early start for Urnes and its stave church where raspberries grow nearby in season. Norway's oldest *stavkirke* was built around 1130 and has been a UNESCO World Heritage Site since 1979. Its north facade frames an imposing portal decorated with exquisite carvings. Take a ferry across the fjord and head to Borgund to see yet another stave church that has been fantastically well preserved and is probably the most spectacular of them all. Near the church, Vindhellavegen, an ancient trade route, winds its way up the hillside and is definitely worth the detour.

DAY 5: FROM BORGUND TO HEMSEDAL

Keen anglers will be delighted by this last section—the Hemsila river has the best trout fishing in Norway. Fly fishing enthusiasts come from all over the world to stand in their waders here for days on end, with an immense waterfall providing a backdrop. It is the perfect way to round off a beautiful trip in the peace and quiet of natural surroundings.

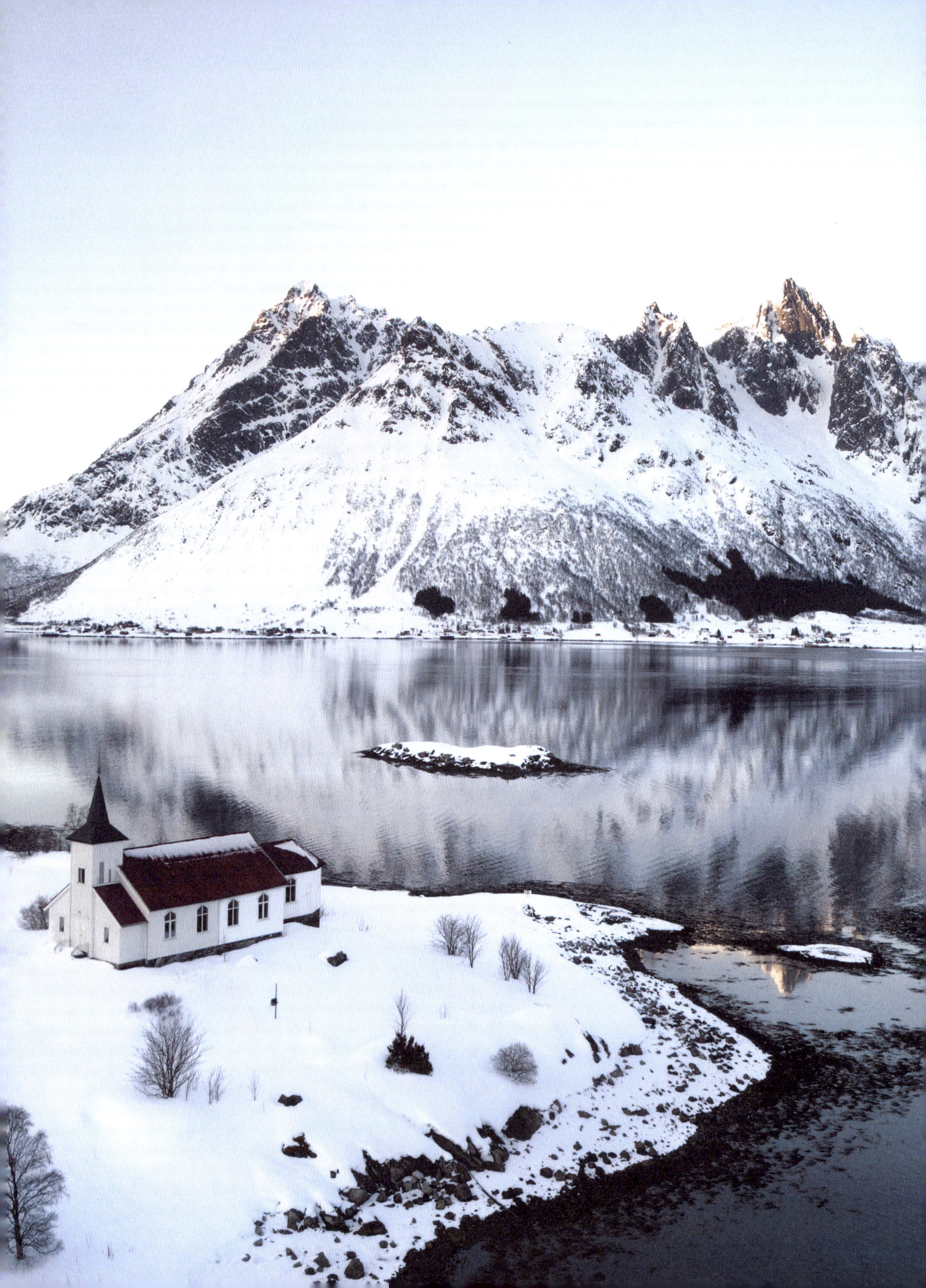

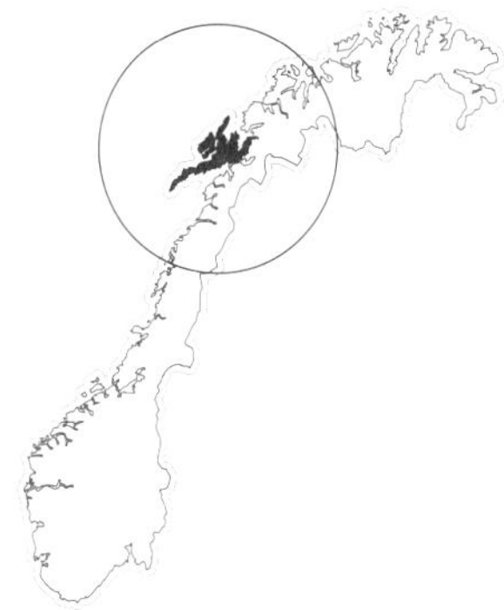

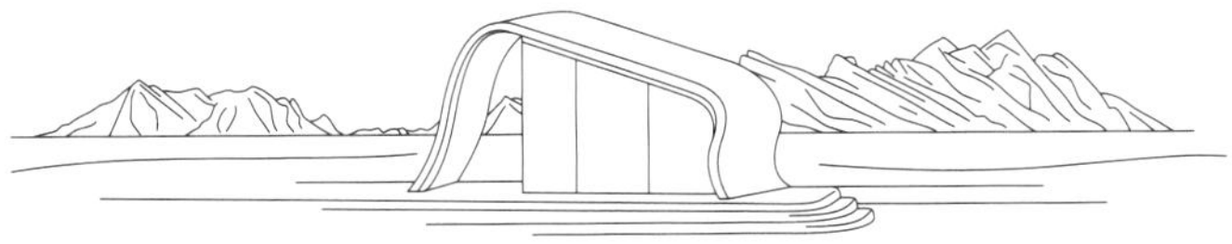

THE ISLANDS

LOFOTEN AND VESTERÅLEN

A region that is simply unmissable, especially for lovers of nature in its most unspoiled state.

P.158

Sildpollnes church draws crowds of tourists deep into Austnesfjorden, a fjord that extends for 8 miles (13 km).

OPPOSITE

Heading further south, the landscape becomes more rugged and the mountains of the Lofoten Islands are lost in the clouds.

With its snowy peaks dropping vertiginously down to crystal-clear waters and beaches of white sand, the region of the Lofoten Islands and Vesterålen has a charm all of its own, with scenery that is quite unusual for the Arctic.

Having been cut off from civilization for generations, these archipelagos now have an excellent road network that includes a host of bridge and tunnels connecting the islands to one another and providing a link with the mainland. The climate is extremely mild, thanks to the Gulf Stream, with temperatures generally hovering around freezing even in the depths of winter, and it is these unique conditions that attract the annual influx of *skrei* (cod)—between January and April, millions of this fish migrate from the Barents Sea to spawn in the waters around the Lofoten Islands. No sooner have the first fish arrived than dozens of trawlers leave port, the processing plants fire up, and a relentless flurry of activity begins to catch and prepare the cod for delivery to the rest of Europe.

Some 1.3 billion barrels of crude oil are estimated to lie buried off the coast, but extraction of these oil reserves is banned to protect this precious ecosystem. After many years of hesitation, the Norwegian government finally caved in to pressure from residents and environmental groups and ruled on the issue in 2019. This is therefore one of the few of Norway's coastal areas that is yet to be exploited for its black gold, and the decision represents a significant volte-face in Norwegian policy.

Numerous hiking trails crisscross the peaks of the Lofoten Islands, leading to breathtaking vantage points overlooking the archipelago as a whole. Exploring the fjords by sea kayak is also an ideal way to enjoy the midnight sun while gliding silently across the water. If the Atlantic swell obliges, there are sure to be waves on Unstad Beach, an Arctic surfing Mecca where enthusiasts from all over the world gather throughout the year.

Lovers of seafood can hop aboard a trawler to catch a delicious cod for supper, while the luckiest visitors might even catch a glimpse of orca or humpback whales hunting for herring, a spectacular sight that will make a trip to the region truly unforgettable.

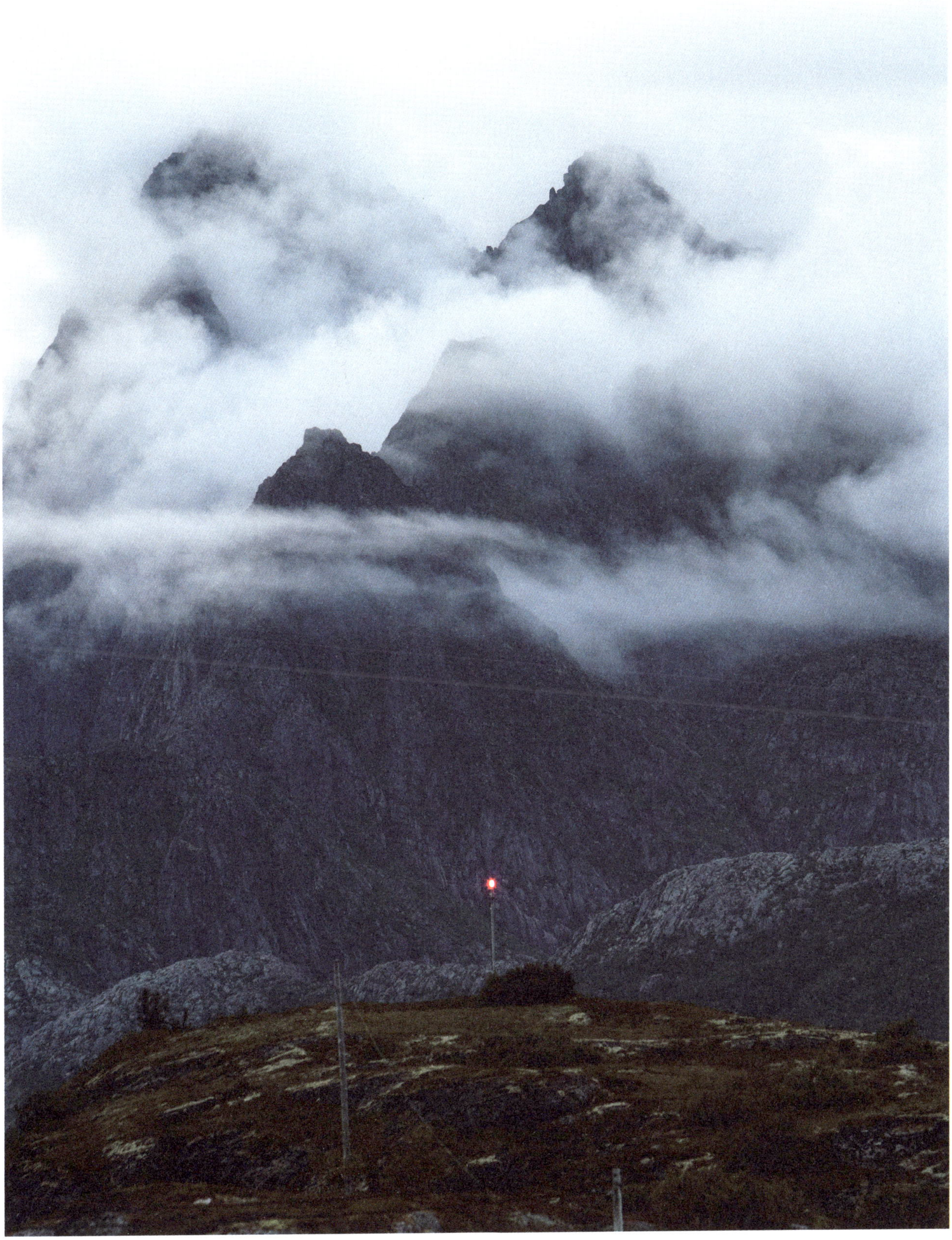

THE ESSENTIALS

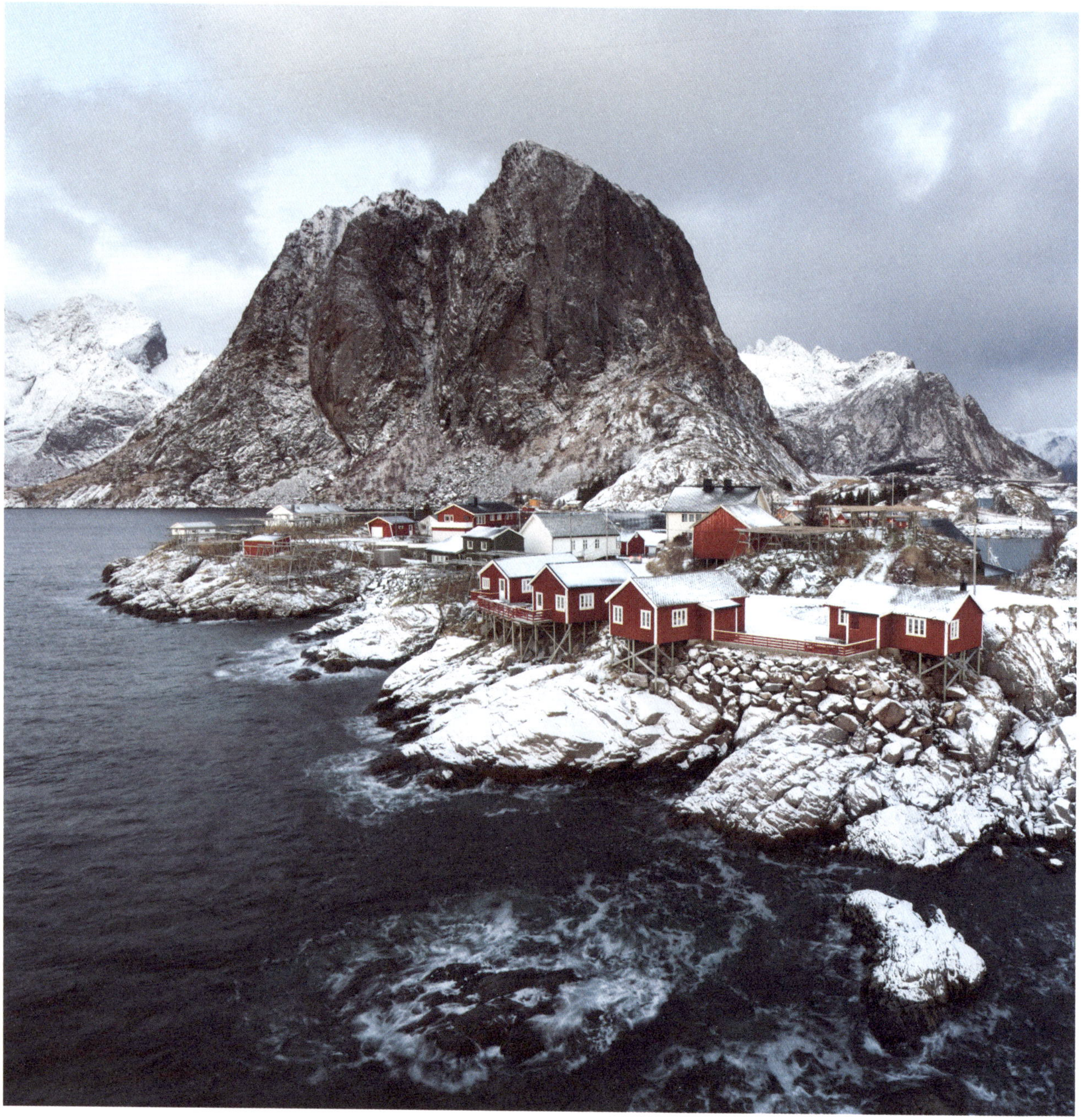

HAMNØY

This view of the fishing village of Hamnøy has to be one of the most famous in Norway. The *rorbuer*, red cabins mounted on stilts, housed fishermen during the cod fishing season every year at the end of winter.

37

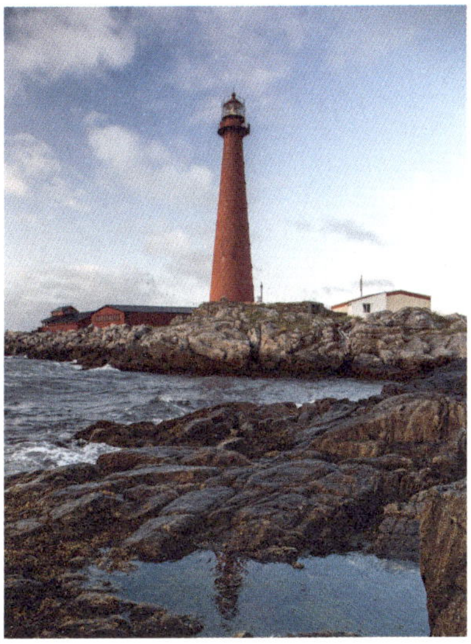

ANDENES

The village of Andenes has a superb lighthouse that is 130 ft (40 m) high; it is also an important center for the study of cetaceans, notably whales.

38

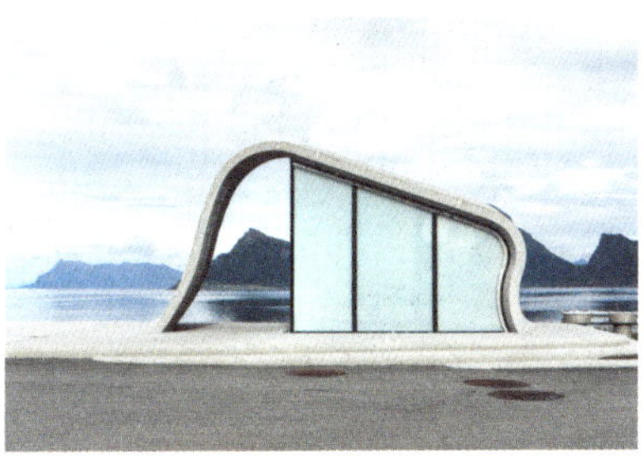

UREDDPLASSEN

The restrooms at this rest area must be some of the best in Norway. The marble used is the same as used in the United Nations headquarters in New York.

39

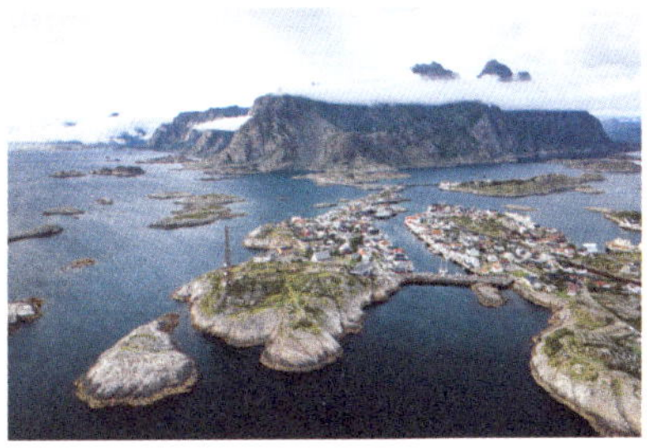

HENNINGSVÆR

This charming and especially well-preserved fishing village has been nicknamed the "Venice of the Lofotens."

40

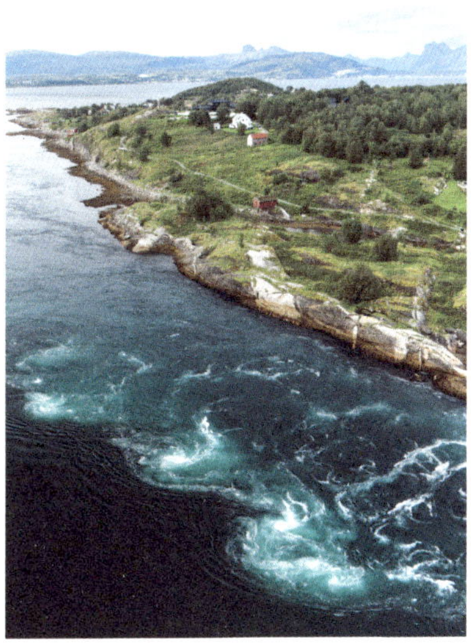

SALTSTRAUMEN

Some of the most powerful tidal currents in the world are found in these narrows, said to have been the inspiration for the Maelstrom in Jules Verne's novel *Twenty Thousand Leagues under the Sea.*

41

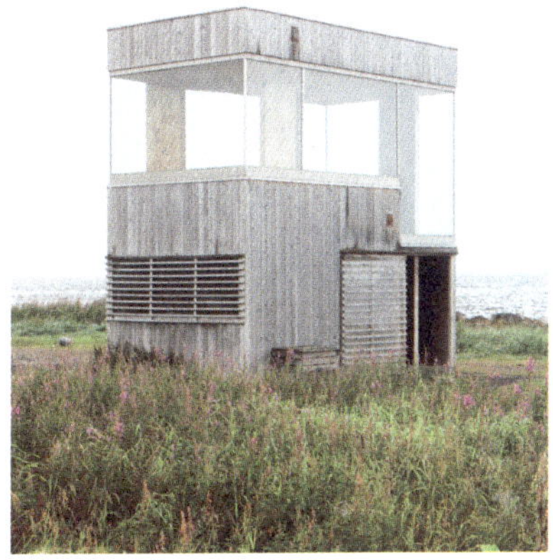

GRUNNFØR

The views from this shelter over the peaks of the islands of Vesterålen are superb. It was designed for cyclists and is open all year round; it is also open for overnight stays.

42

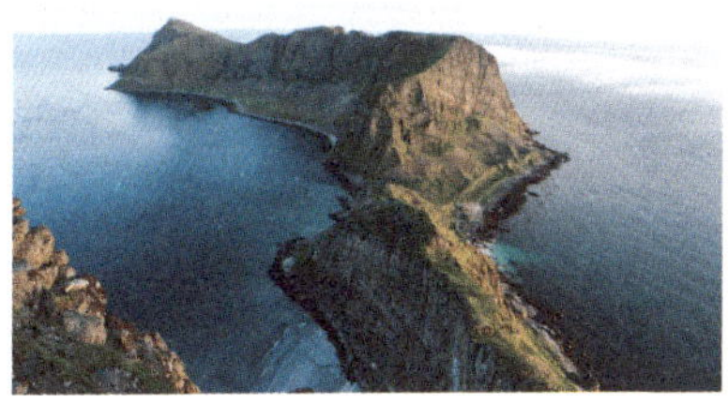

VÆRØY

Don't miss the viewpoint at Måstadfjellet when hiking on the small island of Værøy at the southern tip of the Lofoten Islands.

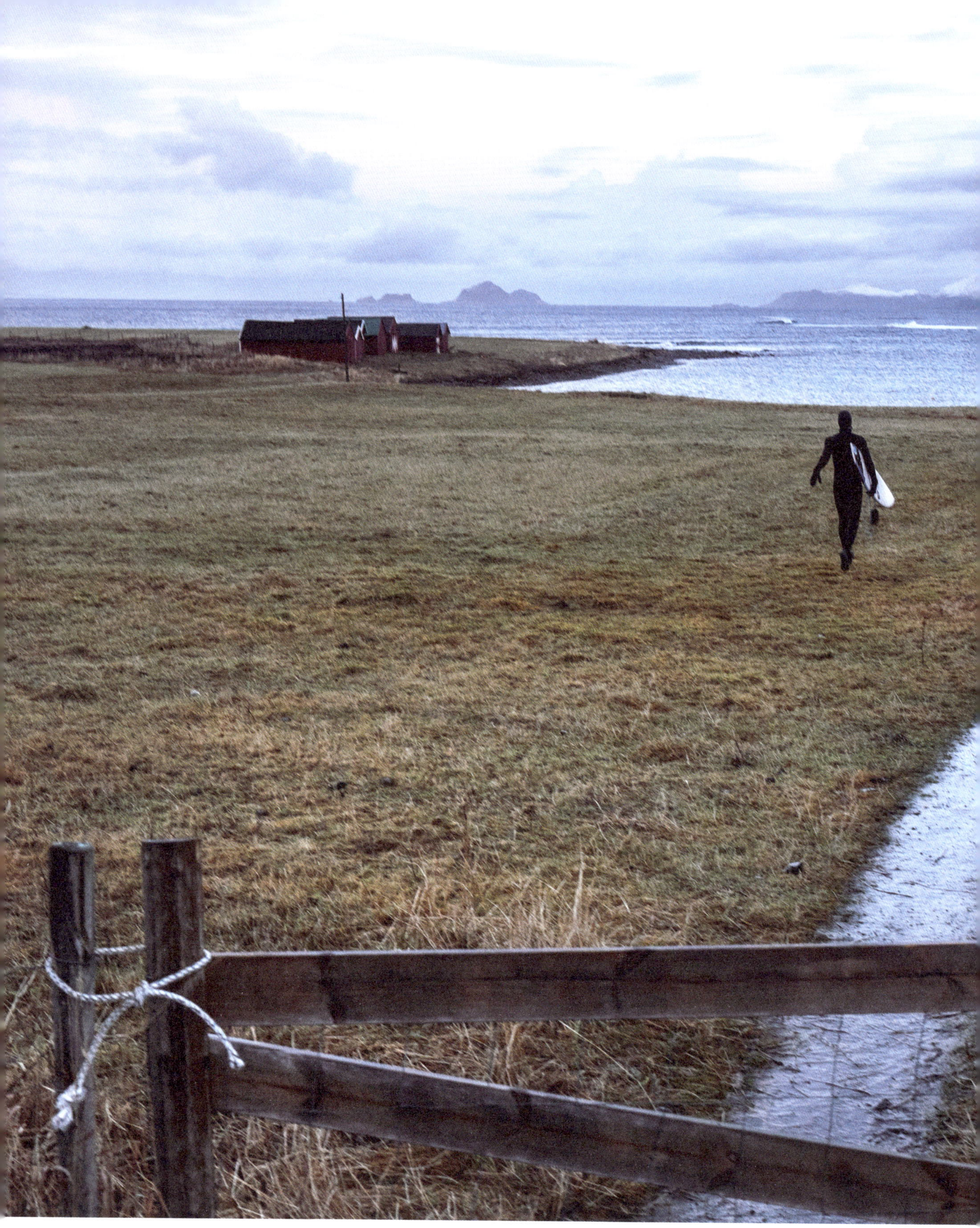

A surfer braves the cold of fall as he crosses a field on the way to his favorite spot.

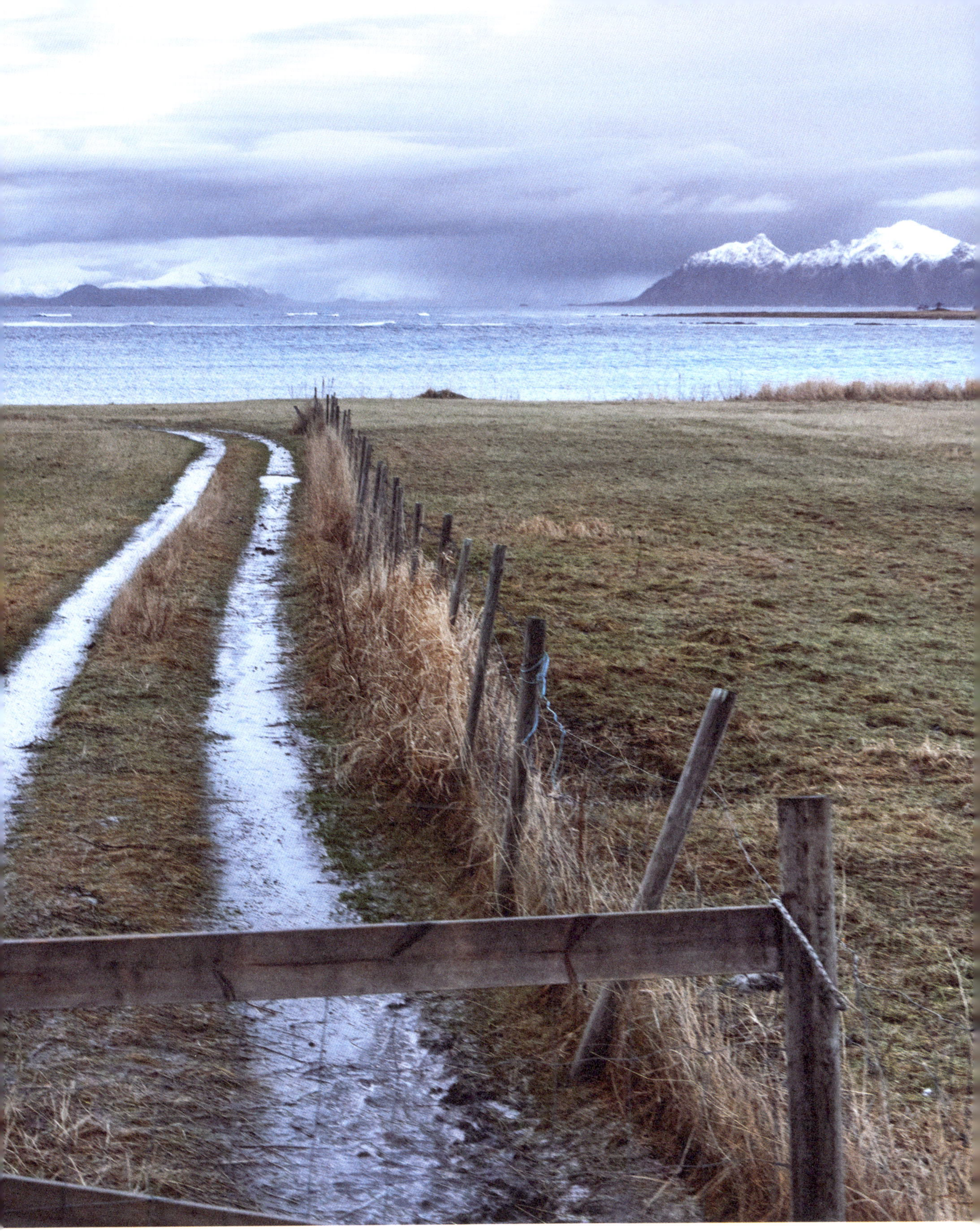

LIFESTYLE

ARCTIC SURFING

Surfing is becoming increasingly popular among locals in the Lofoten Islands, where surfers now form a real community.

The coastline of the Lofoten Islands is pounded by the long and powerful swells of the Atlantic Ocean throughout the year. The water temperatures may be cool in summer and freezing in winter, but this does not seem to put off the local surfers.

"When the swell is good, the waves are of excellent quality! You just have to be prepared to accept a few numbed toes… It may be a bit of a hindrance, but it is worth it!" says Lisa Blom, a Swedish-born hotel manager and surfer who moved to the islands a few years ago.

It is true to say that the wild nature and sublime scenery surrounding the surfing sites only accentuate the unique character of the experience, and surfers may even be lucky enough to catch a glimpse of some marine wildlife. In 2017 several orca even dropped in on surfers taking part in the Lofoten Masters competition, the northernmost surfing contest in the world—possibly a little scary but also a spectacular sight for the athletes in the water that day.

If the waves are right, no one cares about the weather conditions—the surfers have all the right equipment and are always ready to hit the water. Because of the warm currents of the Gulf Stream, the seas around the Lofoten Islands never freeze, even in winter. That said, temperatures never rise much higher than 40°C (4°C), which limits sessions to an hour or two.

One highly effective technique used locally is to wear woolen socks inside surf shoes to keep toes warm. Match these with a thick wetsuit, gloves, and a balaclava, and the Arctic surfer is good to go.

The cold is addictive for such athletes, who emerge from their surf sessions invigorated and euphoric. After a couple of hours in the water, they pry off their thick wetsuits (despite the numbness in their fingers) before taking refuge in their cars or in the surf school's sauna to warm up, the perfect way to get some heat back into the extremities before returning to the water for another session.

As spring comes, the swells of winter give way to summer waves that are smaller and more suitable for beginners. Temperatures rise and the midnight sun shines out over the archipelago for several weeks. As soon as the brief summer comes to an end, however, the waves grow in size again and surfers from all over the world set off in the hope of catching the biggest waves of the season. Night sets in again as fall comes to an end and the Northern Lights take their place in the sky, only enhancing the magic of these exceptional surfing locations.

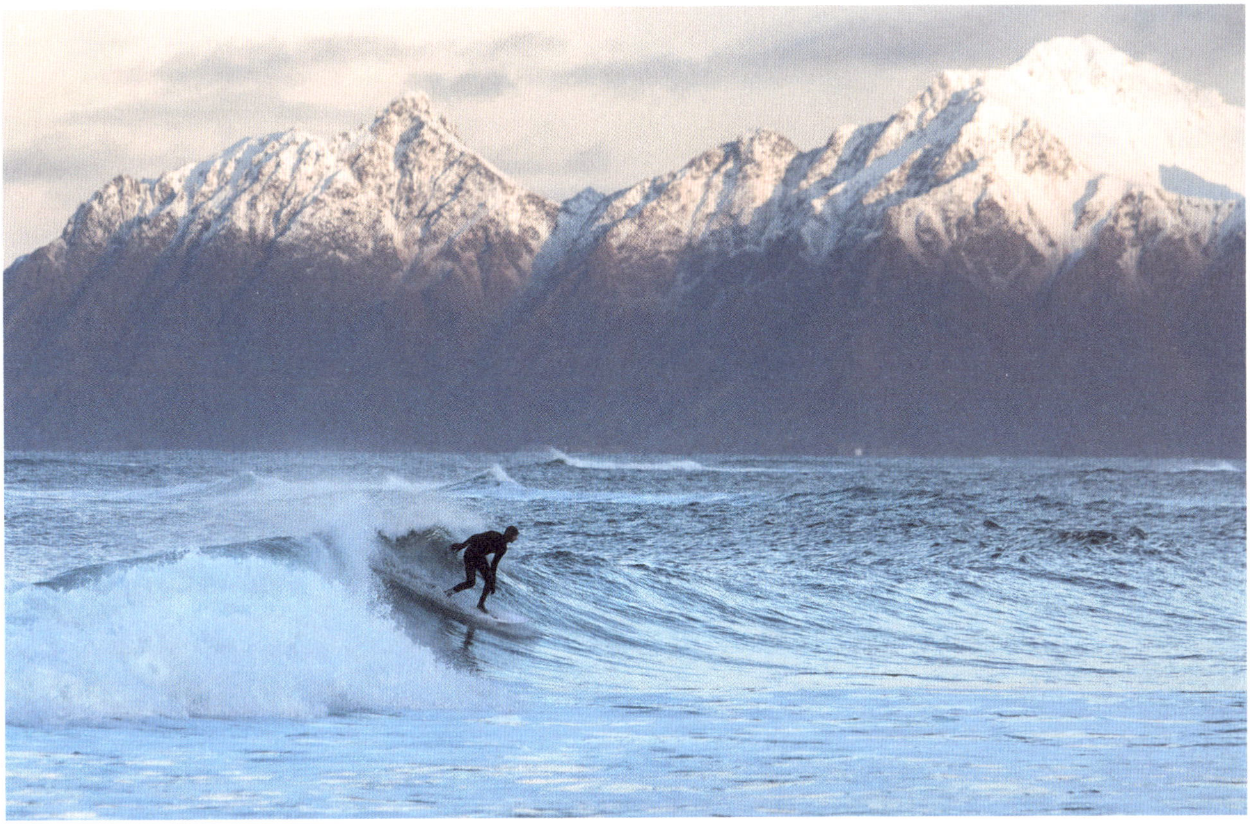

2

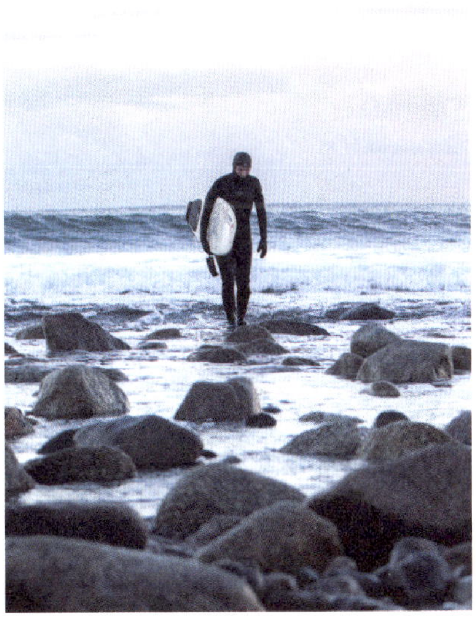

3

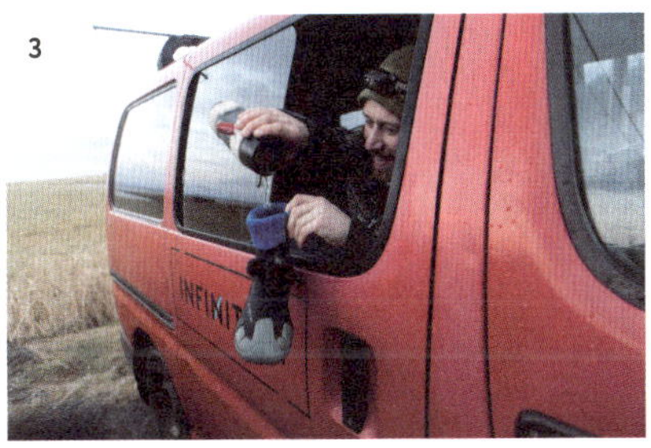

4

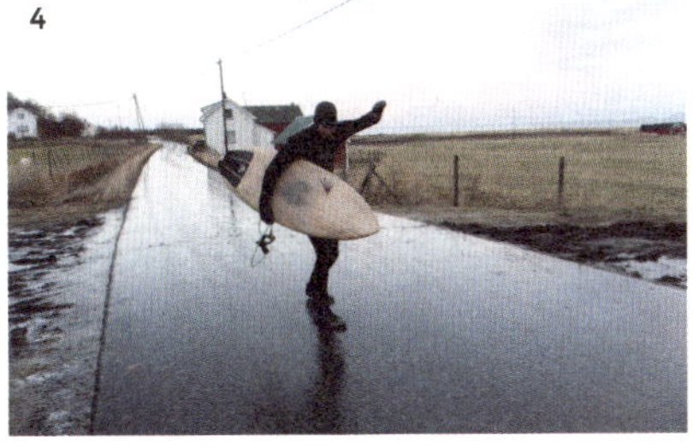

5

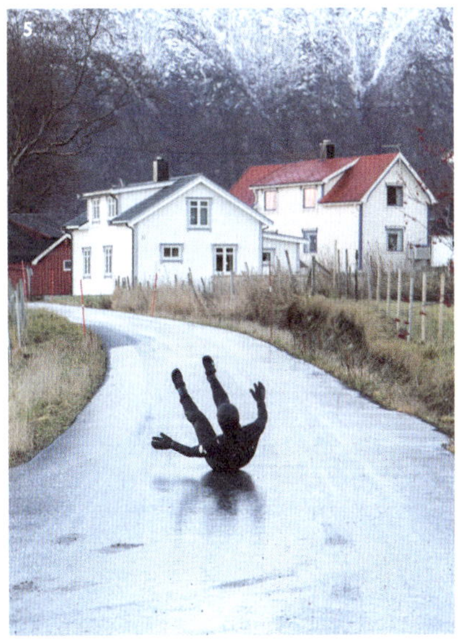

1/ 2/ A SECOND SKIN

The wetsuits worn by the islands' surfers in winter are ¼ in (7 mm) thick, but gloves and a balaclava are essential as well.

3/ FROZEN TOES

Any way is a good way if it keeps feet warm. Some locals wear woolen socks to stop their toes from going numb.

4/ 5/ FROST SURFER

Professional surfer Maria Petersson from Sweden having fun skidding along an ice-covered road.

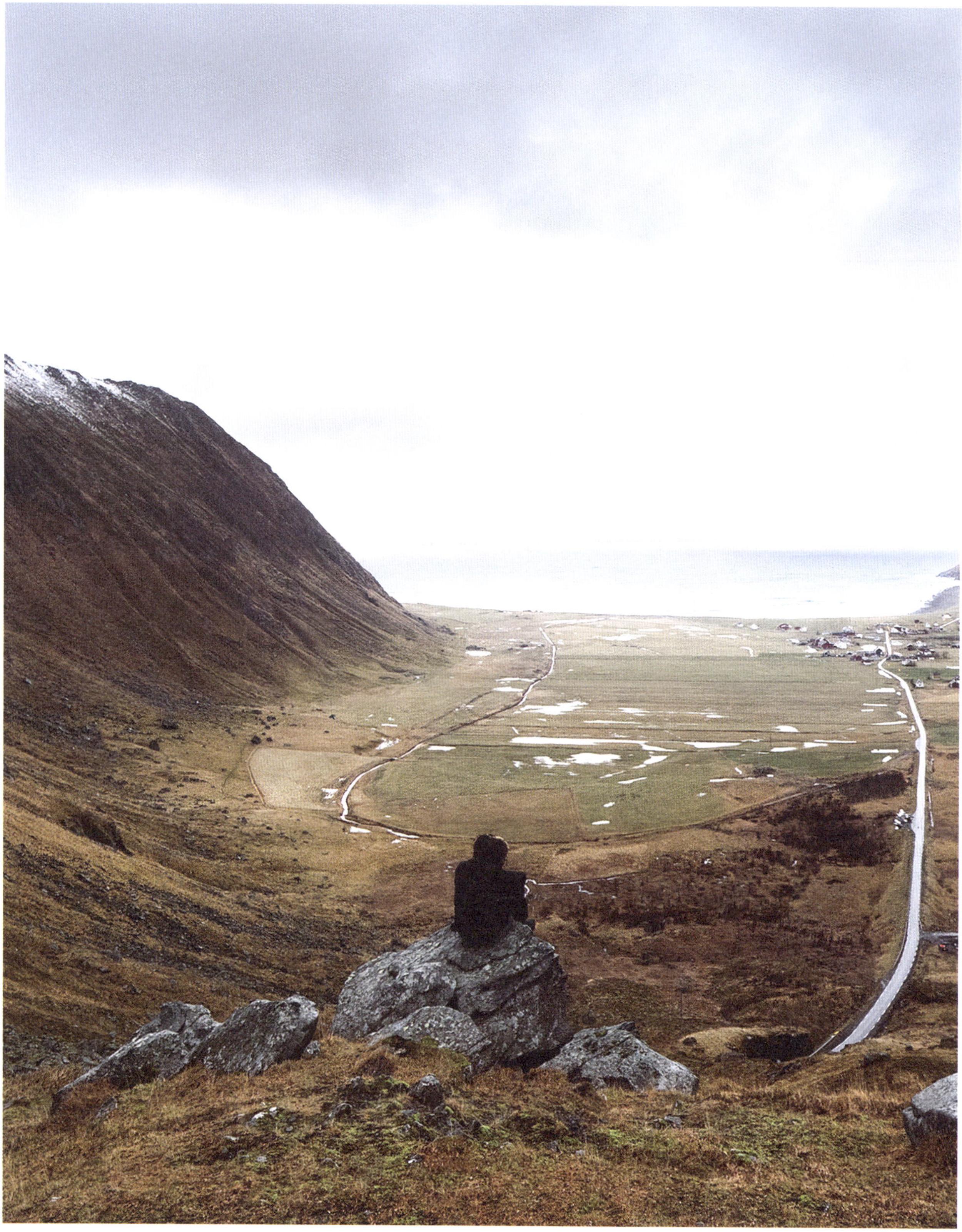

The tiny fishing village of Unstad has become a surfer's paradise; the waves can be 10 ft (3 m) high here.

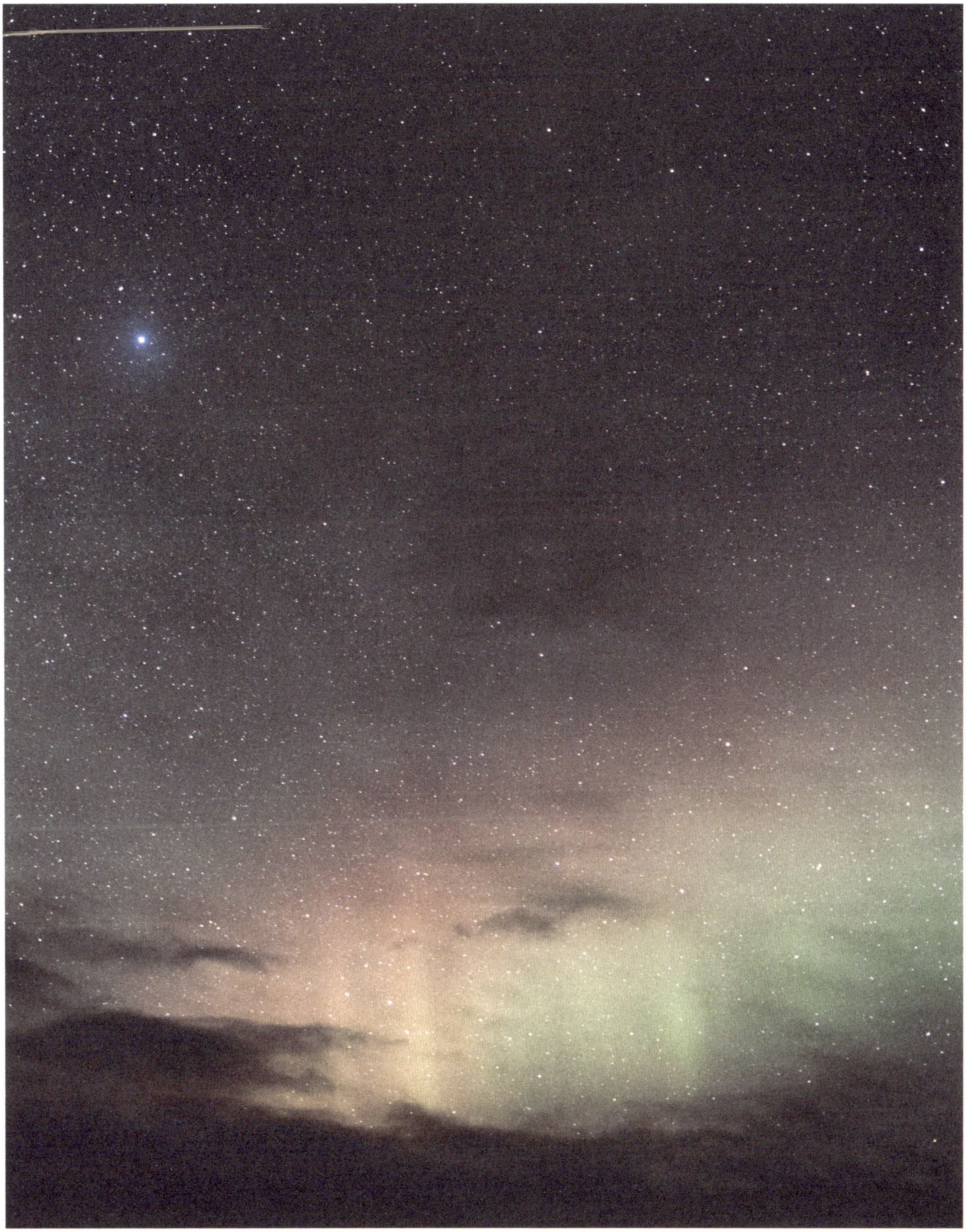

The Northern Lights peek through a break in the clouds to light up the whole Lofoten archipelago.

NATURE

COD FISHING

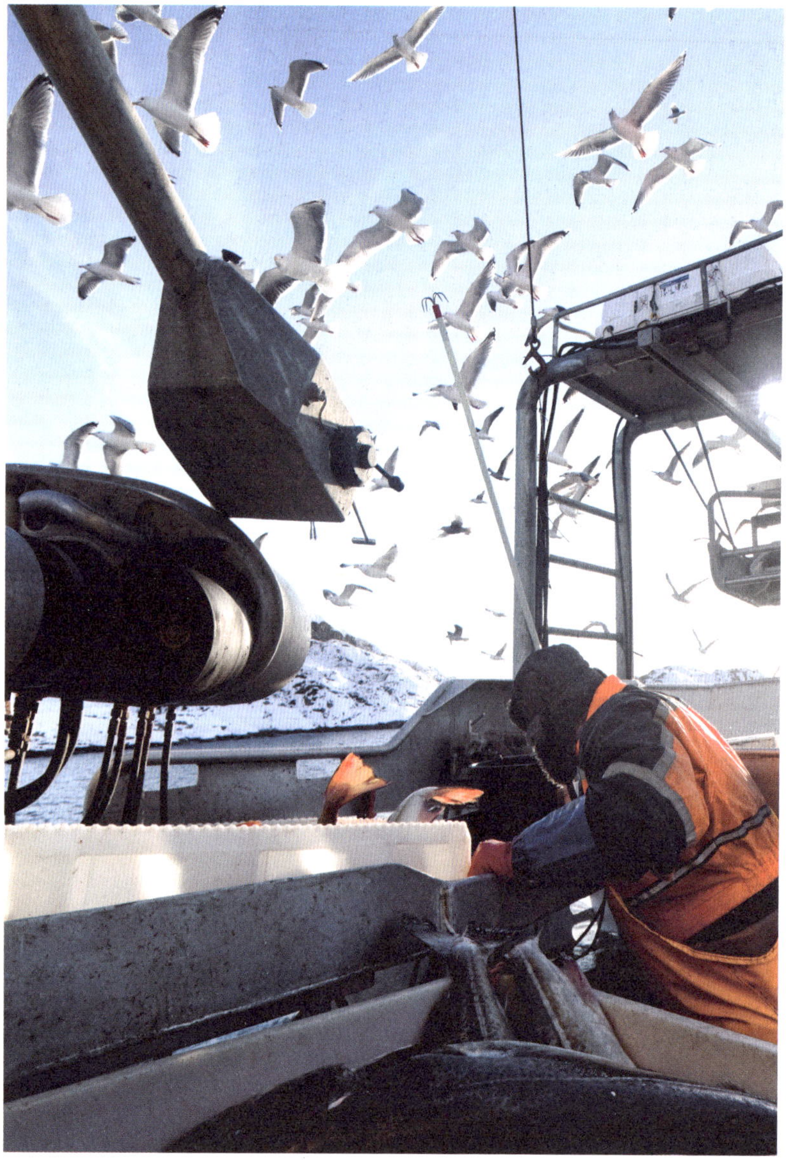

THE FISHING SEASON

As the first cod make an appearance around the Lofoten Islands at the end of February, the fishing villages stir into life, the factories are restarted, and boats cast off from the quays in their dozens.

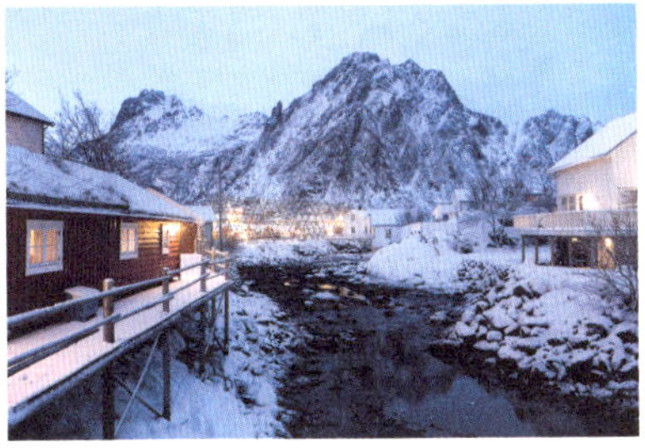

RORBUER

Living conditions were Spartan in these fishing huts mounted on stilts.

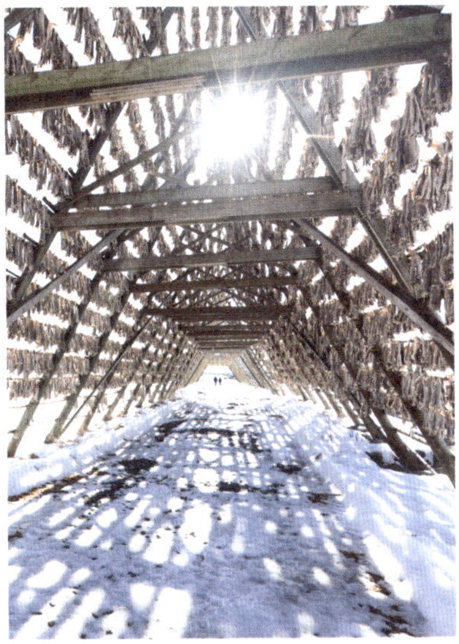

CATHEDRALS

Enormous wooden drying racks stacked with fish in Svolvær.

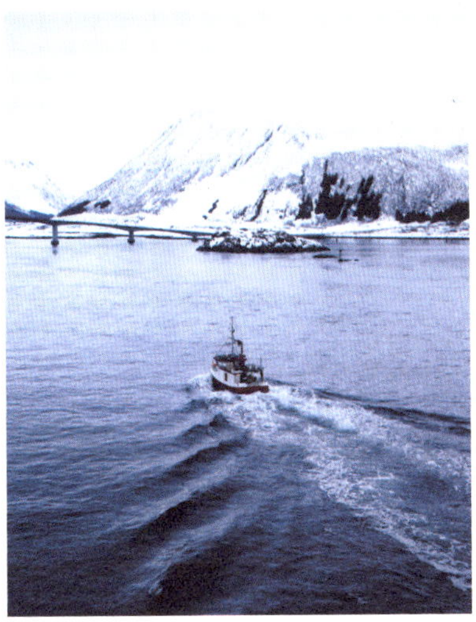

HEADING FOR THE HORIZON

A trawler leaves the islands' tranquil waters to go fishing on the high seas.

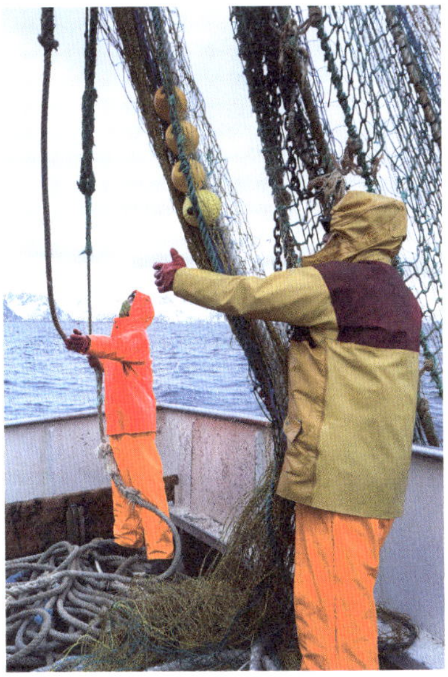

HARD WORK

Fishermen wear oilskins, gloves, and boots to combat exposure to water and cold.

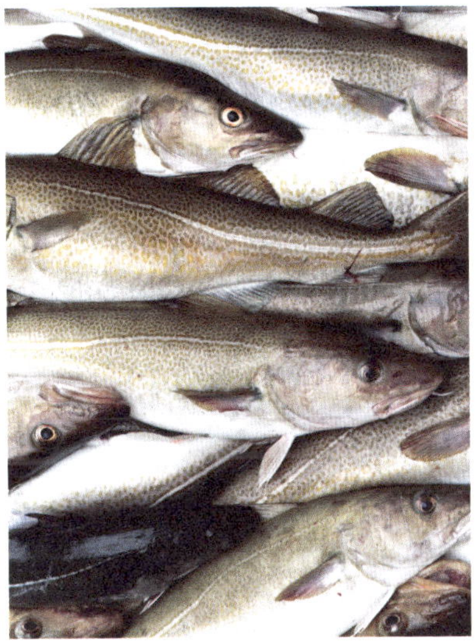

COD AND KLIPPFISK

Millions of cod migrate from the Barents Sea every winter to breed in the Lofoten Islands. Once the fish have been dried and salted, they are known as *klippfisk*.

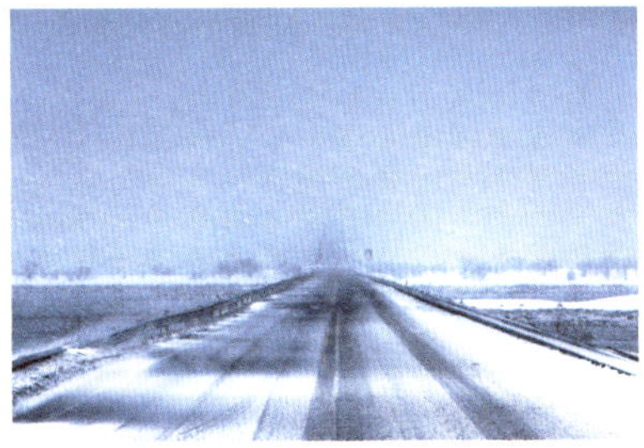

STORMY WEATHER

The weather and atmospheric conditions change completely during the many gales of winter.

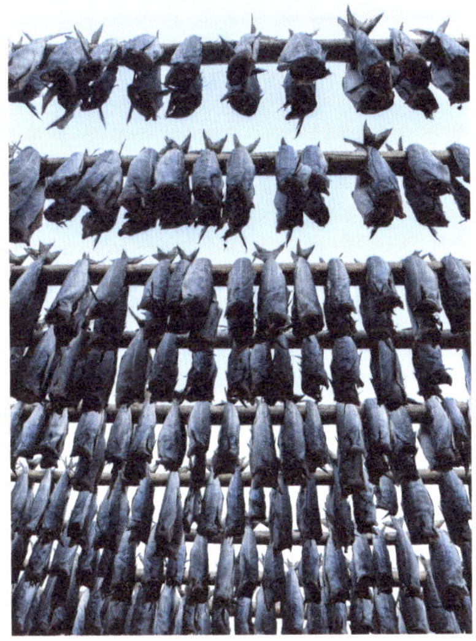

POLLOCK

Besides cod, pollock is also preserved by drying.

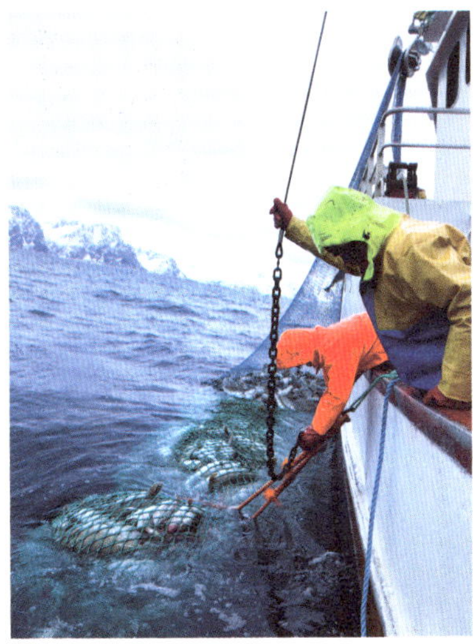

QUOTAS

Very strict quotas have been imposed to prevent the extinction of Norwegian cod.

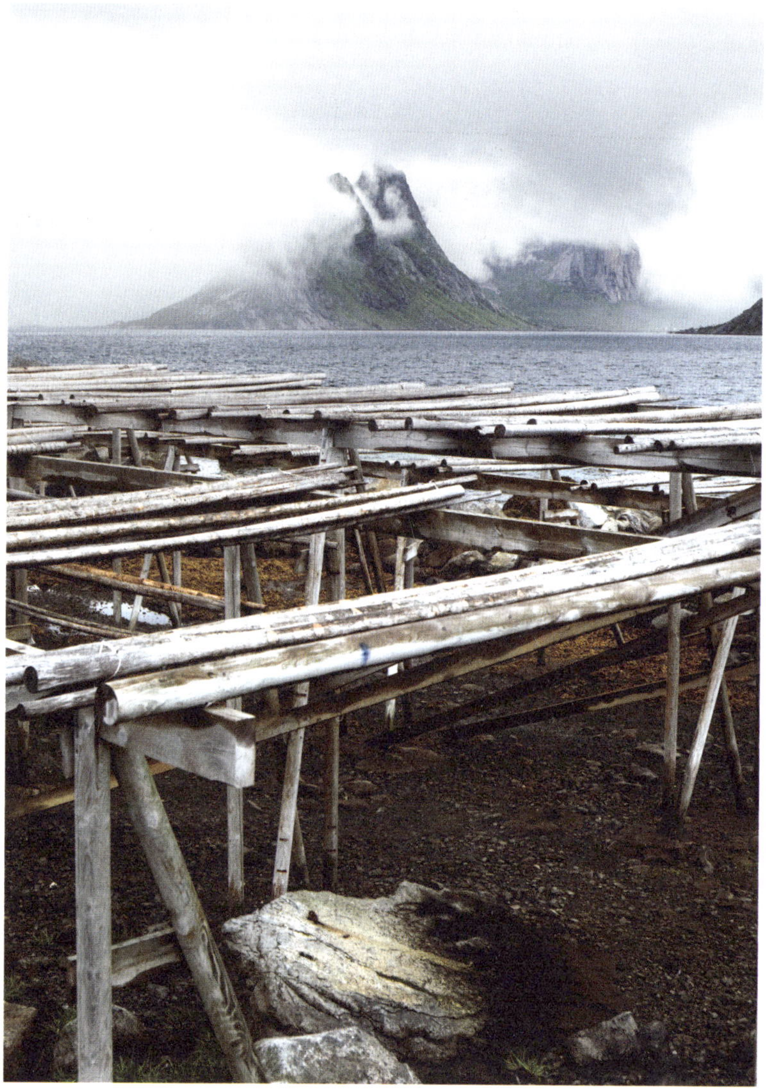

ABOVE

Fish are left on the drying racks between the end of winter and the end of spring. Once dried and salted, cod will keep for several years.

OPPOSITE

The rorbuer have been renovated and are now let out to passing tourists, who enjoy staying in these picturesque homes.

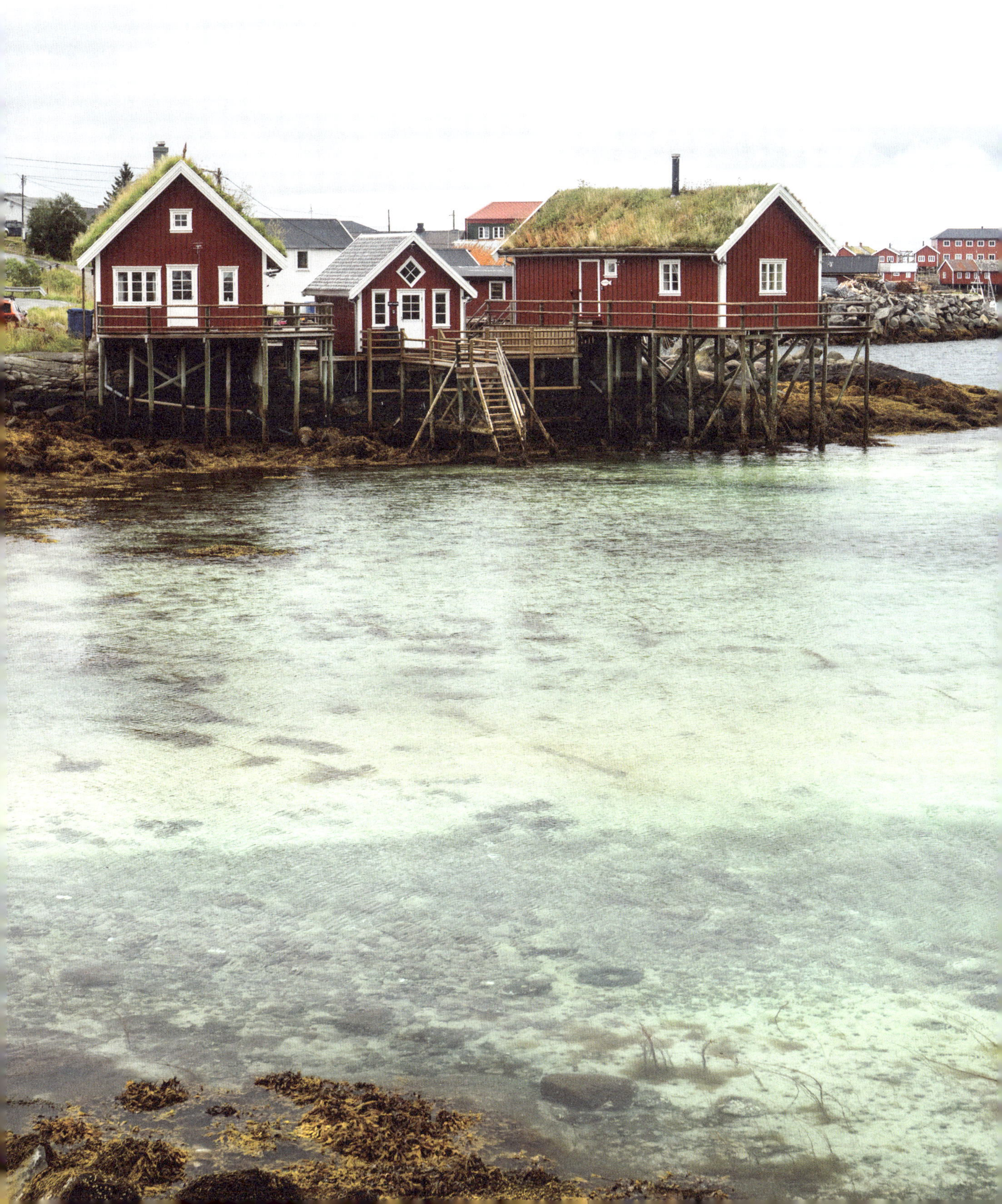

DEEP DIVE

THE NORTHERN LIGHTS

This spectacular phenomenon, a regular sight in the far north, was unexplained for many years.

In the darkness of the polar night colorful lights sometimes appear swirling across the sky. Initially faint and barely visible, the lights awaken slowly with a low glow before increasing in intensity and suddenly bursting into life. These are the world-famous polar lights, a phenomenon that can be seen around both the North Pole (aurora borealis) and the South Pole (aurora australis).

Because of its clear skies, long nights, and northern latitudes, Northern Norway has become a particularly popular destination for scientists and Northern Lights hunters alike. Tromsø is also one of the world's key cities from where the Northern Lights can frequently be observed.

The lights are shrouded in myth and legend. In the Middle Ages, they were thought to be the reflection of celestial warriors engaged in battle, while in Finland, there was even a tale suggesting that it was a magical fox who created the lights as it swept snow from the Earth's surface with its tail.

To understand the true origins of the phenomenon, we must look to the Sun. This star emits a constant stream of electrically charged particles known as solar wind, which flows in all directions at great speeds of between 200 and 620 miles per hour (300 and 1,000 km per hour). The influx of particles is particularly high during magnetic storms, events that arise in the wake of a solar flare. Most of these particles bounce off the Earth's magnetic field and continue their journey out into deep space.

The particles that manage to enter our magnetic field are attracted to the North and South Poles. When they penetrate the upper atmosphere (more than 50 miles/80 km high), these solar particles (electrons, protons, and positive ions) excite atoms which, as they return to their initial state, release the energy they have received from this collision in the form of gigantic swirls and veils of color.

The lights are generally green but may also contain blue, red, and indigo, depending on the nature of the gases (nitrogen, hydrogen, helium...) with which the solar particles interact. The various chemical components present in the atmosphere can be identified using spectrographic analysis.

The most common color is a shade of yellow-green emitted by oxygen atoms at a distance between 60 and 75 miles (100–120 km) above the Earth's surface. These same oxygen atoms produce a red-violet light when struck by electrons at altitudes above 95 miles (150 km). By contrast, ionized nitrogen molecules emit violet light at low altitudes between 50 and 60 miles (80–100 km). This is difficult to see with the naked eye but shows up well in photographs.

AURORA BOREALIS

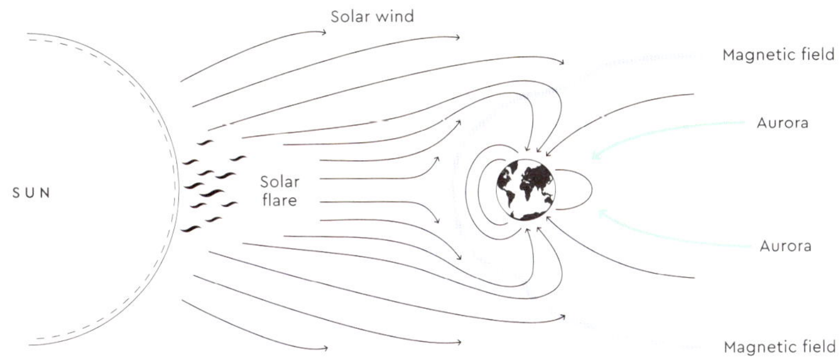

MAGNETIC STORM

Polar auroras are caused when charged particles from solar wind interact with the upper atmosphere of the Earth, usually at the magnetic poles.

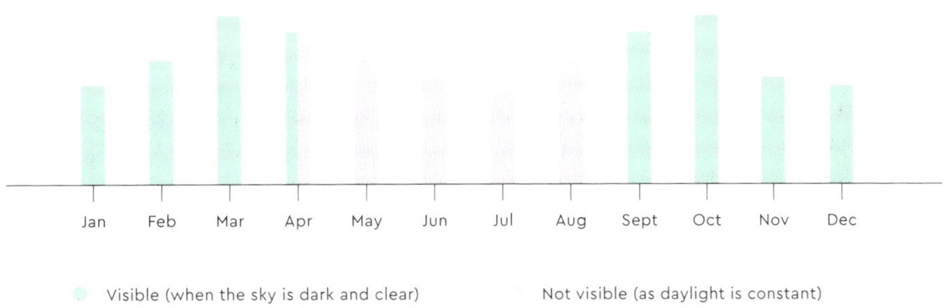

KP INDEX	GEOMAGNETIC LATITUDE	AURORAL ACTIVITY
KP 0	66,5° OR MORE	VERY QUIET
KP 1	64,5°	QUIET
KP 2	62,5°	QUIET
KP 3	60,4°	UNSETTLED
KP 4	58,3°	ACTIVE
KP 5	56,3°	MINOR STORM
KP 6	54,2°	MODERATE STORM
KP 7	52,2°	STRONG STORM
KP 8	50,1°	SEVERE STORM
KP 9	48,1° OR LESS	EXTREME STORM

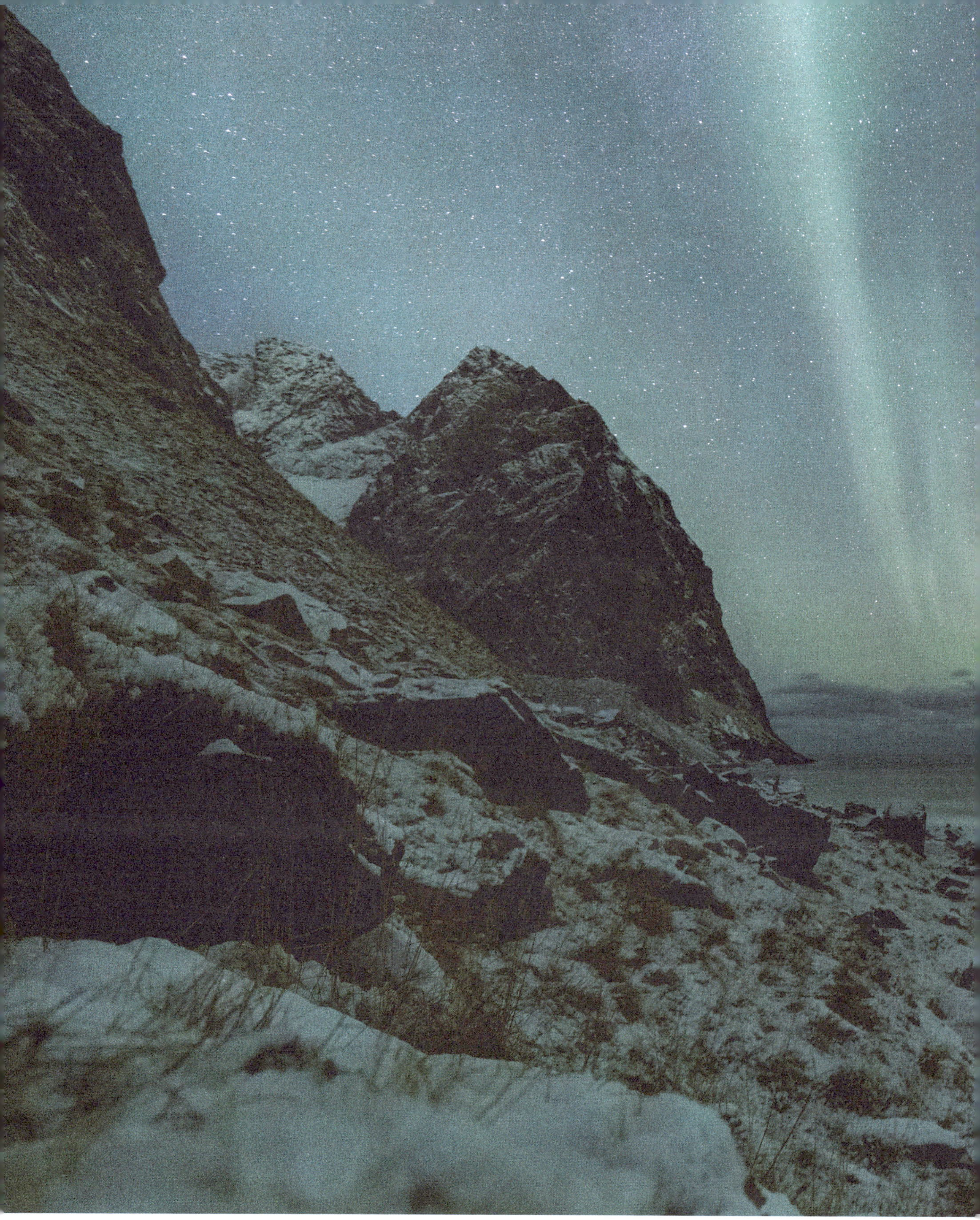

The aurora borealis illuminates the sky as light escapes from a cabin built among the rocks on Kvalvika Beach, a popular location with hikers.

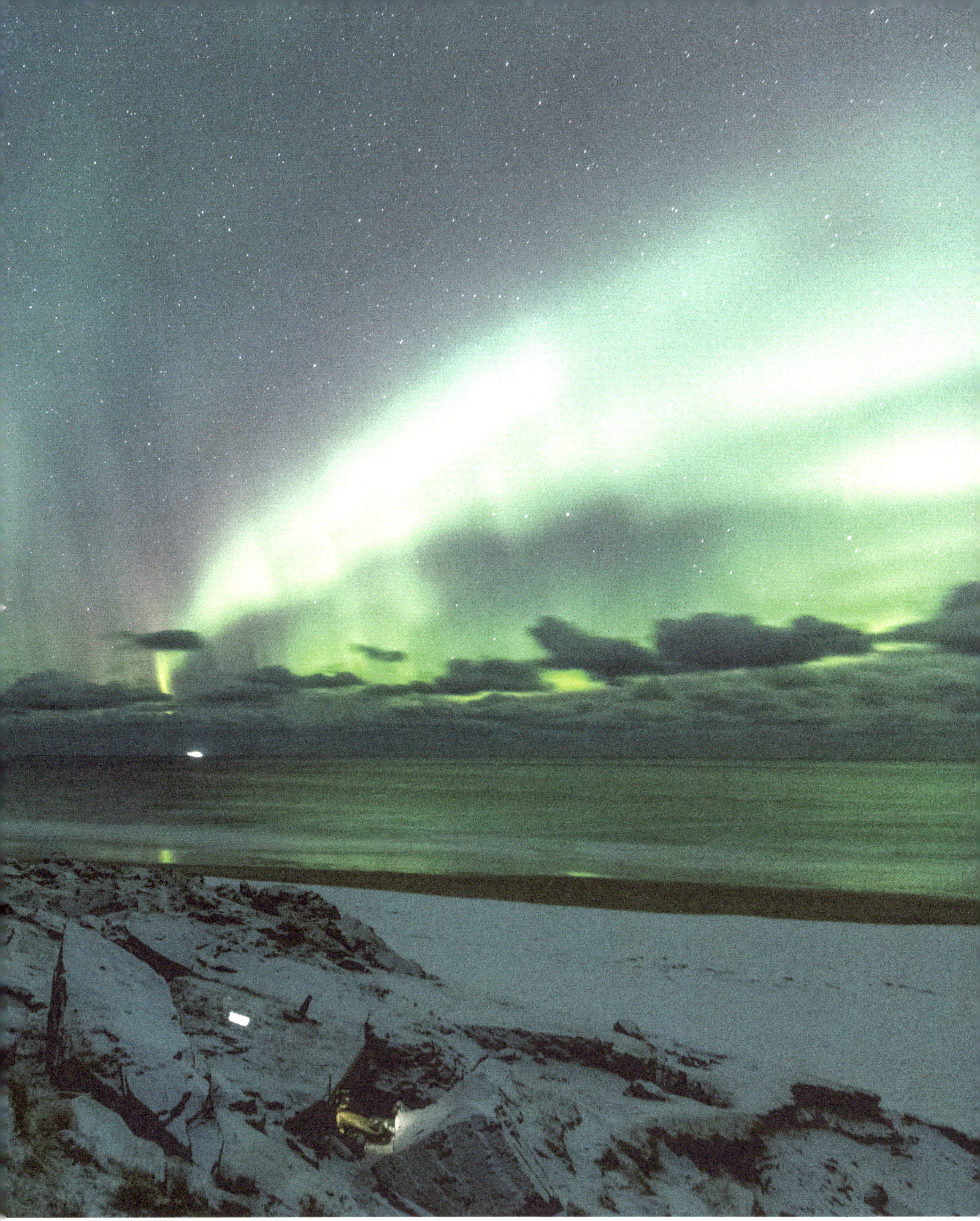

PORTRAIT

ELENA

LIGHTHOUSE KEEPER

Elena has taken up residence in the old lighthouse keeper's cottage on a tiny, remote island looking out over the Lofoten Islands.

After a hectic life spent traveling the world in pursuit of her career in journalism, Elena Hansteensen fulfilled a long-held dream by settling in the far north of Norway, where she bought a lighthouse from the Norwegian Coastal Administration. She moved in alone and has made numerous improvements and alterations, helped by volunteers who came to stay for a few weeks at a time in exchange for bed and board.

The lighthouse's tranquility and proximity to nature were exactly what Elena had been looking for. "This is the perfect place for me. It is where I can reflect on the life I have lived." Her day-to-day existence is not all a bed of roses, however, as she points out, "It isn't necessarily a more relaxed lifestyle, as I have a plenty to do, but it is a different kind of work, more physical. Nature is so close, and I feel privileged to live here."

In 1895, when the advent of motorized boats prompted fishing crews to relocate to a less remote area, there were around eight hundred and seventy-five people living on the island. They left and took the village with them, dismantling the houses plank by plank and reassembling them on the mainland. All that remains from this period are some foundations and the island's jail, which has a few stories to tell—the tiny cell could house no more than a single prisoner at a time and was occasionally used as a drunk tank.

Elena is the sole year-round inhabitant of this rocky island outcrop and watches the ocean change with the seasons. She compares the spectacle of the weather to a kaleidoscope because of its infinite variety of light conditions. Other islands rise up proudly in the distance, occasionally disappearing behind a veil of rain. From her house, Elena will occasionally catch a glimpse of the orcas and humpback whales that stray into the small cove where she moors her boat. When the wind picks up, bald eagles come to play in the air currents flowing past her large picture windows.

To buy groceries, collect her mail, and pick up her guests, Elena has to take her boat into the village, which can take about twenty minutes if the sea is calm, or longer if the swell picks up. This latter-day lighthouse keeper is well aware of her limitations, however, and knows to wait a couple of days before taking the boat out to avoid those real storms of winter when they hit the coast.

Elena started out on this venture all alone, but no longer lacks for company. She now has the support of a partner and has also opened a guest house with three rooms for visitors seeking tranquility, unspoiled nature, and views of an endless horizon—a magical place that seems like the far corner of the world.

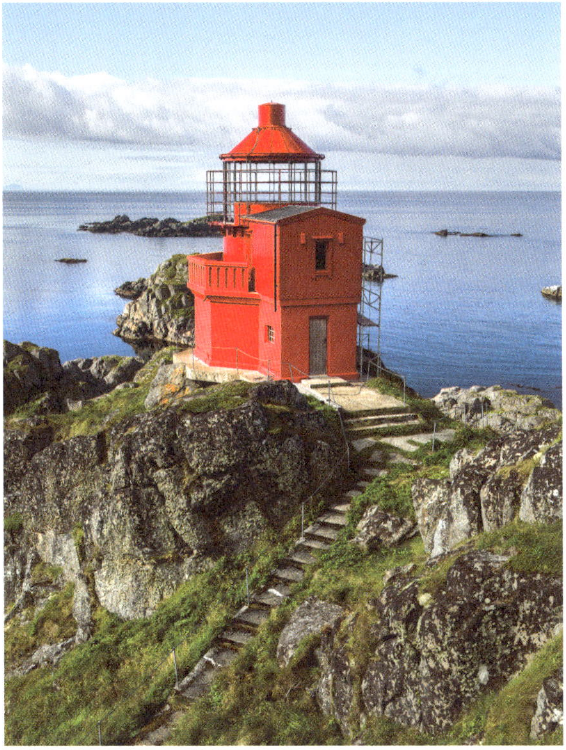

ALONE IN THE WORLD

Elena's nearest neighbors are in the village of Bø, nearly four miles (6 km) away. Elena makes regular visits to pick up her mail and stock up on provisions.

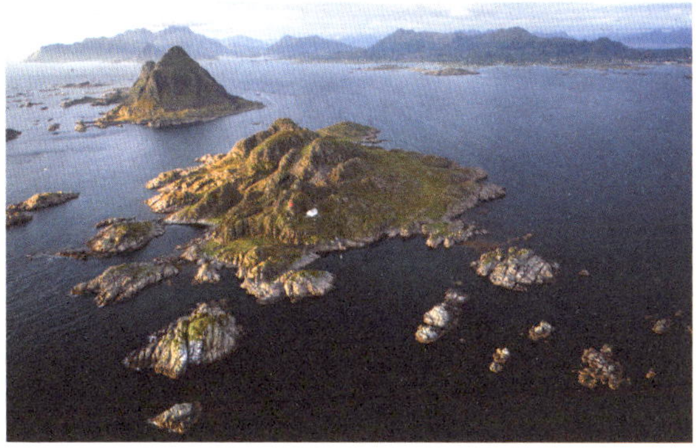

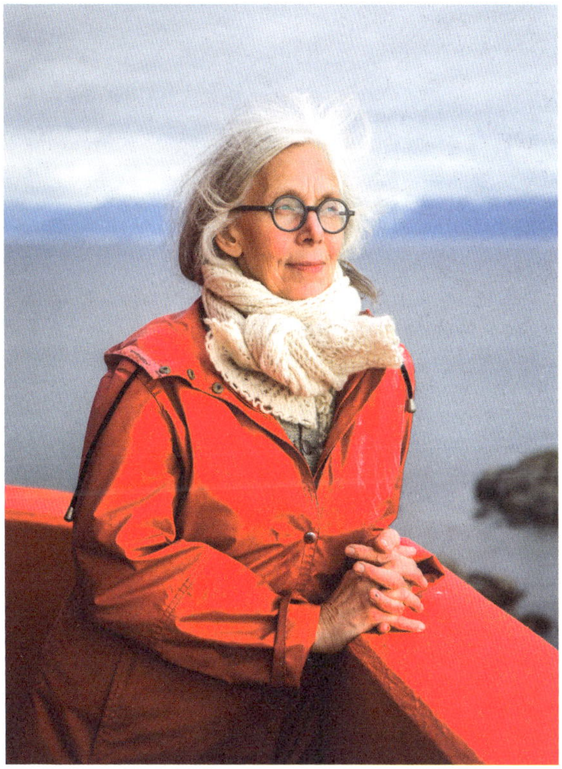

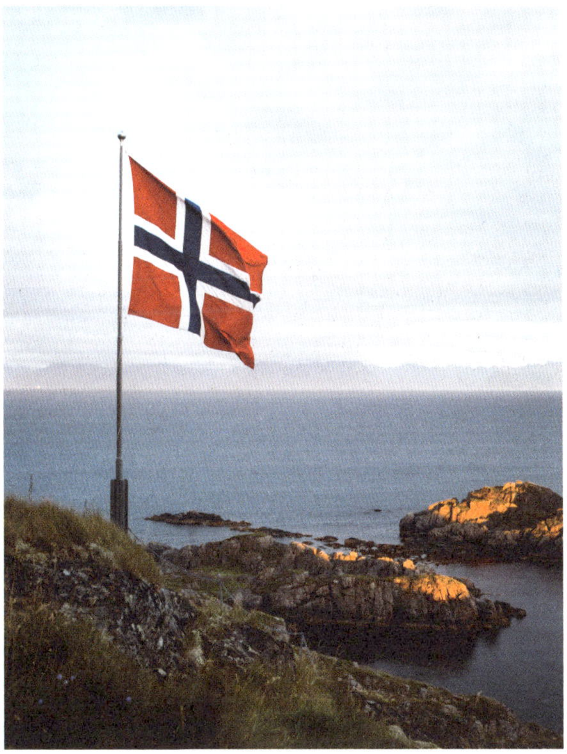

FRESH FISH

A fishing boat stops off on its return voyage to sell Elena some fresh fish and catch up on the latest news.

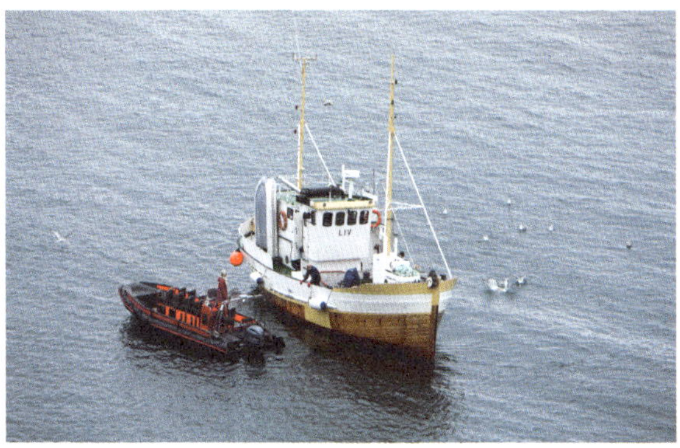

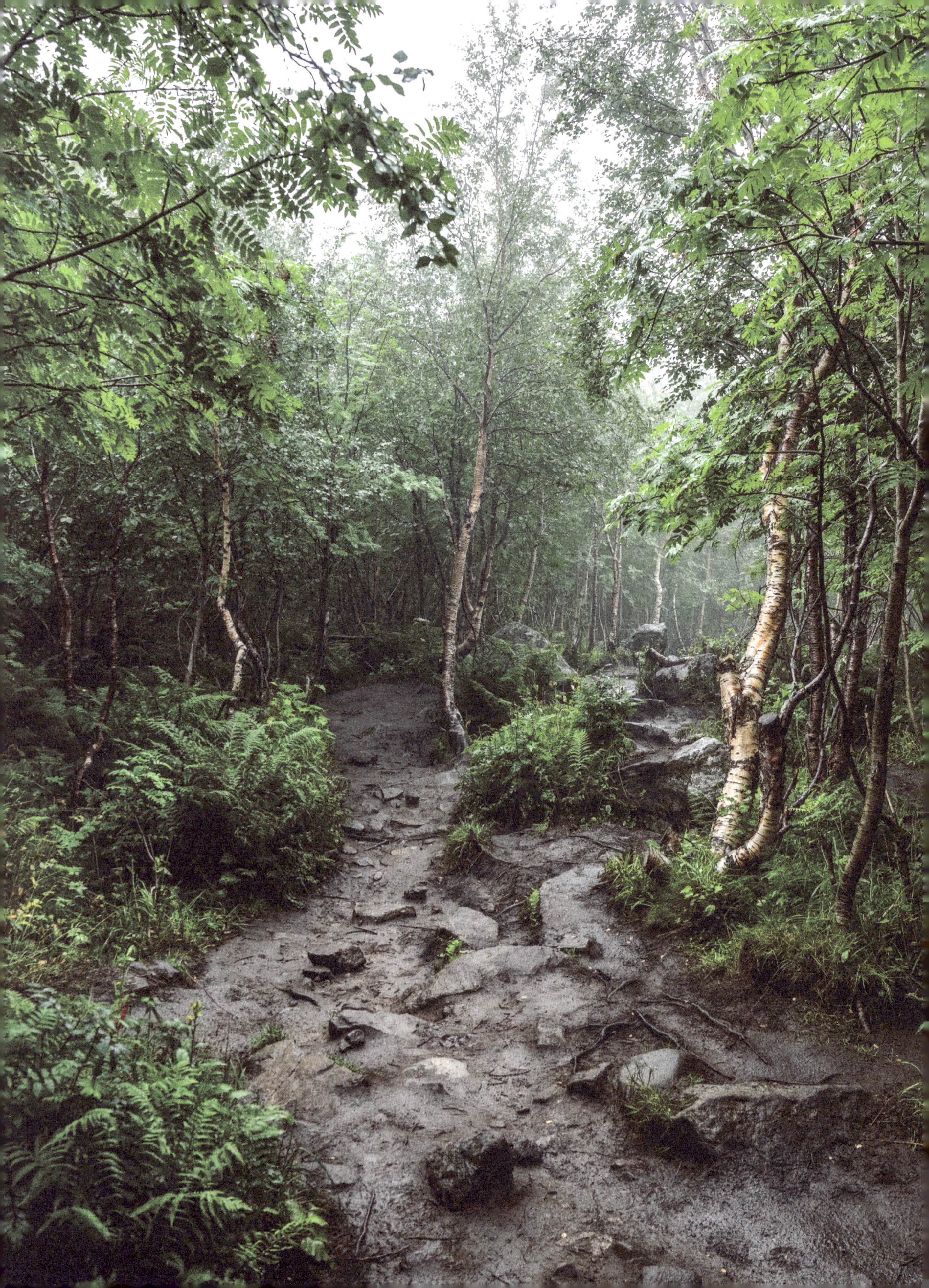

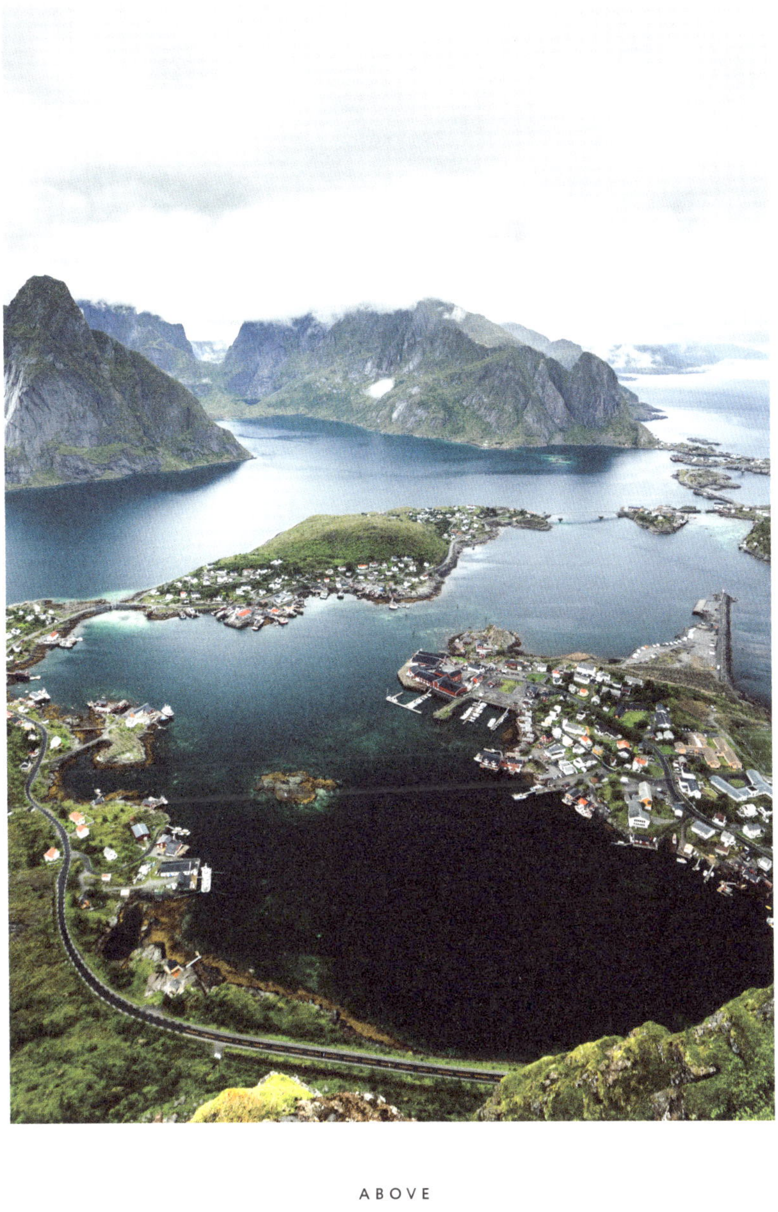

ABOVE

Enjoy superb panoramic views of the Lofoten Islands and the village of Reine from the hiking trail at Reinebringen.

OPPOSITE

The trail looks more like a tropical rainforest when the rain sets in.

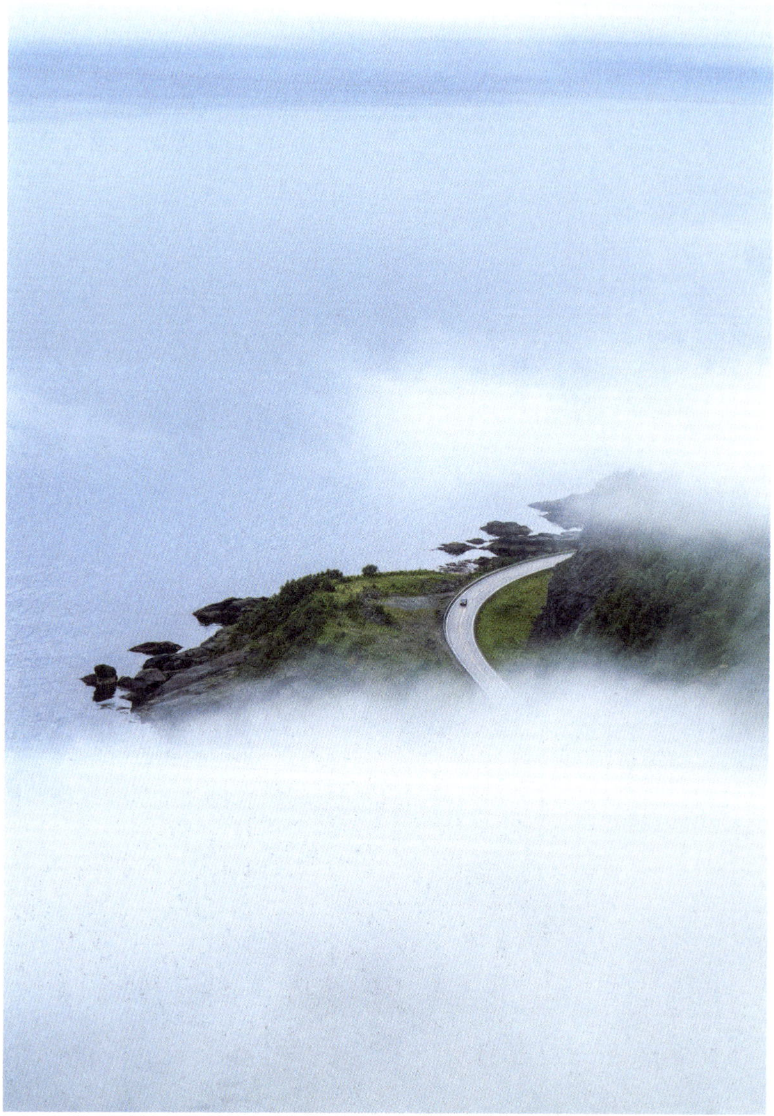

ABOVE

The E10 highway crossing the Lofoten Islands from north to south is just visible between the clouds

OPPOSITE

The road is an ideal way to explore the archipelago's scenery in every season of the year.

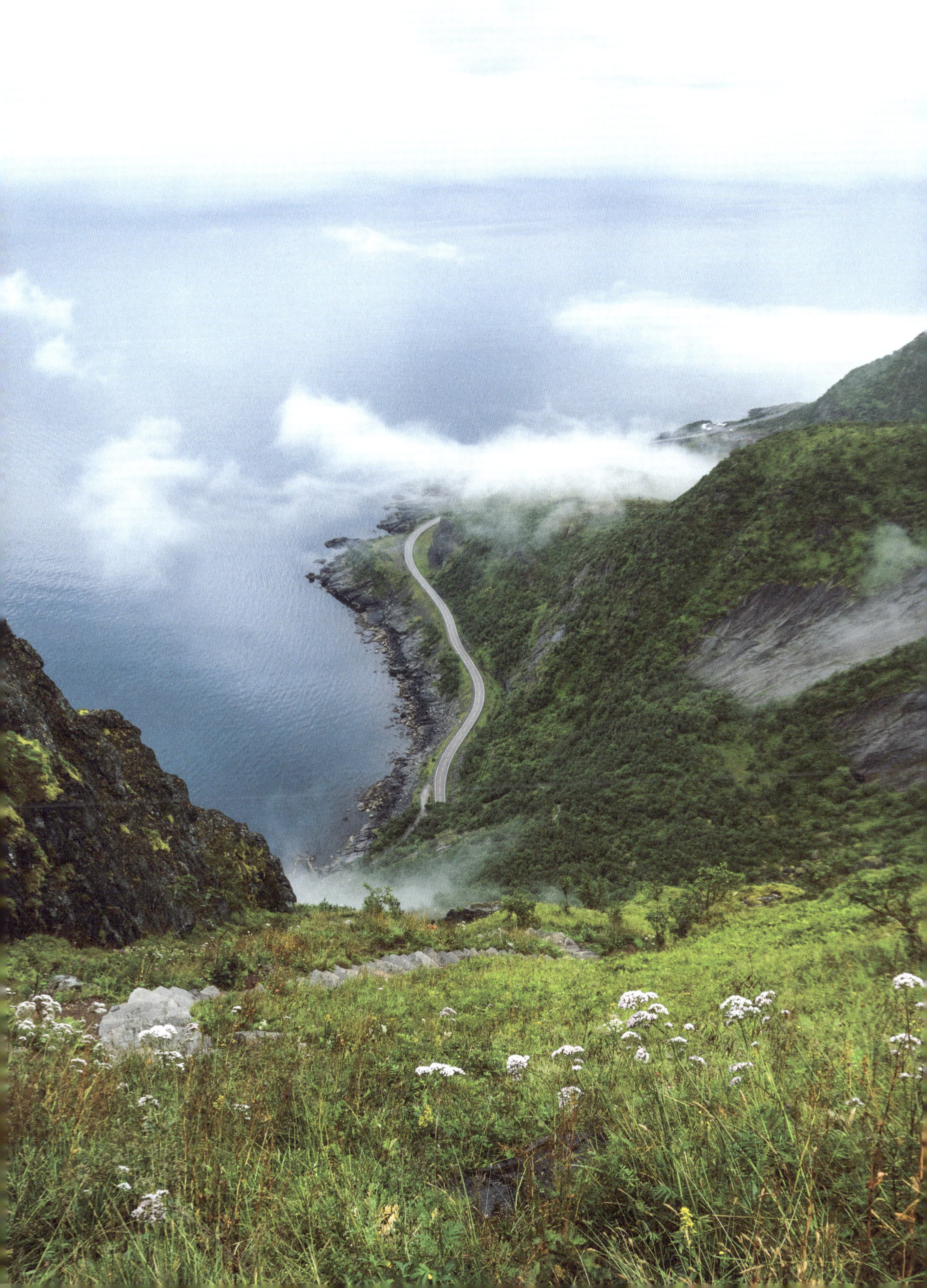

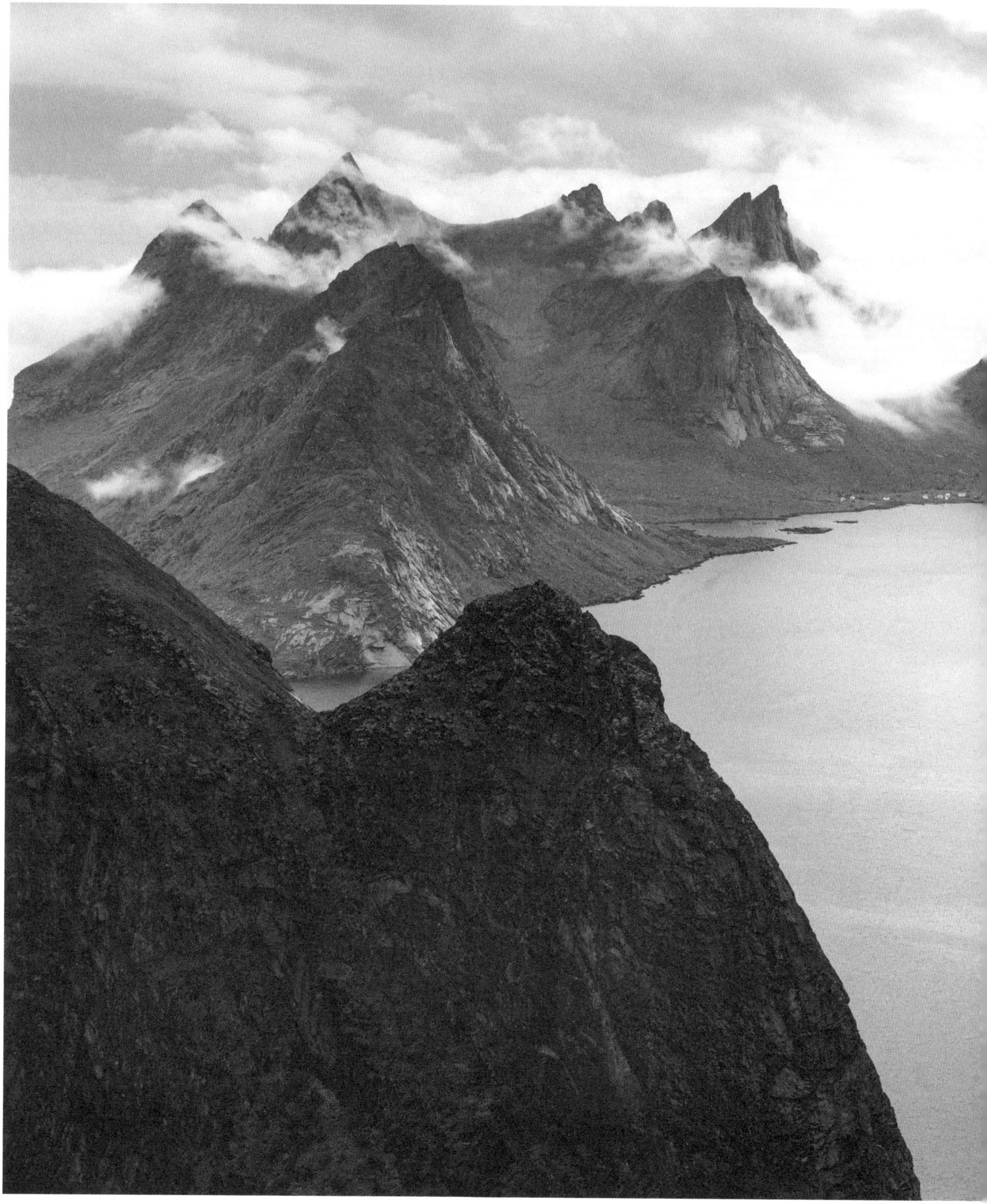

The jagged peaks of Moskenesøya, the main island of the Lofoten chain, lie shrouded in mist after a morning downpour.

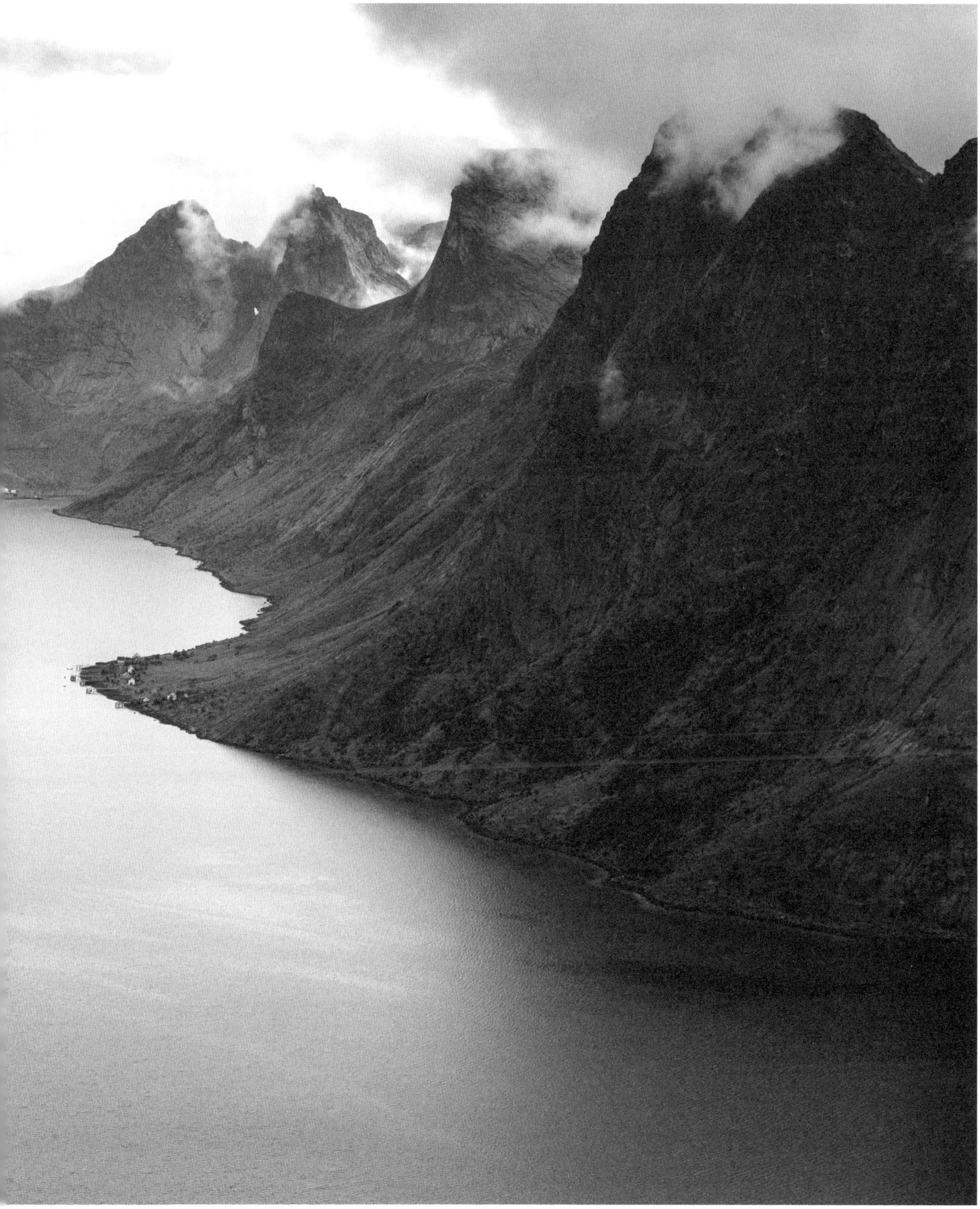

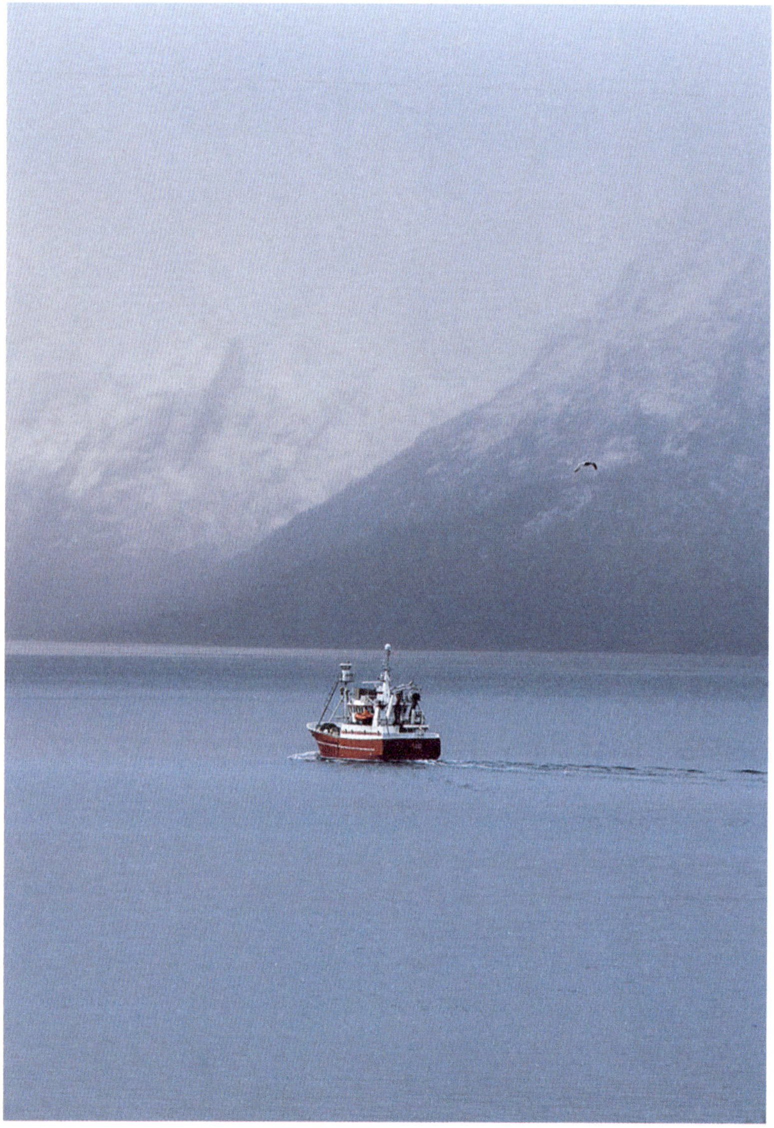

ABOVE

A trawler from the Lotofisket, Norway's largest seasonal cod-fishing fleet, makes its way up the fjord.

OPPOSITE

The mountains plunging steeply down to the fish-laden waters of the Lofoten Islands were carved out by glaciers.

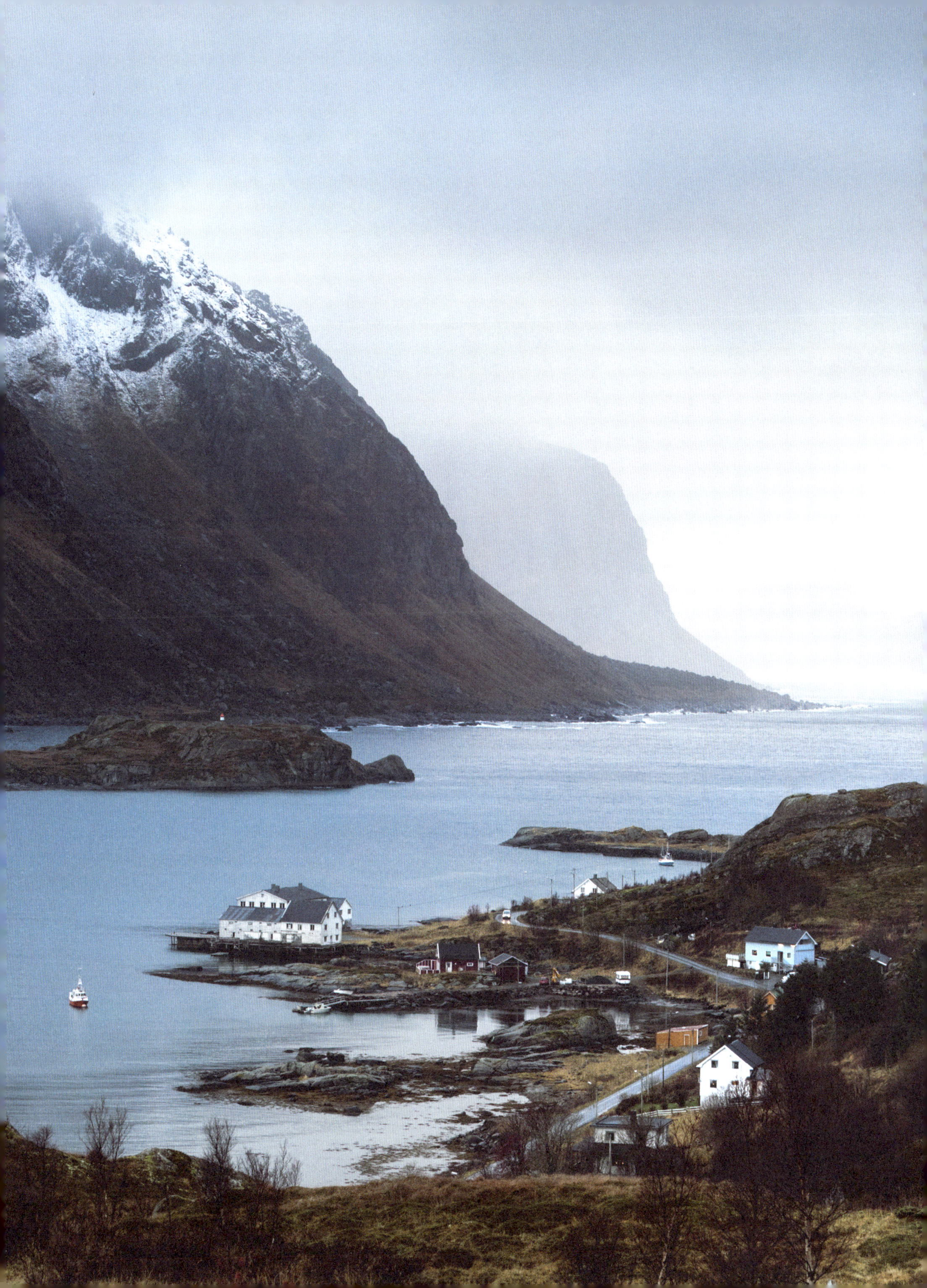

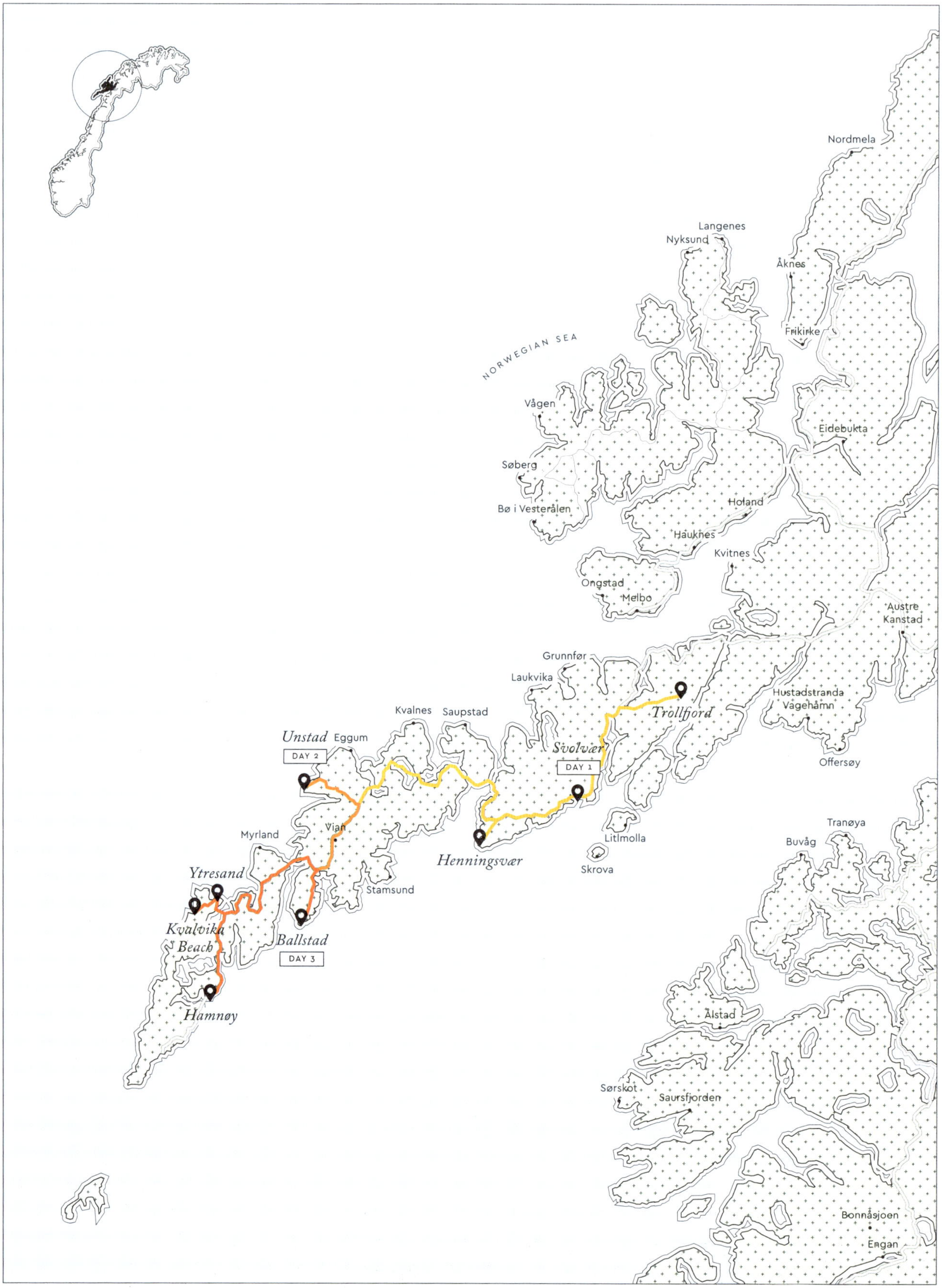
NORWEGIAN SEA
Nordmela
Langenes
Nyksund
Åknes
Frikirke
Vågen
Eidebukta
Søberg
Bø i Vesterålen
Holand
Haukenes
Kvitnes
Ongstad
Melbo
Austre Kanstad
Grunnfør
Laukvika
Trollfjord
Hustadstranda
Vågehamn
Kvalnes
Saupstad
Unstad
Eggum
DAY 2
Svolvær
DAY 1
Offersøy
Vian
Myrland
Henningsvær
Litlmolla
Skrova
Tranøya
Buvåg
Ytresand
Stamsund
Kvalvika Beach
Ballstad
DAY 3
Hamnøy
Alstad
Sørskot
Saursfjorden
Bonnåsjoen
Engan

ITINERARY

THREE DAYS IN THE LOFOTEN ISLANDS

Enjoying the scenery of the Lofoten archipelago has to be the highlight of any trip to Norway, whatever the season.

DAY 1: FROM SVOLVÆR TO HENNINGSVÆR

Svolvær may be first and foremost a fishing town, but it also boasts a number of top-notch restaurants and is an excellent base from which to explore the islands. Take a boat trip to discover Trollfjord (literally, the "fjord of the trolls"), a narrow inlet barely a mile (2 km) long that is also on the Hurtigruten Coastal Express itinerary. Passengers en route may be lucky enough to spot sea eagles fishing on the surface. Keep an eye out also for human fishing crews, who will sometimes throw the eagles some bycatch. Once back on terra firma, head south toward Henningsvær, a charming small village nicknamed the "Venice of the Lofotens." The old fish processing facilities have recently been converted into accommodation for tourists, and the municipality boasts one of the northernmost football pitches in the world, along with an art gallery named the Kaviar Factory. Numerous works by the street artist Pøbel are scattered across the islands, several of which can be seen in the village.

DAY 2: FROM UNSTAD TO BALLSTAD

In a few short years, Unstad Beach has become an essential port of call for surfers, as this is where the annual Lofoten Masters is held, one of the few surfing competitions in polar latitudes. If the water is a bit chilly, don't panic—a cinnamon bun, a steaming coffee, and a nice hot sauna will no doubt get you back on your feet. Head to the village of Ballstad and put to sea with a cod fishing crew. This is also where head chef Roy Magne Berglund presides at the Lofoten Food Studio, an unusual restaurant where Norwegian dishes can be sampled directly from the chef's table. Round off the day with an overnight stay in a *rorbu*, a traditional wooden cabin mounted on stilts, which provides an insight into the lives of the Norwegian fishermen who lived here during the *skrei* season.

DAY 3: FROM BALLSTAD TO HAMNØY

On the way to Ytresand take a short hike to a viewpoint from where you can admire the magnificent turquoise waters of the Lofoten chain. It is almost enough to make you forget you are north of the Arctic Circle. Nearby Kvalvika Beach was made famous as the place where Inge Wegge and Jørn Ranum lived for a whole winter in a cabin built from objects picked up from the shore. They made a film telling the story of their adventure called *North of the Sun*. The more adventurous can sleep in their cabin or on magnificent Kvalvika Beach itself. Finally, head south toward Hamnøy Bridge to see the most famous view in the Lofoten Islands. The hiking trail around Reinebringen may involve negotiating some steep slopes, but the reward is an incredibly panoramic vantage point, undoubtedly one of the most beautiful in the whole archipelago.

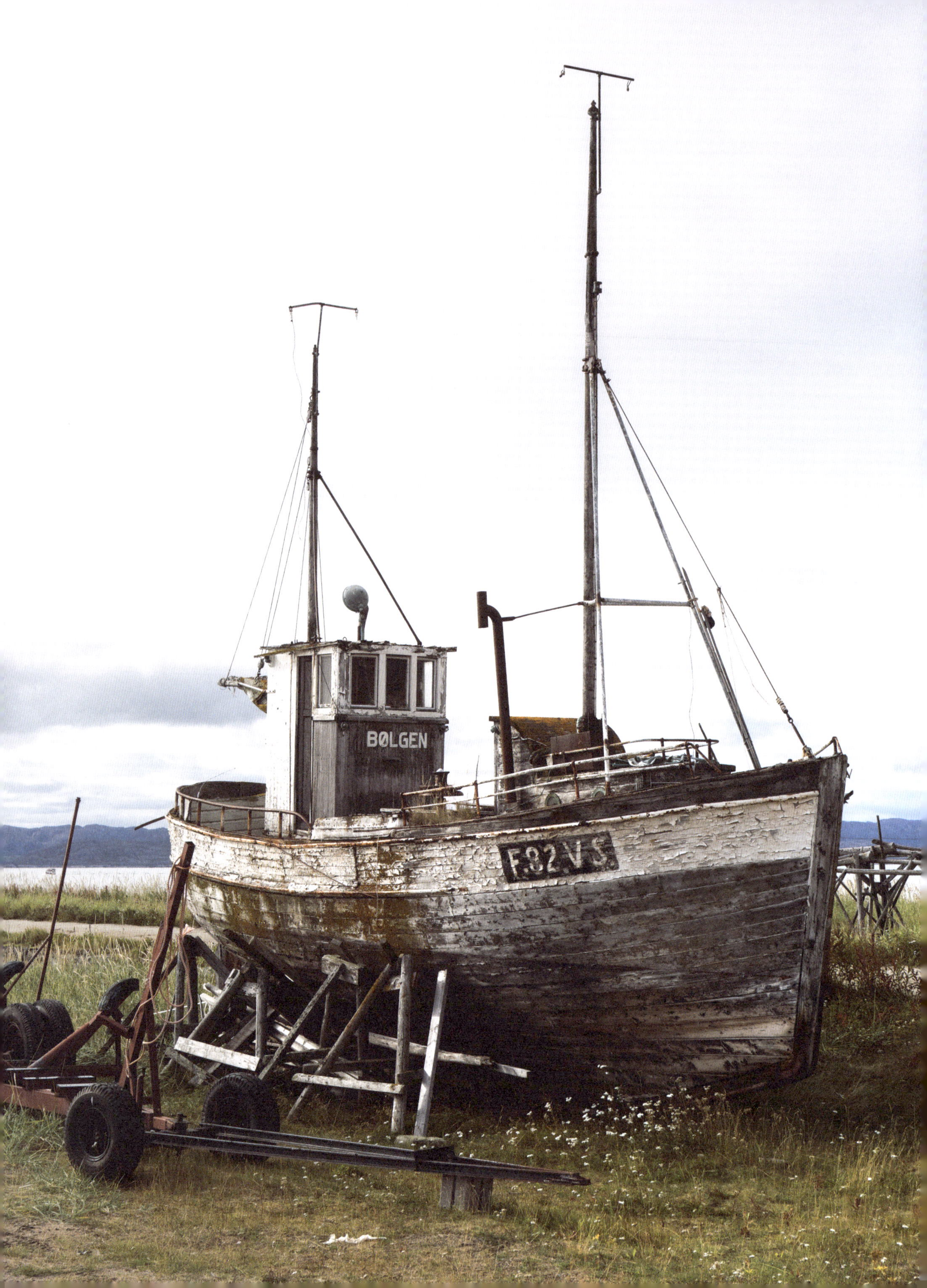
BØLGEN
F-82-V-S

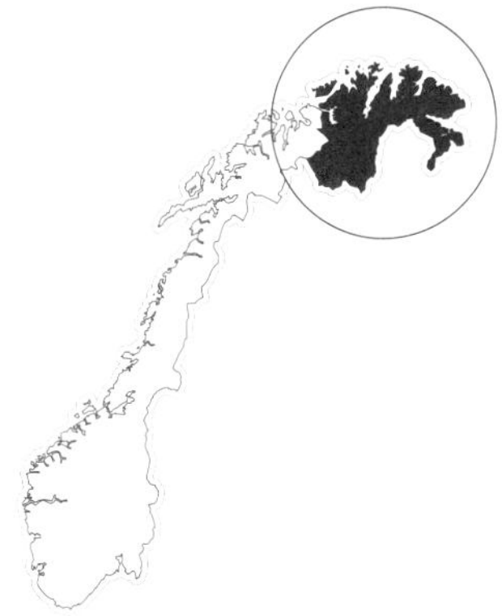

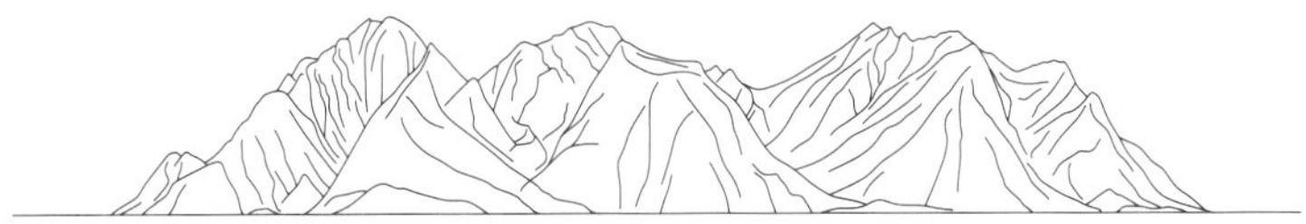

THE FAR NORTH

FINNMARK

The land of the Sámi and midnight sun, Finnmark is a region of mystery located at the same latitudes as Alaska and Siberia.

P.190

An old boat that was built in 1913 awaits better days on the Varanger Peninsula.

OPPOSITE

Norwegians flock to the Lyngen Alps to go skiing in the spring, when the days are lengthening and the mountains are blanketed in snow.

The vast and sparsely populated region of Finnmark enjoys a continental climate with the sort of temperature extremes you might expect in Eastern Siberia, recording highs of 91°F (33°C) in summer and a possible −60°F (−51°C) in January.

Finnmark, the land of polar nights and the Northern Lights, has been inhabited since the end of the last Ice Age more than ten thousand years ago. Some three thousand rock carvings found at Hjemmeluft, near the municipality of Alta, help us to understand the lives of the first hunter-gatherers of the far north many millennia ago.

The local people were evacuated to southern parts of Norway during the Second World War, and many buildings were destroyed by the Germans, who resorted to a scorched-earth policy when forced to retreat, torching homes and infrastructure as they went. As a result, much of Finnmark's present architecture is quite recent and lacks the charm of the older houses to be found elsewhere. The good news is that the scenery is anything but short of character, however, and Reisa National Park is one of the wildest and most remote areas in the country—it is possible to hike for days on end in unspoiled nature.

The northernmost point of Continental Europe, the famous North Cape, also lies in Northern Finnmark and is a must-see for many visitors. The drive is definitely worth it—it feels as though you have reached the ends of the earth. This sometimes desolate-looking landscape (animated by the occasional herd of reindeer) is also rich in wild berries, including the curious cloudberry and the delicious wild bilberry.

The rivers in the region teem with wild salmon and Arctic char (which has made them extremely popular with the fly-fishing community) and there is no shortage of land-based fauna either, with moose, foxes, wolverines, and lynx all present. The Alta region also boasts the country's greatest concentration of brown bears.

Approaching the Russian border, *fjell* dominate the landscape. This scenery is typical of Lapland and features high plateaus of glaciated rocks surrounded by a host of small lakes. We are now a long way from the fjords, and to the south the proximity of Finland and the Kola Peninsula in Russia can be sensed.

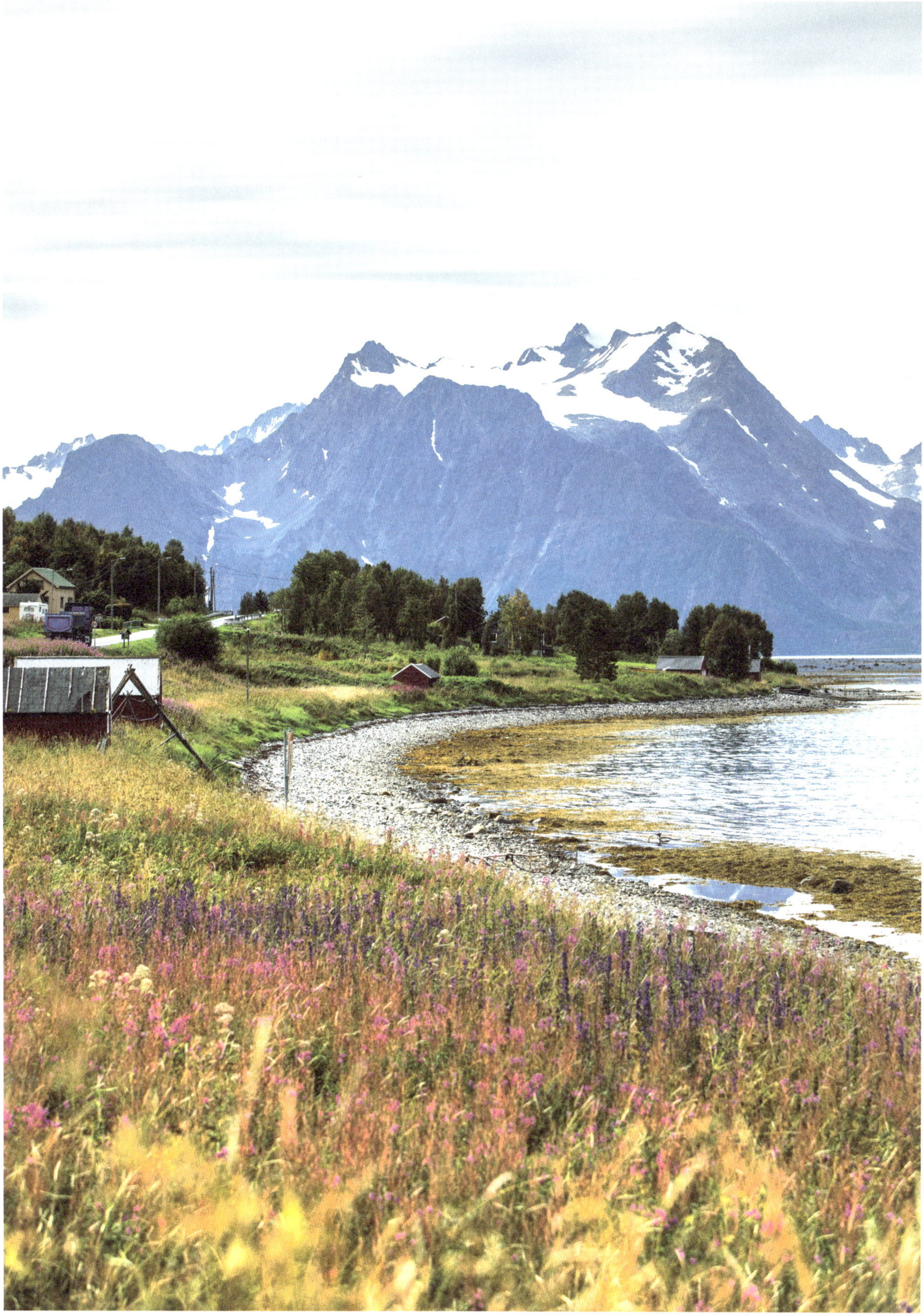

THE ESSENTIALS

43

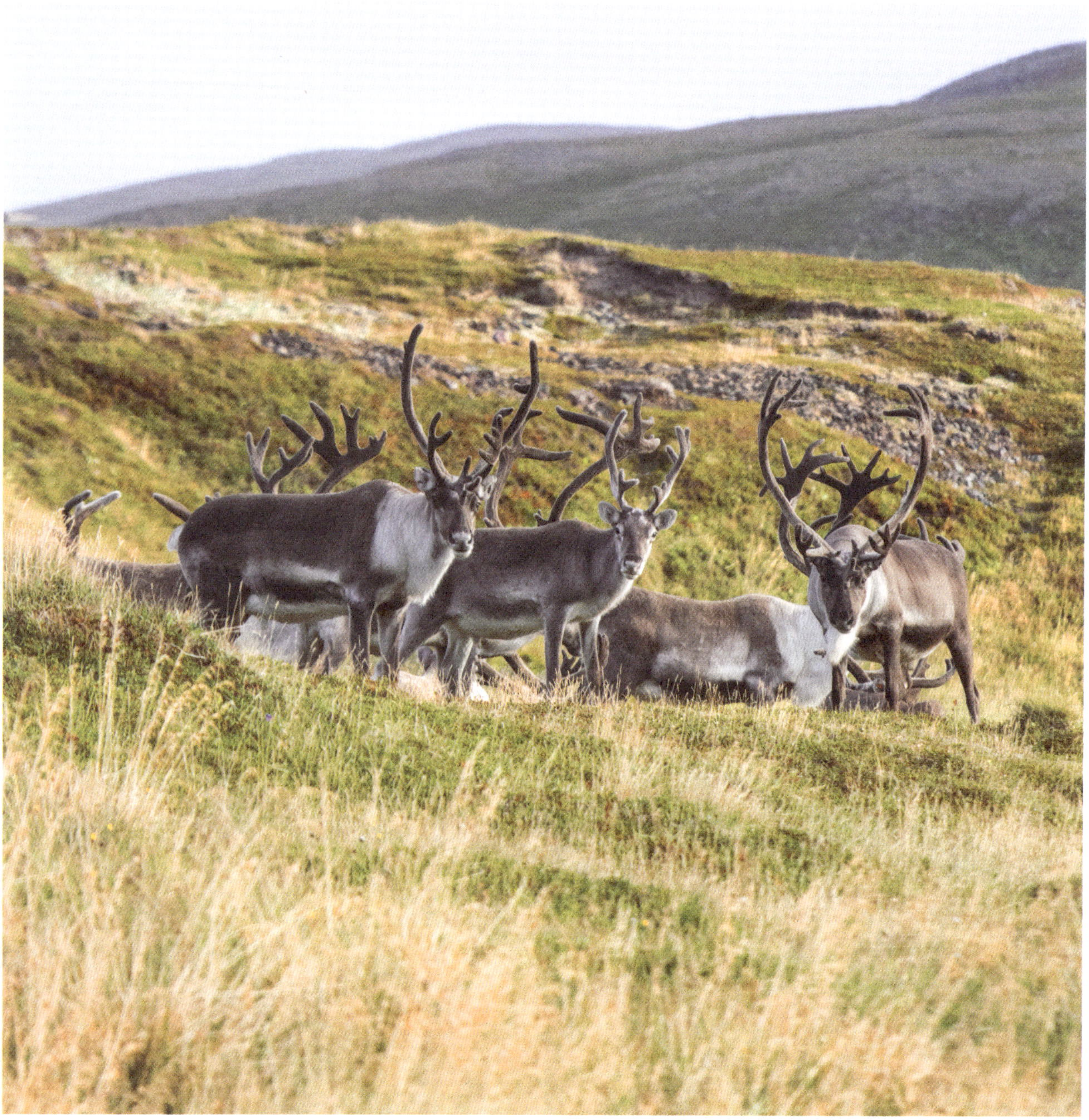

THE ROAD TO HAMNINGBERG

The road eventually peters out into a dead end, but the detour is worth it for its unique atmosphere—you might even catch a glimpse of animals, such as foxes, eagles, and reindeer.

44

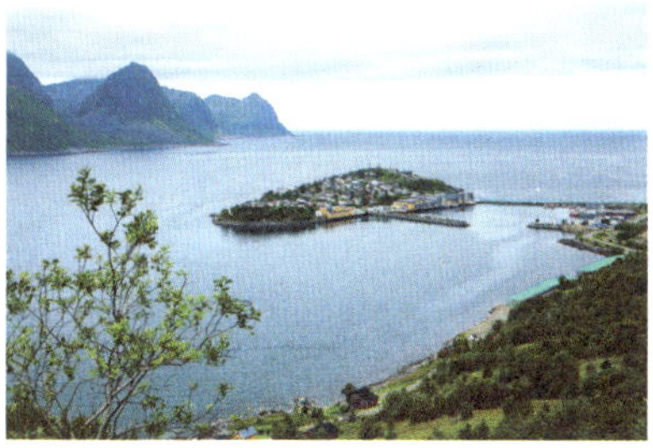

HUSØY

This small hamlet of three hundred residents is one of the most dynamic fishing communities on the island of Senja.

45

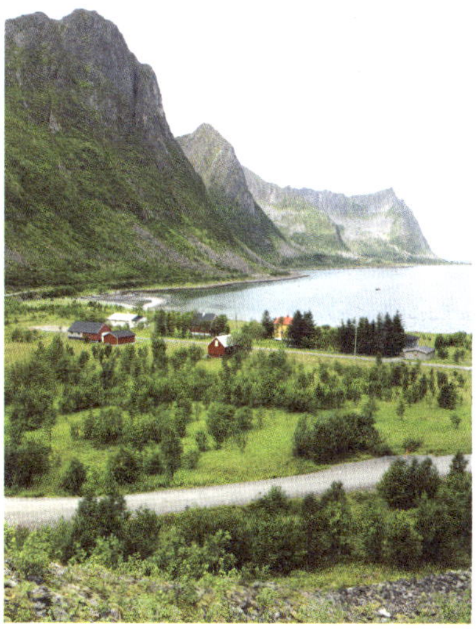

SENJA

Most tourists overlook the scenery of this wild and unspoiled island, but it is well worth a visit.

46

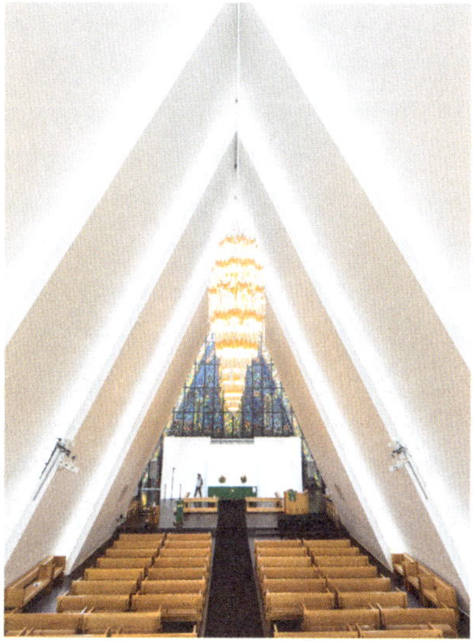

TROMSØ CATHEDRAL

The Arctic Cathedral has become an icon of the city of Tromsø.

47

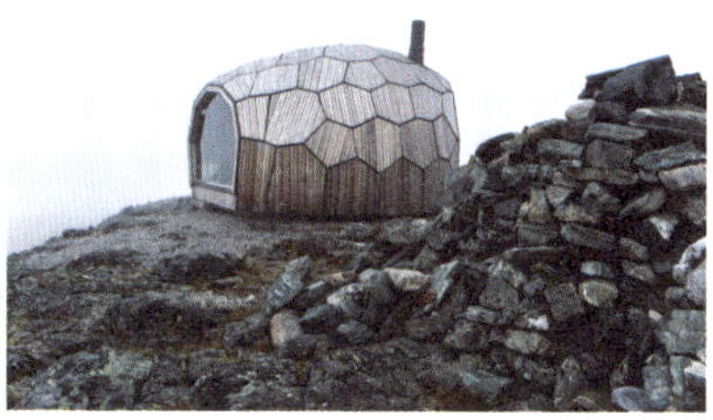

STORFJELLET

This shelter lies on the summit of Storfjellet, a peak in the uplands looking down over Hammerfest. The Northern Lights can sometimes be seen from here in winter.

48

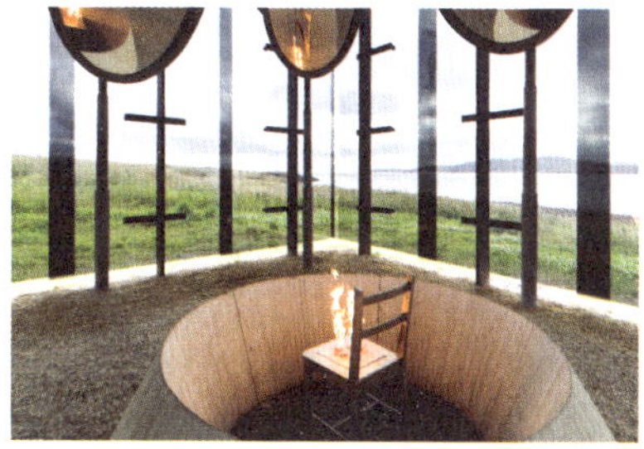

STEILNESET MEMORIAL

A monument designed by the artist Louise Bourgeois and the architect Peter Zumthor to commemorate the Vardø witch trials during the seventeenth century, which resulted in the execution of ninety-one people for witchcraft.

49

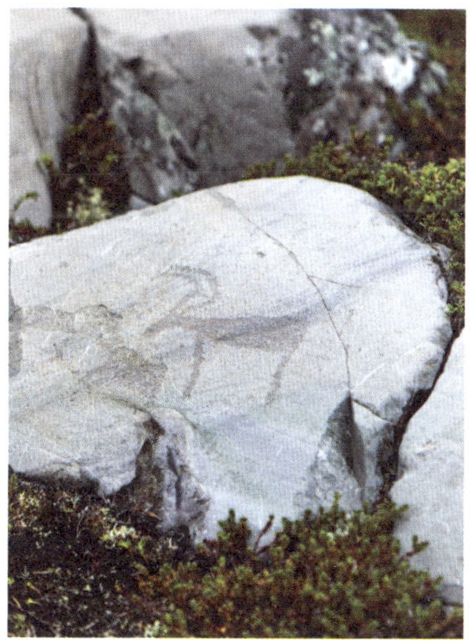

ALTA PETROGLYPHS

There are thousands of rock carvings depicting the lives of the region's first inhabitants several millennia ago.

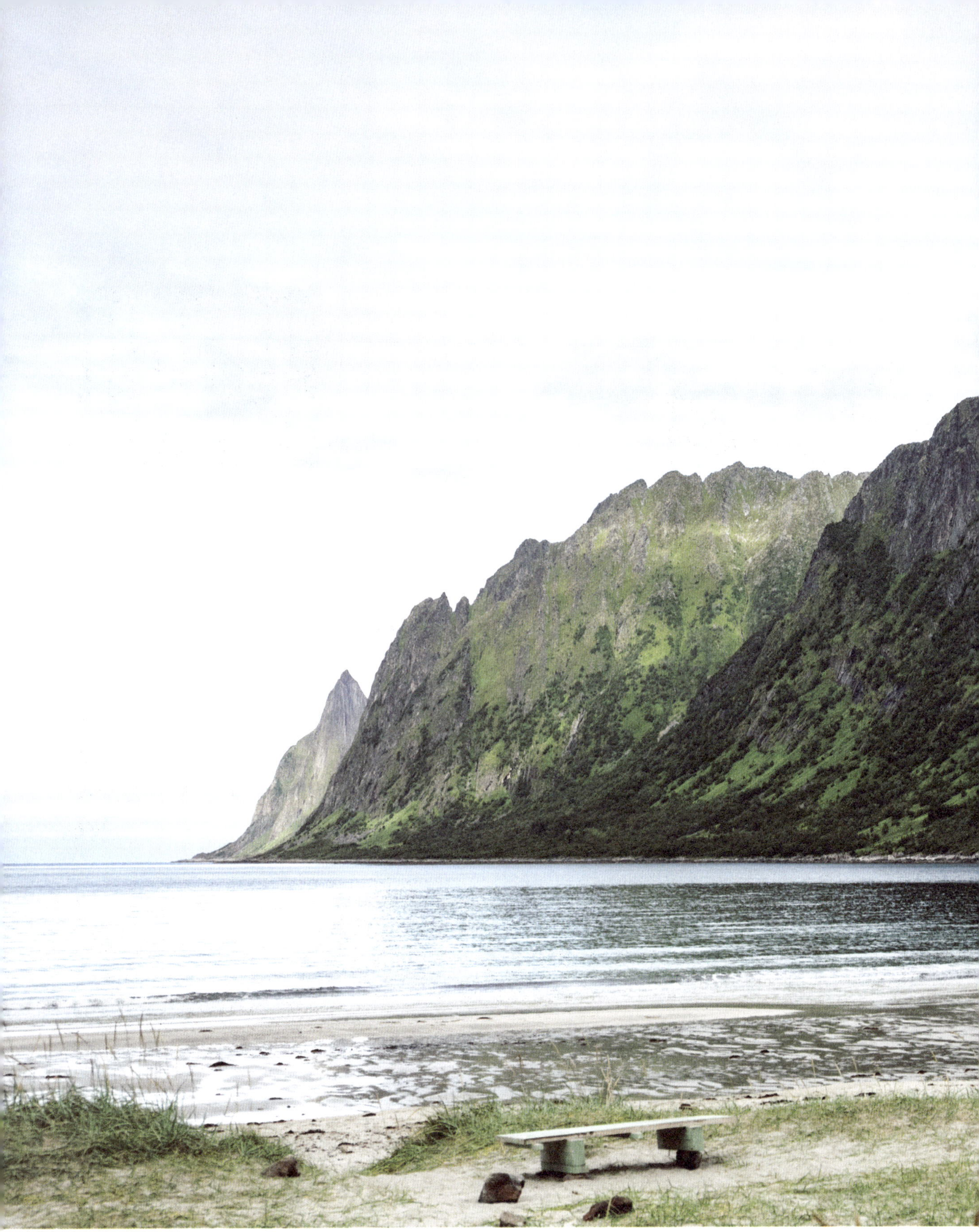

The turquoise waters and fine sand of Ersfjord Beach on the island of Senja make it the perfect place for visitors wishing to spend an evening around the campfire, gazing up at the Northern Lights.

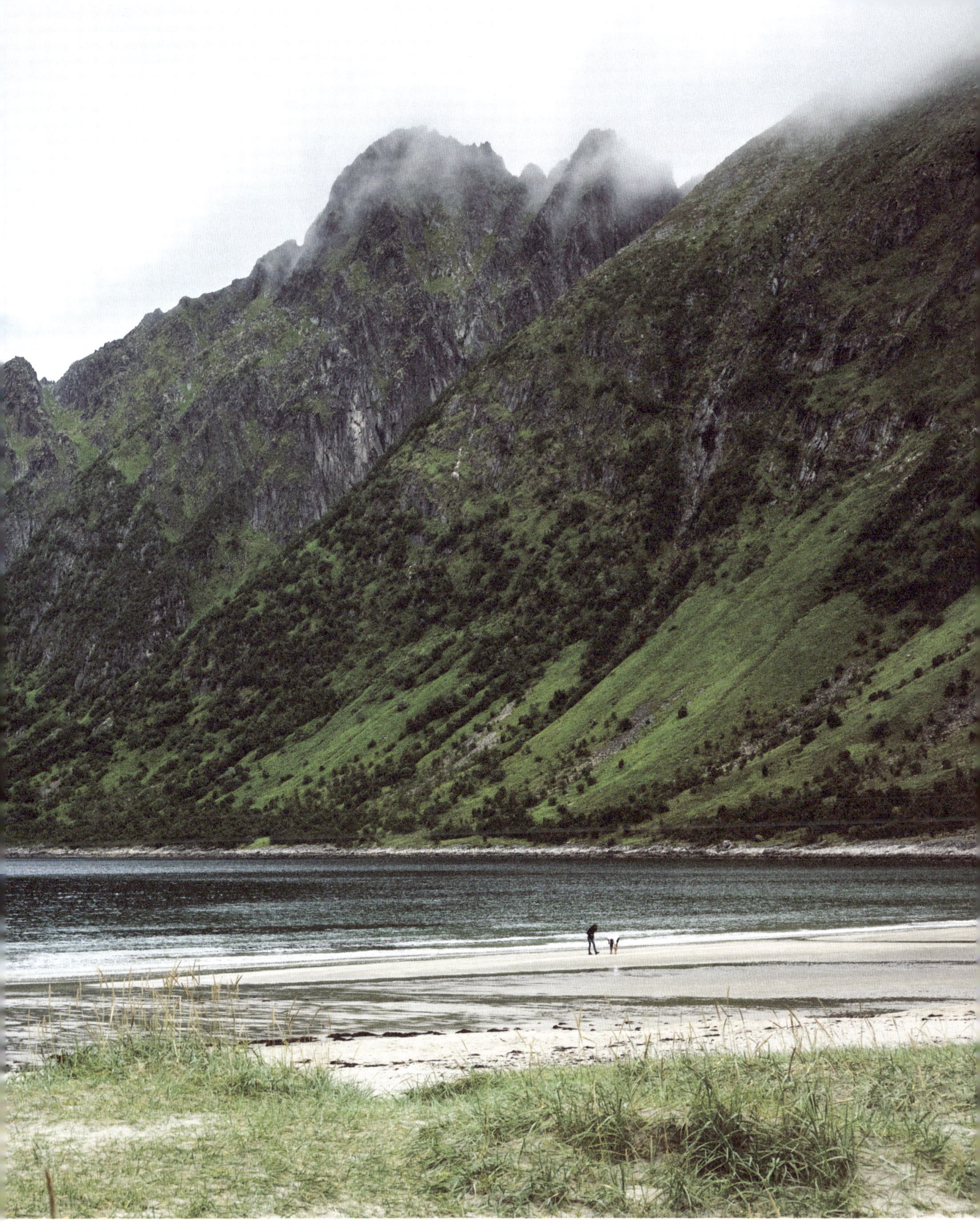

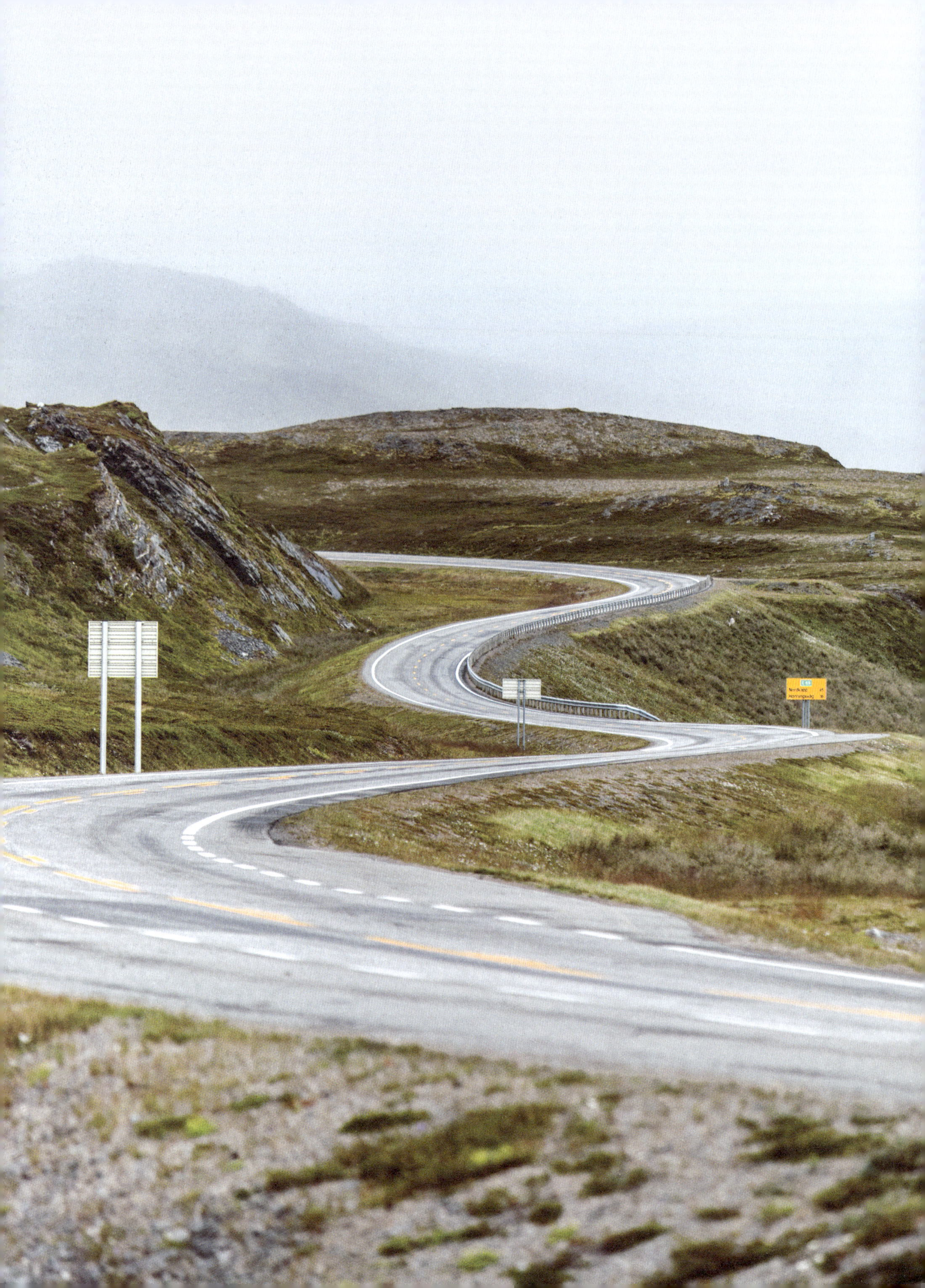

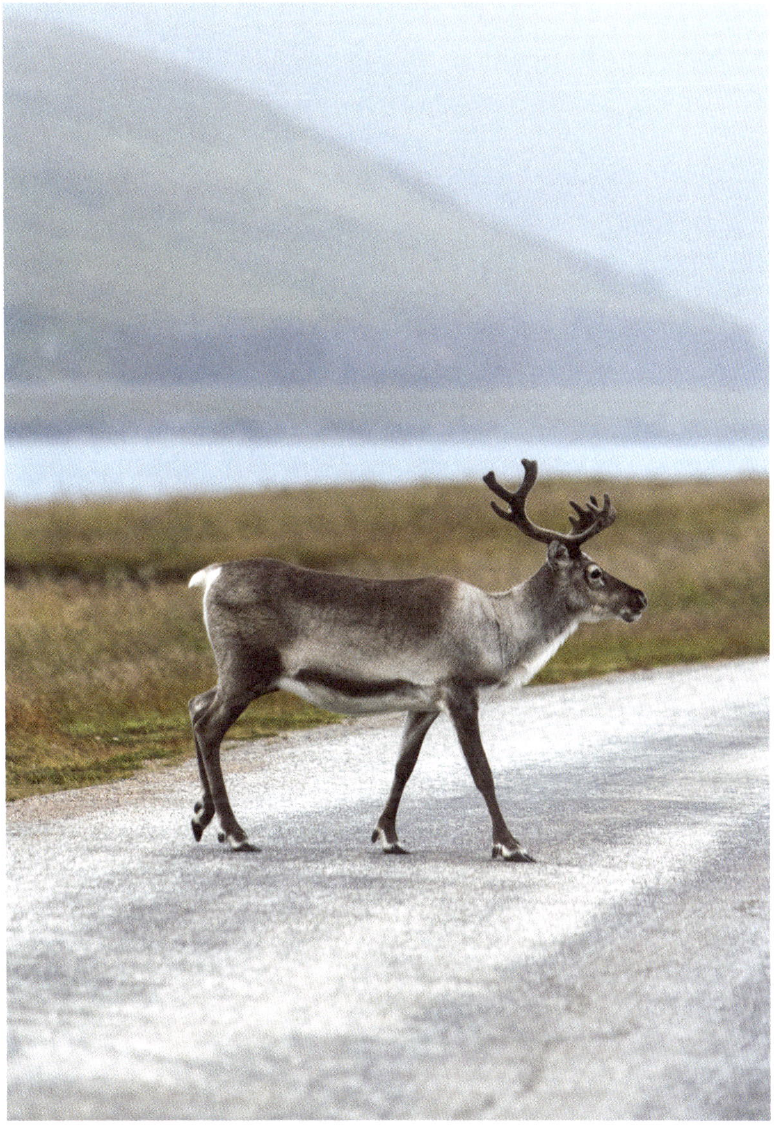

ABOVE

A reindeer crossing the road that leads to the North Cape. Large herds come to graze on the pastureland near the coast during summer.

OPPOSITE

The long and winding road to the North Cape. Weather conditions in winter are so unpredictable that cars can only travel in convoy, as it would be too dangerous to venture out alone.

CULTURE

THE SÁMI

REINDEER HERDERS

The only indigenous people in Europe to be recognized as such, the Sámi, with their millennia of history, are being met with some very contemporary challenges.

For nearly eight thousand years, the Sámi people have inhabited a territory that extends across several countries, including Norway, Sweden, Finland, and Russia. The population is now estimated to number around eighty thousand, with some fifty thousand living in Norway alone. In Norway, the Sámi consist of three groups: those who live in the mountains and subsist by herding reindeer; those who inhabit the river banks and support themselves with agriculture as well as hunting, fishing and gathering; and finally, those who live along the coast and fish but who also enjoy a way of life very similar to other Norwegians.

Under the pressure of European incursions during the seventeenth century, the nomadic Sámi people were forced to turn their hand to herding semi-domesticated reindeer, moving with their animals to find pastureland rich in lichen as the seasons changed.

At one time the Sámi would follow their reindeer on skis and make camp in a *lavvu*, a kind of teepee-shaped tent, but the arrival of snowmobiles and GPS tracking has completely revolutionized their lives. Very few of the Sámi are still entirely nomadic; most have a fixed base but continue to follow their herds as they migrate, often spending long periods of time far from home in the mountains. As well as playing a central role in their lives in terms of economic activity, reindeer herding is a way of life around which all the most significant moments of the year are organized. Today the modern world is disrupting the balanced life the Sámi have built for themselves to date. The mining industry is expanding in the Finnmark region, where there is great potential for extracting the rare earth metals used in advanced technology. Forestry, road-building, and hydroelectric dams all fragment and change the landscape that is essential to reindeer survival.

Like all those who live in the far north, the Sámi are on the front line of climate change. Alternating periods of frost with unseasonal warmth in winter result in the formation of layers of ice that trap the lichen on which the reindeer rely as their principal source of food. Episodes of thaw increase animal mortality and are a source of major concern among the Sámi herders.

Toward the end of the twentieth century, the Norwegian Parliament issued a decree to the effect that the Sámi and Norwegian languages and cultures were to be placed on an equal footing, and a Sámi Parliament was duly convened in Karasjok in 1989 to represent the Norwegian Sámis' socio-economic interests more forcefully. This has proved a useful additional means of addressing the many challenges that lie ahead in the twenty-first century.

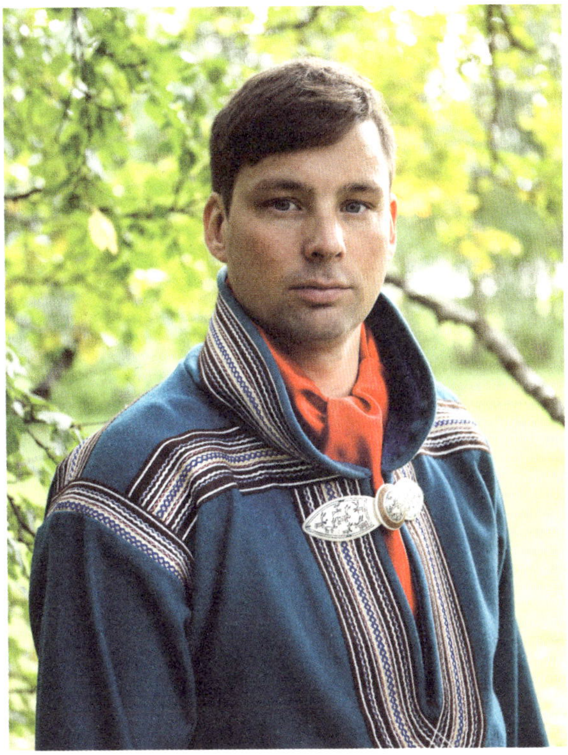

JUHAN

Juhan is a reindeer herder living in Karasjok. He is wearing a *gákti*, traditional Sámi dress that is worn for ceremonial purposes as well as for working with the reindeer.

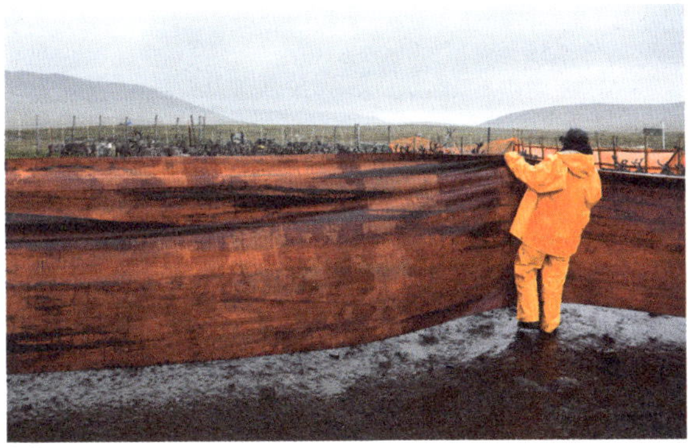

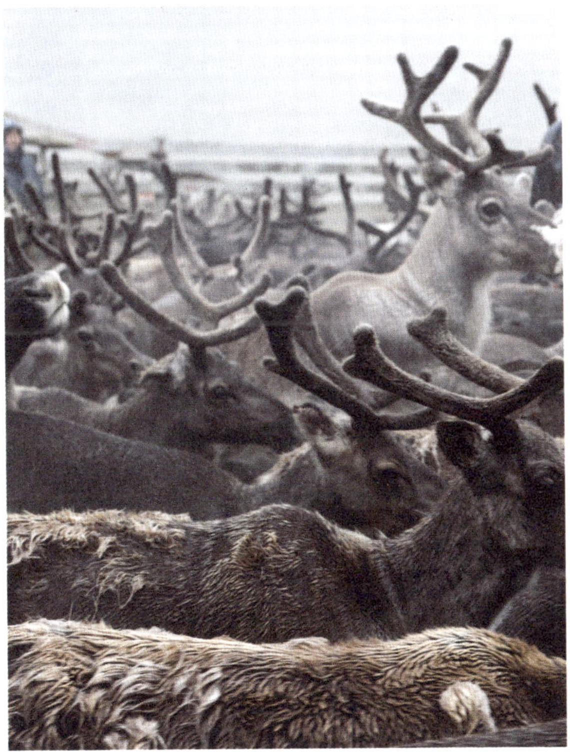

BIRET

Biret is employed by the administrative council for the county of Troms and Finnmark, where she works to preserve the Sámi way of life and promote the interests of reindeer herders.

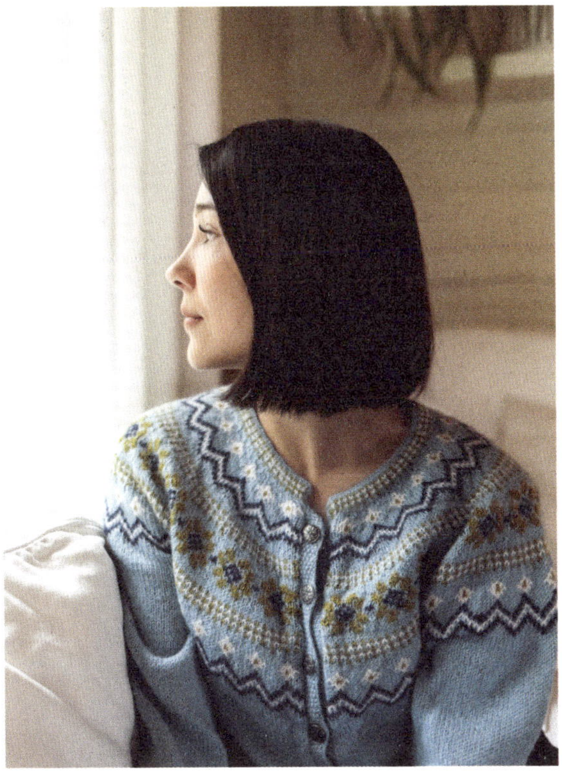

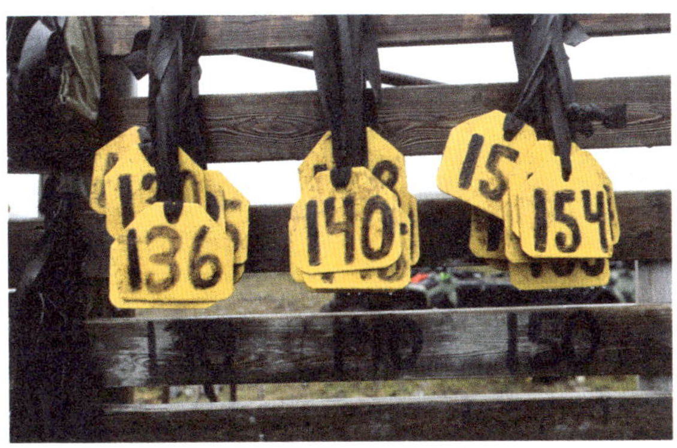

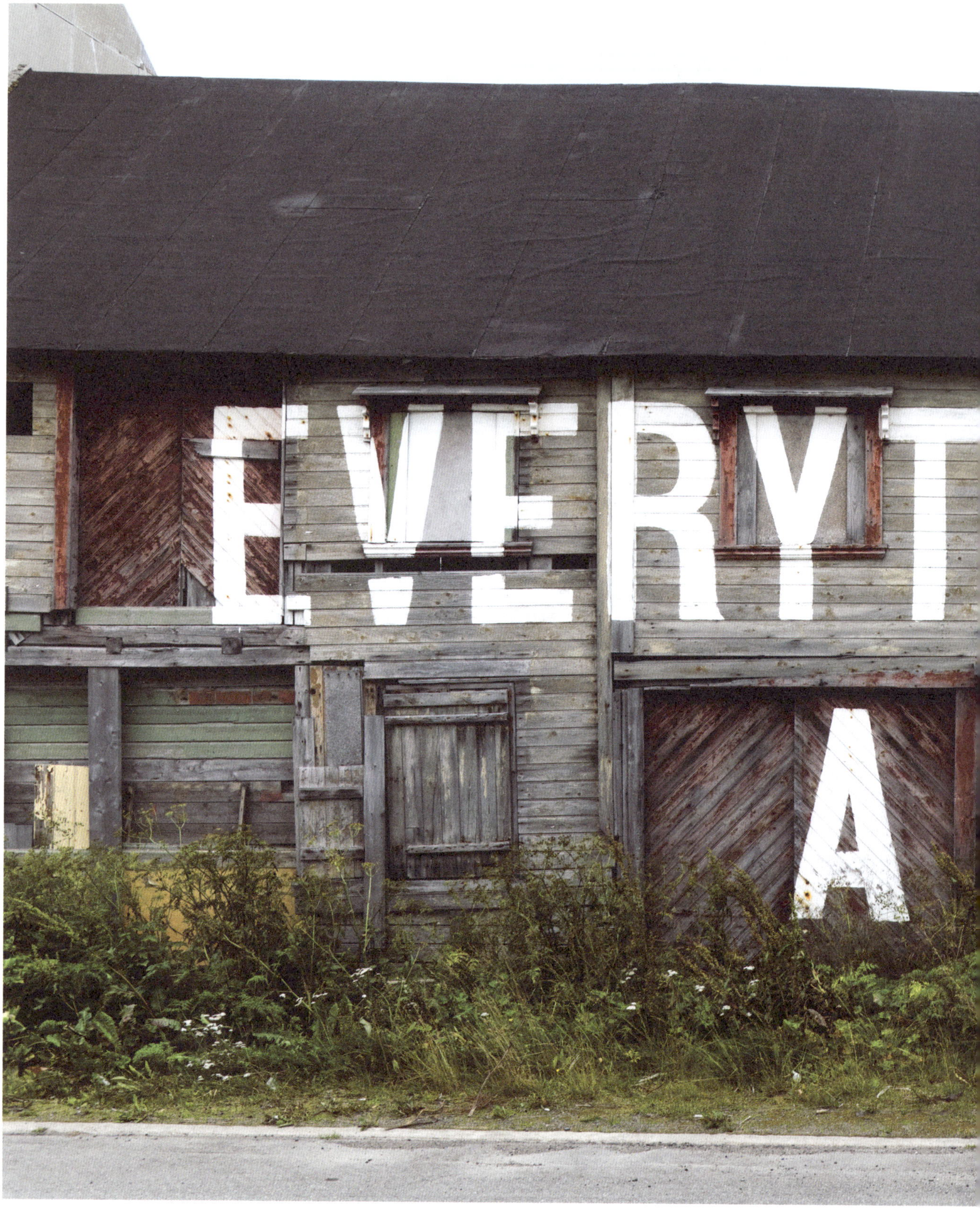

A work by Norwegian street artist Pøbel in the small town of Vardø, situated on the Barents Sea in the far northeast of the country.

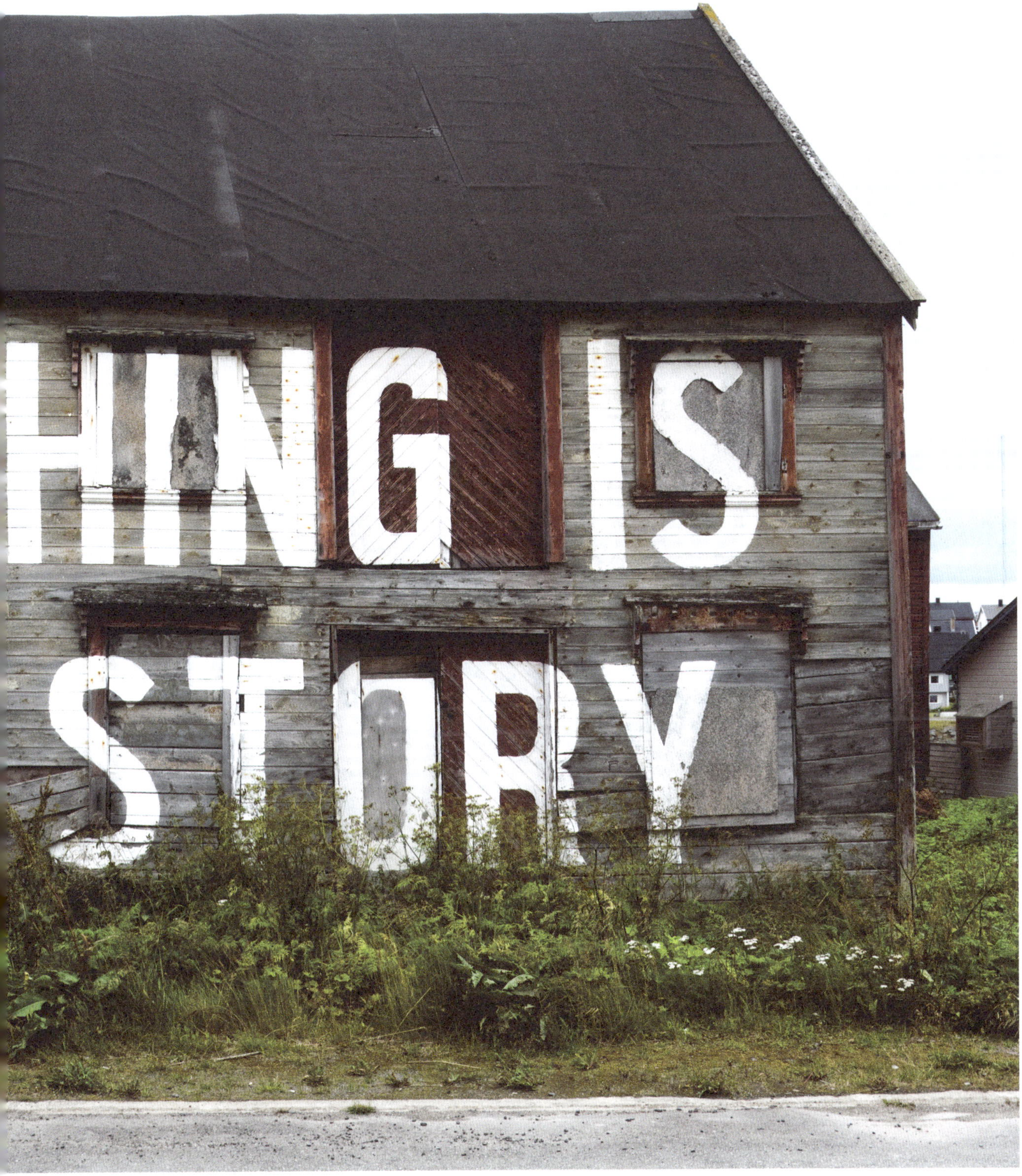
HING IS
STORY

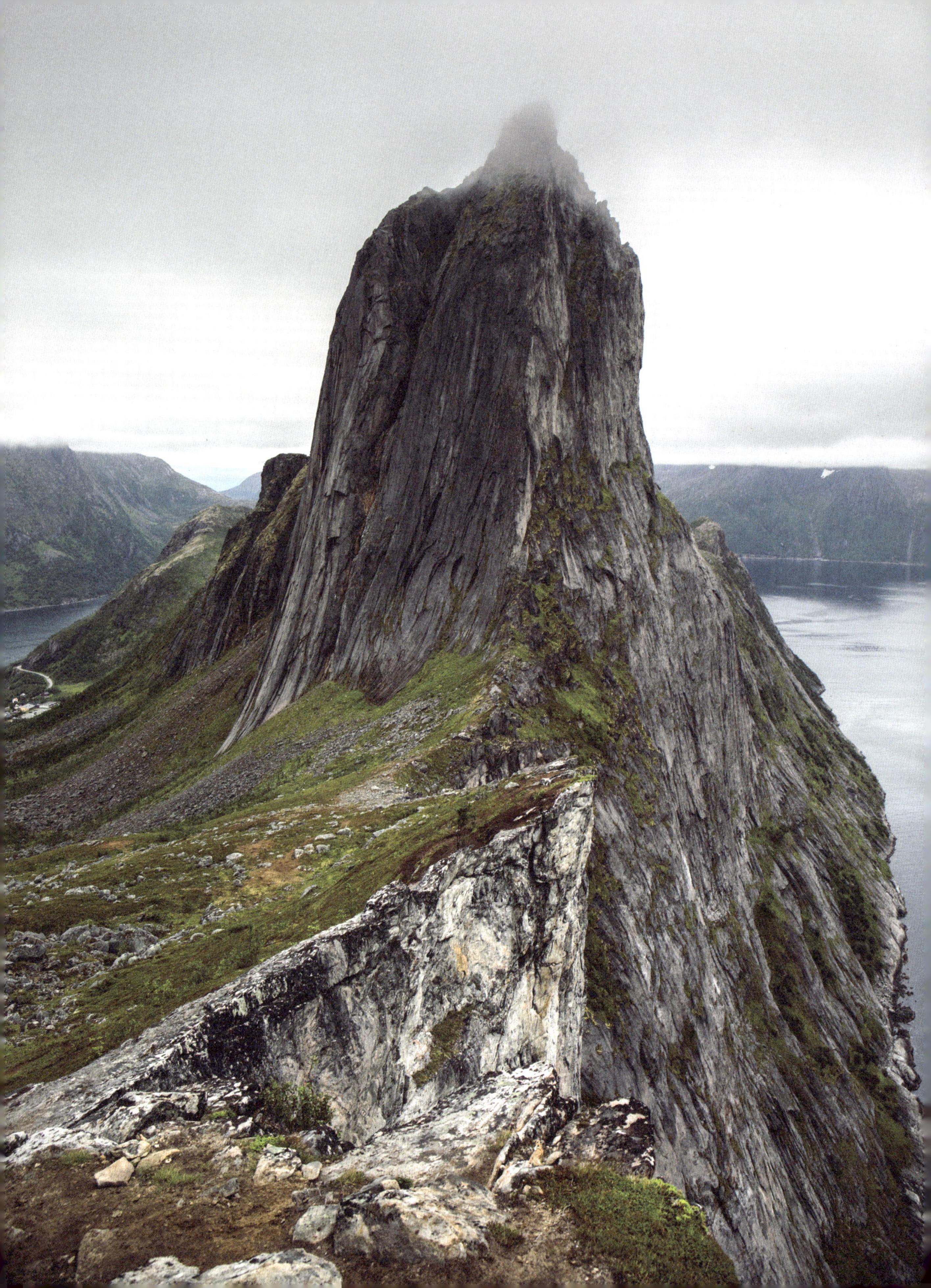

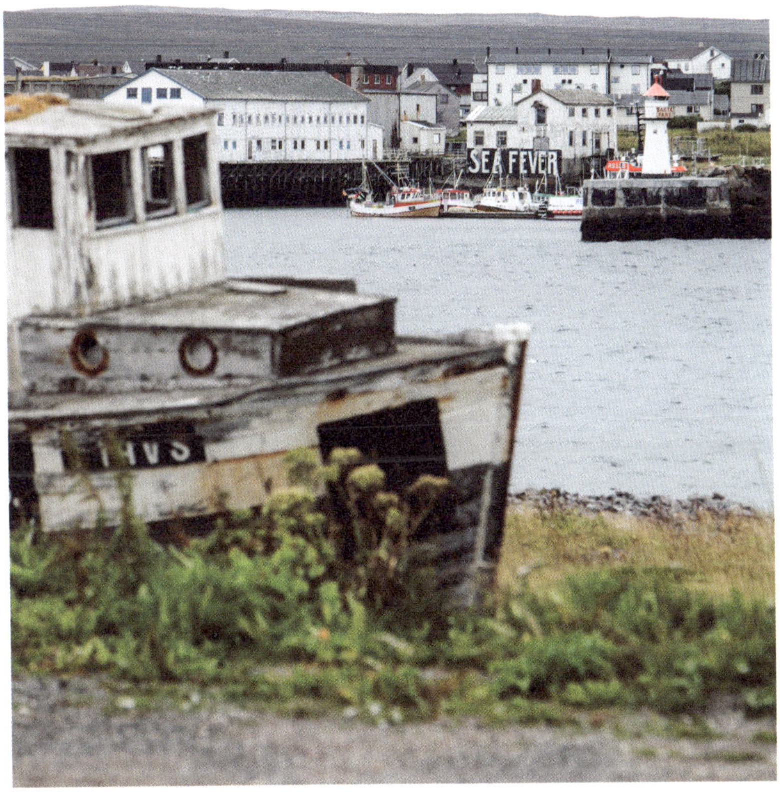

ABOVE

The port of Vardø on the Varanger Peninsula is accessible all year round thanks to the currents of the North Atlantic Drift, which bring in warm water from the Gulf Stream.

OPPOSITE

Don't miss the magnificent trail to the rocky summit of Segla on the island of Senja.

DEEP DIVE

ROALD AMUNDSEN

CONQUERING THE SOUTH POLE

Many trailblazing Norwegians have left their mark on the history of exploration, from Erik the Red to Cecilie Skog, but Roald Amundsen is undoubtedly the most famous of them all.

What makes Norwegians so ready, willing, and able to explore new territories? Is it the country's rugged geography, or maybe its jagged coastline, battered by winter storms? Between 1893 and 1912, the explorers Fridtjof Nansen, Otto Sverdrup, and Oscar Wisting all set off in turn aboard the *Fram* (which translates as "Forward"), the polar exploration vessel that they soon made world famous. Designed to be lifted, rather than crushed, by the ice floes of the North Pole, the three-masted schooner provided accommodation for a crew of sixteen.

In 1908 the explorer Roald Amundsen addressed the Norwegian Geographical Society to announce that he would be embarking for the North Pole aboard the *Fram* to carry out a four-year scientific and geographical mission. The king of Norway and the Norwegian Parliament were much taken with the idea and offered financial support for the project. On learning in September 1909 that the Americans Frederick Cook and Robert Peary had beaten him to the punch, however, Amundsen decided to change tack and instead attempt to conquer the South Pole. The Antarctic was familiar territory for the explorer, as he had been part of an expedition led by Belgian naval officer Baron de Gerlache de Gomery a dozen or so years previously.

Fearing that the Norwegian government might withdraw its financial aid, Amundsen kept his project a secret until the vessel docked in Madeira, the only stop on the voyage to the Antarctic. When he informed his crew of their destination, every member elected to continue, but the news was not well received by the public or the press, who condemned the explorer's decision. Amundsen dropped anchor in the Ross Sea in January 1911 and began preparations.

He set off on October 19, 1911 with four of his crew, fifty-two dogs, and four sleds. The team crossed mountains, glaciers, and crevasse fields before reaching the South Pole on December 14, 1911. Upon completing the return journey to the *Fram*, they had covered a grand total of 2,140 miles (3,440 km) in ninety-nine days. The explorers returned with only two sleds and eleven dogs (some had died of the cold while others had had to be slaughtered to feed the men and the other dogs).

Amundsen and his team were greeted as heroes upon their return and any previous feelings of doubt and reproach were forgotten in favor of the prestige of the exploit they had achieved. The British saluted their accomplishment but criticized Amundsen's hard-headedness. Englishman Robert Falcon Scott and his team were on their way to the South Pole at the same time. They were to reach their objective a month later, only to die on the return journey.

The *Fram* now occupies such an important place in the history of Norway's voyages of exploration that it has been preserved and put on display in Oslo in its own dedicated museum.

THE AMUNDSEN EXPEDITION

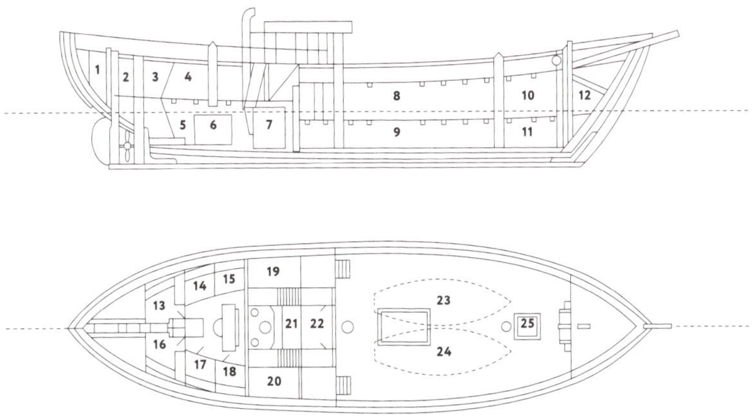

CUTAWAY DIAGRAM OF THE *FRAM*

1 Rudder **2** Propeller **3** Ladder **4** Saloon **5** Engine room **6** Engine **7** Boiler **8** Main hold **9** Lower hold **10** Bow hold **11** Lower hold **12** Bow **13** Cabin **14** Cabin **15** Cabin **16** Cabin **17** Cabin **18** Cabin **19** Storage locker **20** Storage locker **21** Galley **22** Chart room **23** Tender **24** Tender **25** Hatch

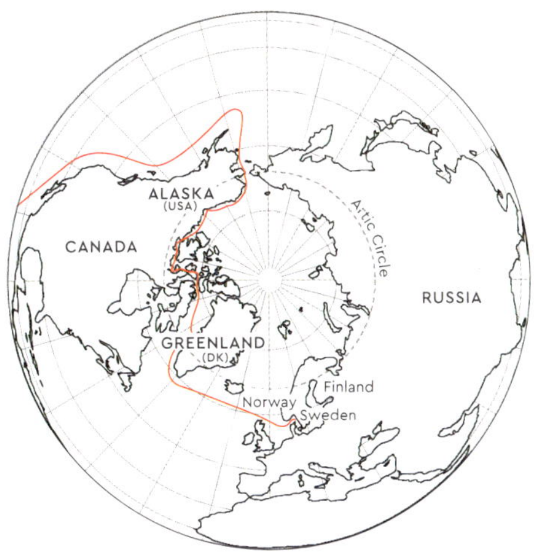

THE NORTHWEST PASSAGE

The Northwest Passage was an expedition personally funded by Roald Amundsen before his trip to the South Pole. His objective was to open up a route linking the Atlantic and the Pacific via the far north of Canada.

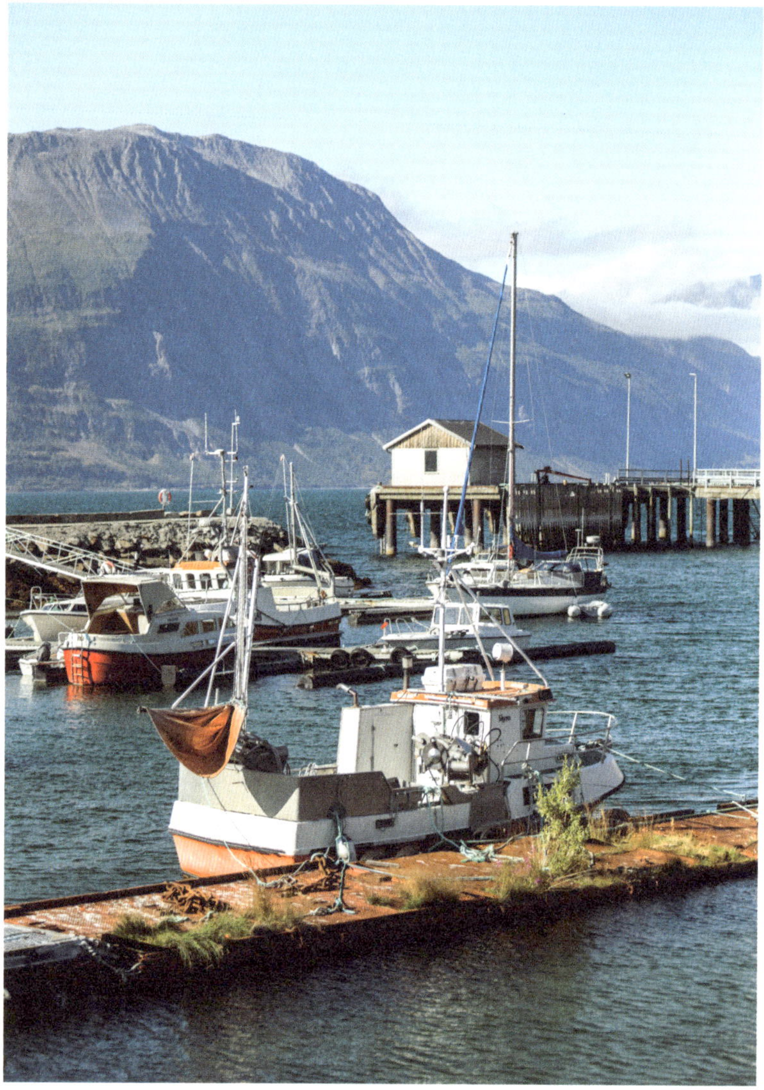

ABOVE

The Lyngen Alps seen from the small fishing port of Skibotn.

OPPOSITE

The Lyngen Alps to the east of Tromsø extend for 56 miles (90 km) from north to south. The summit of Jiehkkevárri, the highest peak in the range, is at a height of 6,014 ft (1,833 m).

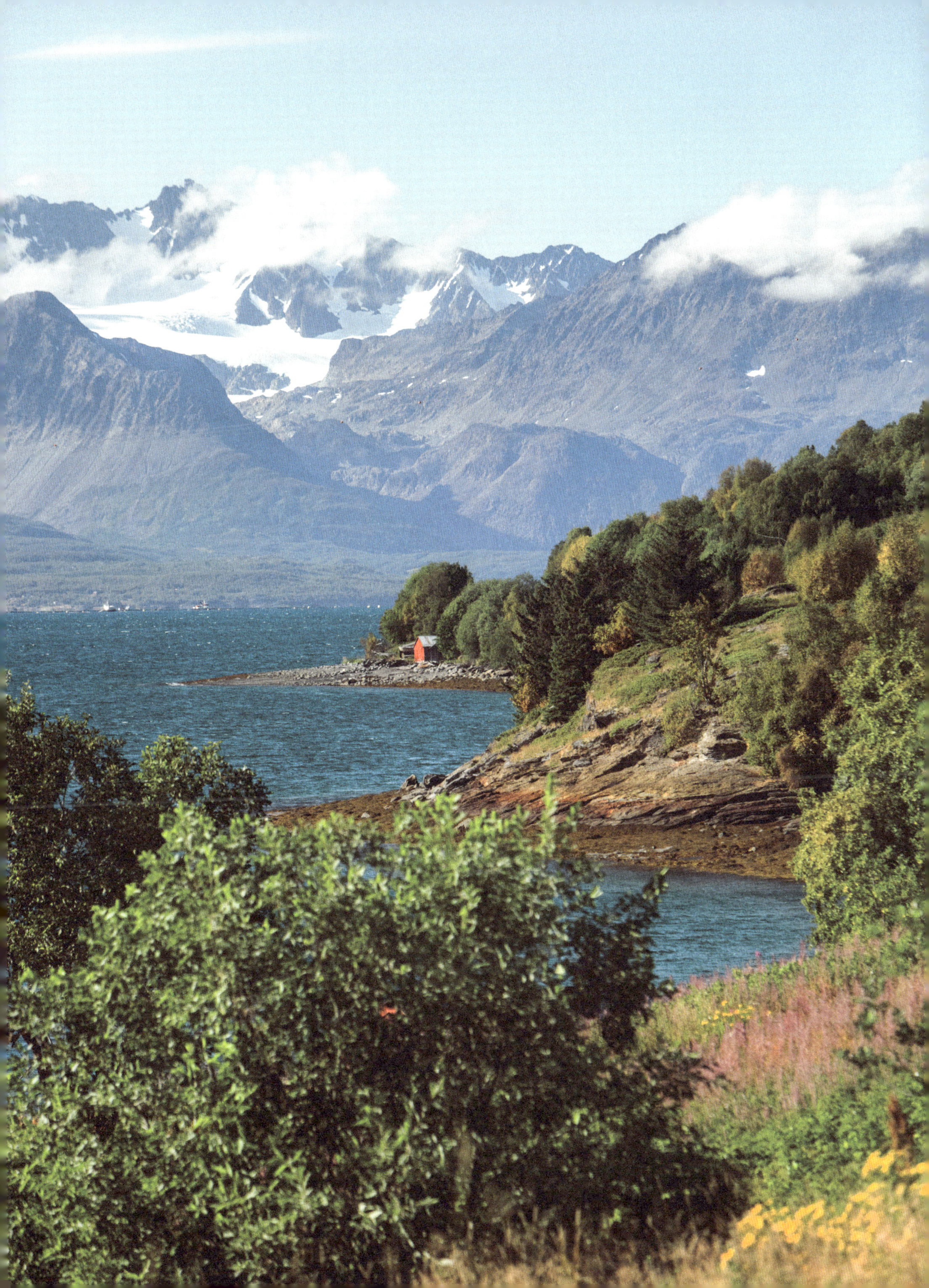

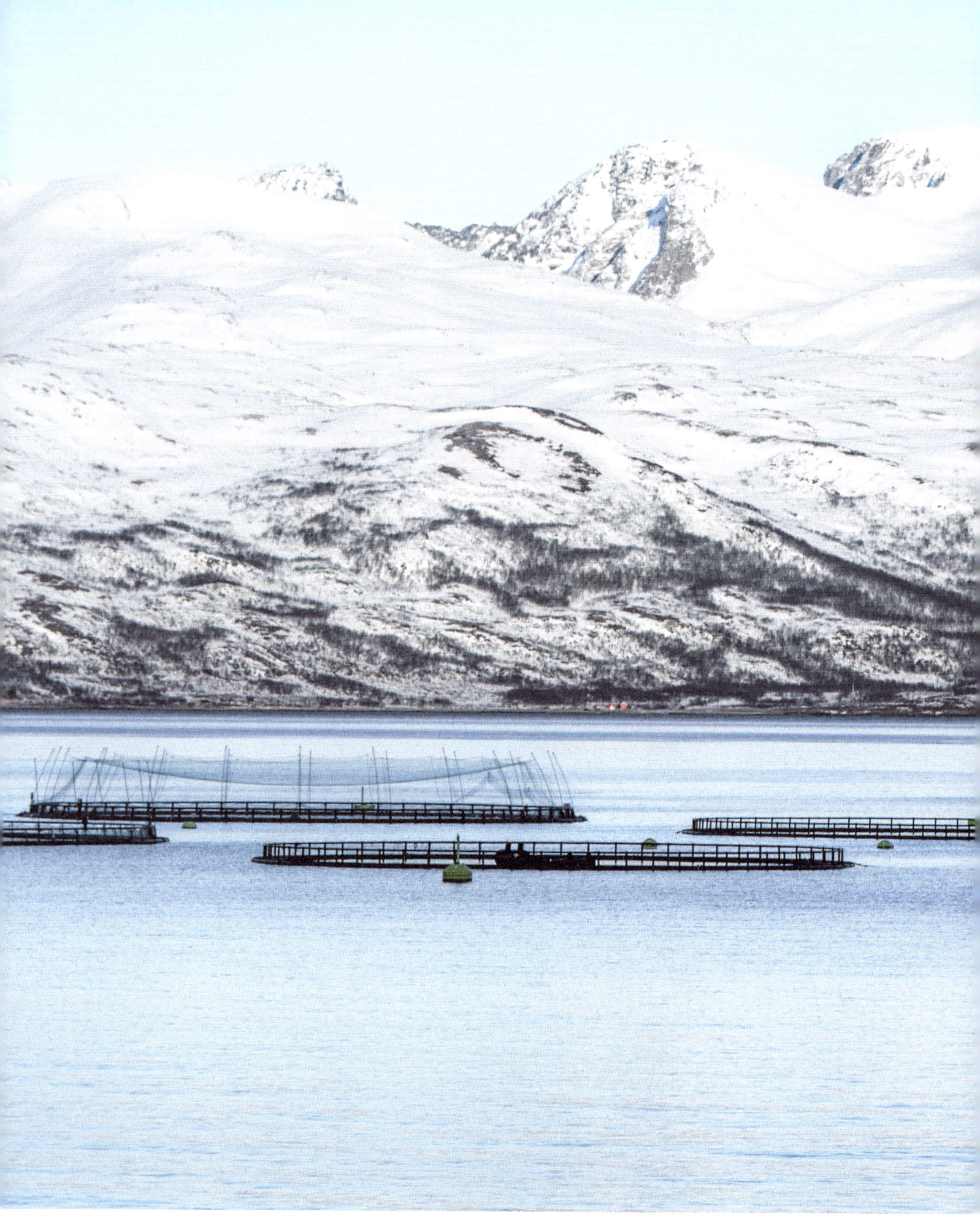

Fish farms near the village of Hansnes. Salmon farming is an important industry in the country's economy.
France and the United States are two of the largest markets for Norwegian salmon.

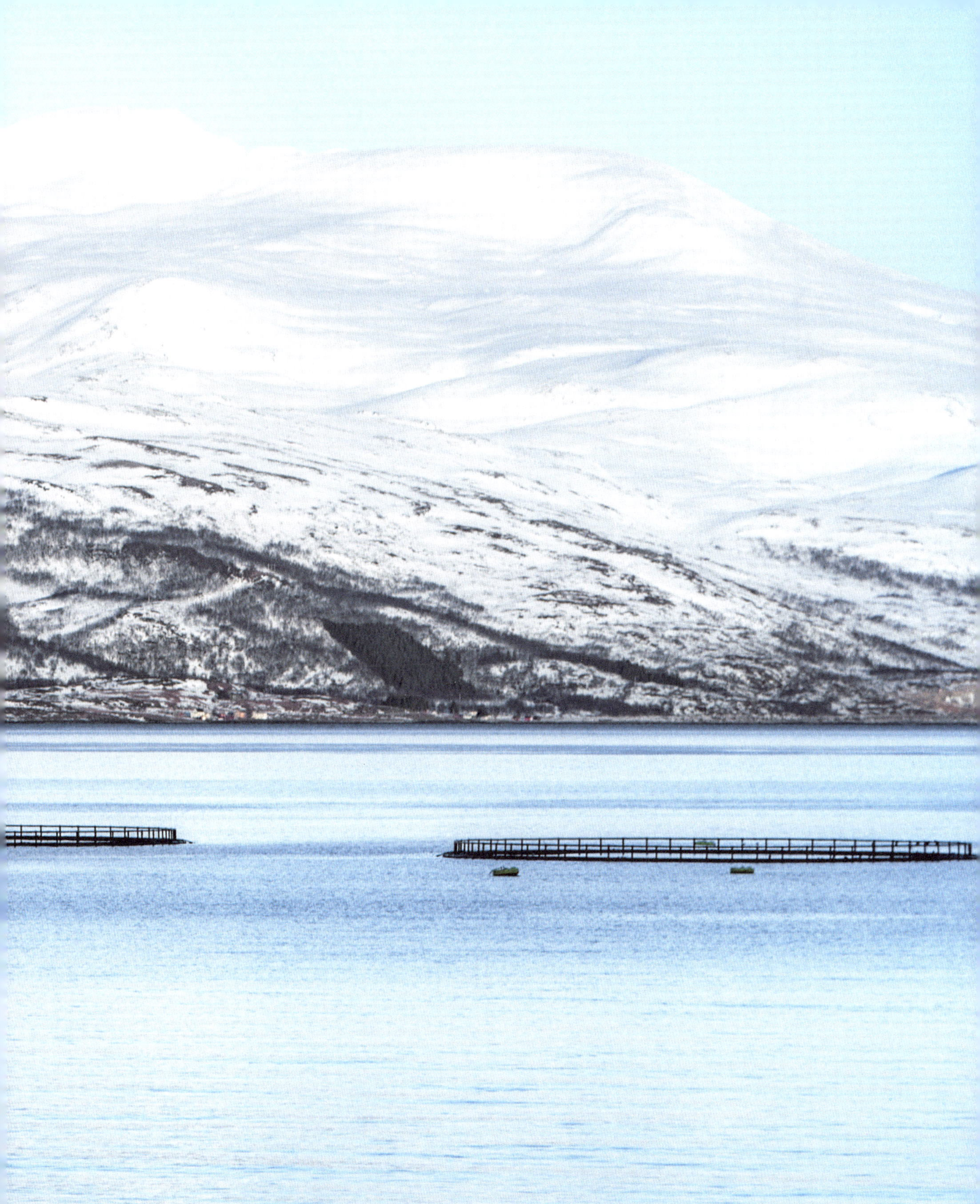

EXCURSION

A TRAVEL DIARY

FROM TROMSØ TO THE NORTH CAPE

No journey to the far north is complete without a stop at the North Cape. This is the tale of a journey into the elements.

After calling in briefly to Tromsø, I hit the road north. I've been crisscrossing Norway for six weeks and the North Cape is an important waypoint. It is a legendary destination and I have heard much about its unpredictable weather—some have come away with fond memories and have even been lucky enough to see the midnight sun, while the less fortunate have found themselves enveloped in thick fog and unable to see their hand in front of their face, let alone the sea. But you have to take it as it comes—it is impossible to predict the weather at these latitudes.

I head north, passing immense, barren valleys smoothed by glaciers. There is less traffic on the roads up here than in the south of the country, even at the height of summer. I am accompanied by a bright, pure light, reminding me of the early fall I spent in Mongolia. I leave the Lyngen Alps to visit Sámi reindeer herders in the Reisa valley. I have been in contact with them for some weeks previously and am determined to meet up with them. After hiking for two hours in the rain, I spot a couple of huts, then some men, and finally a large herd of reindeer. The dogs run up and sniff me but soon realize that I pose no threat to the herd and allow me to come closer. I spend the afternoon with the Sámi herders and before we go our separate ways, we make a promise to meet for longer next time.

There are more reindeer on the road as I continue, and they sometimes decide to cross without warning when a car approaches, so motorists have to stay alert. After spending a night in Repvåg, I stop off in the village of Honningsvåg, which feels somewhat strange and remote. I notice huge flocks of seagulls that seem to be waiting for a storm to break.

The suspicions of the hotelier where I spent the night are seemingly being confirmed. A fog is rolling in, and it only thickens as I continue north. Damn it! It is deep and dense; I am going to get a proper taste of the North Cape.

I have rarely experienced such poor visibility in broad daylight, but I eventually arrive and I find myself almost alone, face to face with the monument symbolizing the North Cape. The visit of the few tourists who have made it up here to snap a photo is curtailed by an icy blast. They scurry indoors to seek shelter in the warm and I take advantage of the ensuing peace and quiet to think back over my journey and the thousands of miles I have covered since Oslo. What a trip! In a way, the conditions here have also left their mark—I've watched a good many sunsets in amazing places, but rarely have I been so completely engulfed by fog. I enjoy the unusual ambience and remind myself that sometimes the journey is more beautiful than the destination.

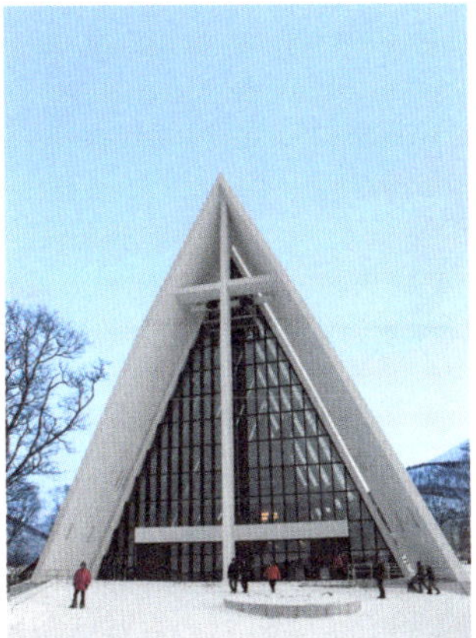

A large glass facade surrounds the entrance of the famous Arctic Cathedral in Tromsø.

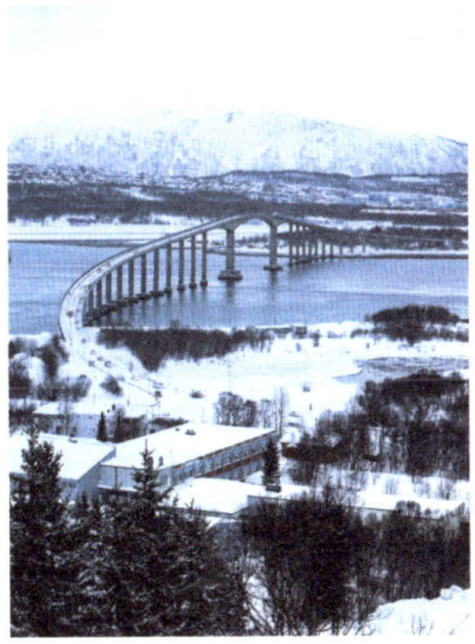

The city of Tromsø was built on an island and is connected to the mainland by several bridges.

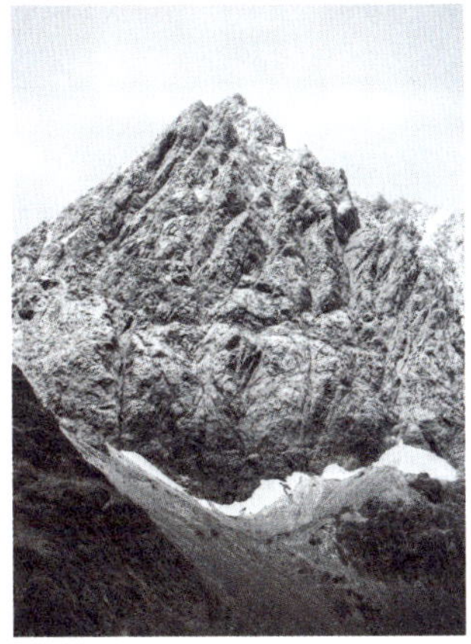

The jagged peaks of the Lyngen Alps are silhouetted against an ominous sky.

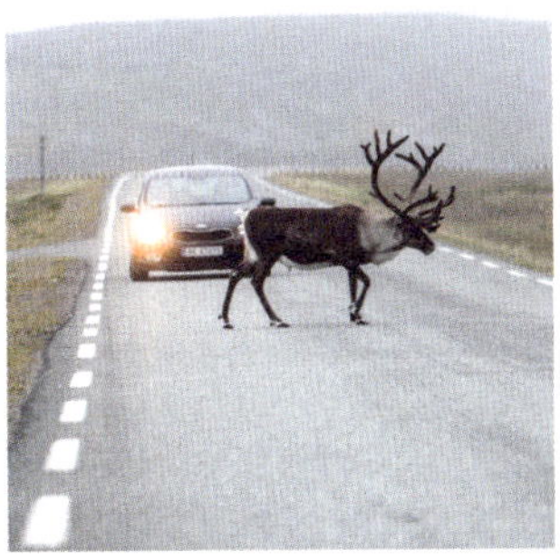

A motorist patiently waiting for a reindeer to cross the road.

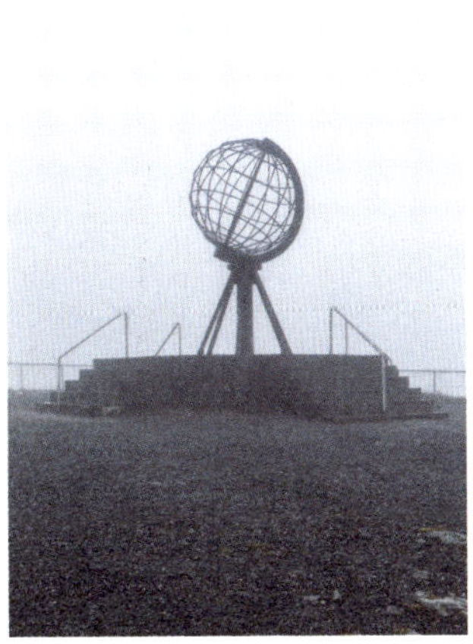

The North Cape is symbolized by the Globe Monument made of steel.

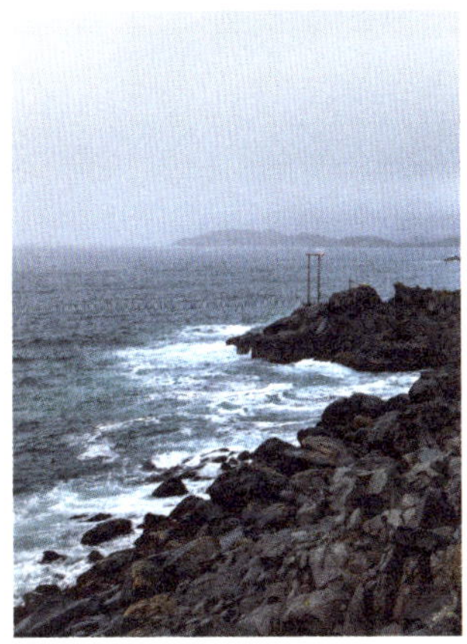

The storm-battered coastline only enhances the unique atmosphere here.

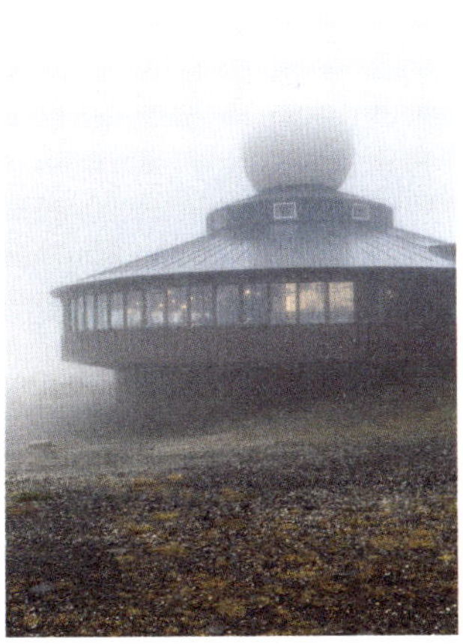

A shelter provides protection for visitors when the weather is bad.

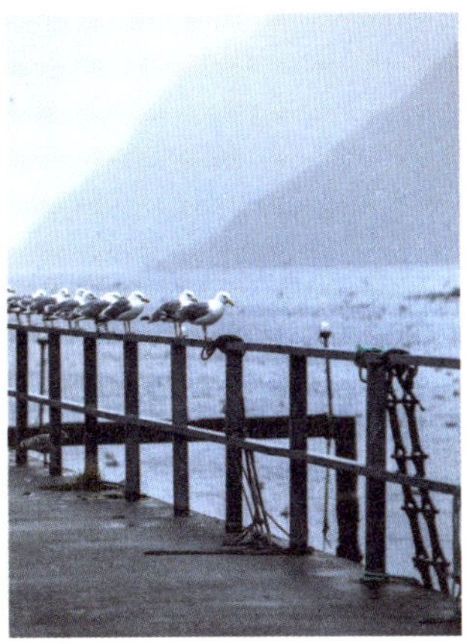

Seagulls awaiting the return of fisherman bringing in a fresh catch.

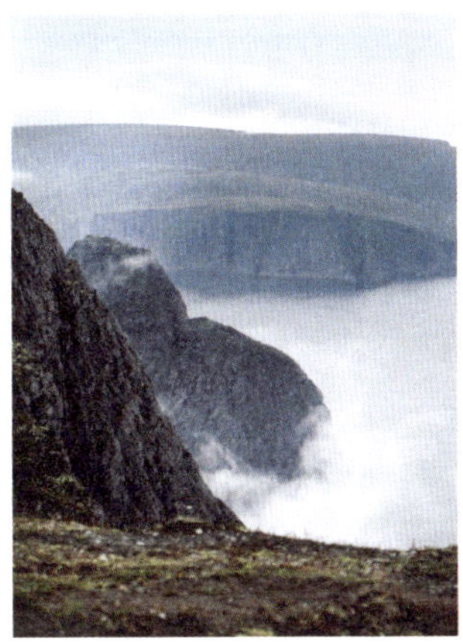

A glimpse of the cliffs of the North Cape through a gap in the fog.

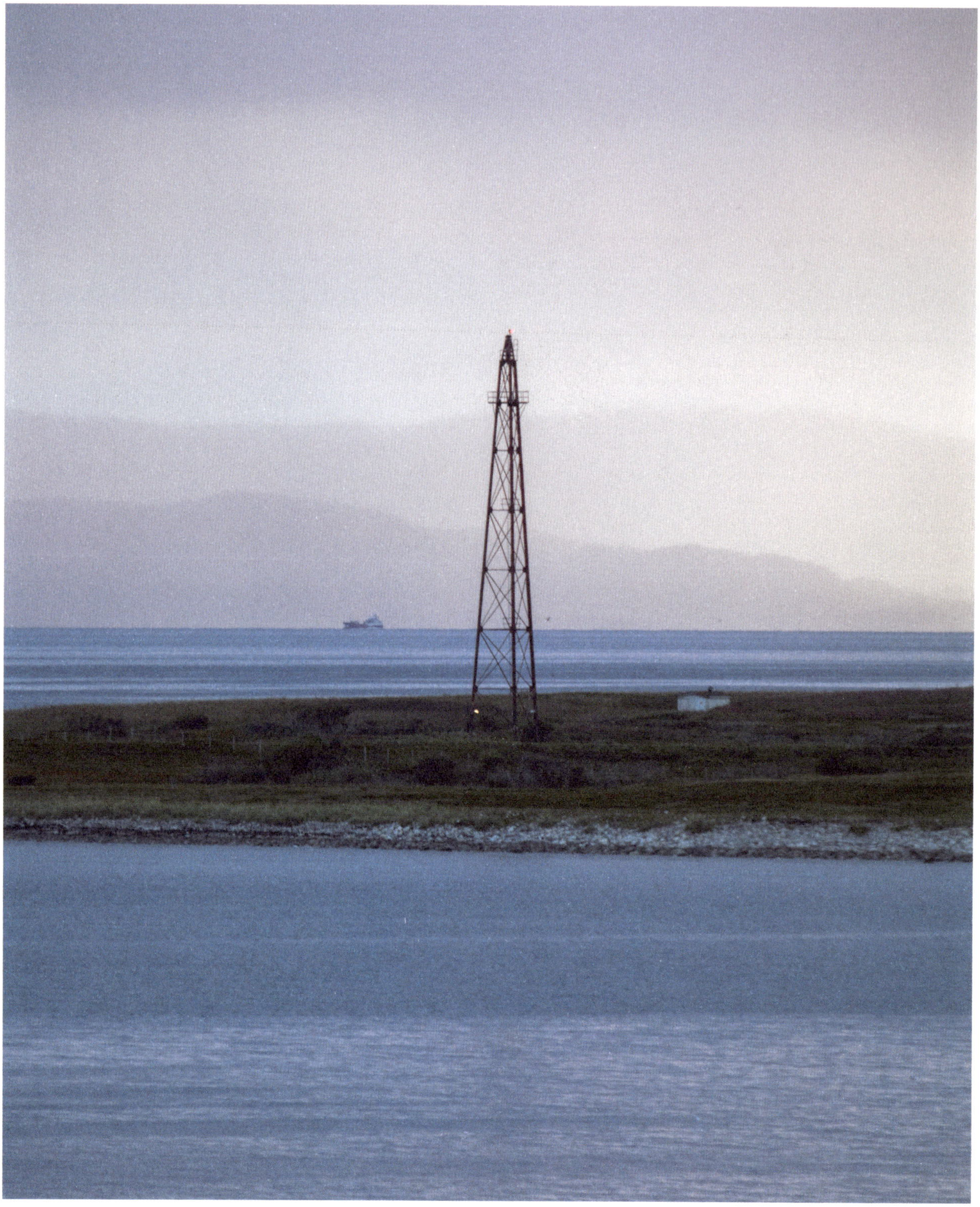

ABOVE

The mooring mast for the Norge airship in Vadsø is a relic of past polar expeditions. It was used by Roald Amundsen for a flight over the North Pole in 1926.

OPPOSITE

Seagulls enjoying the light of early evening on the Barents Sea.

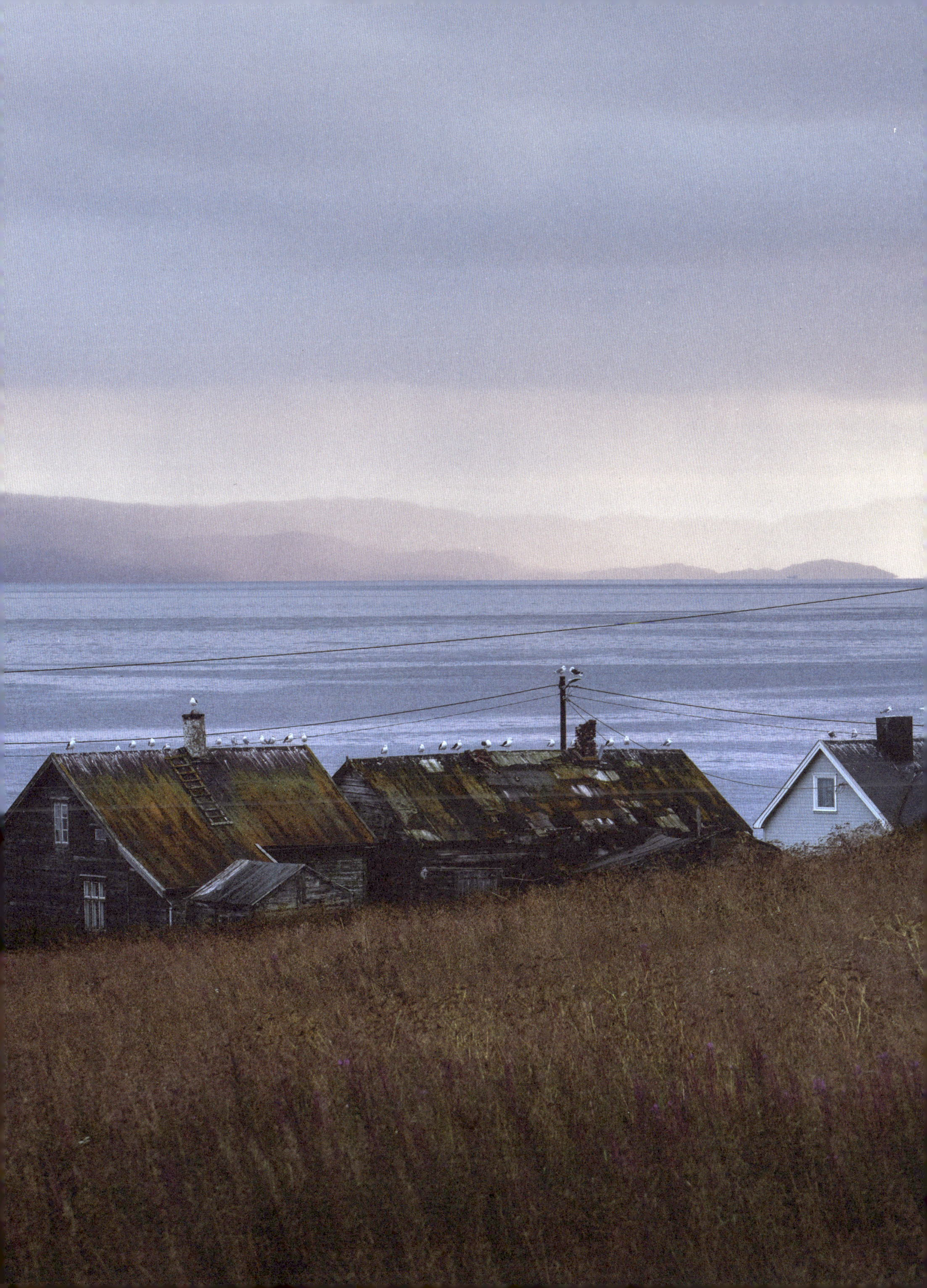

NATURE

NORWEGIAN WILDLIFE

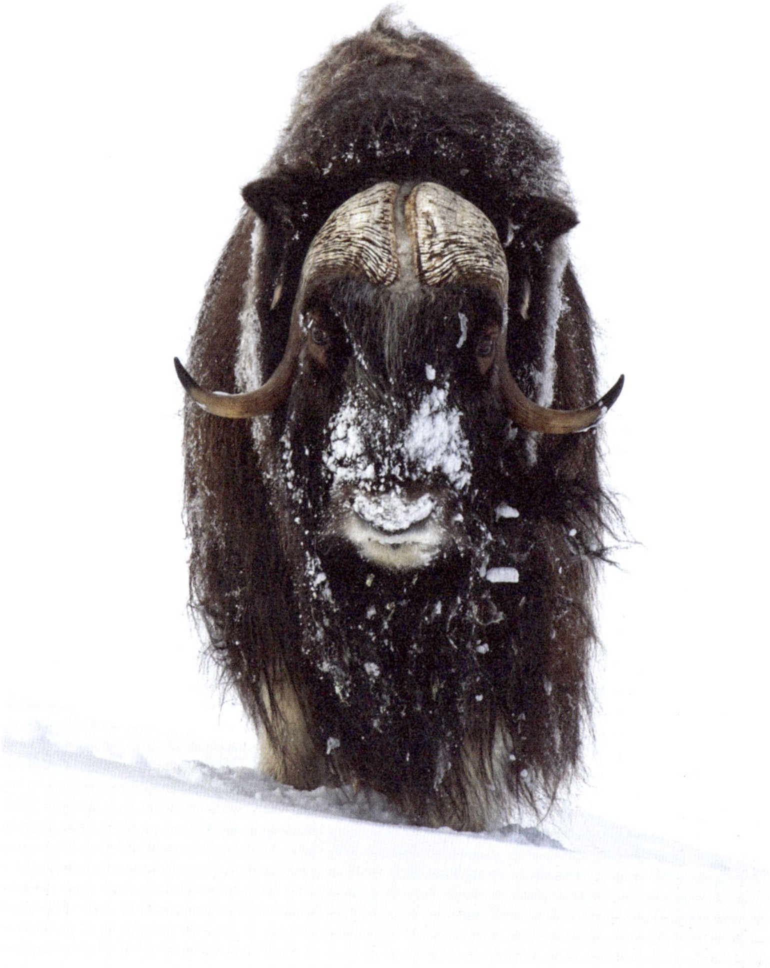

MUSK OX

This impressive beast is found in the mountains of Dovrefjell. It was reintroduced here several thousand years after its extinction.

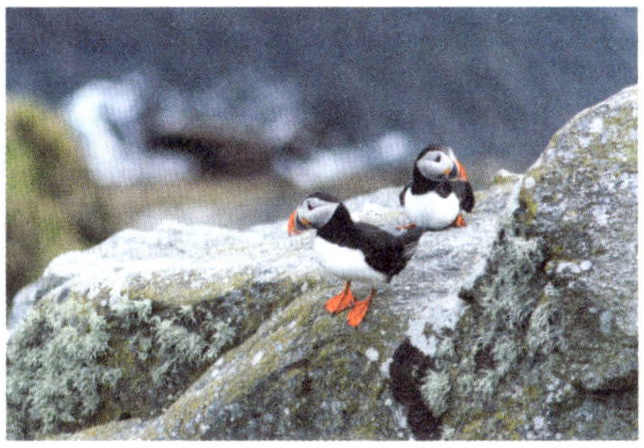

PUFFINS

From spring onward birds flock to nest all along the Norwegian coast.

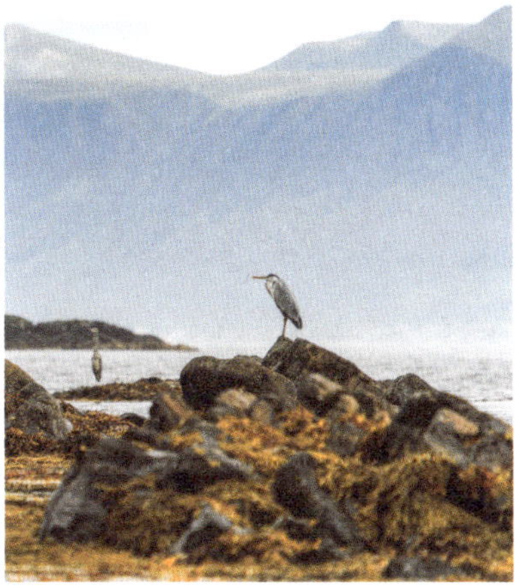

GREY HERON

Herons may be seen at low tide, looking out for fish, which they stab with their sharp bills.

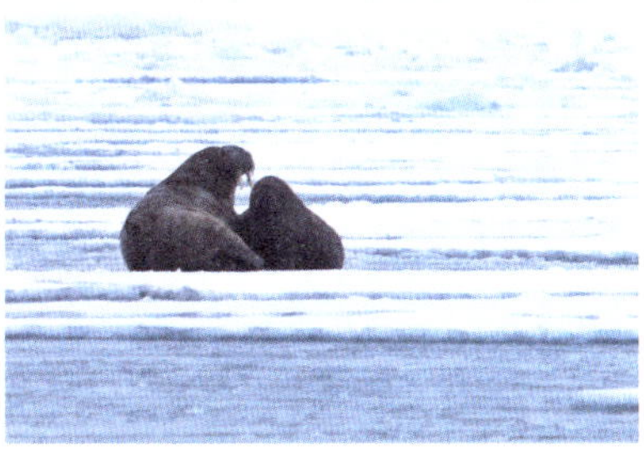

WALRUS

Populations have grown significantly since the walrus became a protected species.

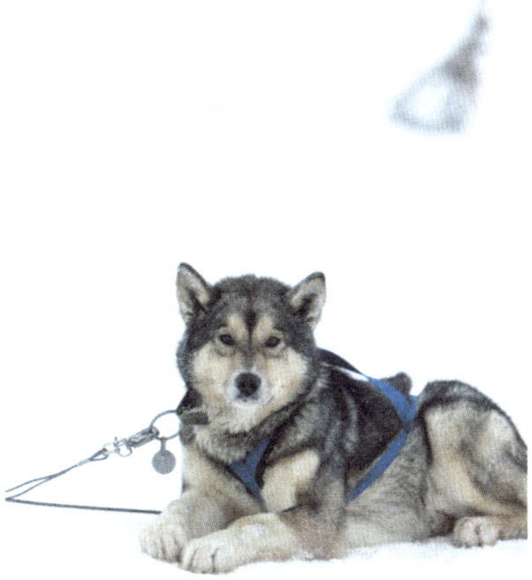

SIBERIAN HUSKY

Mushers could not get about the Svalbard archipelago by dog sled without this breed.

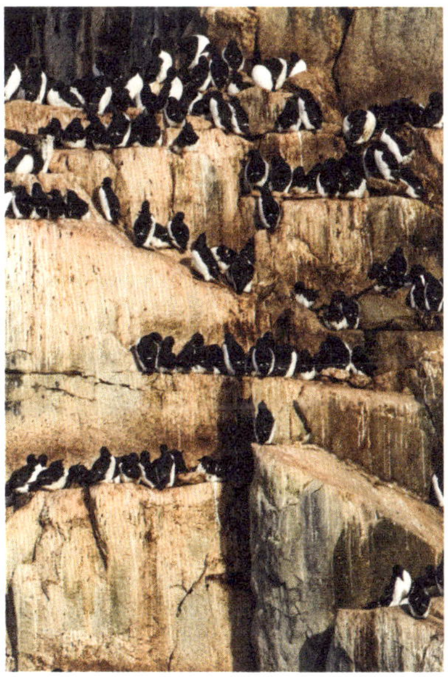

RAZORBILL

Unlike the penguin, which lives in the Antarctic, the razorbill can fly.

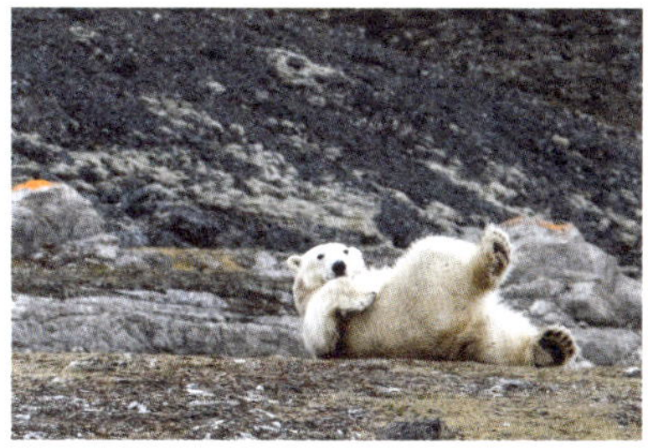

POLAR BEAR

These animals are predators that feed primarily on seals. This one seems to have been caught in the middle of a nap.

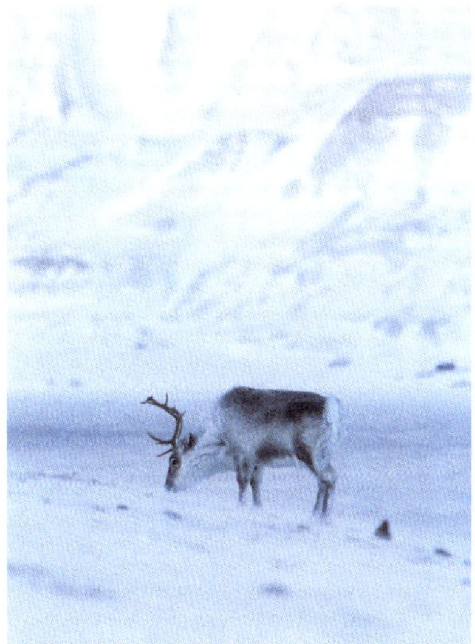

REINDEER

The reindeer on Svalbard are wild but have little fear of humans.

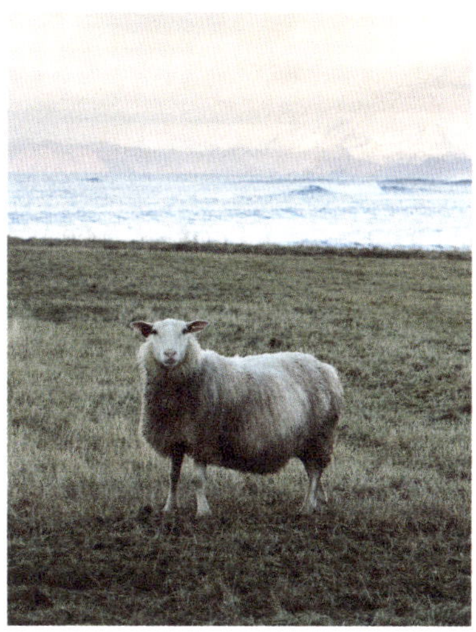

SHEEP

Sheep wool is used to knit the famous, traditional Norwegian jumpers.

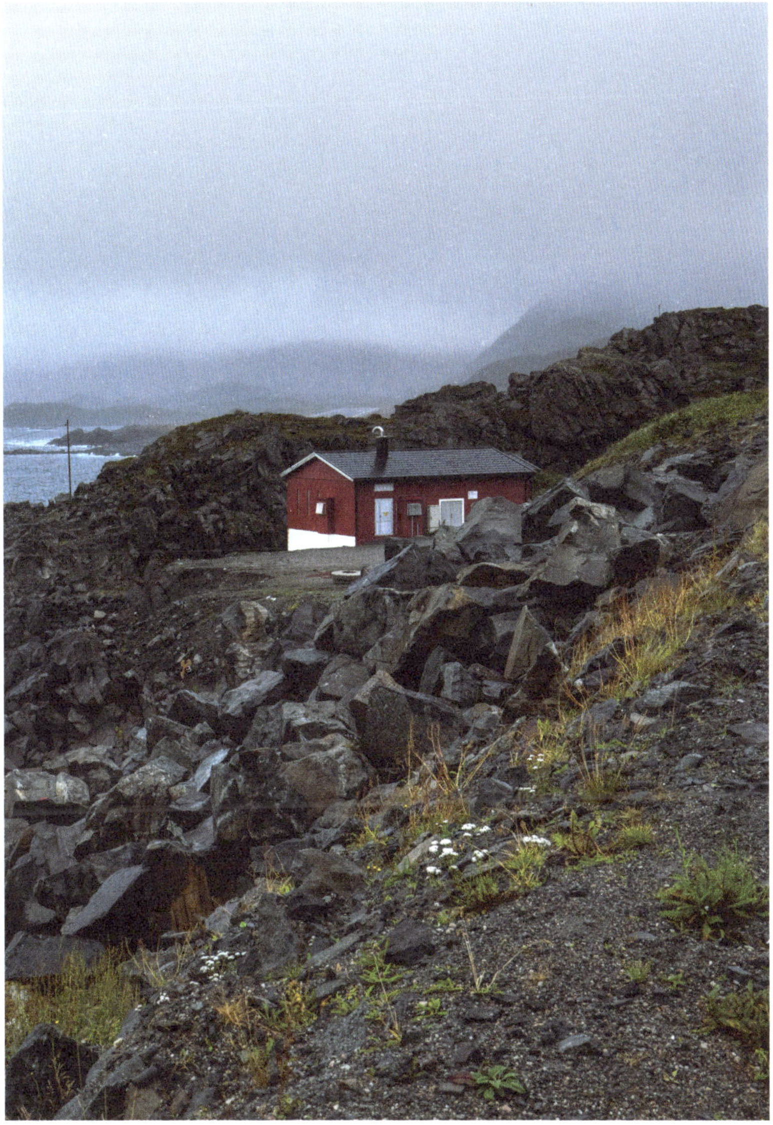

ABOVE

A house tucked away in the heart of the kind of scenery that is typical of the road to the North Cape. An aura of mystery sets in as the fog falls.

OPPOSITE

The closer you get to the North Cape, the steeper and more forbidding the cliffs become.

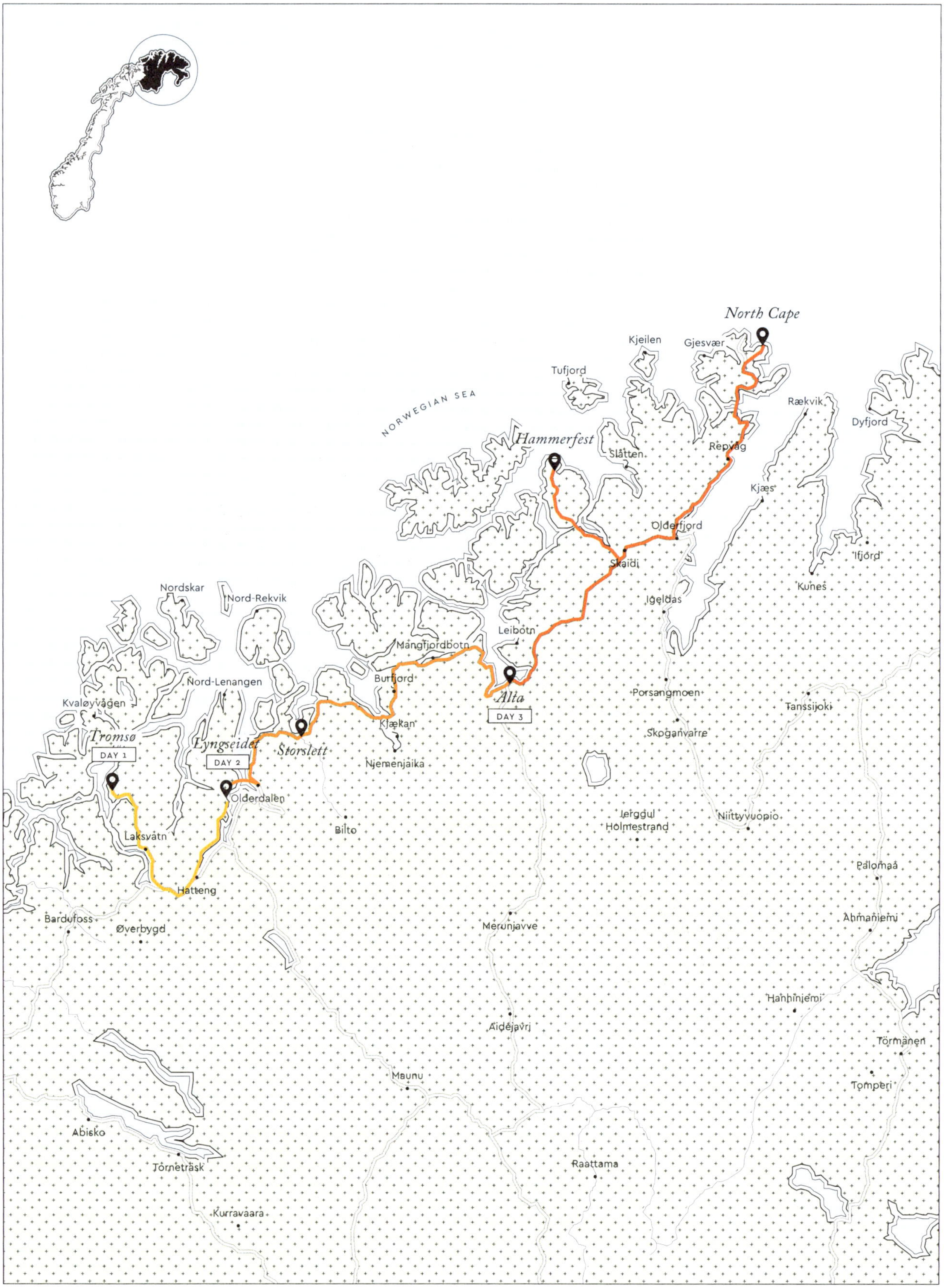
North Cape
Kjeilen
Gjesvær
Tufjord
NORWEGIAN SEA
Rækvik
Dyfjord
Hammerfest
Slåtten
Repvåg
Kjæs
Olderfjord
Ifjord
Skaidi
Kunes
Nordskar
Nord-Rekvik
Igeldas
Leibotn
Mangfjordbotn
Burfjord
Alta
DAY 3
Porsangmoen
Nord-Lenangen
Kvaløyvågen
Tanssijoki
Kjækan
Skoganvarre
Tromsø
DAY 1
Lyngseidet
DAY 2
Storslett
Njemenjaika
Olderdalen
Jergul
Holmestrand
Niittyvuopio
Bilto
Laksvåtn
Palomaa
Hatteng
Bardufoss
Øverbygd
Merunjavve
Ahmaniemi
Hanhinjemi
Aidejavrj
Törmänen
Maunu
Tomperi
Abisko
Torneträsk
Raattama
Kurravaara

ITINERARY

FROM TROMSØ TO THE NORTH CAPE

The road leading to the North Cape, the northernmost point of Continental Europe, is long and winding, but the scenery and the sense that you have reached the ends of the Earth more than make up for the distance traveled.

DAY 1: FROM TROMSØ TO THE LYNGEN ALPS

Tromsø, known as the "Capital of the Arctic" or "Gateway to the Arctic," was once the starting point for major polar expeditions but is now home to a large student body who attend its famous university, which specializes in the study of phenomena specific to the Arctic regions, among other things. While the wonderful Northern Lights can be seen here in winter, in the height of summer a cable car takes visitors up the Storsteinen mountain to enjoy the midnight sun. Tromsø also makes an excellent base from which to explore the surrounding area and for boat trips to look for the orcas and whales that are attracted to the fjords by shoals of herring as winter draws in.

DAY 2: FROM THE LYNGEN ALPS TO ALTA

Norway is certainly not short of mountains, and many Norwegians come to the Lyngen Alps to ski their steep slopes. On the opposite side of the fjord, the E6 highway offers fine views of these mountains before continuing toward Alta. Keen hikers can take a detour on the way to Reisa National Park, one of the wildest and most remote landscapes the country has to offer. In Alta thousands of rock carvings (dating back from between two thousand and six thousand years) depict scenes from the daily lives of the region's earliest inhabitants. Longships, reindeer, bears, and hunting scenes are among the many petroglyphs at this UNESCO World Heritage Site. A wealth of activities is also on offer in the area, from dog sled excursions to fishing for wild salmon in the Altaelva river or watching for rock ptarmigan.

DAY 3: FROM ALTA TO THE NORTH CAPE

Off to the North Cape! On the way, semi-wild reindeer cross the road without warning. It may feel as though this is the end of the Earth, but take a detour to the town of Hammerfest and visit the wooden cabin on top of Storfjellet as you explore this municipality of ten thousand residents, most of whom make their living from the extraction of natural gas. The gas is transported via an 89-mile (143-km) pipeline and comes straight from the Snøhvit ("Snow White") natural gas field in the Barents Sea. Small fishing villages are scattered across the landscape. Keen anglers should take a trip to sea in search of the famous king crab. The species is originally from Alaska but was introduced to Murmansk by the Soviet Union in the 1960s. It has since gradually made its way along the Norwegian coast and by the 1990s had reached the North Cape region. Once here, purists can continue to Knivskjelodden, the true geographical northern tip of the country, although the journey is not for the faint-hearted and requires a round-trip hike of 11 miles (18 km). A great way to end the journey in style, weather permitting.

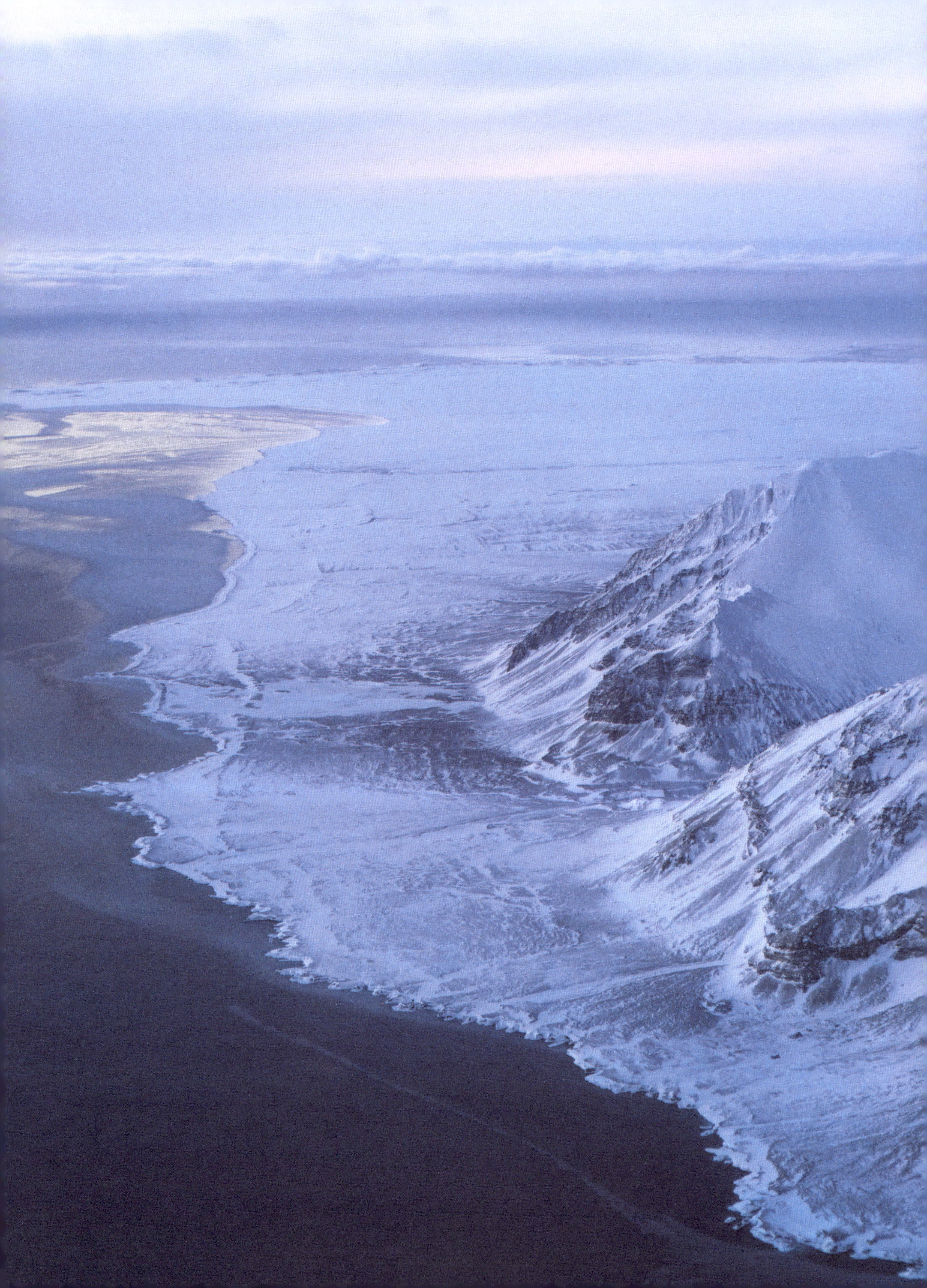

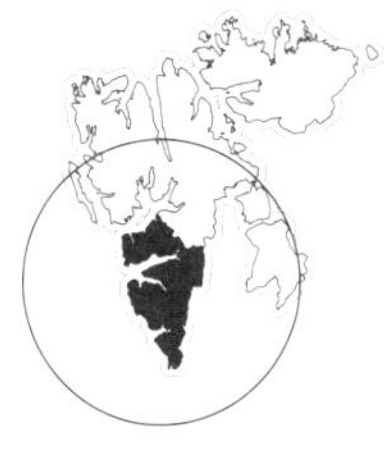

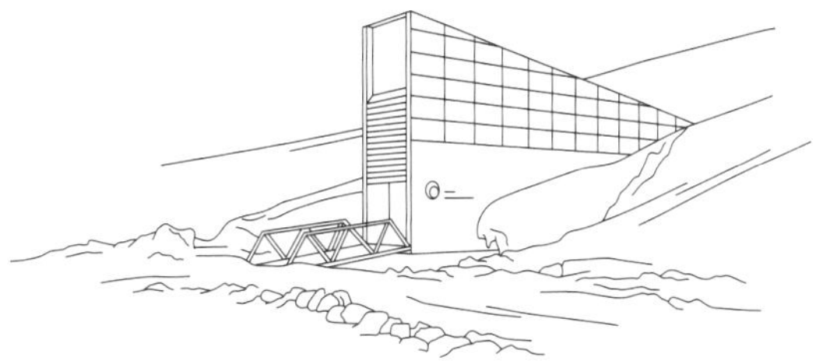

UP CLOSE AND PERSONAL WITH THE NORTH POLE

SVALBARD

Svalbard is a vast wilderness, an archipelago of mountains and ice, where polar bears reign supreme.

P. 222

On a clear day, landing on the Svalbard archipelago is quite a spectacle.

OPPOSITE

An old homestead in the valley at Longyearbyen seems almost dwarfed by the imposing size of the mountain.

The Svalbard islands feature a series of immense fjords lying at a latitude of 78° north, surrounded by sea ice and the jagged peaks of mountain ranges. No less than 60 percent of Svalbard's surface area is covered by glaciers.

Ny-Ålesund, originally established as a mining settlement in the far north of the archipelago, now houses an international Arctic research center. A dozen or so countries have bases here to study permafrost and glaciers, and to carry out meteorological surveys, observations of the Northern Lights, atmospheric measurements, and so on. Scientific research is carried out in a wide range of fields, with the number of scientists and their backup teams ranging from around thirty to one hundred and eighty over the year. The AWIPEV Arctic Research Station, a facility shared by the French Polar Institute Paul-Émile Victor and a German team, can accommodate forty people in high season. This unique site mainly welcomes scientists, but tourists have been known to come for a short stay in the summer.

The Svalbard area enjoys a very special status. The archipelago was declared a demilitarized zone after the First World War and Norway's sovereignty over Svalbard was recognized by the Svalbard Treaty signed in Paris in 1920. Although the signatories to the agreement reserved the right to exploit natural resources (mainly coal) on an "absolutely equal" footing, in practice, only Russia and Norway would actually go on to mine coal on the island. While most of the pits have now been abandoned, a few have remained open to guarantee local supply. This is particularly the case in the village of Barentsburg, which is home to three hundred Russians and Ukrainians.

Another unique feature of the archipelago is the large population of polar bears. The probability of running into one is so high that residents are not permitted to go outdoors unarmed in order to be able to defend themselves against a potential attack. For this reason, many tourists elect to stay aboard a boat to observe and photograph these animals in relative safety. In addition to polar bears, visitors may also see walrus, wild reindeer, and Arctic foxes on the islands, where the presence of humans is but a minor detail among the vast expanses of rock and ice.

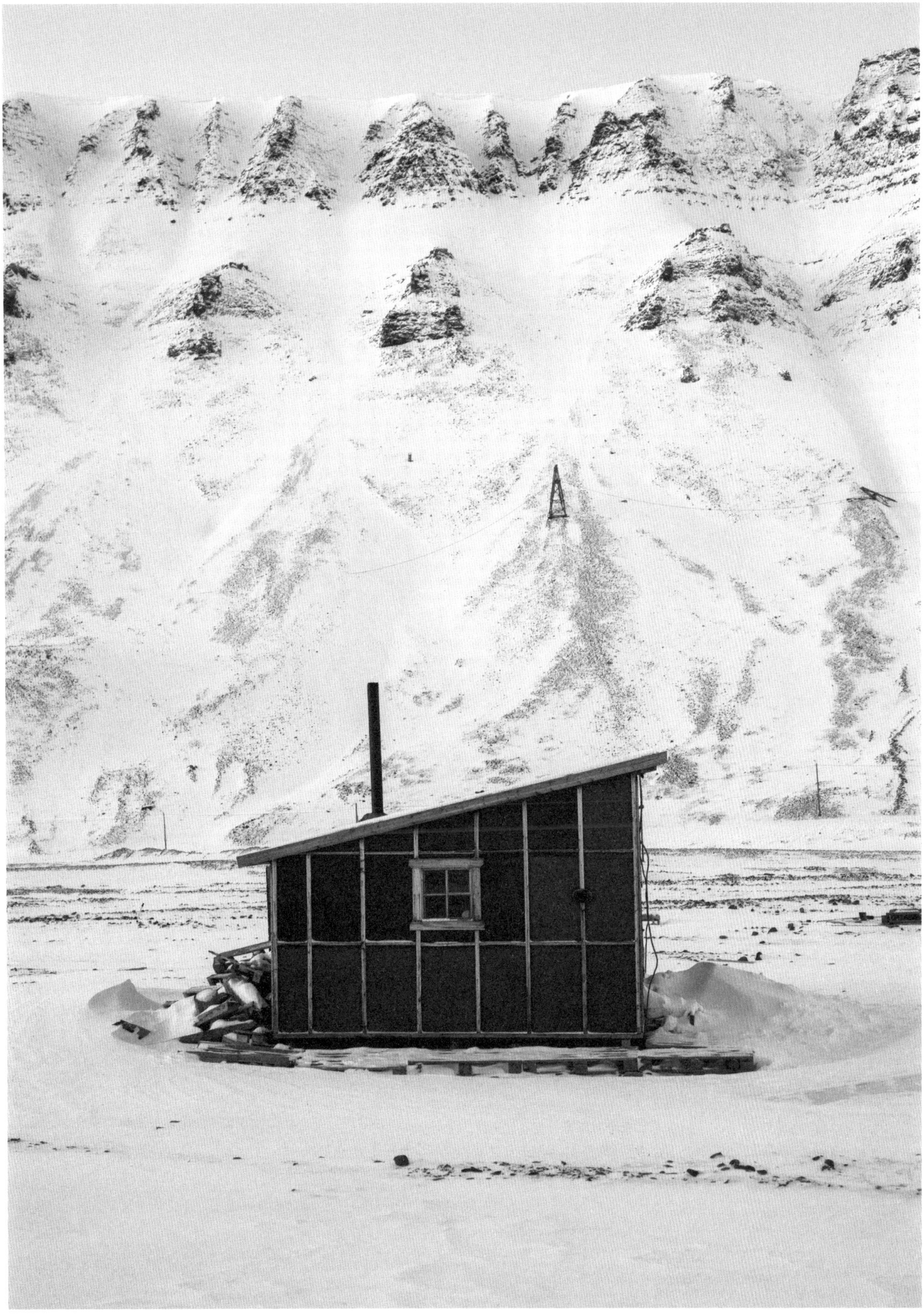

THE ESSENTIALS

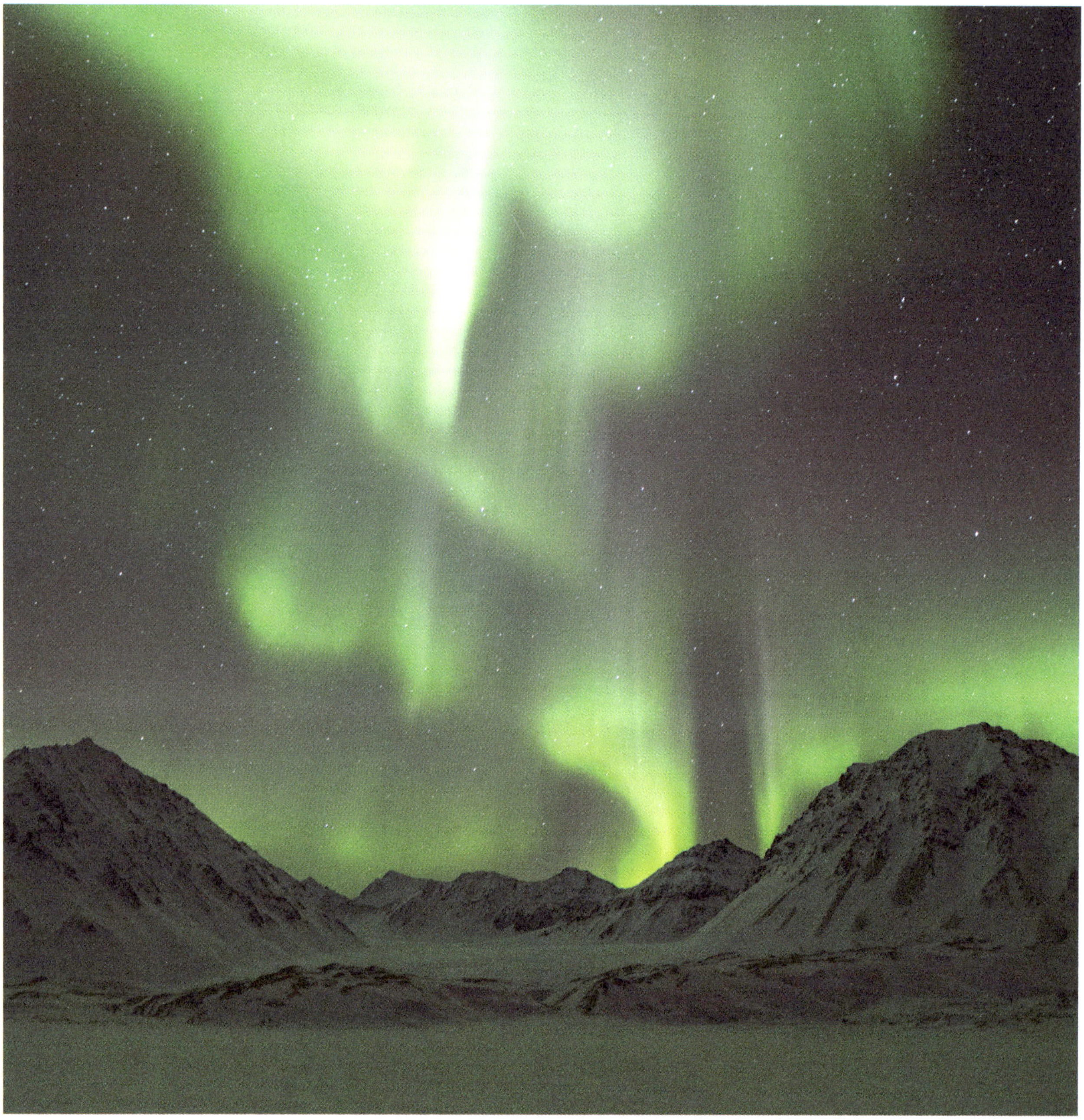

NORTHERN LIGHTS

The aurora borealis frequently lights up the skies of Svalbard during the long months of winter, presenting an endlessly fascinating spectacle.

51

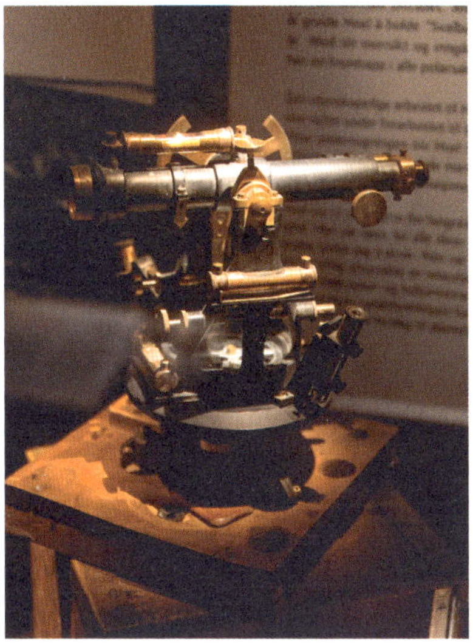

SVALBARD MUSEUM

The history of the archipelago and the lives of its inhabitants are documented in minute detail in this very comprehensive museum.

52

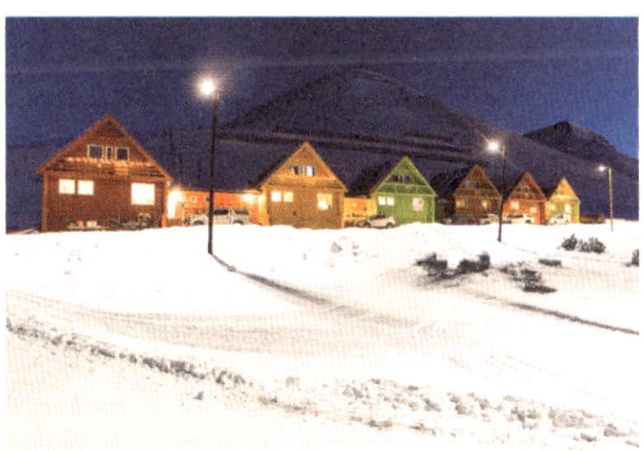

LONGYEARBYEN

Svalbard's main town has 2,417 residents. An old law makes dying here illegal, because the permafrost prevents bodies from decomposing, creating potential health hazards. The lack of hospital means that pregnant women must be transferred to the mainland.

53

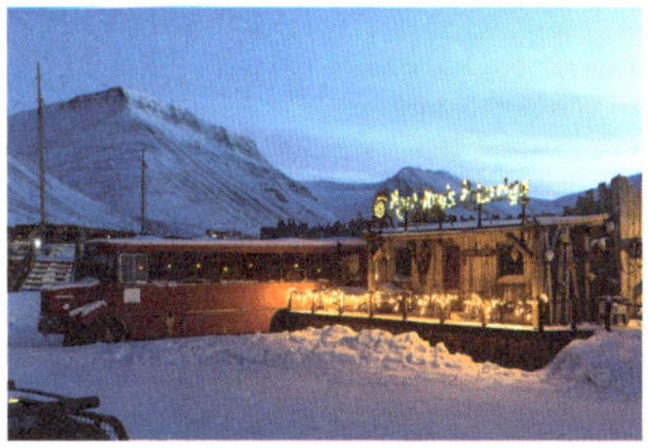

MARY-ANN'S POLARRIGG

A unique hotel in Longyearbyen, established in 1999 by Mary-Ann, something of a local character, in a former miners' barracks.

54

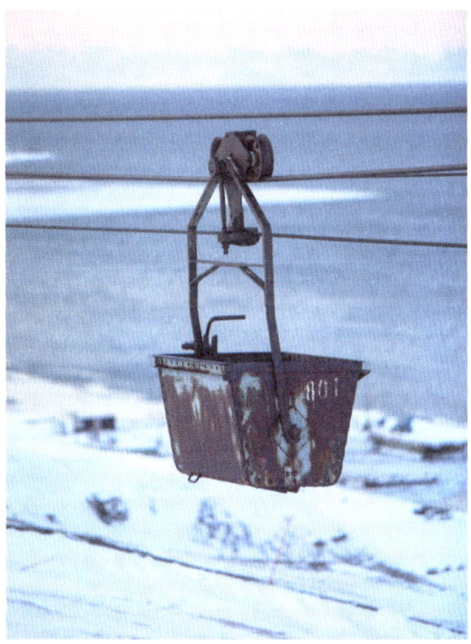

COAL MINE GRUVE 3

Mine number 3 is no longer in operation but is open to the public. Visitors can access the coal seam and learn what the life of a miner is like.

55

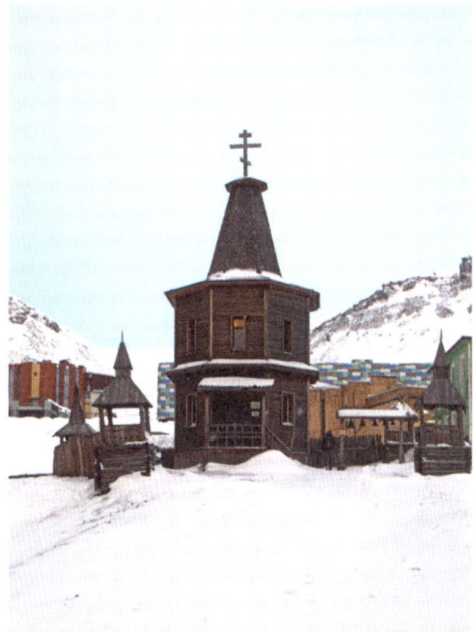

BARENTSBURG

In Barentsburg most people make a living from coal mining. Tourism plays a smaller role but helps to maintain an important connection with the Norwegian community in Longyearbyen and the rest of the world.

56

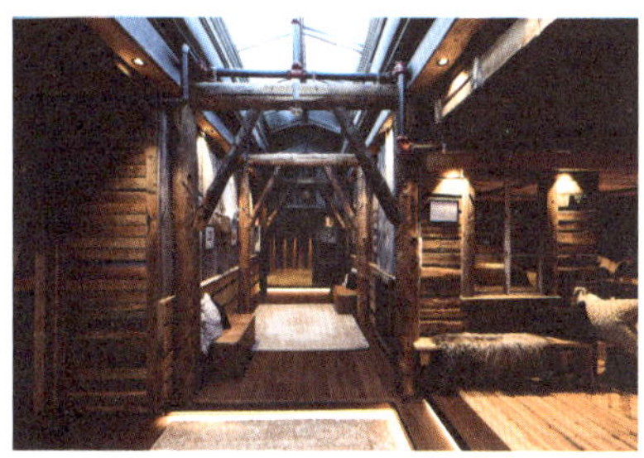

BASECAMP HOTEL

This comfortable hotel takes its inspiration from the fur trappers' cabins that once proliferated on the island. The rooms are wood-paneled from floor to ceiling and feel very cozy.

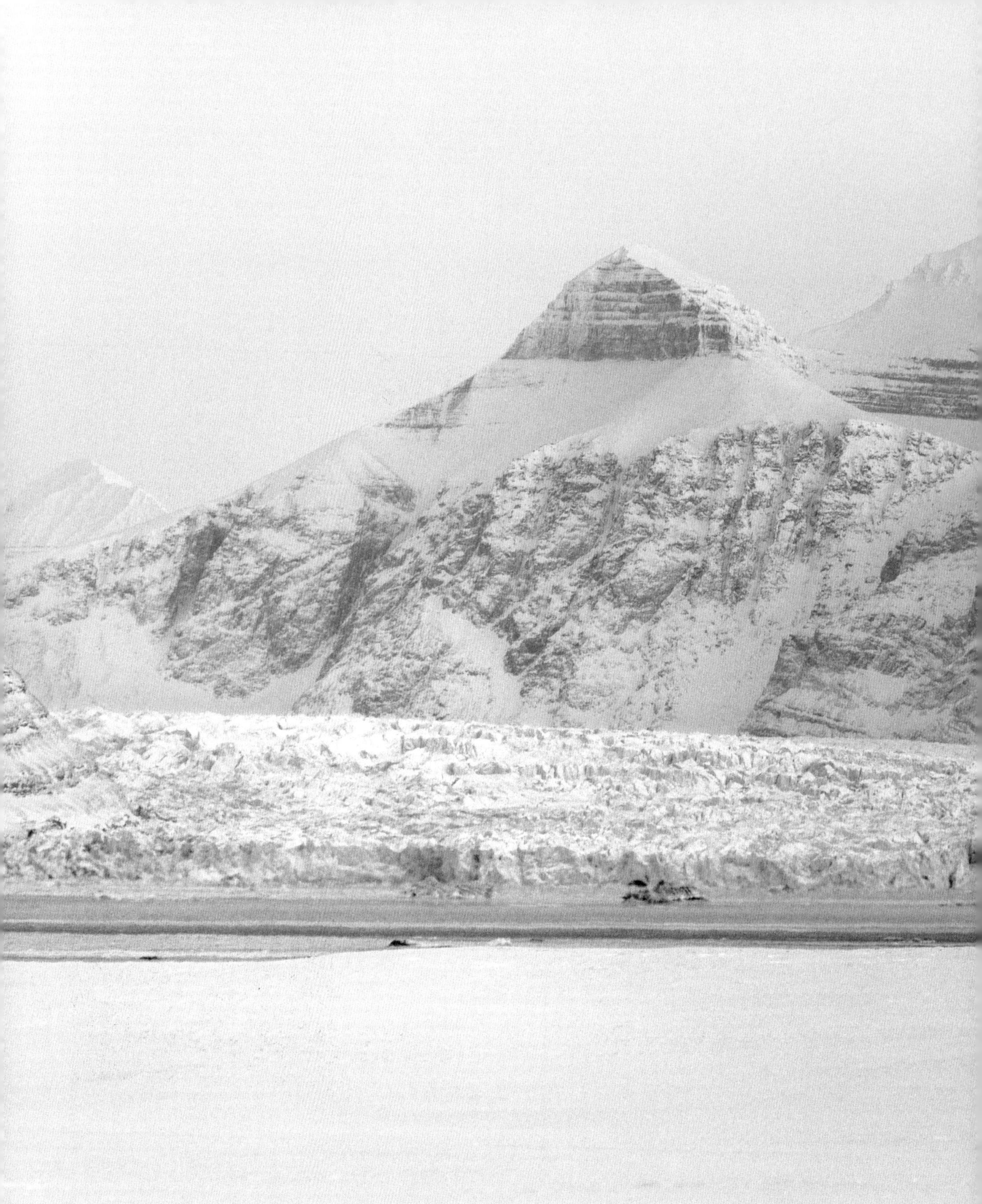

A glacier flows into the Kongsfjorden near Ny-Ålesund. This photograph was taken from the Jean Corbel station, a scientific research facility run by the French Polar Institute.

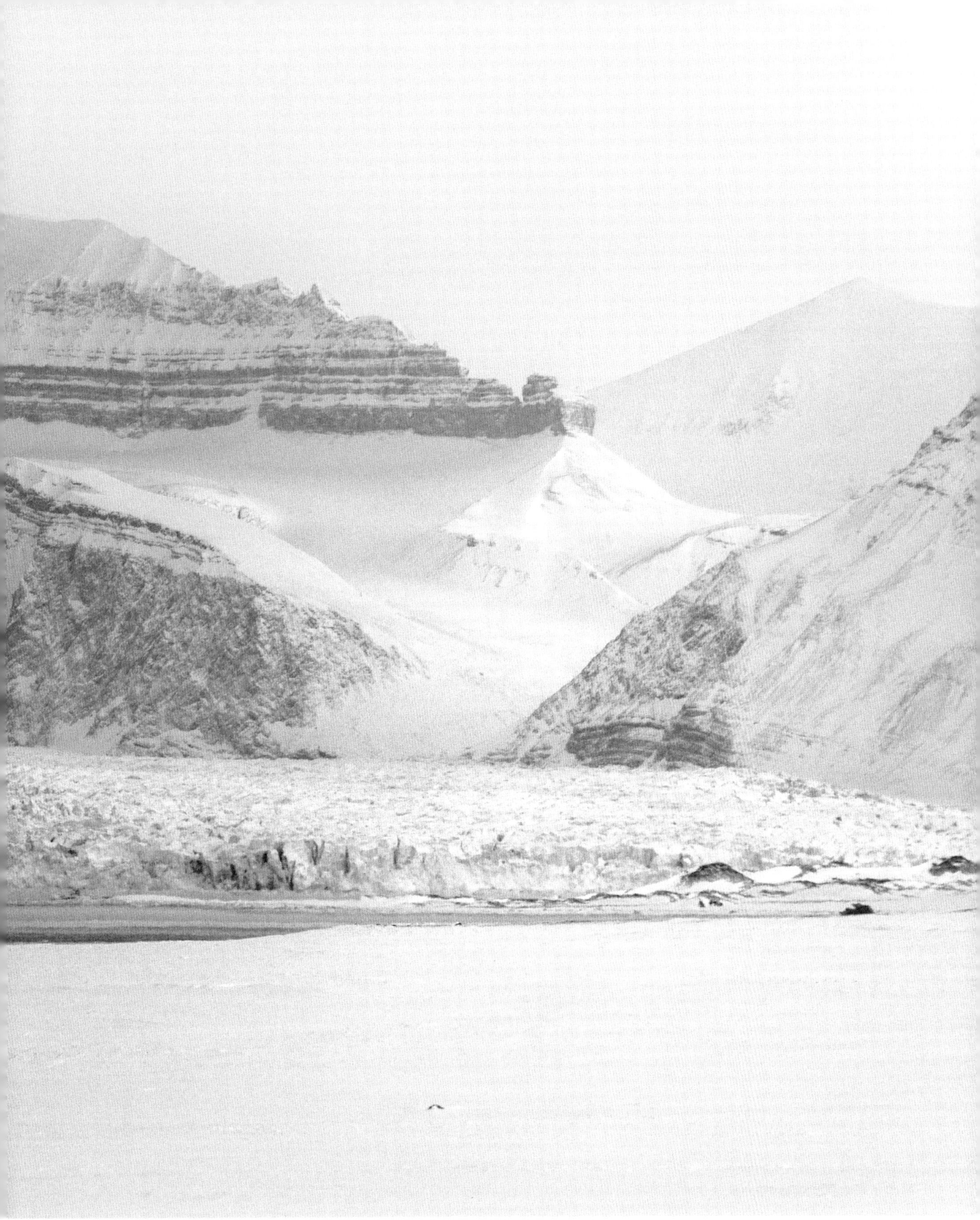

PORTRAIT

MUSHER

Long before snowmobiles arrived on the scene, trappers and other inhabitants of the far north would travel by dog sled.

Today dog sleds are still used on the islands of Svalbard. More than just a method of transport, they have become a way of exploring the archipelago's vast white expanses, gliding silently across virgin snow in breathtaking scenery, without disturbing the wildlife that lives here.

Much like 25 percent of all Svalbard residents, Hana is not Norwegian. She grew up in the mountains of Slovenia and her father, an amateur dog sled racer, passed on his passion for the sport by taking her along to the competitions in which he took part. After several snowless winters, however, he was eventually obliged to give up his sled dogs. A number of years passed, by which time Hana was old enough to leave home and it seemed natural for her to head north to pursue her father's passion and become a full-time musher.

Hana went on to spend several winters in the Finnish and Swedish parts of Lapland, where she found work as a guide and competed in long-distance dog sled races. As a lover of the great outdoors, one day she made for Svalbard, where she bumped into Karina and Martin, two globetrotters who had been working as guides in Greenland for fifteen years before starting Green Dog Svalbard, a business based in Longyearbyen offering dog sled tours.

Hana moved into a small cabin on Svalbard where, for the first few nights, she was unsettled by the slightest noise, fearful of polar bears, although the noises proved to be no more than reindeer searching for dry grass. While this new life brought its own share of unfamiliar dangers, the raw nature that surrounded her fascinated and inspired Hana to embark upon dog sled expeditions lasting several days. As the months passed, she came to appreciate that although she was living in the town closest to the North Pole in the world, she was also at the edge of vast expanses of land that were entirely wild and untouched by human hand. This realization brought her an immense sense of both freedom and humility in the face of the elements.

Hana works with a pack of dogs that she is slowly getting to know, and has learned to appreciate the balance between the uproar before they set off and the silence that follows. "It might seem chaotic and noisy at first—when the dogs are impatient to run, they bark nonstop and jump around. But then I let go of the rope and give them the command to go, and everything calms down. Within minutes, all you can hear are paws hitting the ground and the runners gliding across the snow." This young woman finds fulfillment in a life in the great outdoors that allows her to enjoy her passion to the full, until the day when, perhaps, she will set off once more to explore new horizons.

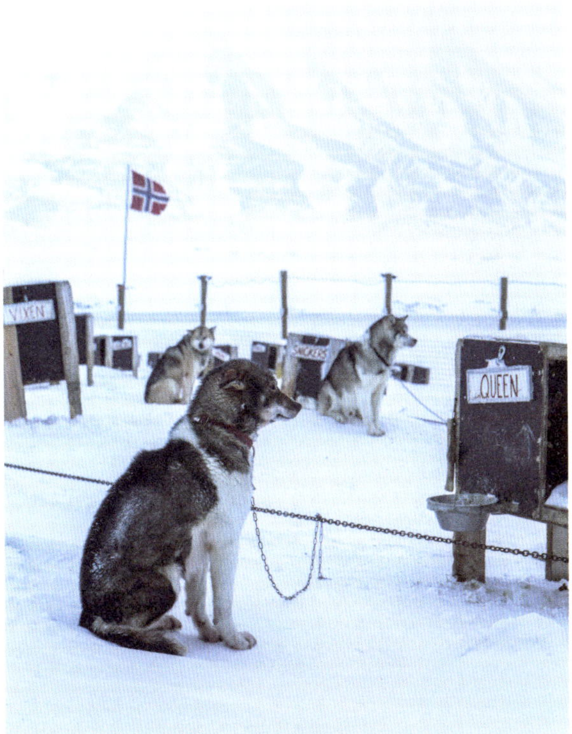

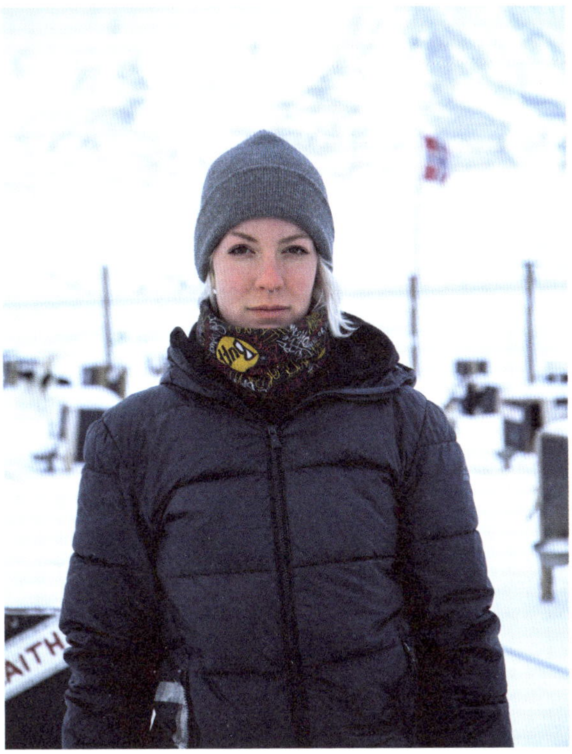

LIFE IN THE GREAT OUTDOORS

Icy conditions hold no fear for a young woman who grew up on her father's sled in the mountains of Slovenia—he too drove dog sleds.

ACROSS THE ICE

Hana works with the same pack throughout the year, and a real bond develops between the musher and the dogs over time.

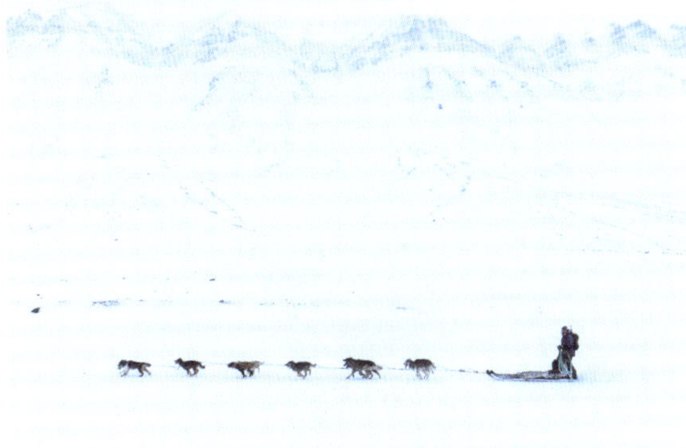

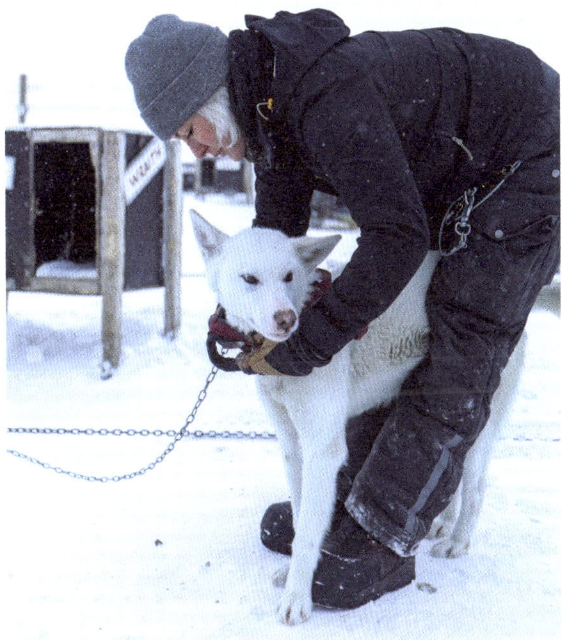

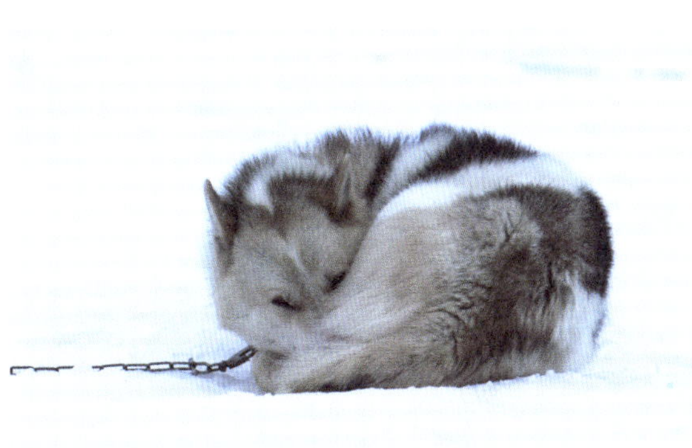

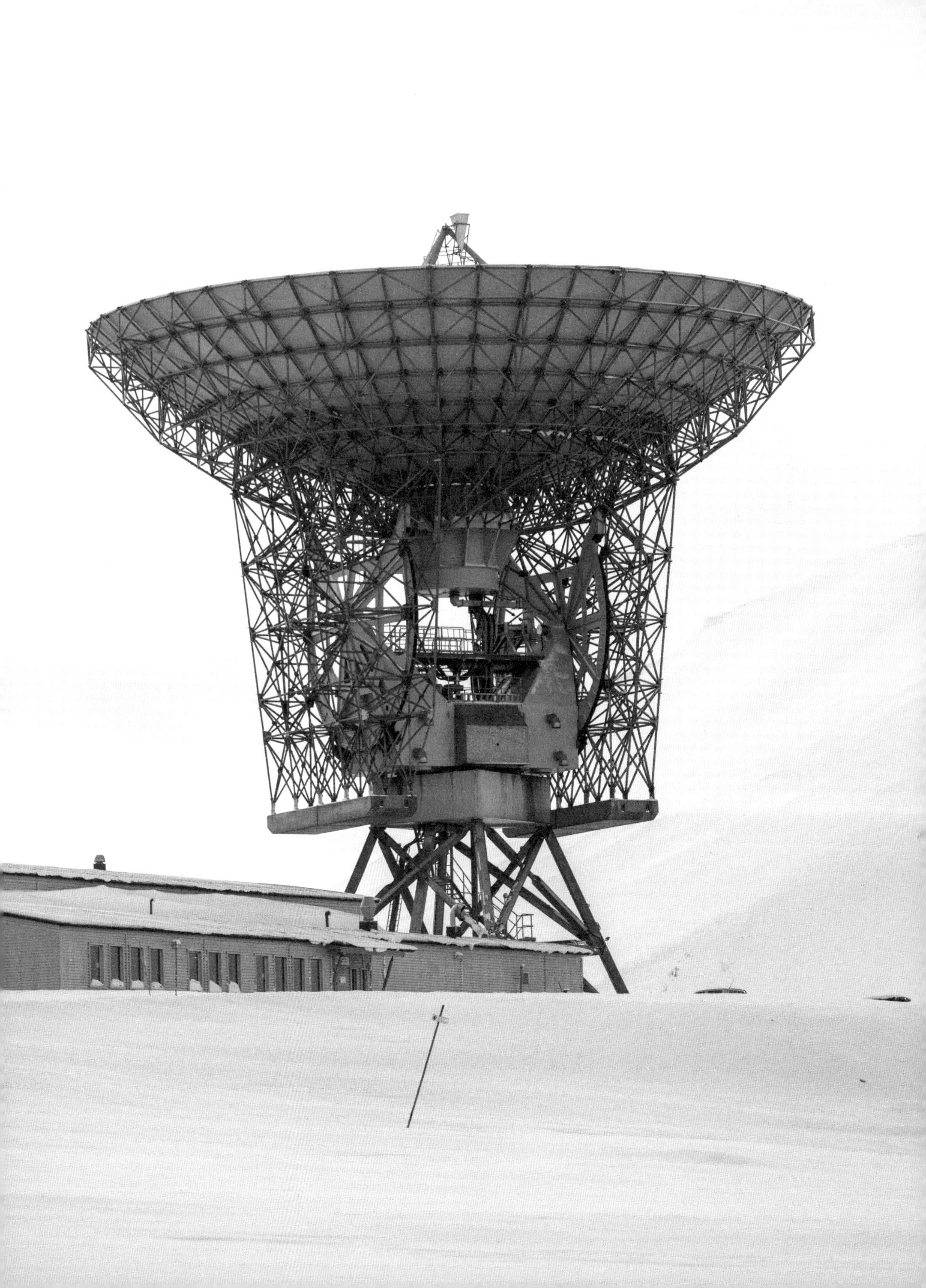

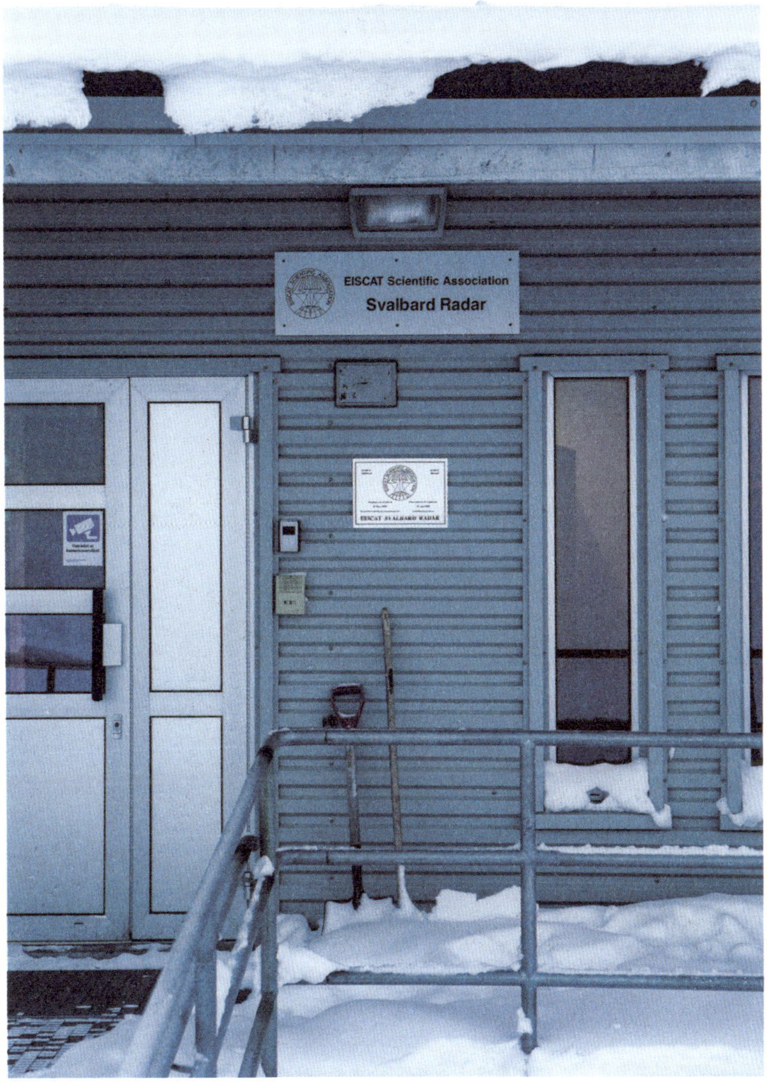

ABOVE

EISCAT is an international scientific association studying the upper atmosphere and the interaction between solar wind and the Earth's magnetosphere.

OPPOSITE

The radar equipment at the EISCAT station in Svalbard includes a 105-ft (32-m) steerable parabolic dish antenna.

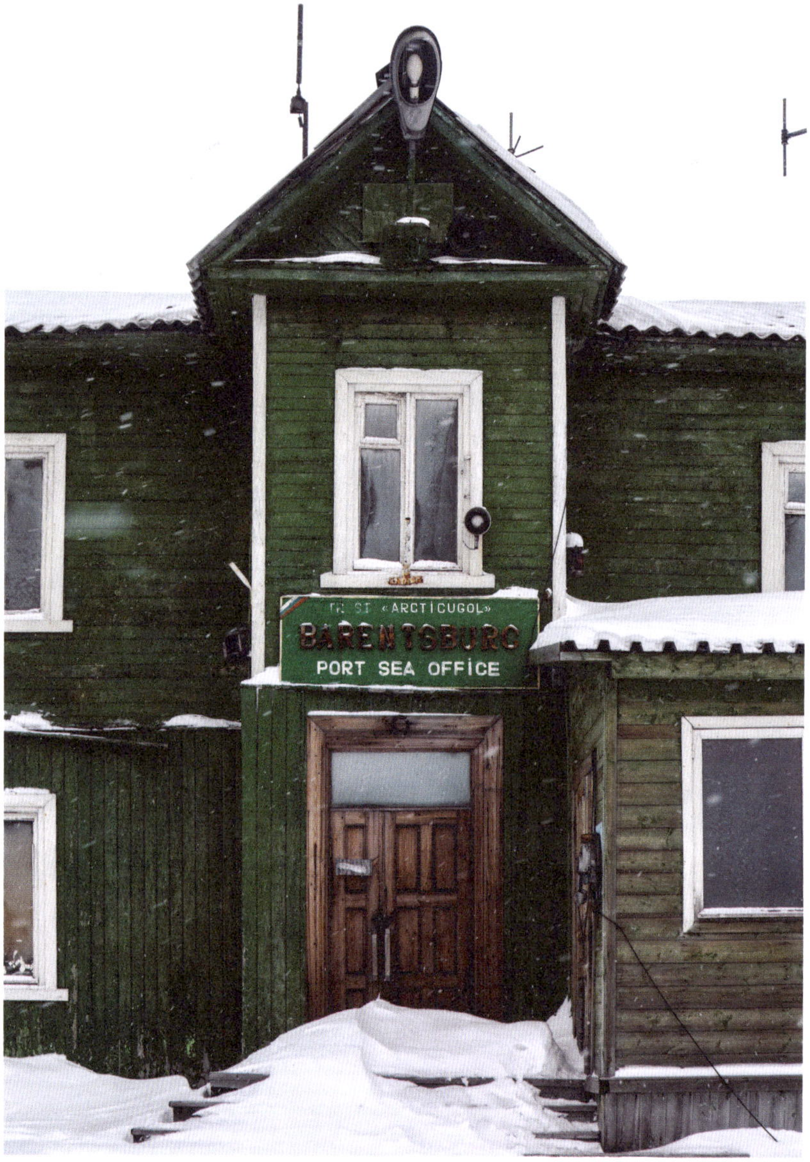

ABOVE

The office of the Arktikugol port authority in the Russian mining village of Barentsburg.

OPPOSITE

Apartment blocks decorated in pastel shades of orange, brown, and gray have replaced the wooden buildings in this small town that once had two thousand inhabitants and are reminders of the Russian presence on the island.

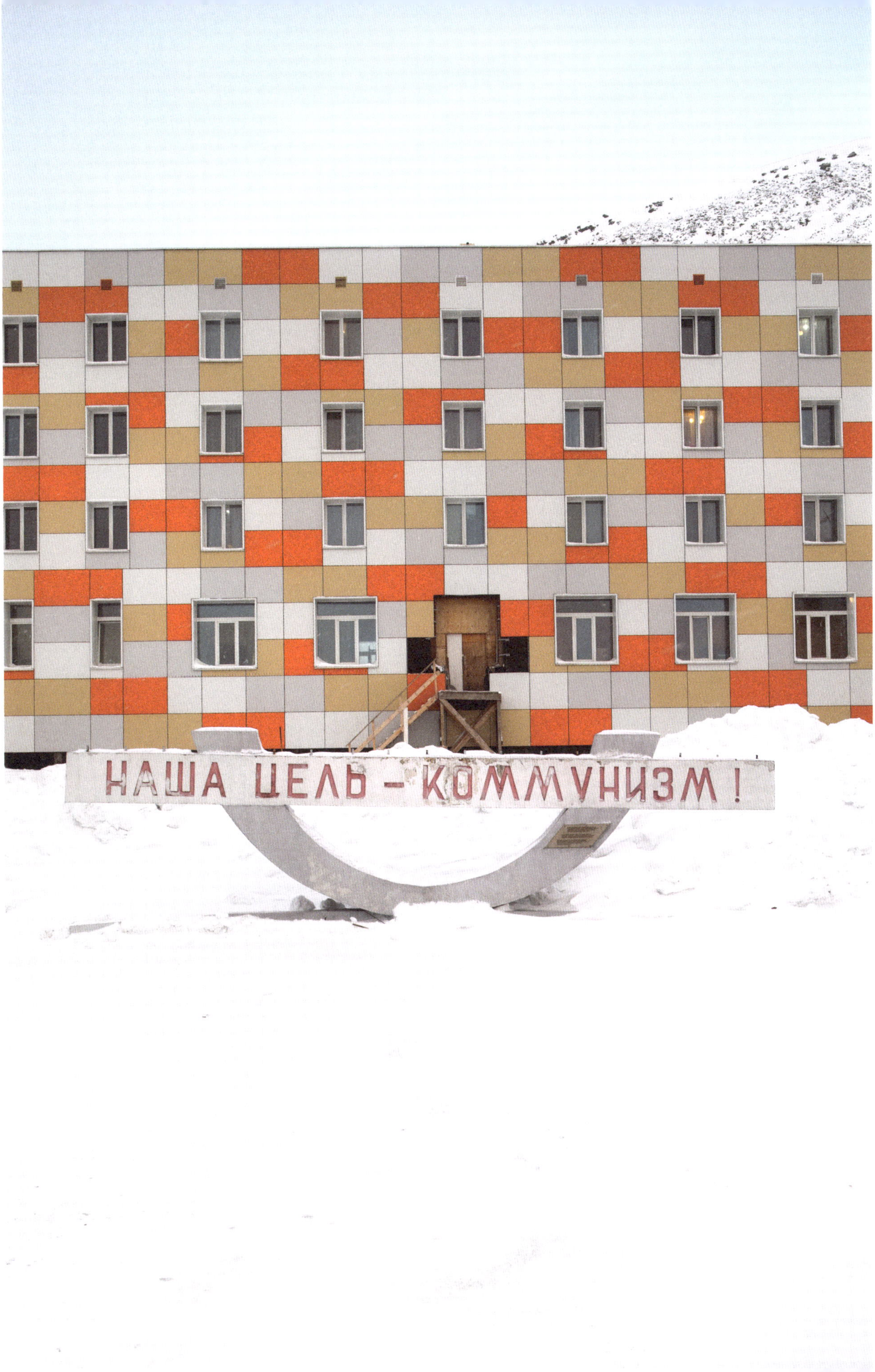
НАША ЦЕЛЬ - КОММУНИЗМ !

SCIENCE

NY-ÅLESUND RESEARCH STATION

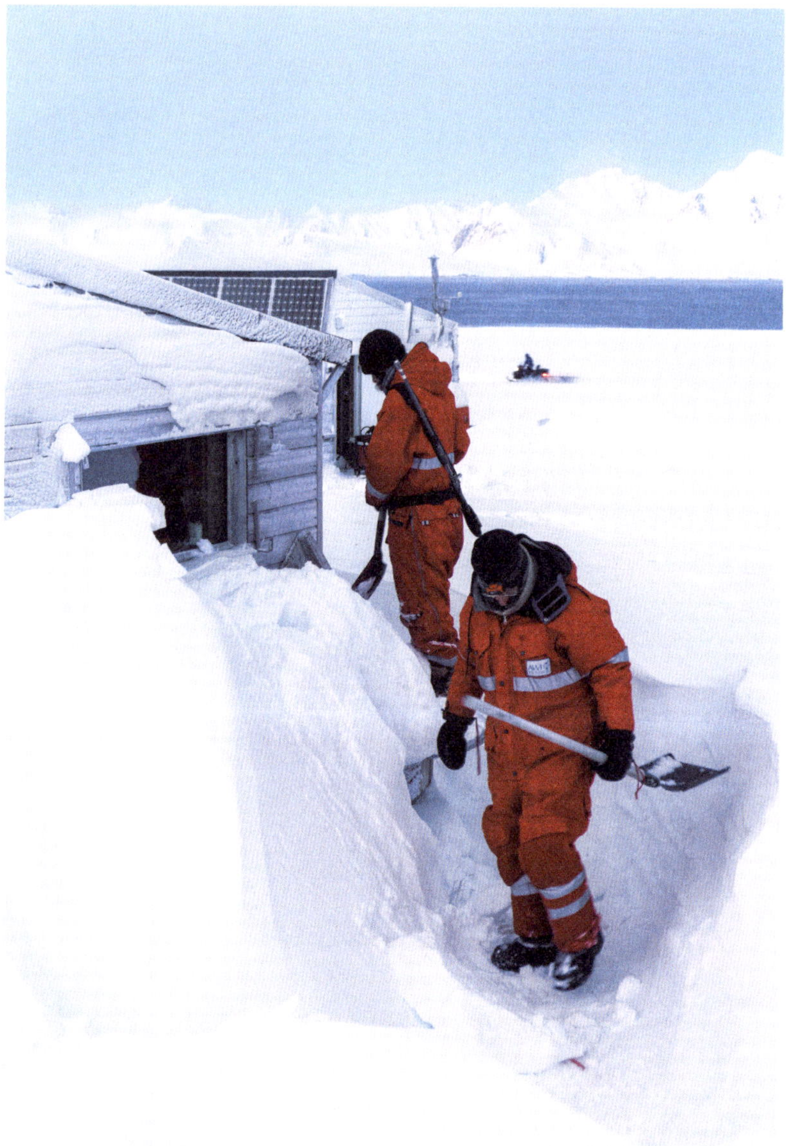

JEAN CORBEL STATION

Jean Lilensten and Léo Bosse clearing snow from the windows of the research station. They have come to take measurements of the visible spectrum of the aurora borealis, far from any sources of light pollution.

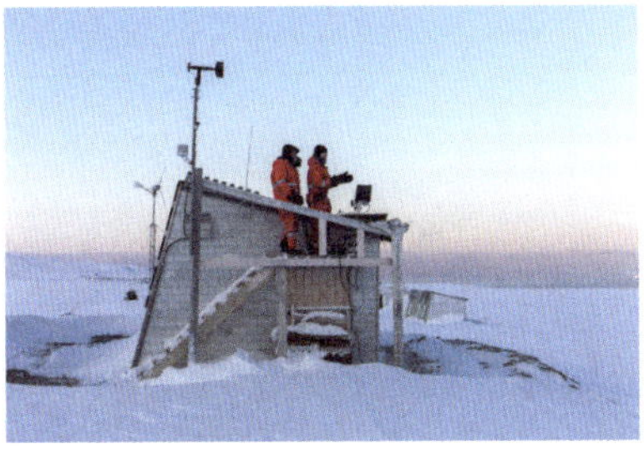

THE BIG FREEZE

Handling equipment is made more difficult by freezing cold air at temperatures of -22°F (-30°C).

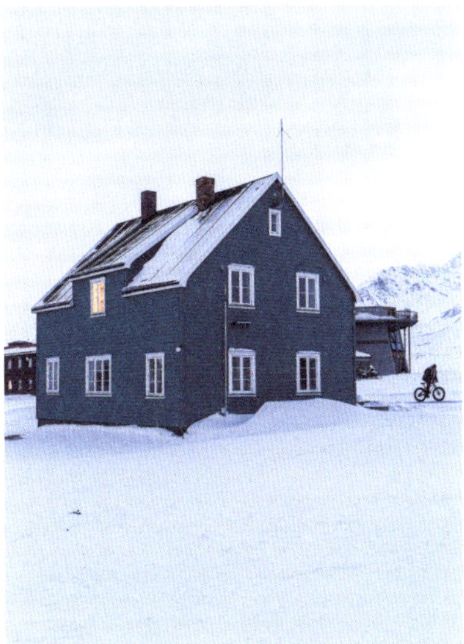

THE BLUE HOUSE

This building is home to the Franco-German AWIPEV team.

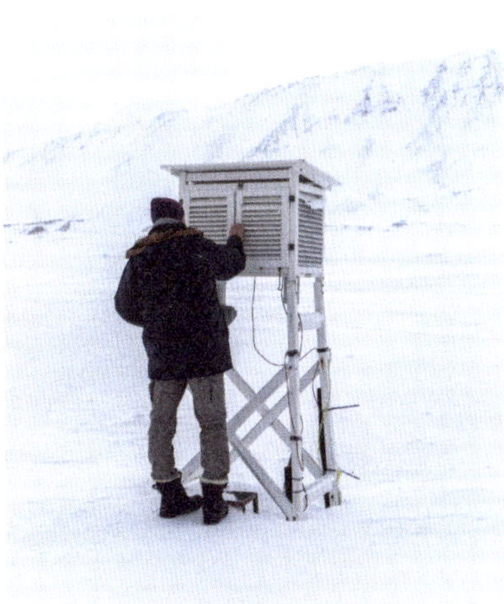

RECORDING TEMPERATURES

Readings are taken every day of the year.

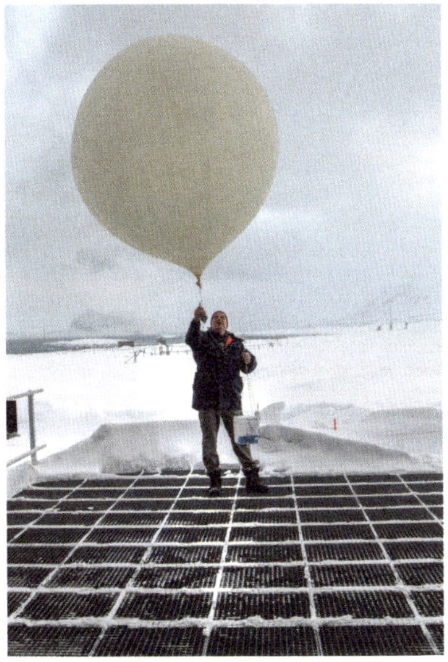

WEATHER BALLOON

Ingo, one of the German scientific team, releasing an atmospheric probe to gather data used in weather forecasting.

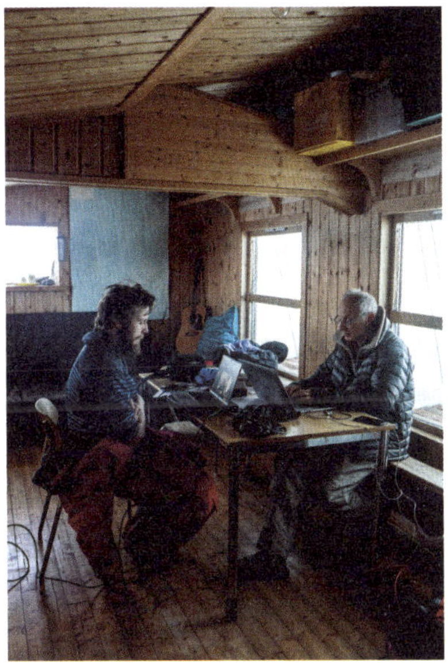

JEAN LILENSTEN AND LÉO BOSSE

The two scientists are conducting studies on electrical activity in the Northern Lights with the support of the French Polar Institute.

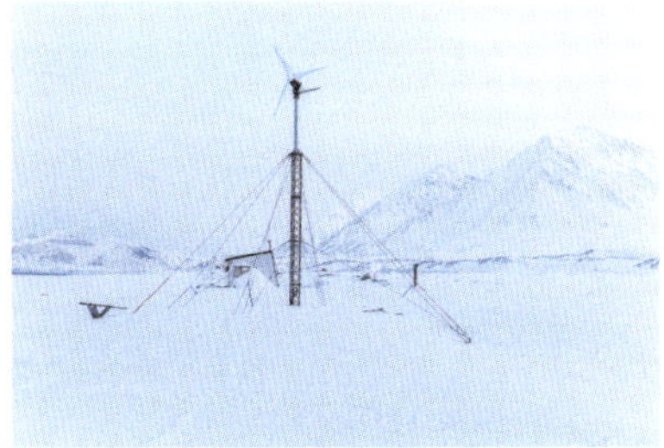

OUT ON ITS OWN

Jean Corbel station is entirely self-sufficient in terms of energy during the summer months.

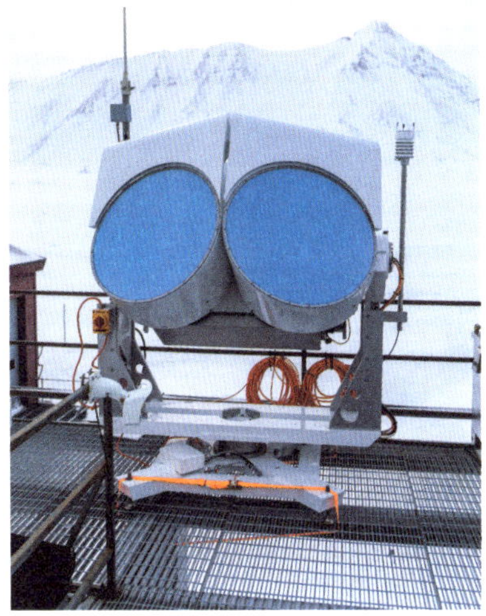

MEASURING THE ATMOSPHERE

A whole array of measuring equipment has been installed on the roof of the AWIPEV research station.

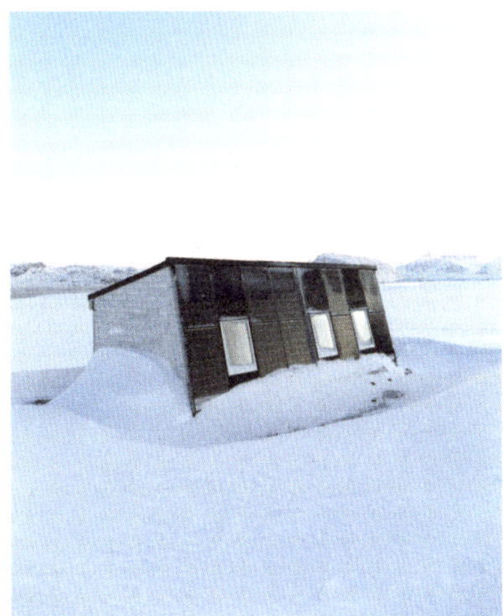

JEAN CORBEL STATION

The base was built by geographer Jean Corbel in 1956 and can accommodate eight people, summer and winter.

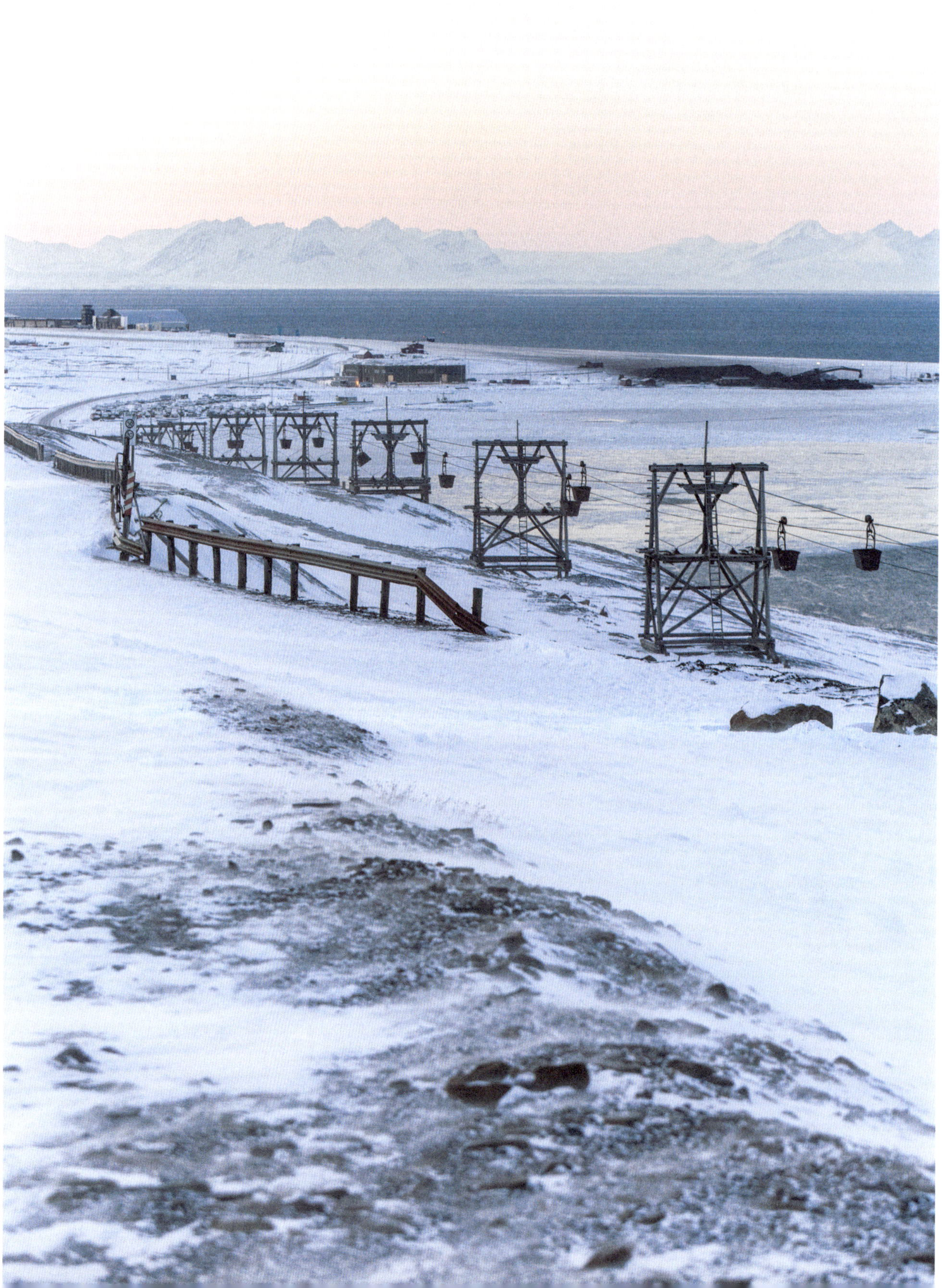

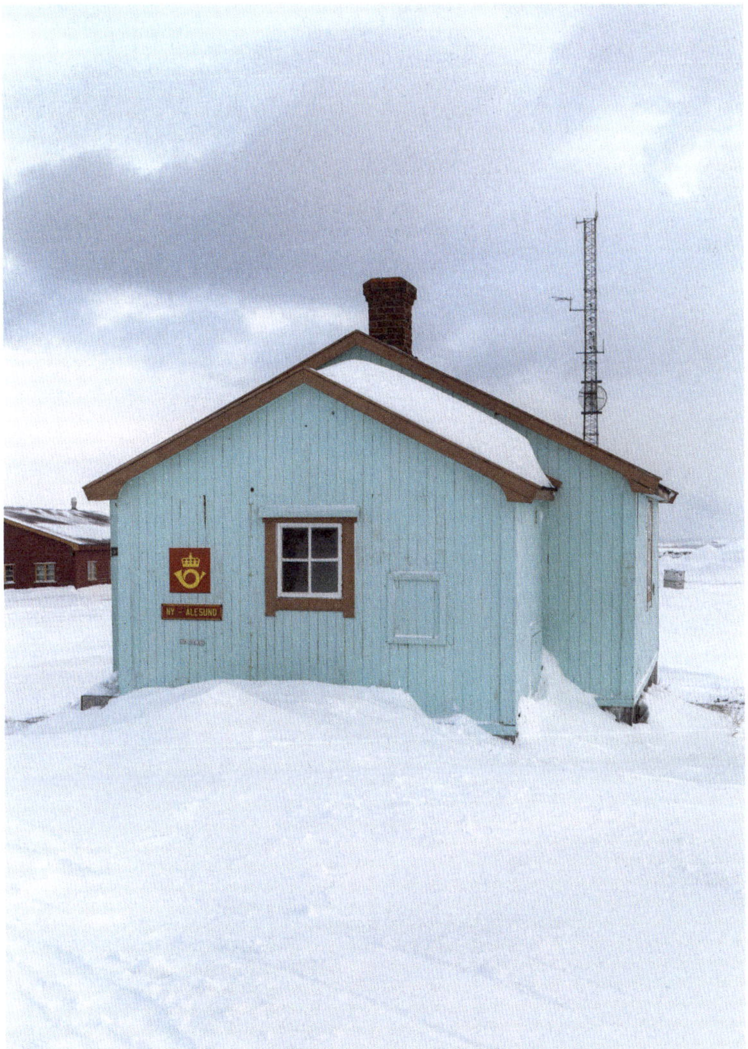

ABOVE

The former post office in Ny-Ålesund is thought to be the northernmost in the world.

OPPOSITE

Coal was once brought from the mines to the port of Longyearbyen by means of cable car.

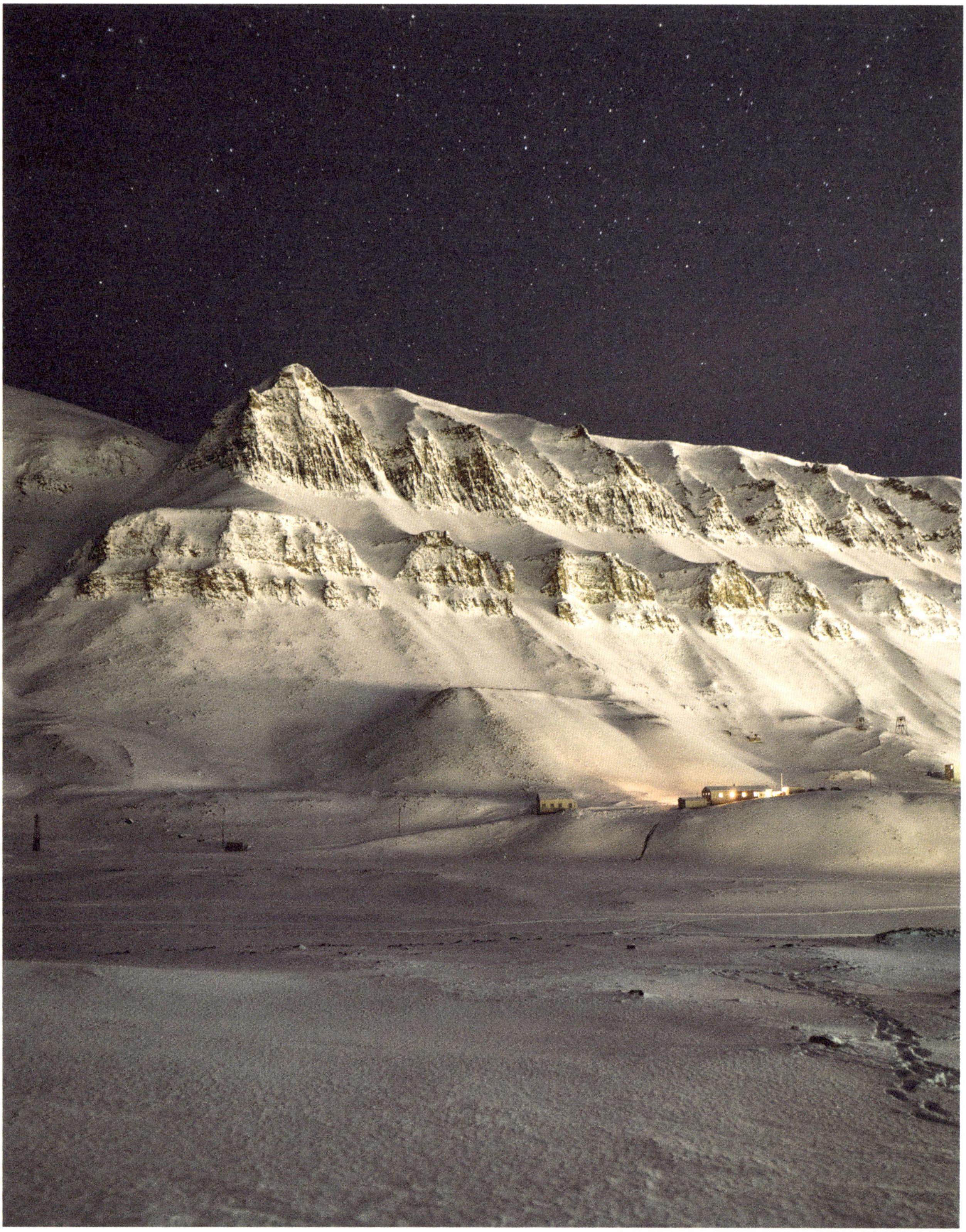

The town of Longyearbyen is ringed by mountains, and illuminated by powerful street lights during the long polar nights.

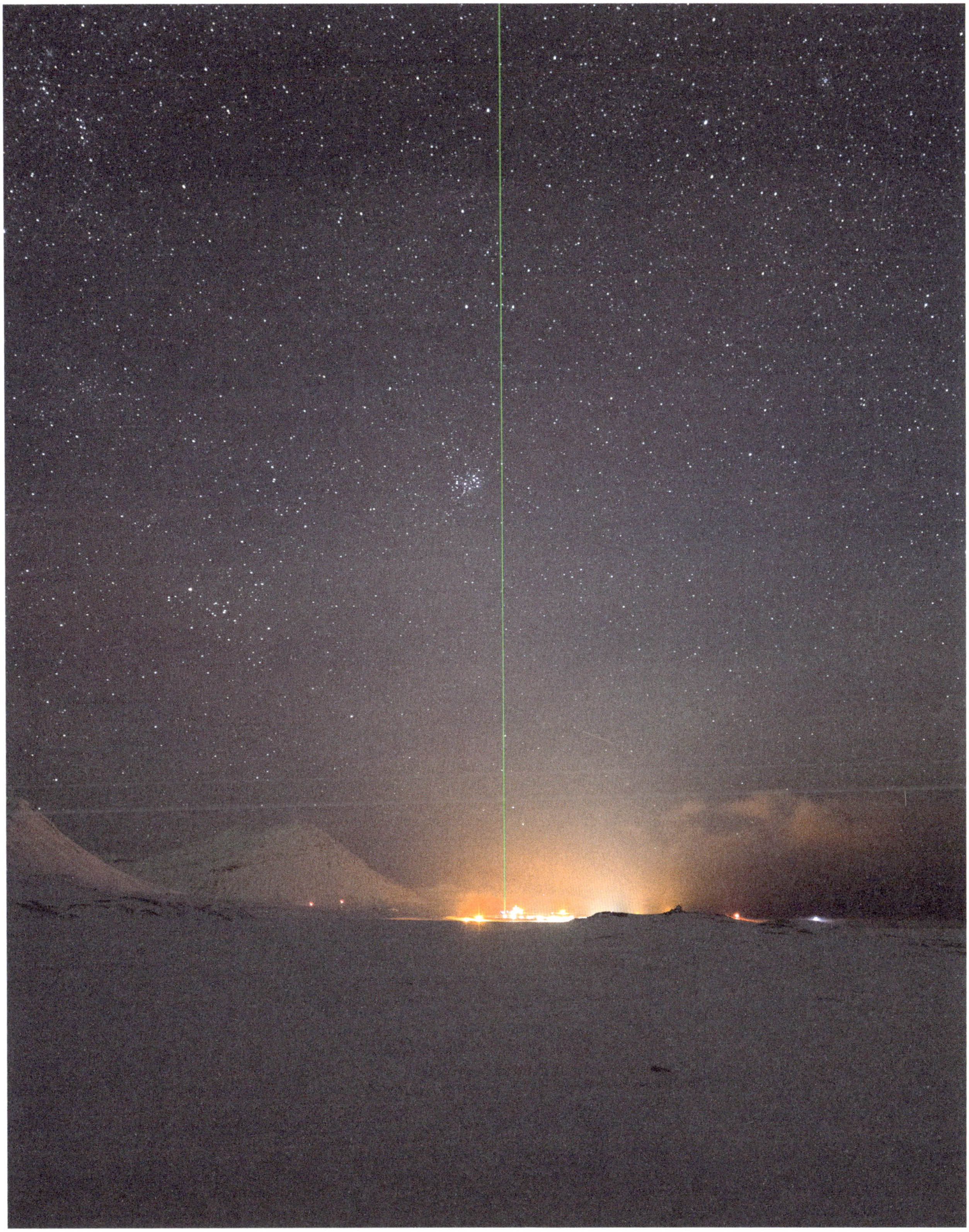

LIDAR is a laser system used to measure the atmosphere. The beam is emitted from the AWIPEV, a Franco-German Arctic research station housing both the French Polar Institute and Germany's Alfred Wegener Institute.

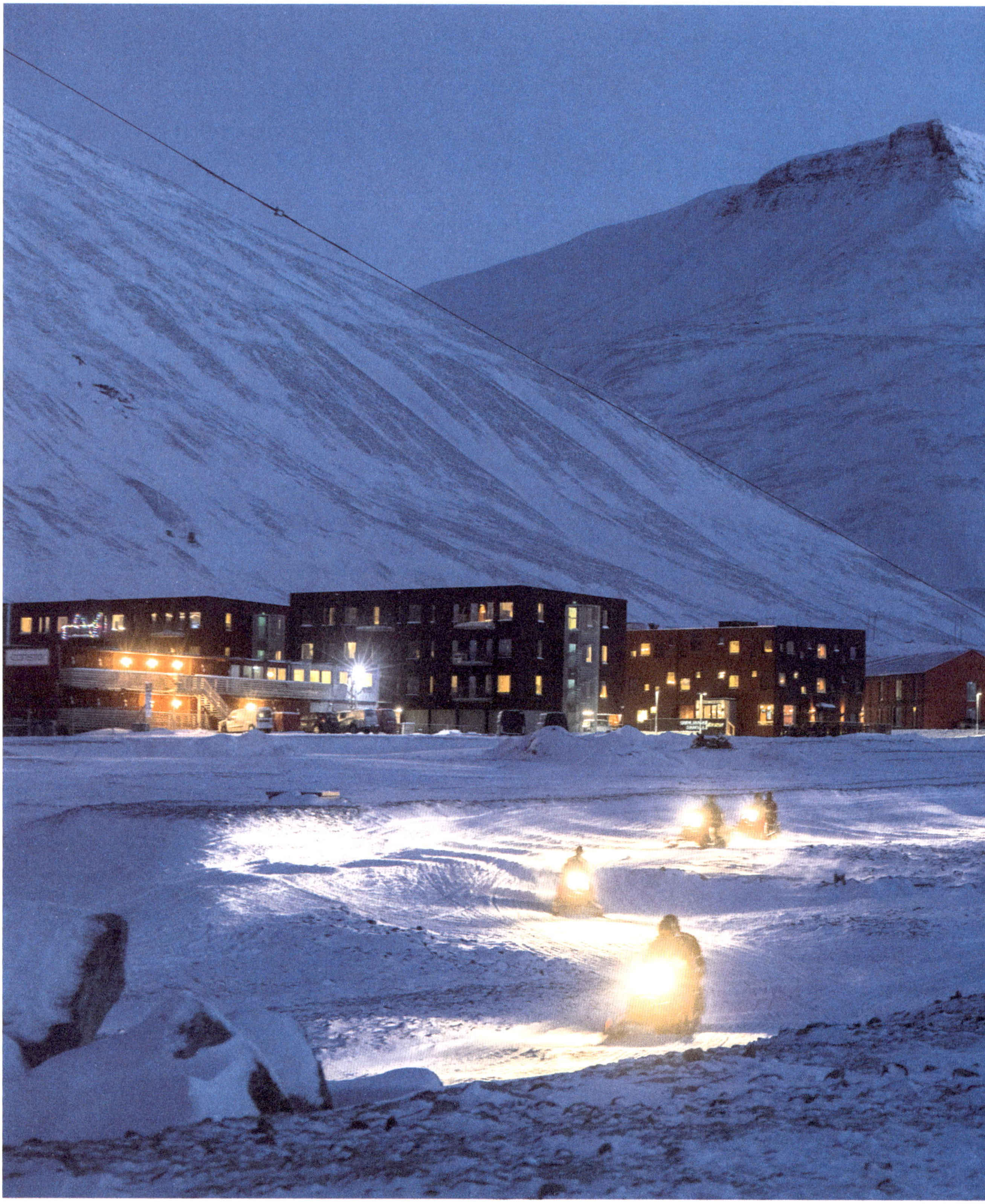

A group of tourists returning from a snowmobile excursion. For the residents of Svalbard, this is an essential way of getting about in winter.

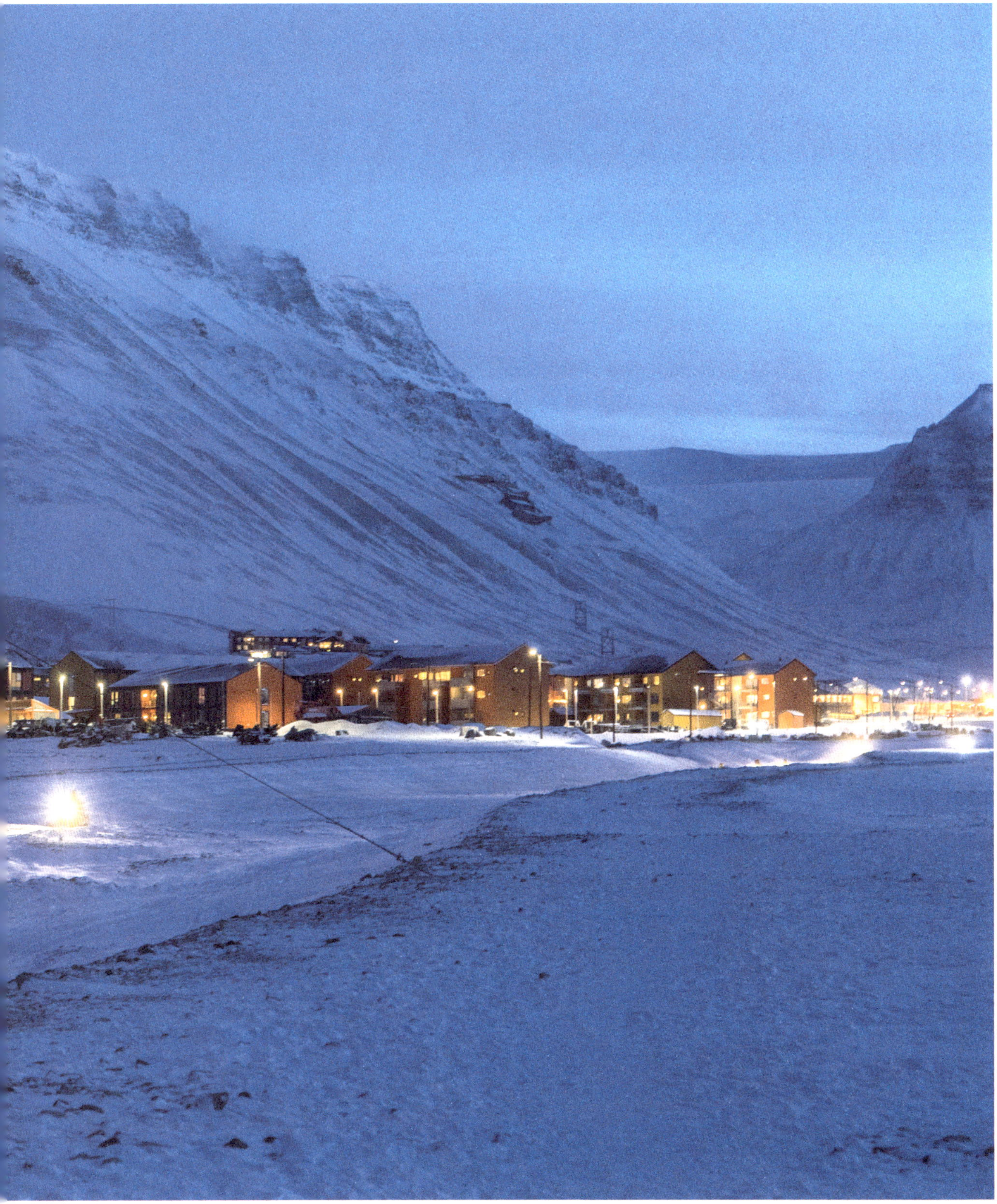

DEEP DIVE

THE MIDNIGHT SUN

This unique phenomenon lights up the skies for several weeks at a time, lending summer nights an unreal atmosphere.

The midnight sun refers to a period in the year, typical of polar regions, when the sun does not actually set—as the day comes to an end, the sun dips low in the sky, blazing with golden light as it grazes the horizon, before rising again. In Norway this phenomenon occurs around the summer solstice.

People living in the latitudes of the Arctic Circle are exposed to the midnight sun only briefly, but the further north you go, the more days without darkness there are. The residents of Svalbard, for example, can see midnight sun for four whole months between April 20 and August 22, while at the North Pole, this period lengthens to the six months between the March and September equinoxes. There is a simple explanation for this fascinating phenomenon, however—it is an inevitable consequence of the tilt of the Earth's axis relative to the plane of its orbit.

When spring arrives the sun is positioned vertically above the equator, illuminating both poles. As the weeks progress, it gradually moves northward until the Arctic is illuminated continuously. The term "polar day" is also used to describe the period when the North Pole is exposed to the sun's rays for a consecutive series of days in summer.

These extended periods of daylight are a godsend for summer visitors to Norway. There's no need to hurry back from hiking a trail and, in the evening, the landscape is bathed in a golden light as an endless sunset prolongs the day with mild temperatures. It is an ideal time to take a kayaking trip on the calm waters of a lake or a dip in the sea after a sauna. It can take a few days to adapt, although in the absence of darkness, the body tends to feel less fatigue and you can go about your business without worrying about the time. For this reason, Norwegians fit their houses with blackout blinds so they can sleep in the dark.

The phenomenon of "white nights" occurs at lower latitudes, between the Arctic Circle and around 60°. Although the sun goes down, it does not disappear completely below the horizon to create proper darkness. Towns remain in twilight all night, a phenomenon that can be observed in Oslo, St Petersburg, Stockholm, and Helsinki. Once winter arrives, however, the opposite is the case and the sun disappears for months on end. This is the beginning of the polar night that plunges the far north into a protracted period of darkness.

THE MIDNIGHT SUN

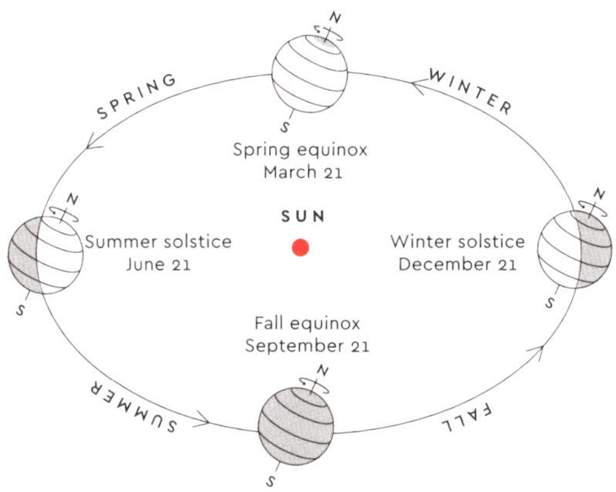

THE SUN'S CYCLE

Because the Earth's axis is tilted, not every part of the planet is illuminated at the same time—the North Pole is continuously exposed to the sun's rays between the spring and fall equinoxes, for example. In winter, the opposite occurs and the sun does not rise at the pole at all during the polar night.

MONTH	SUNRISE	SUNSET	DURATION OF DAYLIGHT
JANUARY	POLAR NIGHT	POLAR NIGHT	-
FEBRUARY	11:20 am	13:02 pm	1hr 42mins
MARCH	06:24 am	17:48 pm	11hrs 25mins
APRIL	02:24 am	23:29 pm	21hrs 5mins
MAY	POLAR DAY	POLAR DAY	-
JUNE	POLAR DAY	POLAR DAY	-
JULY	POLAR DAY	POLAR DAY	-
AUGUST	POLAR DAY	POLAR DAY	-
SEPTEMBER	05:44 am	20:12 pm	14hrs 39mins
OCTOBER	09:19 am	16:06 pm	6hrs 48mins
NOVEMBER	POLAR NIGHT	POLAR NIGHT	-
DECEMBER	POLAR NIGHT	POLAR NIGHT	-

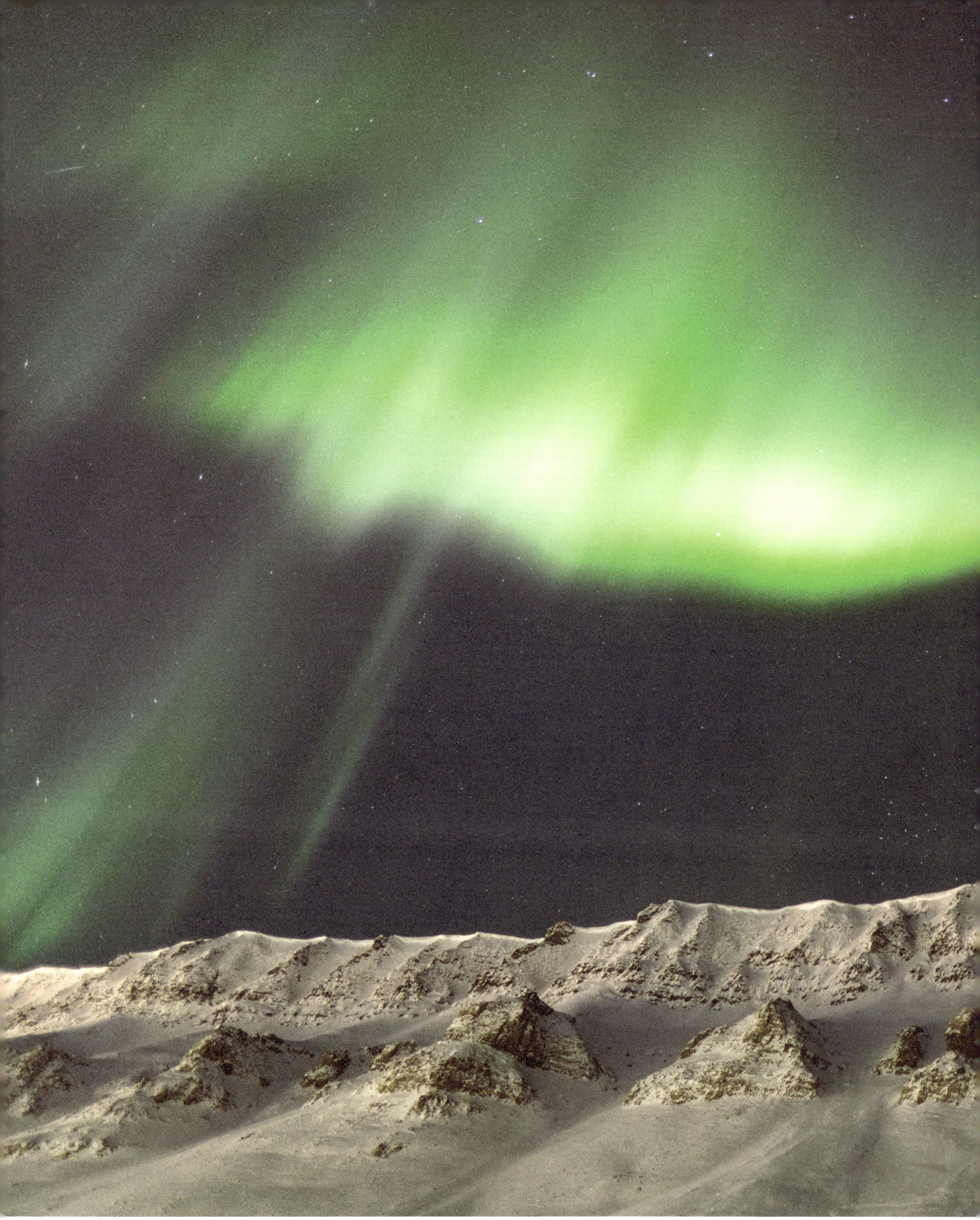

The Northern Lights dancing above the town of Longyearbyen.

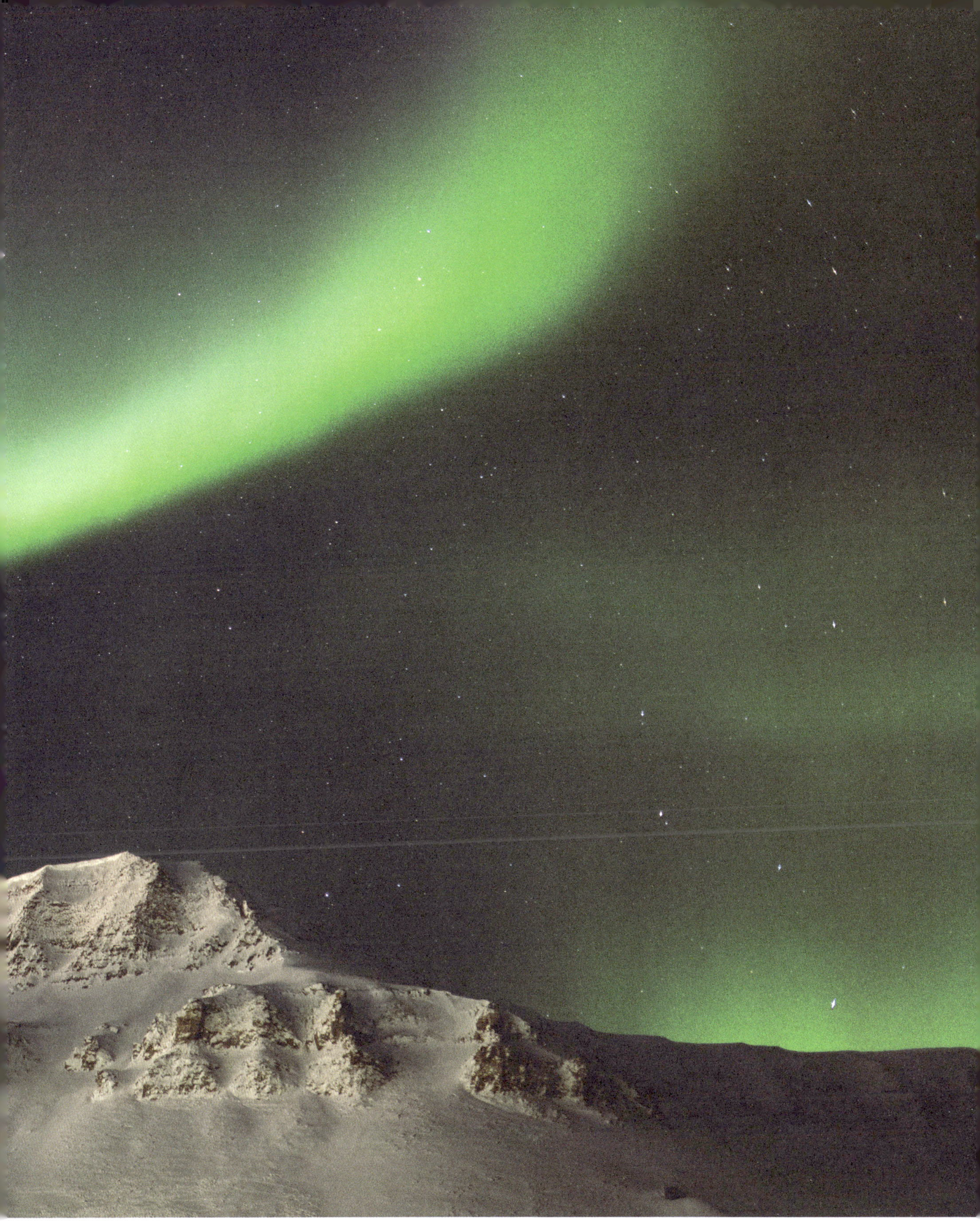

EXPERIENCE

THE SVALBARD GLOBAL SEED VAULT

A SUBTERRANEAN STRONGROOM

This underground vault housing countless varieties of seeds from all over the world is truly a latter-day Noah's Ark.

The Svalbard Global Seed Vault is a project backed by the Norwegian government. The facility, which opened its doors in 2008, was designed by Norwegian architect Peter W. Söderman. Its simple mission is to protect the genetic diversity of the world's plants in the event of war, environmental disaster, or human error.

Svalbard's thick layer of permafrost and the absence of any tectonic plates in the area make it the perfect location for a conservation project of this kind. The facility has been built 400 ft (120 m) underground in an old nuclear shelter, but as the site is still 430 ft (130 m) above sea level, it would remain protected should the ice melt and water levels rise.

At the end of a corridor 330 ft (100 m) long, three rooms, each with floor space of about 2,700 square feet (250 m^2), house seed samples from all over the world. A total of some 4.5 million seeds can be stored in this repository, which has a total volume of 53,000 cubic feet (1,500 m^3).

When the seeds arrive in the facility, they are meticulously packed in heat-sealed bags to prevent the growth of mold and are then stored at a temperature of −0.4°F (−18°C). Among these millions of seeds are those from all kinds of plants, from Thai rice to Israeli wheat and even the corn held sacred by the Cherokee nation. Although the maximum shelf life of wheat seed does not exceed 1,693 years, sunflower seeds can only be stored successfully for fifty-five years, so these seeds are regularly renewed (every ten years or so) to ensure the supply is as fresh as possible.

There are now nearly one thousand seven hundred seed banks located all round the world, and though some conduct agricultural research, their primary purpose is to protect the diversity of the world's plants by preserving seeds to safeguard existing biological diversity and prevent the extinction of certain species.

In 2015 the Svalbard Seed Vault was contacted by researchers from ICARDA (the International Center for Agricultural Research in the Dry Areas) now based in Beirut, Lebanon. Its previous headquarters in Aleppo, Syria, were looted during the Syrian Civil War, but ICARDA had entrusted the Svalbard facility with a duplicate of its collection. This was the first time a request of this kind had been received by the vault and the circumstances confirmed its importance and interest in remaining in a region that on the face of it is well protected from natural shocks and political risk. The vault is now managed by the Global Crop Diversity Trust, a body founded by the UN and financed by an association of organizations and nation states, including the Gates Foundation, DuPont, France's INRAE, Australia, the United States, Germany, Switzerland, and Sweden.

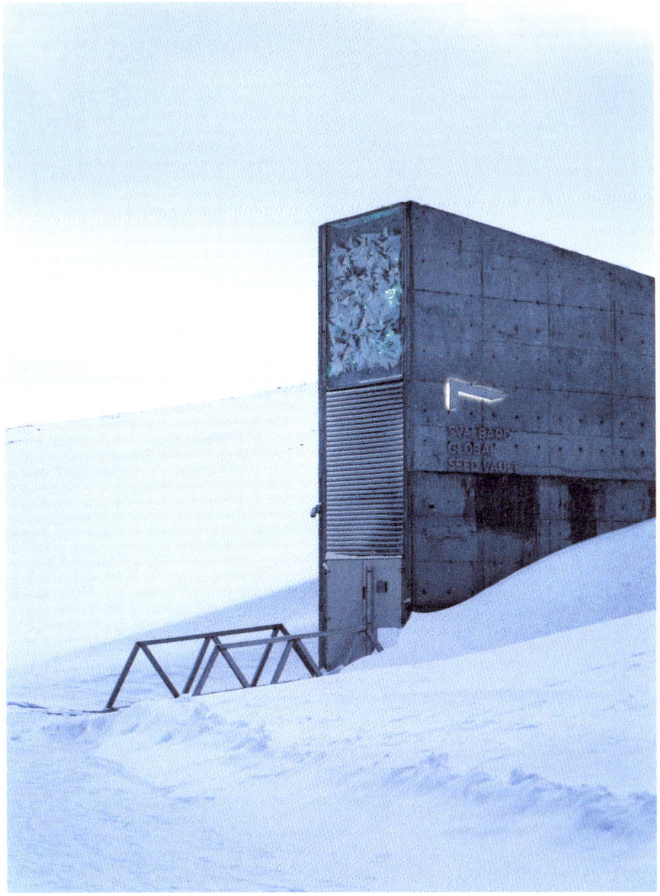

1/ NOAH'S ARK

The seed bank can hold 4.5 million seeds in its three underground vaults.

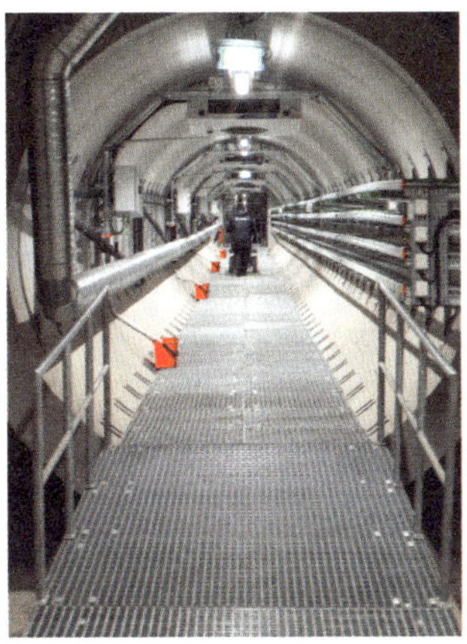

2/ TUNNEL

The vault is accessed via a tunnel 330 ft (100 m) in length.

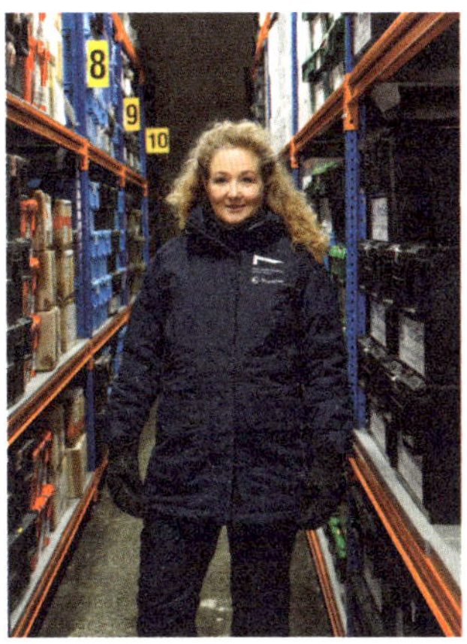

3/ LISE STEFFENSEN

The executive director of NordGen on a visit to the seed vault.

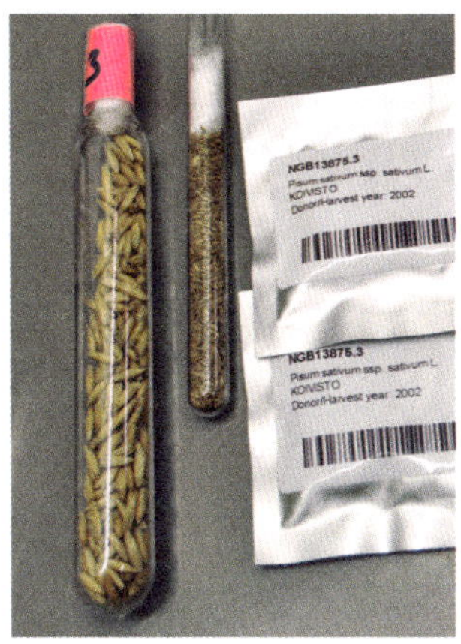

4/ SEEDS

A range of different conservation options are applied, depending on the nature of the seeds.

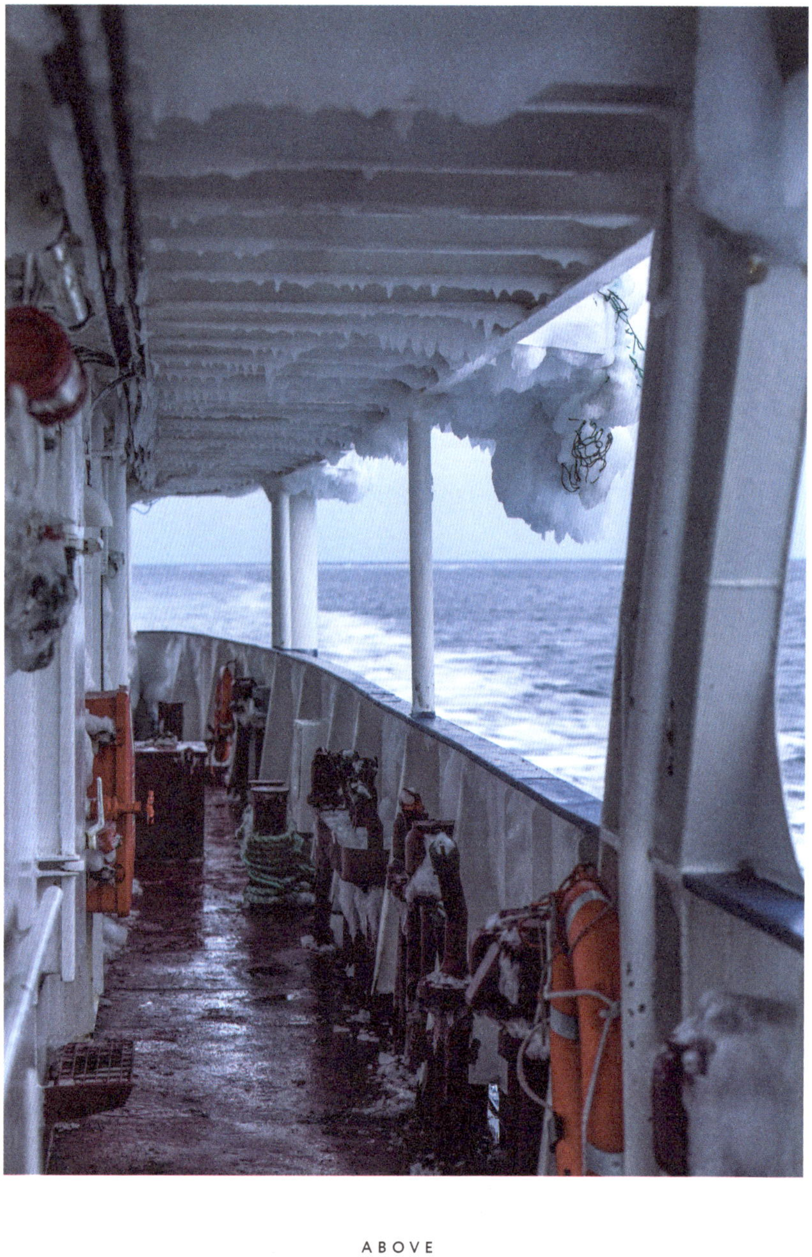

ABOVE

Spray from the sea has frozen on this ship's bridge after a passage on the high seas.

OPPOSITE

Sea ice begins to form when the water temperature drops below 28.75°F (-1.8°C), which happens every winter in Svalbard.

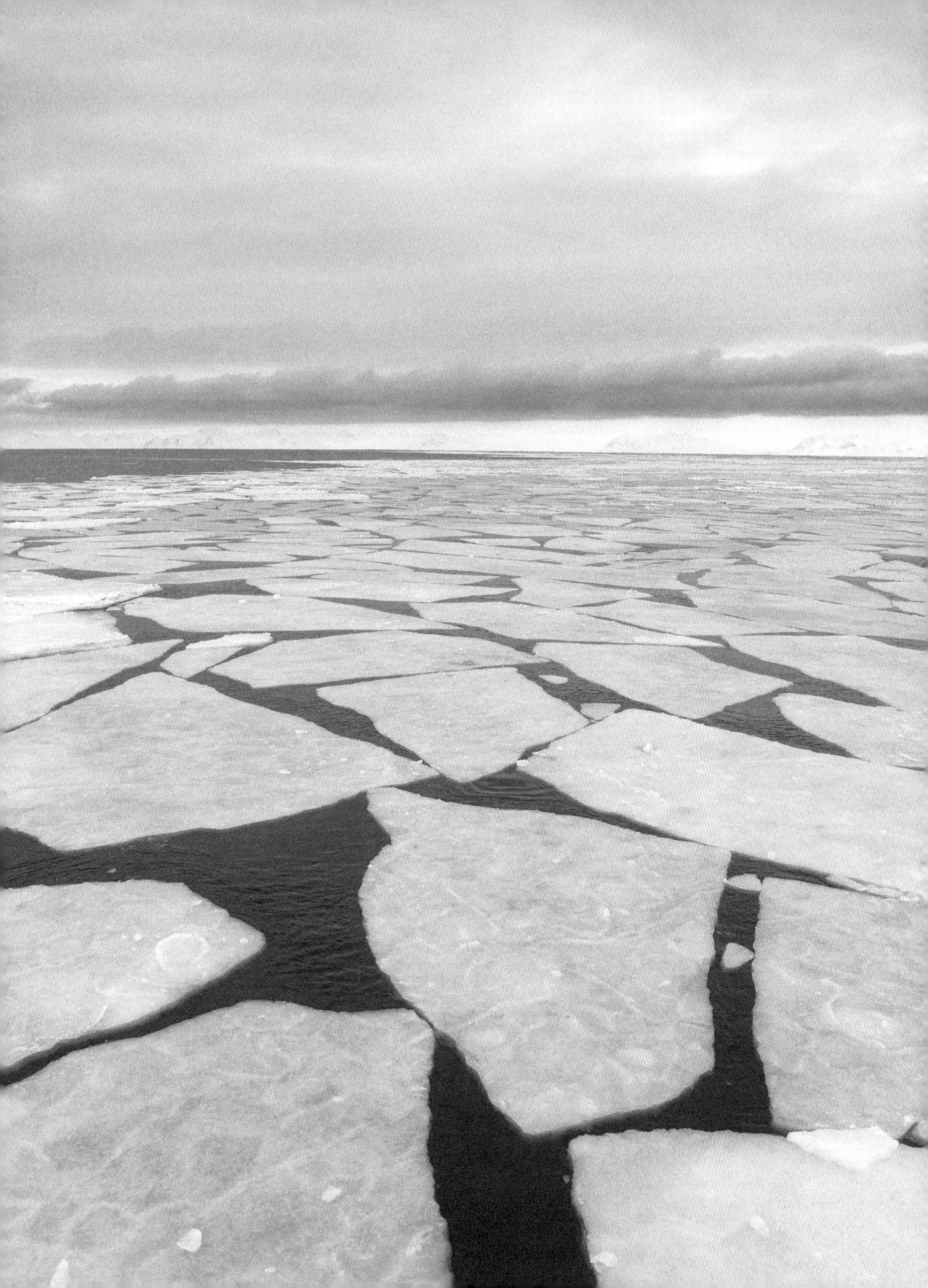

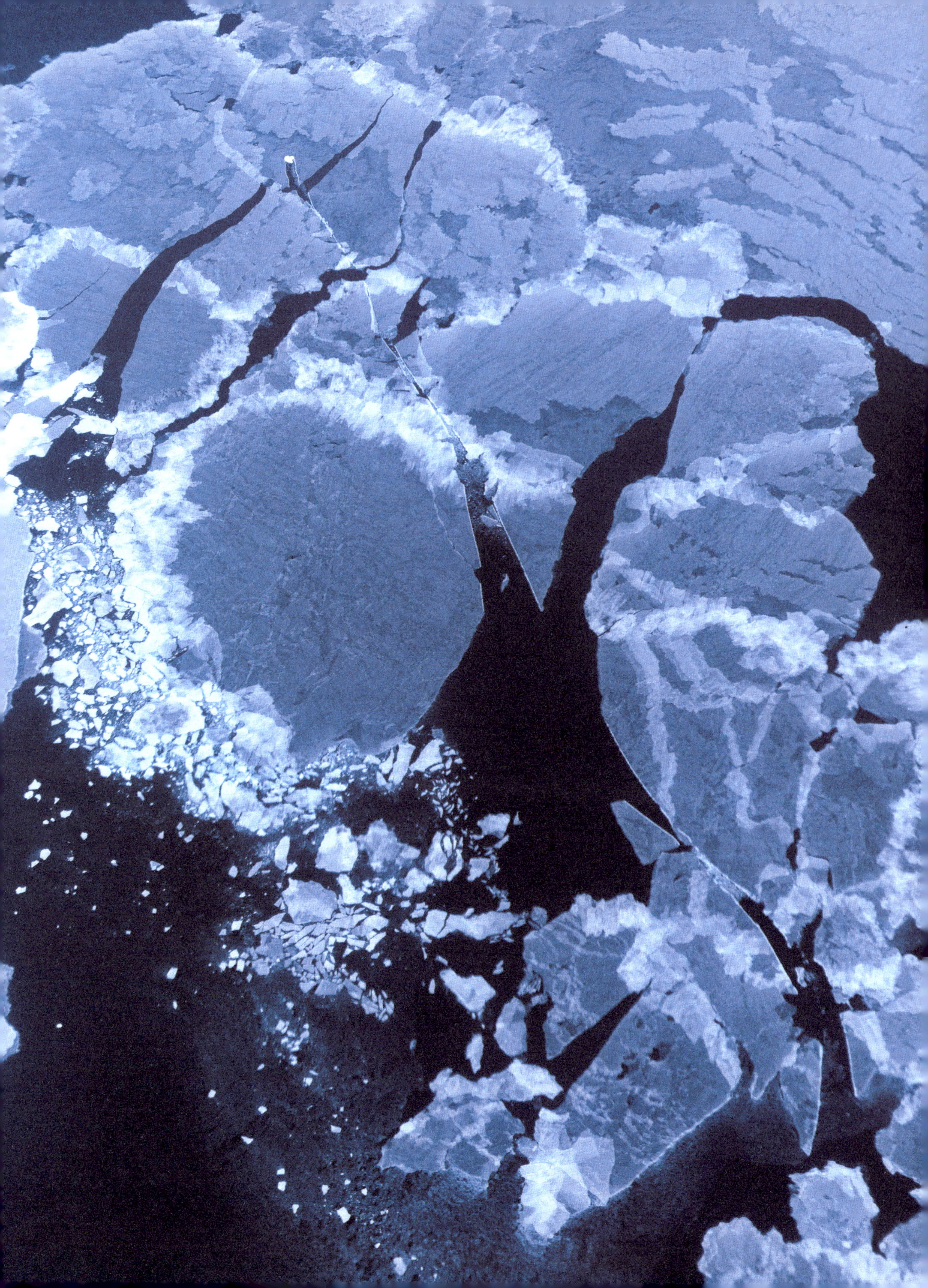

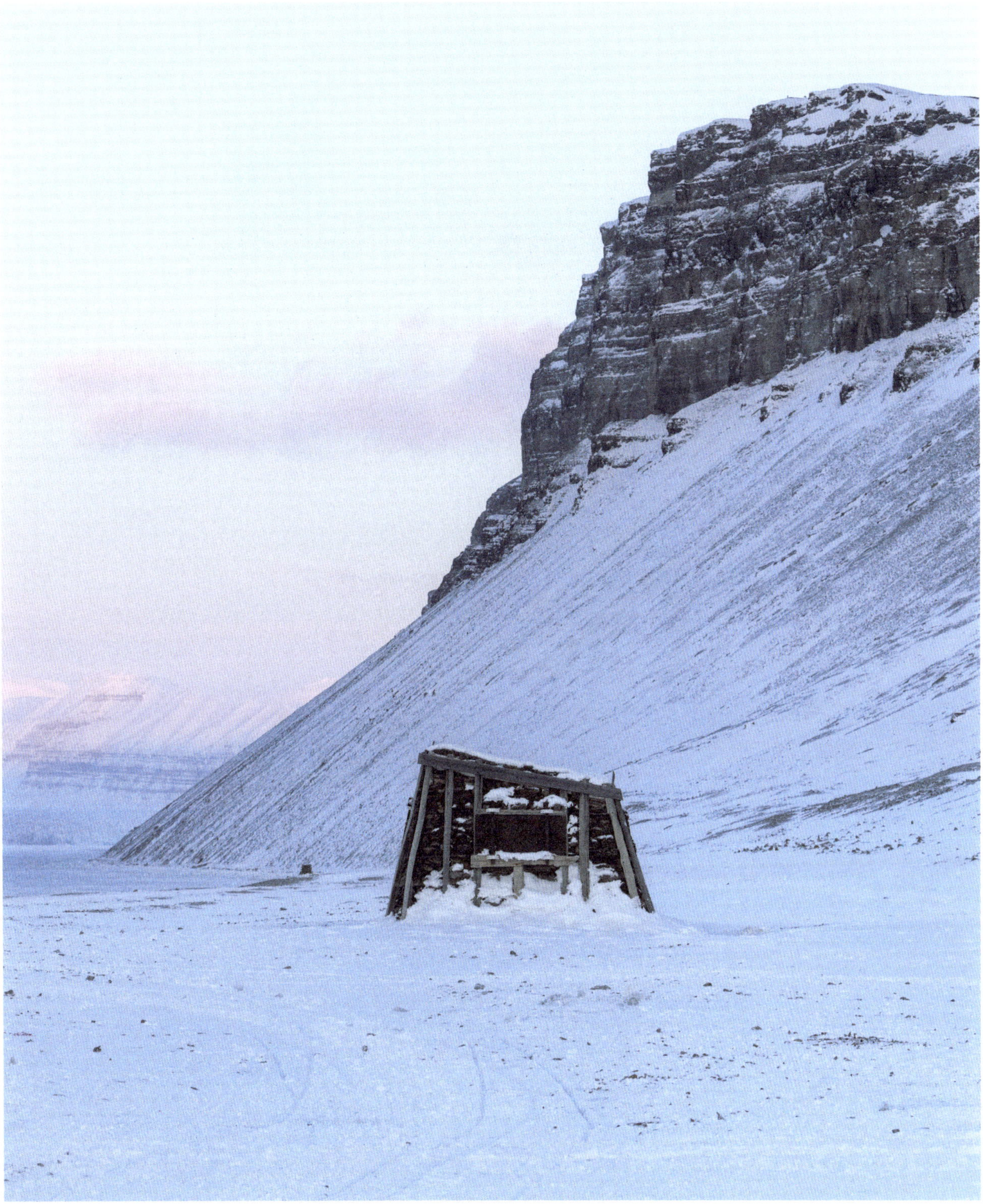

ABOVE

A relic of a bygone era—a former trapper's shack in Tempelfjord.

OPPOSITE

Sea ice is a vital habitat for many marine animals, including walruses, seals, and polar bears.

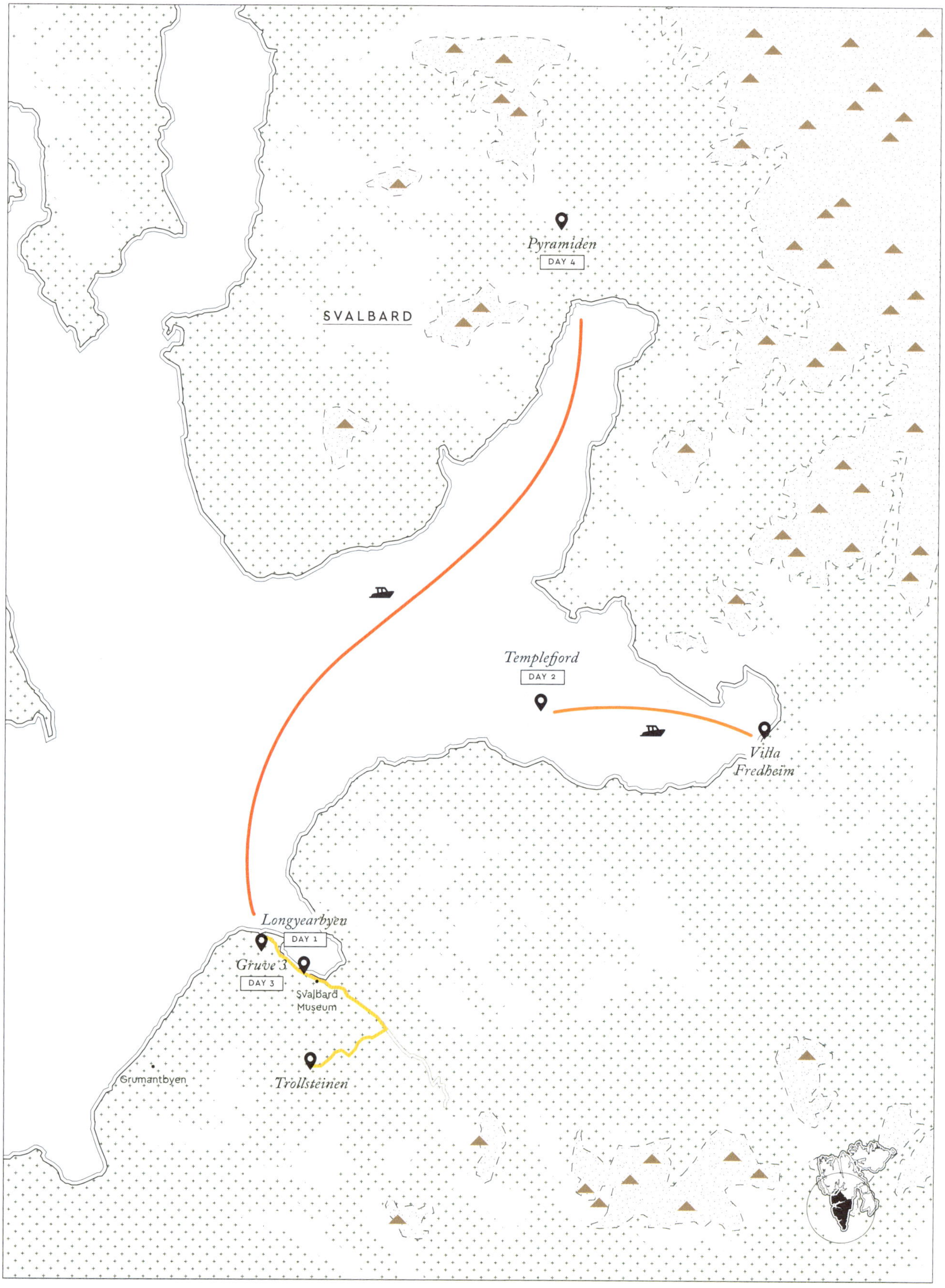
SVALBARD
Pyramiden
DAY 4
Templefjord
DAY 2
Villa Fredheim
Longyearbyen
DAY 1
Gruve 3
DAY 3
Svalbard Museum
Trollsteinen
Grumantbyen

ITINERARY

FOUR DAYS IN SVALBARD

From glaciers to abandoned mining towns, discover everything there is to see in this fascinating archipelago.

DAY 1: LONGYEARBYEN

Longyearbyen, Svalbard's administrative center, is home to two thousand residents. Visit Svalbard Museum to absorb a little of the local atmosphere and come face to face with a polar bear—although the one here is stuffed and mounted. You can also learn about the history of the archipelago and the methods used by trappers to survive the long months of winter. On the way to Restaurant KROA for a hearty supper a few blocks away, there is every chance of seeing some of the wild reindeer (actually quite tame) that roam freely in Longyearbyen.

DAY 2: TEMPLEFJORD

Before the advent of the snowmobile, the principal way of getting around on the islands was dog-powered, and you can still jump aboard a sled (in summer and winter alike) to explore the local scenery at a totally different pace. On the trip to Templefjord, stop off at Villa Fredheim to see the famous cabin in which the trapper Hilmar Nøis lived for most of his life. Juva Cabin, on the way, is an ideal place for an overnight stay in the wilderness. Relax in the sauna and see the Northern Lights, far from the bright lights of the town.

DAY 3: GRUVE 3

Svalbard's history of mining is an important chapter in its story, and it is no coincidence that a statue of a miner stands proudly on the town's pedestrianized high street. Visit Gruve 3 coal mine and imagine living the life of a miner. Or, if you prefer to remain above ground, visit the Svalbard Seed Vault. While not open to the public, the building itself, sitting low in the landscape, has an interesting history and design. For the chance to enjoy the midnight sun from a vantage point (or the Northern Lights in winter), try a short walk in the hills above the town.

DAY 4: PYRAMIDEN

Head for the docks and jump aboard a boat bound for the old Russian mining town of Pyramiden. Unlike its counterpart Barentsburg, Pyramiden has been completely abandoned and lies frozen in time since the last inhabitants left in 1998. It represents a true journey back into the past and an opportunity to find out a bit more about the archipelago's unique status. On the way, the luckiest visitors might be able to spot a polar bear, a walrus or two, or even some seals. Only Svalbard's ptarmigans remain on the islands throughout the year, the only land-inhabiting birds to do so, but in the summer many bird species make a brief stopover here to breed in the far north.